Trump's America

New Perspectives on the American Presidency
Series Editors: Michael Patrick Cullinane and Sylvia Ellis,
University of Roehampton

Published titles
Constructing Presidential Legacy: How We Remember the American President
Edited by Michael Patrick Cullinane and Sylvia Ellis

Presidential Privilege and the Freedom of Information Act
Kevin M. Baron

Forthcoming titles
Obama v. Trump: The Politics of Rollback
Clodagh Harrington and Alex Waddan

Series website: <https://edinburghuniversitypress.com/new-perspectives-on-the-american-presidency.html>

TRUMP'S AMERICA

Political Culture and National Identity

Edited by Liam Kennedy

EDINBURGH
University Press

For Milla
S.B.S.

Edinburgh University Press is one of the leading university presses in the UK. We publish academic books and journals in our selected subject areas across the humanities and social sciences, combining cutting-edge scholarship with high editorial and production values to produce academic works of lasting importance. For more information visit our website: edinburghuniversitypress.com

© editorial matter and organisation Liam Kennedy, 2020, 2022
© the chapters their several authors, 2020, 2022

Edinburgh University Press Ltd
The Tun – Holyrood Road
12(2f) Jackson's Entry
Edinburgh EH8 8PJ

First published in hardback by Edinburgh University Press 2020

Typeset in 11/13 Adobe Sabon by
IDSUK (DataConnection) Ltd

A CIP record for this book is available from the British Library

ISBN 978 1 4744 5887 0 (hardback)
ISBN 978 1 4744 5888 7 (paperback)
ISBN 978 1 4744 5889 4 (webready PDF)
ISBN 978 1 4744 5890 0 (epub)

The right of Liam Kennedy to be identified as the editor of this work has been asserted in accordance with the Copyright, Designs and Patents Act 1988, and the Copyright and Related Rights Regulations 2003 (SI No. 2498).

Contents

List of Tables and Figures vii
Acknowledgements viii
Notes on Contributors ix

    Introduction: Making Sense of Trump's America   1
    Liam Kennedy

Part One: Paradigm Shift

1. Donald Trump's Settler-Colonist State (Fantasy): A New Era of Illiberal Hegemony?   23
   Donald E. Pease

2. Caesarism Revisited: Cultural Studies and the Question of Trumpism   53
   Stephen Shapiro

3. Hegemoronic Vistas: The Pseudo-Gramscian Right from the Powell Memorandum to the 'Flight 93 Election'   72
   Frank Kelleter

4. Women Voters and Activists in Trump's America   107
   Melissa Deckman and Kelly M. Gardner

Part Two: Foreign Policy and Global Relations

5. Angry at the World: Progressive Possibilities in Trump's Disruption of the Current Order   135
   Patrick McGreevy

CONTENTS

6. Trump or the Cultural Logic of 'Late' Democracy 150
   David Ryan

7. The End of the Age of Three Worlds and the Making of the Trump Presidency 177
   Penny Von Eschen

8. Trumpism and the Future of US Grand Strategy 204
   Jack (John M.) Thompson

9. From George W. Bush to Donald Trump: Understanding the Exceptional Resilience of Democracy Promotion in US Political Discourse 222
   Eugenio Lilli

Part Three: Identity Politics and the Politics of Spectacle

10. 'If You Want to Know Why 2016 Happened, Read This Book': Class, Race and the Literature of Disinvestment (the Case of *Hillbilly Elegy*) 247
    Hamilton Carroll

11. Ivanka Trump and the New Plutocratic (Post)feminism 268
    Diane Negra

12. Trump and the Age of Hybrid Media Communicators 289
    Alireza Hajihosseini

13. 'Reality Has a Well-Known Liberal Bias': The End(s) of Satire in Trump's America 310
    Liam Kennedy

14. Spectacle of Decency: Repairing America after Trump 335
    Scott Lucas

Index 366

Tables and Figures

Table 2.1	The kit of social convergences at analogous crisis years/conjunctures	69
Figure 4.1.	Vote (percentage) for Trump and Clinton in 2016: women only	109
Figure 4.2.	2016 Presidential vote choice among white women by religion, education, age and gender attitudes	111
Figure 4.3.	Percentage of women approving of Trump's job performance	116
Figure 11.1.	In their cameo appearance in an episode of teen drama *Gossip Girl*, Ivanka Trump and Jared Kushner are presented as an exemplary 'power couple' on the rise	273
Figure 11.2.	The failure of Ivanka Trump's 2017 self-help book *Women Who Work: Rewriting the Rules for Success* augured a shift in her marketability	278
Figure 11.3.	Ivanka Trump's tweeted photo with son Theodore gained notoriety as a display of triumphalist privilege in 2018 when Donald Trump's government was separating asylum seekers at the US border from their children	281
Figure 11.4.	Meghan McCain drew plaudits for her speech at John McCain's funeral in which she repudiated Donald Trump's 'Make America Great Again' slogan	282
Figure 13.1.	'The Deplorables' meme	323

Acknowledgements

This volume began as a conference at the Clinton Institute at University College Dublin. I owe thanks to Catherine Carey for her help in organising that event and supporting this project in many ways. Thanks to Scott Lucas, Donald Pease and Stephen Shapiro for their enthusiasm and ideas along the way.

Contributors

Hamilton Carroll is Associate Professor of English at the University of Leeds. He is the author of *Affirmative Reaction: New Formations of White Masculinity* (2011) and editor of 'Fictions of Speculation', a special issue of the *Journal of American Studies* (2015).

Melissa Deckman is the Louis L. Goldstein Professor of Public Affairs at Washington College, whose area of specialities include gender, religion and political behaviour in American politics. Her latest book is *Tea Party Women: Mama Grizzlies, Grassroot Leaders, and the Changing Face of the American Right* (2016). She also co-authored the bestselling textbook *Women and Politics* (2007) with Julie Dolan and Michele Swers. In addition, she is the author or co-author of more than a dozen scholarly articles. Her first book, *School Board Battles: The Christian Right in Local Politics* (2004), won the Hubert Morken Award, given by the American Political Science Association biennially to the best work on religion and politics.

Kelly M. Gardner graduated *summa cum laude* from Washington College in 2019 with a Bachelor of Arts in political science and sociology and a minor in gender studies. At Washington College, she served as Dr Melissa Deckman's research assistant, studied abroad at the London School of Economics and Political Science, and interned with the Governance Studies programme at the Brookings Institution. Her undergraduate research focused on women in politics, public policy and gender discrimination.

CONTRIBUTORS

Alireza Hajihosseini has worked as a producer in Tehran covering Iranian current affairs for an international audience and was working for Al Jazeera English in the network's heyday during the Arab Spring. He is currently the executive producer of CNN International's flagship current affairs programme *Connect the World with Becky Anderson*, broadcast from the network's Middle East broadcasting hub in Abu Dhabi.

Frank Kelleter is chair of the Department of Culture and Einstein Professor of North American Cultural History at John F. Kennedy Institute, Freie Universität Berlin. He is the director of the Popular Seriality Research Unit (PSRU), a transdisciplinary group consisting of thirteen projects, funded by the German Research Association (2010–16). His monographs include *David Bowie* (2016), *Serial Agencies: 'The Wire' and Its Readers* (2014) and *Con/Tradition: Louis Farrakhan's Nation of Islam, the Million Man March, and American Civil Religion* (2000). His edited volumes include *Media of Serial Narrative* (2017), *Populäre Serialität* (2012), *American Studies as Media Studies* (2011) and *Melodrama! The Mode of Excess from Early America to Hollywood* (2007).

Liam Kennedy is Professor of American Studies and director of the Clinton Institute for American Studies at University College Dublin. He is the author of *Susan Sontag* (1995), *Race and Urban Space in American Culture* (2000) and *Afterimages: Photography and US Foreign Policy* (2016). His edited books include *Urban Space and Representation* (1999), *The Wire: Race, Class, and Genre* (2012), *The Violence of the Image: Photography and International Conflict* (2014) and *Neoliberalism and Contemporary American Literature* (2019).

Eugenio Lilli is a lecturer at the Clinton Institute for American Studies, University College Dublin. Previously, he lectured at King's College London, the UK Defence Academy and John Cabot University in Rome. He was also an honorary visiting research fellow at City University in London. He obtained his PhD from the War Studies Department at King's College London. Recent publications include the book *New Beginning in US–Muslim Relations: President Obama and the Arab Awakening* (2016).

CONTRIBUTORS

Scott Lucas is Professor of International Politics at the University of Birmingham. He has also been a professional journalist since 1979, and is the founder and editor of *EA Worldview* (www.eaworldview.com), a leading website in daily news and analysis of Iran, Turkey, Syria and the wider Middle East, as well as US foreign policy. He is the author of *The Betrayal of Dissent: Beyond Orwell, Hitchens, and the New American Century* (2004), *Freedom's War: The US Crusade against the Soviet Union 1945–56* (1999) and *The Lion's Last War: Britain and the Suez Crisis* (1996), and editor of *The Trials of Engagement: The Future of US Public Diplomacy* (2012) and *Challenging US Foreign Policy: America and the World in the Long Twentieth Century* (2011).

Patrick McGreevy is dean of the Faculty of Arts and Sciences at the American University of Beirut (AUB) and formerly director of the Prince Alwaleed bin Talal bin Abdulaziz al Saud Center for American Studies and Research at AUB. He is the author of *Imagining Niagara: The Meaning and Making of Niagara Falls* (1994) and *Stairway to Empire: Lockport, the Erie Canal, and the Shaping of America* (2009). He is the editor of *Liberty and Justice: America and the Middle East* (2008) and *Connections and Ruptures: America and the Middle East* (2011).

Diane Negra is Professor of Film Studies and Screen Culture and head of film studies at University College Dublin. A member of the Royal Irish Academy, she is the author, editor or co-editor of ten books, including *The Aesthetics and Affects of Cuteness* (2016), *Extreme Weather and Global Media* (2015), *Gendering the Recession* (2014), *Old and New Media after Katrina* (2010), *What a Girl Wants? Fantasizing the Reclamation of Self in Postfeminism* (2008), *Interrogating Postfeminism: Gender and Politics of Popular Culture* (2007), *The Irish in US: Irishness, Performativity, and Popular Culture* (2006) and *Off White Hollywood: American Culture and Ethnic Female Stardom* (2001). She currently serves as co-editor-in-chief of *Television and New Media*.

Donald E. Pease Jr is the Ted and Helen Geisel Third Century Professor in the Humanities and chair of the Masters of Arts in Liberal Studies Program at Dartmouth College. He is the founder and director of the Futures of American Studies Institute at Dartmouth and editor of Duke University Press book series The New Americanists. He is the author of *Visionary Compacts: American Renaissance Writings in Cultural Context* (1987), *The New American Exceptionalism* (2009) and *Theodor Seuss Geisel* (2010), and editor of several collections, among them *National Cultures of United States Imperialism* (1992), *Identities and Postnational Narratives* (1994) and *Revisionary Interventions into the Americanist Canon* (1994).

David Ryan is Professor of History at University College Cork. He has published extensively on contemporary history and US foreign policy, concentrating on interventions in the post-Vietnam era. His books include *US Foreign Policy and the Other*, edited with Michael Cullinane (2015), *Obama, US Foreign Policy and the Dilemmas of Intervention*, co-authored with David Fitzgerald (2014), *Frustrated Empire: US Foreign Policy from 9/11 to Iraq* (2007), *Vietnam in Iraq: Tactics, Lessons, Legacies and Ghosts*, edited with John Dumbrell (2007), *The United States and Europe in the Twentieth Century* (2003), *US Foreign Policy in World History* (2000) and *US–Sandinista Diplomatic Relations: Voice of Intolerance* (1995).

Stephen Shapiro is Professor of English at Warwick University. He is the author of *The Culture and Commerce of the Early American Novel: Reading the Atlantic World-System* (2009) and *How to Read Marx's Capital* (2008), and co-author of *Pentecostal Modernism: Lovecraft, Los Angeles, and World-Systems Culture* (2017), *Combined and Uneven Development: Towards a New Theory of World Literature* (2015) and *How to Read Foucault's Discipline and Punish* (2011). His edited books include *The Wire: Race, Class, and Genre* (2012) and *Revising Charles Brockden: Culture, Politics and Sexuality in the Early Republic* (2004).

Jack (John M.) Thompson is a senior researcher in the Global Security Team at the Center for Security Studies at ETH Zurich. He is the editor of *Progressivism in America: Past, Present, and Future* (2016) and *America's Transatlantic Turn: Theodore Roosevelt and the 'Discovery' of Europe* (2012).

CONTRIBUTORS

Penny Von Eschen is Professor of History and William R. Kenan, Jr, Professor of American Studies at the University of Virginia. She is the author of *Satchmo Blows Up the World: Jazz Ambassadors Play the Cold War* (2004) and *Race against Empire: Black Americans and Anticolonialism 1937–1957* (1997), and editor of *American Studies: An Anthology* (2009) and *Contested Democracy: Freedom, Race, and Power in American History* (2007).

Introduction: Making Sense of Trump's America

Liam Kennedy

For a great many Americans, America changed on 9 November 2016. Recall the references to unreality and dislocation expressed by so many; some commentators spoke of a form of collective trauma.[1] To be sure, the shock and outrage was being experienced mostly by liberals and others who had not voted for the new president and for whom Donald Trump's election unsettled assumptions and beliefs about the order of things and most fundamentally about the America they thought they knew. Yet, all were left staring at an uncertain future and with a new sense of the fault lines and divisions in the US.

It is too early to offer historical assessments of Trump's presidency but it is timely to present considered scholarly interpretations of its political and cultural significance. Already this presidency is viewed as a seismic shock to the American political system and more broadly to political culture and the public sphere in the US – and beyond, given the influence of the US across the world. *Trump's America* analyses the shockwaves and the underlying paradigm shift signified by the advent of Trump. A unifying theme of the book is the challenge to understand the nature of this disruption, to identify and critically illuminate some of its key cultural and political facets.

The political rise of Trump is proving challenging to comprehend and interpret well after the immediate impact of his election as president. Even as the dust clears and the initial shockwaves recede and we begin to formulate frames and narratives to explain what happened and what it means, there is something excessive and confounding about this presidency that not only beggars belief but impedes critical interpretation – a sense that the very grounds of analysis and argument have shifted. Part of this difficulty is that fundamental assumptions about truth and democracy have been called into question, and conventions of political culture and critique are being compromised if not rendered obsolete. Another part of the difficulty is the 'mind warp' – the cognitive overload and mental exhaustion – that has become a common ground tone surrounding the Trump presidency, amplified but also normalised by endless cycles of outrage. As Masha Gessen has observed:

> The overstimulation of the age of Trump ... makes us lose track of time and whatever small sense humans normally have of themselves in history. We forget what happened a month ago. If we look away for a day, we miss news that seems momentous to others – only to be forgotten, too, in a week. Living in a shared reality with our fellow-citizens is an endless triathlon of reading, talking, and panicking. It creates the worst possible frame of mind for answering vexing moral questions.[2]

This overstimulation has been a marked feature of 'the age of Trump', in part due to the impact of the Internet and social media on the public sphere but also because Trump has turned up the volume in ways which have deepened distrust in media and hastened talk about a 'post-truth' America.[3]

Trump has tested the institution of the presidency. His disdain for institutional norms has flummoxed many observers. Again and again, though with decreasing frequency, commentators have looked for some kind of return to normality: the idea that as president-elect Trump would suddenly learn or at least mimic civility, or later that the Office of the Presidency would curb and reshape his wayward temperament; that the role would subsume the man as we are often told it does. Mark Danner, observing the early weeks of the Trump presidency, remarked that they 'have been an ongoing seminar on where norms end and laws begin, of how much of what we relied on when it came to the president's conduct rested largely on a heretofore unquestioned foundation of centuries-old custom'.[4] This desire for normality reflects a concern that the election of Trump is something more, something different from the normal run of Republican and Democrat presidencies.

INTRODUCTION

That is also a concern for scholars and other commentators seeking to 'make sense' of this presidency, with much of the discussion to date hinging on questions of rupture or continuity – does Trump represent a radical break in American political history and culture, or, despite the chaos he creates, does he fundamentally continue Republican conservative traditions? To be sure, there is much evidence in both directions. Some are keen to highlight the differences between style and substance in the Trump presidency and argue he has delivered little in policy terms.[5] Others suggest that the change he is fomenting is substantive, representing a 'radical restructuring of the entire political space'.[6] However, the binary choices of rupture or continuity, or of style or substance, are ultimately limiting in trying to make sense of what we term 'Trump's America'. This requires what Stephen Shapiro (following Antonio Gramsci) in his chapter calls a 'conjunctural analysis', cognisant of the complex interactions of immediate crisis and long-term structural conditions of change, 'in order to better ascertain the pattern within the noise'.

The desire for normality also indicates a deeper, more existential anxiety, that beyond his contempt for institutional norms Trump has ignited a devastating attack on liberal democracy that may prove epochal. The contradictions and tensions in American liberal democracy have been forcefully revealed with his presidency, which has taken advantage of the gap between declared liberal values and political reality and appealed to the discontents of the growing constituencies of people who have been disenfranchised by the promises of liberal democracy. That gap has long existed, as David Ryan reminds us in his chapter, where he points to the historical locus of the tensions between liberty and expansion and between dominion and freedom in American exceptionalism. Trump not only exploits that gap; he speaks to latent desires in the body politic and emboldens expressions of identity that had been marginalised or silenced by the hegemony of liberal democracy. In this, he is not interested in illuminating the hypocrisies of liberal values but rather in displacing them with nativist and conservative ones that have remained as submerged but powerful currents of American political culture. He is certainly not the first American president to do so and we do not have to go back to Andrew Jackson for an obvious example. Writing in 1960, observing the ascent of John F. Kennedy to the presidency, Norman Mailer described him as an 'existential hero' who could tap into the drives that roil the national unconscious.[7] This reflected Mailer's romantic vision of American history:

> Our history has moved on two rivers, one visible, the other underground; there has been the history of politics, which is concrete, factual, practical and unbelievably dull ... and there is a subterranean river of untapped, ferocious, lonely and romantic desires, that concentration of ecstasy and violence which is the dream life of the nation.[8]

In Kennedy, Mailer saw someone who could fuse these historical currents and potentially renew the nation. Is Trump an existential hero in the mode Mailer described? There is no doubt that he has channelled the discontents of the nation and tapped into angers and resentments that are more than politics as usual. He dares to say what should not be said, shocking the political and cultural elites, speaking to and for the 'real Americans' in their language, giving voice to their inarticulate anger and thwarted dreams. Trump's call to 'Make America Great Again' is in some part an articulation and legitimisation of what has been disavowed in the making of a liberal democracy. He promises national renewal, but not the progressive, forward-looking renewal promised by Kennedy. Instead, he offers a regressive, backward-looking nationalism, one which is highlighted by Donald Pease in his chapter, where he argues that Trump 'animates his populist movement' by manipulating a resurgence of 'white settler-colonist attitudes and animosities'.

In Trump's language as well as that of his acolytes we see explicit efforts to reformulate core myths and narratives of American national identity and civic community. A key example is the consistent efforts to debunk the myth of America as a nation of immigrants. In 2018 the US Citizenship and Immigration Services (USCIS) dropped the phrase 'nation of immigrants' from its mission statement.[9] More recently, the acting director of USCIS has proposed a new interpretation of the famous welcome lines written by Emma Lazarus that appear on the Statue of Liberty, to read

INTRODUCTION

'Give me your tired and your poor who can stand on their own two feet and who will not become a public charge' – this was said in the context of Trump's decision to impose a wealth test on immigrants.[10] Of course, this myth of America as a nation of immigrants was always a questionable fiction used to exclude and silence certain constituencies and their stories – an example of that gap between liberal principles and realities. Nonetheless, Trump's attack on the myth is intended not to question its efficacy but to insert a new foundational myth that serves the desires of his base, one which requires the explicit and repeated demonisation of immigrants.

This contested view of American origin stories and concomitant identities is also evident in the frequent denunciation by Trump and conservative commentators of liberal ideas of progress and justice. A common example is the questioning or mocking of President Obama's favoured phrase borrowed from Martin Luther King that 'the arc of the moral universe bends toward justice', and his many iterations of his belief that 'we are on the right side of history'.[11] Against this view, the text of the 2017 National Security Strategy states, 'There is no arc of history that ensures that America's free political and economic system will automatically prevail.'[12] Such statements are intended to explicitly counter the belief in the inevitability of liberal democracy and replace it with a belief in 'continuous competition'.[13] To the extent that Trump articulates a worldview, which might be titled 'America First', it is driven by this belief in competitive struggle for gain, which is clearly evident in his aggressive pursuit of trade wars and rejection of a rules-based international order. In such articulations we see a struggle over the meaning of America, which is also apparent domestically in the intensification of the culture wars.

Trump's 'illiberal' perspective can also be seen in the verve with which he took up and avidly politicised a discourse of decline that was already well established in US media and some broader literature from the 1990s onwards. The discourse served to focus anxieties about the dissolution of the national culture, about citizenship and about race relations.[14] For many commentators, America's decline is writ largest in a domestic crisis of liberal democratic citizenship, a fracturing or unravelling of civil society and an atomisation of the populace. The political scientist Robert Putnam famously drew attention to this in 2000 when he argued that Americans were increasingly 'bowling alone'.[15] More recently, in 2014, the journalist George Packer described an 'unwinding' of the nation: 'In the space of a generation, [America] has become more than ever a country of winners and losers, as industries have failed, institutions have disappeared and the country's focus has shifted to idolise celebrity and wealth.'[16] Though short on solutions, Packer offers resonant claims, that 'the game is rigged' and the 'social contract is shredded'. This language of decline was magnified by Trump as he spoke to the sense of disinheritance and declining expectations expressed by many Americans and particularly by middle-aged lower-educated white people. During the election he tapped into a language of fear and paranoia, stoking the anger of his supporters, reminding them that the country they knew was in decline: 'Our country is falling apart. Our infrastructure is falling apart . . . Our airports are, like, Third World.'[17]

It is race that structures much of the discontent that Trump taps into as he gives voice and credence to white nationalist anxieties and grievances, most potently in his scapegoating of immigrants, which was a particularly effective tool in his rise to power and continues to be a key lever in his efforts to undermine liberal concepts of nationhood. Race is often encoded in the discourse of domestic decline, perhaps most insidiously in discussions of urban poverty and disorder, which frequently conjoin race and decline and so displace responsibilities for inequalities and injustices. Trump activates the discourse in many of his comments on black culture and urban life, such as his claim that Elijah Cummings's congressional district in Baltimore is a 'disgusting, rat and rodent infested mess'.[18] From the deaths of African-American men at the hands of police in Ferguson, Chicago and elsewhere to the water crisis in Flint, there is evidence of structural violence and neglect and of unanswered questions about the value of black lives in America. Trump not only ignores this evidence but promotes populist law-and-order perspectives that explicitly devalue black lives. He has tweeted a picture of a black gunman beside a series of bogus statistics stating 'Whites Killed by Blacks' and has repeatedly said at his rallies, 'Police are the most mistreated people in this country.'[19] It is worth recalling that Trump in part built his profile as a presidential candidate on claims that Obama was not born in the US and so not a 'real American' nor a legitimate president. These claims have proved significant for his followers, soothing an existential threat to white status, and the constant attacks on Obama and his legacy have been central to Trump's mobilisation of a white nationalist identity politics.[20]

It is Trump's construction of a compelling fantasy for his supporters that is one of the most extraordinary features of his presidency, as is his capacity to project this as their desired reality. (Several of the authors here comment on Trump's use of fantasy – see the chapters by Pease, McGreevy, Negra, Kennedy and Lucas.) In this, he may be said to be actively creating a public through his performances and narrativisations of that fantasy. His stories connect with his followers in a visceral way, and he imaginatively and emotionally empowers them by 'offering them a place in the stories from which they were left out'.[21] This is a common feature of authoritarian populist leadership. The Spanish journalist Andrés Miguel Rondón distils the populist appeal of an alternative reality:

> Populism is not a system of facts or solutions, operating in the complex world of policy and legislation, but rather an interactive fiction, borne of posturing and symbolism, where whole countries can become not what they are, but what they believe themselves to be.[22]

Trump's populist appeal in the US posits just such an interactive fiction, a dramaturgy of the president's making and orchestration, of continual disruption and outrage. His deceptions are widely endorsed as an alternative reality – the frightening story is not that Trump lies but that he is mandated to do so; his very performance of lies and fabrications is what designates his reality for his supporters.[23]

'Trump's superpower is his shamelessness,' Max Boot observes.[24] Fintan O'Toole has provided an incisive commentary on Trump's genius for 'the game of distraction', arguing that he 'disorients us by wearing his most contemptible qualities as though they were crown jewels' and that the 'flaunting of his most shameful qualities deflects damage that any revelation can do to him'.[25] O'Toole writes:

> Trump confounds us by using as distractions the very things that other politicians want to distract us *from*. In democracy as we think we have known it, the art of governance is, in part, the skill with which our attention is diverted from the sordid, the shameful, the thuggish. Yet these same qualities are the gaudiest floats in Trump's daily parade of grotesqueries. This is his strange, and in its own way brilliant, reversal: instead of distracting us from the lurid and the sensational, Trump is using them to distract us from the slow, boring, apparently mundane but deeply insidious sabotaging of government.[26]

Trump hides his sabotaging in plain sight and this can deflect critique and charges of accountability; it underlines the inadequacy of exposing Trump's lies and deceits, for these are already apparent. The French philosopher Alain Badiou has argued the need to 'think beyond the affect' caused by Trump's presidency; he warns that if we do not 'we are only in the fascination, the stupidity of fascination, by the depressive success of Trump'.[27] Or as Frank Kelleter observes in his chapter here, 'the liberal order has lost – and keeps losing – a battle over public meaning and public affect . . . We all live in Trump's reality.'[28]

The transformation of the public sphere in the US, radically reconfigured by new and social media, has facilitated Trump's promotion of a populist alternative reality. Some have charged that mainstream media in the US normalised Trump's ascendancy; they certainly have provided him with a great deal of free press coverage. Trump successfully played off mistrust of establishment media, discrediting them with casual claims of 'fake news' and even calling the media the 'enemy of the people'.[29] Discrediting the media is not new in the US and conservative attacks on 'liberal media' have been loud since the 1970s, though again we see a new ferocity in the attacks by Trump and a deepening of silos due in part to the workings of the Internet and social media in becoming the major sites of news for Americans. For journalists the challenge has been to understand and respond to the dynamics and consequences of what has come to be called 'post-truth' politics, where conviction trumps facts and the norms of political communication have been radically disrupted. *New York Times* White House correspondent Peter Baker has asked, 'Does it ever go back? Have we changed something in a fundamental way in terms of the relationship between the person in the White House, people in power, and the media?'[30]

A similar question could be asked about the fracturing of the polity and loss of a sense of shared reality in Trump's America. Has something changed in a fundamental way in terms of the relationship between the people and the state? The civic crisis in the US is mirrored by a political sclerosis, nationally symbolised by the ideological paralysis in Washington but also affecting the body politic more broadly. With such a dysfunctional system there is limited remedial action to address many problems and a concomitant lack of accountability. Political nihilism is growing more evident, no longer masked by the rhetoric of liberal democracy, while polarisation and partisanship are solidifying political balkanisation. Bill Bishop, who identified the anti-democratic tendencies of Americans in the early 2000s moving to live among like-minded neighbours – what he termed 'the big sort', commented on voting patterns in the 2016 election:

> 8 out of 10 US counties gave either Trump or Hillary Clinton a landslide victory. In these increasingly homogenous communities, nobody need bother about compromise and the trust it requires . . . At the last count, 1 in 4 Americans supports the idea of their state seceding from the union.[31]

One clear message emerging from the overstimulated United States is that party politics and the political sensibilities of the populace are out of synch. Whether this means the American experiment is irremediably broken or at an end is too soon to say. At some point, there will need to be a realignment of relations between the individual and the state, and a rebalancing of rights and responsibilities. While the American capacity for regeneration should not be underestimated, the growing tribalisation and toxic political debate are not conducive to making America great again.

Trump's victory and presidency should remind Americans just how fragile the social and political order so many take for granted is. Is it not a little shocking that Americans should need to be reminded of this? Perhaps not, perhaps the amnesia is a component of the American worldview.[32] Might it be that the import of Trump's election is better or at least more readily understood in other countries where there is a living memory of the pains of populist authoritarianism, where people are more familiar with how reality can be dismantled? The Bosnian-American writer Aleksandar Hemon suggested as much when, in the wake of Trump's election, he commented, 'In America, a comfortable entitlement blunts and deactivates imagination – it is hard to imagine that this American life is not the only life possible, that there could be any reason to undo it.'[33] Hemon filters his perspective through his experiences and insights from living in Sarajevo during the Bosnian war, 'through a time when what cannot possibly happen begins to happen, rapidly and everywhere'.[34] Chastising Americans for their 'scramble for the ontological blanket of reality inertia' following Trump's election, Hemon wryly notes that '"Reality" has finally earned its quotation marks'.[35] The Russian-American writer Masha Gessen has a similar outsider perspective informed by her experiences in chronicling culture and politics in Russia.[36] Reflecting on moral and intellectual challenges posed by Trump's ascendency, she writes:

> Thinking morally about the Trump era requires a different temporal frame. It requires a look at the present through the prism of the future. There will come a time after Trump, and we need to consider how we will enter it. What are we going to take with us into that time – what kind of politics, language, and culture? How will we recover from years of policy (if you can call it that) being made by tweet? How will we reclaim simple and essential words? Most important, how will we restart a political conversation?[37]

These are important questions and while we do not directly answer them all here their spirit guides much of the critical reflections that follow.

* * *

The first section of the book provides varied perspectives on the realignments of political culture in the US that signify a paradigm shift, a radical disruption of fundamental, naturalised beliefs and values about the political process and about national identity. Donald Pease argues that Trump's populist insurgence is antagonistic to American democratic investments in liberal principles and that it constitutes the advent of 'illiberal democracy' in the US (and beyond). In this he sees a resurgence of 'settler-colonist attitudes and animosities' first manifested in eighteenth- and nineteenth-century nativist negations of native peoples. He argues that Trump reanimates these animosities as a white supremacist fantasy for his followers, directing hostilities at the figure of the immigrant as the locus of contestation between liberal and illiberal conceptions of America. Stephen Shapiro looks back and across the Atlantic to another moment of authoritarian populism, that of 'Thatcherism' in the UK, to ask if there is such a thing as 'Trumpism' in the US today. He frames much of his analysis through the lens of the work of the British cultural studies theorist Stuart Hall, who wrote insightfully about how Thatcherism was a 'project . . . to transform the State in order to restructure society'. He does not believe Trumpism constitutes a project in this sense yet argues it represents a Caesarist moment in the absence of compelling alternative political visions on the left. Perhaps most usefully, Shapiro argues that Hall (following Gramsci) helps us to ask 'the right kinds of questions' about the politics of the present and to begin the daunting task of creating a new cultural hegemony. Frank Kelleter traces the revolutionary nature of the new American far right, as it is expressed in some of its intellectual precursors and sources, to argue that these documents formulate a fairly consistent political vision, which is fundamentally inspired by initially left-wing and countercultural figures of thought. He argues that this paradoxical combination of insurrectionary victimology with unsubtle assertions of entitlement – encouraging counter-hegemonic disruption while accelerating existing structures of exploitation – accounts for much of Global Trumpism's current popular appeal. Melissa Deckman and Kelly M. Gardner provide us with a more empirical perspective that provides detailed insight on how women voters and activists have responded to Trump during and since his election as president. They ask if his election has significantly altered the political behaviour of women, and their nuanced answers draw on substantive data collections from national surveys and media polls. They remind us that voting by women is not based solely on gender but on many other variables, including partisanship, age, race and religion. They note that Trump's election has propelled American women to run for office in record numbers and galvanised even more towards forms of social and political advocacy commonly identified as the 'politics of resistance'.

The second section of the book focuses on US foreign policy and diplomacy, taking stock of how the Trump presidency has disturbed the international system and US primacy within it. The chapters illuminate linkages between domestic ideologies and foreign policy that help explain this disturbance and also comment on transnational forces that roil domestic politics, such as the effects of an unregulated globalisation. Patrick McGreevy focuses on the extraordinary disruption of the global status quo occasioned by Trump's presidency, suggesting it may be understood as 'Rabelaisian' in its disruptive energies and impacts, suspending conventional modes of international relations and diplomatic conduct. He explores the relation of the Trump phenomenon to broad discontents with the current global economic and political order and argues that Trump performs a fantasy of global domination for his domestic audience. He views the geopolitical present as 'unmoored', an interregnum of both danger and hope. David Ryan takes a long view on Trump's disruptions and the loss of a grand narrative of American exceptionalism. He outlines the defining tensions in the exceptionalist American origin story, between liberty and expansion and between dominion and freedom, which has run its course in the belated cultural logic of 'late democracy', evident in the US's relative decline since the end of the Cold War. Remarking on how Trump reformulates the concept of the US national interest, he argues that the emphasis is on accentuating 'zero-sum political tribalism' and fear of the Other. Penny Von Eschen too takes a look back to the moment when the US basked in the 'end of history' and the triumph of market capitalism to argue that American leaders then and since failed to learn the value of democratic ideals and norms that had supposedly been fought for. She explores the roots of the Trump presidency in the new geopolitical order that emerged in the

INTRODUCTION

aftermath of the collapse of the Soviet Union. Trump's contempt for diplomacy, his bellicose militarism, his wanton shattering of rules and norms, and his xenophobic white nationalism – all of these, she argues, can be traced to developments after the collapse of the Eastern Bloc. Jack Thompson analyses the impact of Trump's presidency on the long-standing consensus about the nation's internationalist grand strategy – a commitment to free trade, security alliances in Europe and east Asia, multilateral institutions and democratic values and norms. He argues that Trump's extremist conservative populism consciously channels widespread concern about the nation's apparent downward trajectory and poses the most pressing threat to the future of US internationalism. Eugenio Lilli notes that proclamations of the end of democracy promotion in US foreign policy have been frequent in US history and sees reason to believe that the rhetoric of democracy promotion will outlast Trump's presidency. He argues that it has an instrumental value even for those US leaders who do not share the Wilsonian belief that promoting liberal democratic values abroad increases national security and improves the chances for a more peaceful world. What might alter this continuity, he suggests, is structural change in the values associated with US national identity and/or in the international distribution of power.

The Trump reality show is driven by disruption and distraction – it has transfixed the US and much of the rest of the world. The third section of the book addresses the dynamics and consequences of what has come to be called 'post-truth' politics. Hamilton Carroll examines J. D. Vance's *Hillbilly Elegy* (2016), which was hugely popular and widely praised as providing a unique insight to Trump's election. He analyses the memoir's representations of working-class disaffection and asks what those representations have to tell us about the fault lines of class and race in contemporary America. He argues that as an elegy for privilege lost Vance's memoir is a revanchist text that seeks to reclaim the investments of whiteness by recasting it as a minority identity, and that this chimes with the national animus of white political disinvestment that Trump rode to electoral victory. Diane Negra uses Ivanka Trump as a case study to investigate the nature and functions of a new plutocratic (post)feminism and to assess its value to current hegemonies of class and capital, particularly the regressive adulation of the wealthy. She asks what kinds of fantasies Trump focalises and what her use value is to a political administration seeking to affect a separation from democratic habits, norms and values. She suggests that public fascination with Trump is tied to the pressing question of what women's relationship to crony capitalism is. Trump personifies on the one hand women's traditional moral obligation to stand apart from markets, yet she also epitomises dynastic privilege and capitalist zeal. Alireza Hajihosseini examines today's media ecology to emphasise how old and new media logics are co-evolving to create a hybrid media ecology in which more people have access to greater information and the capacity to intervene in the narrative formation process. This results in bursts of media activity centred around narrative episodes that fit within wider meta-narratives that are dominant within the political landscape. Donald Trump's understanding of media logics helped propel him first into the role of a reality TV star and then that of a presidential candidate. As well as illustrating Trump's manipulation of media logics this chapter argues that a new generation of celebrity politicians, most notably the Democrat Alexandria Ocasio-Cortez, are fast learning to enter the news cycle on their own terms. Liam Kennedy asks if political satire is dead or dying in Trump's America, killed off by fake news and disinformation and fatally compromised by its limited appeals to like-minded audiences in their bubbles or echo chambers. He argues that the derealisation of politics and the public sphere signals a radical decline in the symbolic efficiency of liberal democracy, and satire registers this. Traditionally, satire has functioned as a form of political communication that attacks but also relies on the solid-seeming reality secured by existing institutions and relations of power. In the era of Trump, though, Americans seem to have lost belief in a shared referential world. Can satire be effective if there is no underlying belief system? Scott Lucas evaluates the catalytic moment in which personality, the technology of new media and foreign intervention (by Russia) reshaped US politics. Drawing on ideas of spectacle he notes the common thesis that Trump is a master-manipulator of spectacle, a showman who has rendered his audience complicit

INTRODUCTION

in his games of distraction. Against Trump's manipulation of spectacle, though, he poses spectacles of resistance (the Women's March, the female Democratic legislators' theatrical response to Trump's State of the Union address) and argues that spectacle can be a democratising force, empowering us as citizens and not just as consumers. He concludes with an optimism that spectacular politics of civility and of decency may yet be the most potent form of resistance to what Badiou calls 'the stupidity of fascination' caused by the Trump presidency.

Notes

1. Julie Beck, 'How to Cope with Post-Election Stress', *The Atlantic*, 10 November 2016, <https://www.theatlantic.com/health/archive/2016/11/how-to-cope-with-post-election-stress/507296>; Erin Durkin, 'Trump–Clinton Election Battle Left Students with PTSD Symptoms, Study Finds', *The Guardian*, 23 October 2018, <https://www.theguardian.com/us-news/2018/oct/23/trump-clinton-2016-election-ptsd-students-stressful-experience->; Kali Holloway, 'Trump Trauma Is Real and Affecting Many. We Need to Fight Back', *AlterNet*, 11 July 2017, <https://www.alternet.org/2017/07/trump-trauma-real-it-wont-kill-us> (all accessed 16 January 2020).
2. Masha Gessen, 'In the Trump Era, We Are Losing the Ability to Distinguish Reality from Vacuum', *New Yorker*, 25 May 2018, <https://www.newyorker.com/news/our-columnists/in-the-trump-era-we-are-losing-the-ability-to-distinguish-reality-from-vacuum> (accessed 16 January 2020).
3. To speak of the 'age of Trump' or 'the Trump era' already indicates the mark this president has made on public perception and discourse.
4. Mark Danner, 'What He Could Do', *New York Review of Books*, 23 March 2017, <https://www.nybooks.com/articles/2017/03/23/what-trump-could-do> (accessed 16 January 2020).
5. See, for example, Jon Herbert, Trevor McCrisken and Andrew Wroe, *The Ordinary Presidency of Donald J. Trump* (Cham: Palgrave Macmillan, 2019).
6. Slavoj Žižek, 'We Must Rise from the Ashes of Liberal Democracy', *In These Times*, 3 March 2017, <http://inthesetimes.com/article/19918/slavoj-zizek-from-the-ashes-of-liberal-democracy> (accessed 16 January 2020).

7. Norman Mailer, 'Superman Comes to the Supermarket', *Esquire*, November 1960, <http://www.esquire.com/news-politics/a3858/superman-supermarket> (accessed 16 January 2020).
8. Ibid.
9. Richard Gonzales, 'America No Longer a "Nation of Immigrants"', NPR, 22 February 2018, <https://www.npr.org/sections/thetwo-way/2018/02/22/588097749/america-no-longer-a-nation-of-immigrants-uscis-says>; Miriam Jordan, 'Is America a "Nation of Immigrants"? Immigration Agency Says No', *New York Times*, 22 February 2018, <https://www.nytimes.com/2018/02/22/us/uscis-nation-of-immigrants.html> (both accessed 16 January 2020).
10. Jason Silverstein, 'Trump's Top Immigration Official Reworks the Words on the Statue of Liberty', CBS News, 14 August 2019, <https://www.cbsnews.com/news/statue-of-liberty-poem-emma-lazarus-quote-changed-trump-immigration-official-ken-cuccinelli-after-public-charge-law> (accessed 16 January 2020).
11. David A. Graham, 'The Wrong Side of "the Right Side of History"', *The Atlantic*, 21 December 2015, <https://www.theatlantic.com/politics/archive/2015/12/obama-right-side-of-history/420462>; Ben Shapiro, 'Obama's Skewed Moral Universe', *Real Clear Politics*, 27 December 2016, <https://www.realclearpolitics.com/articles/2016/12/27/obamas_skewed_moral_universe_132655.html>; Michael Barone, 'The Arc of History Doesn't Always Bend towards Justice', *Washington Examiner*, 23 November 2016, <https://www.washingtonexaminer.com/the-arc-of-history-doesnt-always-bend-toward-justice>; Mychal Denzel Smith, 'The Truth about "the Arc of the Moral Universe"', *HuffPost*, 18 January 2018, <https://www.huffpost.com/entry/opinion-smith-obama-king_n_5a5903e0e4b04f3c55a252a4> (all accessed 16 January 2020).
12. 'National Security Strategy of the United States of America', December 2017, https://www.whitehouse.gov/wp-content/uploads/2017/12/NSS-Final-12-18-2017-0905.pdf (accessed 16 January 2020).
13. Ibid.
14. See Liam Kennedy, 'America Feels Like It Is in Decline Again – and Trump Is Just a Symptom', *The Conversation*, 19 May 2016, <http://theconversation.com/america-feels-like-its-in-decline-again-and-trump-is-just-a-symptom-56864> (accessed 16 January 2020).
15. Robert D. Putnam, *Bowling Alone: The Collapse and Revival of American Community* (New York: Simon & Schuster, 2000).
16. George Packer, *The Unwinding: An Inner History of the New America* (New York: Farrar, Straus & Giroux, 2014), jacket statement.

INTRODUCTION

17. 'Trump on US Airports: We're Like Third World,' CNBC, 3 March 2016, <https://www.cnbc.com/video/2016/03/03/trump-on-us-airports-were-like-third-world.html> (accessed 16 January 2020). See Kennedy, 'America Feels Like It Is in Decline Again'; Thomas Frank, *Rendezvous with Oblivion: Reports from a Sinking Society* (New York: Metropolitan, 2018).
18. Spencer Kimball, 'Trump Calls Baltimore a "Disgusting Rat and Rodent Infested Mess" in Attack on Rep. Elijah Cummings', CNBC, 27 July 2019, <https://www.cnbc.com/2019/07/27/trump-calls-baltimore-a-disgusting-rat-and-rodent-infested-mess-in-attack-on-rep-elijah-cummings.html> (accessed 16 January 2020).
19. Jon Greenberg, 'Trump's Pants on Fire Tweet that Blacks Killed 81% of White Homicide Victims' *PolitiFact*, 23 November 2015, <https://www.politifact.com/truth-o-meter/statements/2015/nov/23/donald-trump/trump-tweet-blacks-white-homicide-victims>; Cory Bennet, 'Trump Takes Heat for Tweet about Black Murder Rates', *The Hill*, 22 November 2015, <https://thehill.com/homenews/presidential-campaign/261059-trump-takes-heat-for-tweet-about-black-murder-rates>; Nick Wing, 'Donald Trump Says "Police Are the Most Mistreated People" in America', *HuffPost*, 15 January 2016, <https://www.huffpost.com/entry/donald-trump-police_n_569869d1e4b0b4eb759df9b8> (all accessed 16 January 2020).
20. Trump's racism has a long and well-documented history. See 'From Birtherism to Racist Tweets: Trump's History of Inflaming Racial Tensions', *CBS Evening News*, 16 July 2019, <https://www.cbsnews.com/news/from-birtherism-to-racist-tweets-trumps-history-of-inflaming-racial-tensions>; David A. Graham, Adrienne Green, Cullen Murphy and Parker Richards, 'An Oral History of Trump's Bigotry', *The Atlantic*, June 2019, <https://www.theatlantic.com/magazine/archive/2019/06/trump-racism-comments/588067>; Ezinne Ukoha, 'What the Birther Attack on President Obama was Supposed to Accomplish', *Medium*, 18 July 2019, <https://medium.com/@nilegirl/why-wasnt-the-birther-attack-on-president-obama-considered-racist-1e161add21fb> (all accessed 16 January 2020).
21. Nicolas Bencherki and Joelle Basque, 'Why So Many Americans Continue to Believe in Donald Trump', *The Conversation*, 6 August 2018, <https://theconversation.com/why-so-many-americans-continue-to-believe-in-donald-trump-100498> (accessed 16 January 2020). Liberals, including Democratic politicians, have struggled to tell compelling stories about national identity, reflecting their discomfort with the

language of nationalism. See Noam Gidron, 'The Left Shouldn't Fear Nationalism. It Should Embrace It', *Vox*, 8 February 2018, <https://www.vox.com/the-big-idea/2018/2/8/16982036/nationalism-patriotism-left-right-trump-democrats-solidarity>; Jill Lapore, 'Don't Let Nationalists Speak for the Nation', *New York Times*, 25 May 2019, <https://www.nytimes.com/2019/05/25/opinion/sunday/nationalism-liberalism-2020.html>; Fareed Zakaria, 'Democrats Need an Antidote to Nationalism', *Washington Post*, 11 April 2019, <https://www.washingtonpost.com/opinions/democrats-need-an-antidote-to-nationalism/2019/04/11/0ba94fe2-5c95-11e9-a00e-050dc7b82693_story.html>; Joseph O'Neill, 'Real Americans', *New York Review of Books*, 15 August 2019, <https://www.nybooks.com/articles/2019/08/15/jill-lepore-suketu-mehta-real-americans>(all accessed 16 January 2020).

22. Andrés Miguel Rondón, 'Donald Trump's Fictional America', *Politico*, 2 April 2017, https://www.politico.com/magazine/story/2017/04/donald-trumps-fictional-america-post-fact-venezuela-214973.

23. Trump astutely understands his currency as a performer – 'I will be so presidential,' he promised while campaigning – and as a producer – 'I play to people's fantasies,' he remarks in his book *The Art of the Deal*. Scott Detrow, 'Show's Over? Trump Pledges to Be "So Presidential You Will Be So Bored"', NPR, 21 April 2016, <https://www.npr.org/2016/04/21/475126907/shows-over-trump-pledges-to-be-so-presidential-you-will-be-so-bored>; Carlos Lozada, 'How Donald Trump Plays the Press, in His Own Words', *Washington Post*, 17 June 2015, <https://www.washingtonpost.com/news/book-party/wp/2015/06/17/how-donald-trump-plays-the-press-in-his-own-words> (both accessed 16 January 2020).

24. Max Boot, 'Trump's Superpower Is His Shamelessness', *Washington Post*, 12 February 2019, <https://www.washingtonpost.com/opinions/2019/02/12/trumps-superpower-is-his-shamelessness> (accessed 16 January 2020).

25. Fintan O'Toole, 'Saboteur in Chief', *New York Review of Books*, 6 December 2018, <https://www.nybooks.com/articles/2018/12/06/trump-saboteur-in-chief> (accessed 16 January 2020).

26. Ibid.

27. Alain Badiou, 'Reflections on the Recent Election', Verso Books Blogs, 15 November 2016, <https://www.versobooks.com/blogs/2940-alain-badiou-reflections-on-the-recent-election> (accessed 16 January 2020).

28. Trump's promotion of an alternative reality may be seen as continuous with although more avowedly populist than the view associated with

the George H. W. Bush administration in its disdain for 'the reality-based community'. In 2004 a top aide to President Bush (later identified as Karl Rove) told journalist Ron Suskind: 'We're an empire now, and when we act, we create our own reality. And while you're studying that reality – judiciously, as you will – we'll act again, creating other new realities, which you can study too, and that's how things will sort out. We're history's actors . . . and you, all of you, will be left to just study what we do.' Ron Suskind, 'Faith, Certainty and the Presidency of George W. Bush', *New York Times Magazine*, 17 October 2004, <https://www.nytimes.com/2004/10/17/magazine/faith-certainty-and-the-presidency-of-george-w-bush.html> (accessed 16 January 2020). This was a statement about political power but also a warning that the action of those in power was not answerable to discernible reality. It also foreshadowed 'the psychic logic of the Trump candidacy'. Adam Haslett, 'How the Bush Dynasty's Tactics Birthed the President Trump Nightmare', *The Guardian*, 19 February 2016, <https://www.theguardian.com/us-news/2016/feb/19/bush-dynasty-donald-trump-south-carolina-adam-haslett> (accessed 16 January 2020).

29. David Smith, '"Enemy of the People": Trump's War on the Media Is a Page from Nixon's Play Book', *The Guardian*, 7 September 2019, <https://www.theguardian.com/us-news/2019/sep/07/donald-trump-war-on-the-media-oppo-research>; Martin Pengelly, '"The President's Insane": Book by CNN's Jim Acosta Charts Trump War on Press', *The Guardian*, 25 May 2019, <https://www.theguardian.com/us-news/2019/may/25/jim-acosta-cnn-white-house-trump-book-enemy-of-the-people> (both accessed 16 January 2020).

30. Jack Goldsmith, 'Will Donald Trump Destroy the Presidency?', *The Atlantic*, October 2017, <https://www.theatlantic.com/magazine/archive/2017/10/will-donald-trump-destroy-the-presidency/537921> (accessed 16 January 2020).

31. Bill Bishop, 'Americans Have Lost Faith in Institutions: That's Not Because of Trump or "Fake News"', *Washington Post*, 3 March 2017, <https://www.washingtonpost.com/posteverything/wp/2017/03/03/americans-have-lost-faith-in-institutions-thats-not-because-of-trump-or-fake-news> (accessed 16 January 2020).

32. The American writer Tom Wolfe echoed this amnesia in mocking fashion when he remarked that the 'dark night of fascism is always descending in the United States and yet lands only in Europe'. Tom Wolfe, 'The Intelligent Coed's Guide to America', in *Mauve Gloves & Madmen, Clutter & Vine, and Other Stories, Sketches, and Essays* (New York: Farrar, Straus & Giroux, 1976), 117.

33. Alexsandar Hemon, 'Stop Making Sense, or How to Write in the Age of Trump', *Village Voice*, 17 January 2017, <https://www.villagevoice.com/2017/01/17/stop-making-sense-or-how-to-write-in-the-age-of-trump> (accessed 16 January 2020).
34. Ibid. Hemon writes: 'People asked me if I had known the war was coming – I did, I'd say, I just didn't know I did, because my mind refused to accept the possibility that the only life and reality I had known could be so easily annihilated. I perceived and received information but could not process it and convert it into knowledge, because the mind could not accept the unimaginable, because I had no access to an alternative ontology.'
35. Ibid.
36. Gessen notes: 'You always have the ability to "other" the reality in which you live, which I think is an essential skill for a writer.' Phoebe Neidl, 'Masha Gessen: A Russian's Perspective on Trump's Autocratic Impulses', *Rolling Stone*, 31 August 2017, <https://www.rollingstone.com/politics/politics-features/masha-gessen-a-russians-perspective-on-trumps-autocratic-impulses-128037> (accessed 16 January 2020).
37. Gessen, 'In the Trump Era'.

Part One

Paradigm Shift

1
Donald Trump's Settler-Colonist State (Fantasy): A New Era of Illiberal Hegemony?

Donald E. Pease

The election of Donald Trump was the signature event in a series of electoral insurrections that empowered voters across Europe and the United States to elect populist candidates to express their intense dissatisfaction with long-standing geopolitical arrangements and institutions. Arbiters of conventional wisdom routinely characterise populism as a threat to democracy *tout court*. However, the political theorists Jan-Werner Müller and John B. Judis have analysed this populist insurgence as symptomatic of a political contradiction intrinsic to *liberal* democracy.[1] Both theorists define liberal democracy as a structure of governance that values popular sovereignty and majority rule but that aims to avoid the emergence of the tyranny of the majority through institutions – an independent judiciary, a free press, regulatory agencies – commissioned to guarantee fundamental rights such as freedom of expression and the protection of minorities. Building on this insight, Fareed Zakaria has diagnosed the Trump populist movement's antagonism to American democracy's investments in liberal principles and institutions – equality under the law, impartial and independent courts and tribunals, separation of Church and state, the protection of basic liberties of speech, assembly, religion and property, checks on the power of each branch of government – as the constitutive disposition of the emergent political formation he calls illiberal democracy.[2]

For the last seventy-five years of United States history, the liberal strand of American democracy seemed so deeply interwoven into the political fabric that it could not be pulled apart from it without doing irreparable damage to the nation. Liberal democracy was the favoured self-representation of the United States throughout the post-World War II era, when an illiberal 'authoritarian Other' represented the political figure against which US liberal democracy was set in a relation of insuperable antagonism. Moreover, for the close to three decades since the fall of the Berlin Wall, globalism emerged as the ideology through which the US model of liberal democracy became hegemonic in the New World Order.[3]

However, as the political scientist Philippe Schmitter points out, 'liberalism, either as a conception of political liberty, or as a doctrine about economic policy, may have coincided with the rise of democracy. But it has never been immutably or unambiguously linked to its practice.'[4] Throughout his term of office, Donald Trump has done his best to disconnect American democracy from the liberal principles and the liberal institutions that Zakaria describes as foundational to its workings: he has trampled on the rights of immigrants, Muslims and other ethnic, religious and gender minorities; he has usurped the responsibilities and ignored the mandates of the legislative branch of government; he has ruled by executive decree; he has based his appointments to the Supreme Court and the Federal Reserve Board on political criteria; he has condoned Russian meddling in the electoral process; he has cast the free press as an enemy of the people.

But Trump has not confined his efforts to unseat the hegemony of liberal democracy to the territorial boundaries of the United States. He coined the electioneering imperatives 'America First!' and 'Make America Great Again!' in response to beliefs shared by a broad swathe of his illiberal populist supporters. Trump's followers do not merely believe that the US liberal elite establishment – the media, the academy, the government and the foreign policy community – is responsible for advancing minority rights within the domestic sphere. They are also convinced that liberal elites have used the International Monetary Fund (IMF), the World Bank, the World Trade Organization (WTO), the United Nations, NATO and other institutions within the 'Liberal International Order' to remove important economic, military and security issues from the national political agenda and assign them to multinational global agencies insulated from public scrutiny.

However, the two key slogans of Donald Trump's presidential campaign – 'America First!' and 'Make America Great Again!' – are declarations neither of American isolationism nor of the United States' withdrawal from global dominance; they are the exact opposite. In the remarks that follow I intend to examine the Trump administration's intention to exercise global hegemony but without appealing to liberal norms and institutions – American exceptionalism, NATO, the United Nations, the WTO, multilateral trade agreements, the export of US democracy – to legitimate US super-imperialism. I also hope to show how white settler-colonist attitudes and animosities with which he animates his populist movement re-direct onto the territorial United States Trump's hostility to international liberal institutions and norms so as to target the rights of immigrants and minority groups within the domestic sphere as well as the liberal institutions – the free press, the courts, free and fair elections, regulatory agencies – that safeguard these rights. The overall purpose of this two-tiered strategy is to decouple US hegemony from the liberal norms and institutions that formerly legitimated US global leadership nationally and internationally, and to inaugurate what the MIT political theorist Barry Posen and other foreign policy experts have called a grand strategy of 'illiberal hegemony'.[5]

Anti-globalist globalisation, Trump's grand strategy of illiberal hegemony

Over the past three decades Democratic and Republican administrations devised a globalist grand strategy for harnessing the political principles and commercial aspirations of liberal democracy to the formation of a 'Liberal International Order' – a system of free trade managed through US- and European-dominated institutions like NATO, the United Nations, the World Bank, the IMF, the WTO and the General Agreement on Tariffs and Trade (GATT), which they dubbed liberal hegemony.[6]

This grand strategy was hegemonic in that the United States aimed to maintain its post-Cold War economic superiority and power advantage by building overwhelming military strength that would defend, enforce and sustain a rules-based global order regulated by these multilateral institutions and thereby transform other states into market-oriented democracies freely trading with one another. The grand strategy was liberal in that it was based on Woodrow Wilson's conviction that the United States can only be reliably safe in an international order filled with states founded on US liberal democratic values.

The architects of the ideology of globalism undergirding the grand strategy of liberal hegemony represented international security, free trade, technological progress, human rights, global economic integration, open borders, interdependent economies and the spread of democracy as self-evidently universal ideals that, in so far as they purportedly expressed the aspirations of nations across the globe, fully legitimated a US-led liberal world order. Prior to Trump, as John J. Mearsheimer has remarked in his monograph *The Great Delusion: Liberal Dreams and International Realities*, foreign policy elites were so invested in pursuing liberal hegemony that they cultivated this globalist mindset to foster the twinned beliefs that globalisation – the unimpeded movement across borders of commodities, capital and people – is natural and good, and that global governance should expand as national sovereignty contracts. The foreign policy community also believed that the hegemonic values propagated by globalism would produce a world so consonant with US values and interests that the United States would never again be required to go to war or even to work particularly hard to fulfil its security obligations.[7]

Since 1989, successive US administrations have pursued policies that promoted this globalist perspective in the expectation that tearing down national barriers to the movements of labour, capital and goods would result in a more peaceful and more prosperous world. This globalist project did install an intricate web of multinational legal, political, economic and security institutions that implemented strategic preconditions for complex forms of global interdependence. It also helped reduce competitive pressures in international politics, and in the process generated an international environment more conducive to world peace. The grand strategy of liberal hegemony has managed to secure and sustain a durable European peace and to ameliorate as well seemingly intractable east Asian conflicts. But the policy experts who advocated worldwide economic integration seriously underestimated the dangers that the integration of the world's economies would pose to the members of national societies that it left bereft of jobs as well as customary ways of life. Concerted efforts to regain control of their economic livelihood have led Trump's illiberal populist supporters to hold institutions in the Liberal International Order – the European Union, the WTO, NATO, the United Nations and the North American Free Trade Agreement (NAFTA) – chiefly responsible for their economic precarity.

When one of globalism's principal advocates, Bill Clinton, signed NAFTA into law on 8 December 1993, he hailed the accord as the long-awaited peace dividend the world deserved as compensation for enduring the half-century long Cold War: 'I believe that NAFTA will create a million jobs in the first five years of its impact, and I believe that that is many more jobs than will be lost.' However, Clinton and the policy experts who embraced the ideology of globalism as the self-justifying rationale for worldwide economic integration quite seriously underestimated the military conflicts and economic setbacks that would result.[8]

Between 1990 and 2017, the frequency of US military combat – two wars every three years – was six times greater than in the 200 years spanning 1789 and 1989. The expenditures of blood and treasure in the seven wars initiated by the administrations of Bill Clinton, George W. Bush and Barack Obama are unimaginably vast. In addition to the estimated 370,000 civilians and combatants killed, Brown University's Cost of War project puts the price tag for America's post-9/11 wars at roughly $5.6 trillion.[9]

The nation's military commitments in Iraq and Afghanistan and the 2008 global financial catastrophe entrapped the US in contradictory strategies. US capital remained integrated in the world system and committed to free trade globalisation, but the United States also suffered significant economic decline – its share of global gross domestic product (GDP) shrank from 40 per cent in 1960 to 24.32 per cent today. China by contrast witnessed its political, economic and military power all dramatically increase.

According to IMF projections, China's GDP will surpass that of the United States in ten years.[10]

China in fact triggered this crisis in the US grand strategy by posing an unprecedented challenge to Euro-American globalisation. Although they did not anticipate it, the globalists who administered the America-led world order in the 1990s precipitated this crisis when they demanded that China, with its communist-run state capitalism, be granted entry into the WTO. Indeed when Bill Clinton championed China's entry into the WTO, he predicted that this decision would 'likely . . . have a profound impact on human rights and political liberty'.[11] However, China's integration into the world economy advanced a state of affairs the inverse of Clinton's expectations. Rather than accommodating its policies to what the grand strategists of liberal hegemony described as the irresistible allure of liberal democratic values, China entered the US-dominated global system on its own terms. China met its WTO obligations, but it did so by maintaining an artificially cheap currency and discriminating against non-Chinese investors and products. The Chinese imports that flooded US markets wiped out two million jobs. In 1989 China's economy accounted for only 4 per cent of global GDP; now that figure is close to 20 per cent. Over the last three decades, the Chinese state has become even more repressive at home and antagonistic abroad.[12]

Francis Fukuyama's influential claims about the inevitable triumph of liberal democracy fostered a period of optimism that resulted in a dramatic expansion of the list of big-budget US foreign policy objectives. These included propagating democracy in the Middle East, combatting climate change, re-building failed states and protecting the rights of religious and sexual minorities.[13] In explaining why the United States was seemingly incapable of acknowledging the problem with these exorbitantly expensive humanitarian projects of military intervention and full-spectrum global engagement, the political scientist Barry Posen points to the aforementioned domestic ideology of liberal internationalist globalism, which aspired to remake the world order in America's image by using its overwhelming military power to spread free-market democracy around the globe. In his 2014 monograph *Restraint: A New Foundation for US Grand Strategy,* Posen predicted that the

United States would remain trapped in this predicament so long as its national security plans remained tethered to the globally expansive grand strategy of liberal hegemony.[14]

In an article he published in the 4 February 2019 issue of the *Wall Street Journal,* the foreign policy expert Walter Russell Mead proposed that the impasse Posen identifies in *Restraint* should be understood as the site Donald Trump occupied when he launched his presidential campaign:

> What gives Mr Trump his opening is something many foreign-policy experts have yet to grasp: that America's post-Cold War national strategy [of global liberal hegemony] has run out of gas. First, Mr Trump knows that the post-Cold War policies can no longer be politically sustained. Second, he knows that China poses a new and dangerous challenge to American interests. Third, he sees that foreign policy must change in response. The old approach – on everything from trade and development, to military deployments and readiness, to religious freedom and women's issues – must be assessed in the light of today's dangerous world.[15]

Trump's 'America First!' National Security Strategy, which is a marked departure from those of his Republican and Democratic predecessors, has broken with key elements of the foreign policy establishment's consensus on the governance of the global order. Trump's scepticism about the Liberal International Order and the United States' historic alliances has compromised the usage to which Barack Obama put the US arsenal of soft power to improve its standing in the eyes of the world. His depiction of United States NATO allies as freeloaders, and his denigration of free trade and the treaties and institutions supporting it, along with many other examples of his posturing on the world stage, might initially warrant the belief that his administration intends to withdraw the United States from the leadership role it has played in the international arena since the end of World War II. However, if we focus on Trump's policies rather than his rhetoric and the distracting spectacles he mounts on a weekly basis for his travelling carnival show, a quasi-coherent National Security Strategy becomes discernible.

Trump's repeated threats to pull out of NATO and other entangling alliances are clearly not expressions of an intention to disengage America from the global arena. Despite his braggadocio about avoiding costly foreign entanglements, in practice his administration has demonstrated its preparedness to use American military power – from air strikes in Syria, troop surges in Afghanistan and Iraq and regime change in Venezuela to the increased deployments of naval patrols in the South China Sea and the Strait of Hormuz – to secure the nation's imperial interests across the globe.

Moreover, as his administration's immoderate increase in military spending attests, Trump not only wants a huge military but wants to show it off so that countries across the world will be in awe of American power.[16] Indeed throughout his campaign, Trump repeatedly made the puerile claim that he's going to make the military so massive that 'no one will ever want to mess with us'.[17] In addition to his renewed commitment to maintain the nation's strategic military preponderance, the Trump administration has also expressed the intention to remain tied to NATO and America's other formal and informal alliances for as long as the member nations compensate the US for its protection at whatever price he sets.

As Dennis Ross has reminded us, Trump's 'America First!' policies resurrect those of a cadre of politicians and political strategists from the pre-World War II era that the diplomatic historian Manfred Jonas identified in his 1966 monograph *Isolationism in America 1935–41* as 'belligerent isolationists'.[18] The proponents of belligerent isolationism distinguished themselves from their pacifist brethren in that they were not opposed to war as long as it served narrowly defined United States interests. Moreover, like President Trump, they were violently opposed to international institutions and agreements that did nothing for America but enmesh it in costly obligations and constrain its freedom of action. Trump wants the United States to dominate everyone and rule the world, but, like his bellicose forebears, he wants to do so without the costly encumbrances of international institutions and trade agreements.[19]

However, while Trump has not inaugurated an era of American isolationism, the 'America First!' policies he spelled out during his 2016 presidential campaign did introduce drastic changes in the style and conduct of American leadership. In his debates with Hillary Clinton Trump outlined a strategy of economic aggression that would force China to be more helpful in Asia by threatening to use tariffs and other forms of trade restriction: 'We have the leverage. We have the power over China, economic power, and people don't understand it. And with that economic power, we can rein in and we can get them to do what they have to do with North Korea, which is totally out of control.'[20] He also promised to continue existing US alliances with countries in Europe and Asia, but only under the condition that they agree to pay for the cost of their defence. Perhaps more importantly, he pledged to get out of the nation building business and focus instead on creating stability in the world.[21]

Unlike his predecessors in the Oval Office, Trump does not conduct business on the global stage in the name of lofty American values and humanitarian ideals. Rather than devoting the time and effort required to generate international coalitions and fashion carefully negotiated agreements, Trump quite openly demands that other countries put American interests first. Trump's signature forced-choice contract routinely involves confronting his international trading partners with an either–or proposition: either they align their nation's economic interests with US self-interest or they suffer the economic and political consequences.

The days of Barack Obama's imperialism-lite efforts at coalition-building and consensus are gone forever. In his resolve to 'Make America Great Again!' in the international arena, Donald Trump has acted upon the exceptional power of the United States to break multilateral agreements, withdraw from treaties and exempt itself from the international rules and norms that his predecessor endorsed. His resolve to detach such enactments of global dominance from questions of the United States' ethical responsibilities has led Trump to dismantle many of the ideals and institutions installed to promote the aims of the post-war Liberal International Order.

Numerous commentators have argued that President Trump's abrogation of the liberal norms that formerly legitimised American hegemony would necessarily lead to the end of American leadership.[22] However, Trump has given no indication that he intends to surrender his presidential role as chief spokesman for US world leadership. However, in taking on this role, he has replaced President Obama's persona as benevolent global hegemon ready to absorb the costs of the protecting the Liberal International Order with the figure of a coercive global hegemon adamant that he will collect protection fees from allies and client states. Trump's critics specifically complain that at a time when China's power is increasing, the US should strengthen its alliances abroad.[23] Trump and his advisors have taken the opposite view. For them it is precisely in order to face down China that the US must redefine the bases for its international agreements so that they more clearly represent and serve American interests.[24] His demand that allies pay their share of the bills and other examples of his transactional style of governance are founded on cost–benefit calculations that would promote compliance through rewards and punishment rather than transformational practices of leadership.

Characterising the full gamut of US efforts to build democracy abroad as utter failures, Trump scrapped the country's once hegemonic aspiration to spread the US model of liberal democracy to other societies. For example, Trump's Afghanistan policy is not based on securing the Afghan people's constitutional democracy but on bullying the Taliban back to the negotiating table.[25] More alarmingly, Trump has often praised authoritarian leadership styles of foreign dictators, from Vladimir Putin of Russia to Rodrigo Duterte of the Philippines.

While on the campaign trail, Trump impugned the IMF, the WTO and other US-dominated global institutions as partly responsible for the disruptive economic changes that mobilised his political base. During his term in office, Trump's ambition to accrue the economic advantage he believes such treaties should have afforded the United States has caused him aggressively to renegotiate sundry planks of NAFTA, and to abandon the Transatlantic Trade and Investment Partnership and the Trans-Pacific Partnership altogether. He has pulled out of the Paris climate accords because he says they damage the United States economically. All in all Trump's neo-contractualist style of leadership has replaced multilateral with bilateral trade agreements, which he describes as easier to audit and enforce.

One thousand days into the Trump presidency it is an exaggeration to talk of an end to the American world order. With the twin pillars of military and economic dominance still intact, Trump wants to retain the United States' role as security arbiter for most regions of the world, but he has refused the export of democracy and abstained from many multilateral trade agreements. It is most important to recognise that Trump has adamantly refused the creedal dogma informing the grand strategy of liberal hegemony – that United States global dominance can only be justified by recognising and acting upon the nation's exceptional global responsibilities. What political commentators misread as a cessation of US hegemony should instead be understood as Trump's decoupling of basic structures of US global dominance from the grand strategy of liberal hegemony (and the liberal democratic values underpinning this strategy) that formerly provisioned their legitimation.[26] What has also ended in Trump's anti-globalist practices of global dominance is any attempt on his part to offer American liberal democracy as an exemplary political model. Trump has introduced a decisive break with the global strategy Woodrow Wilson inaugurated in World War I when he claimed that American democracy articulated the deepest expression of liberal humanity. In severing liberal principles from US enactments of global dominance, Trump has inaugurated a grand strategy that Barry Posen and other US foreign policy experts have dubbed 'illiberal hegemony'.[27]

In reality the international global order was never in fact compatible with a strictly liberal representation of its workings. A rift has always interposed between the principles of liberal democracy that US leaders invoked to legitimate their governance of the Liberal International Order and their actual practices of governance. Despite their lip service to liberal values, the grand strategists of global liberal hegemony always believed that competition within an international order should be welcomed only so long as its competitors agreed to play by America's rules.[28]

In the past critics deployed the principles of liberal democracy to urge US government officials to close the gap between the ideals they invoked and the policies they practised. Mr Trump is the first post-World War II president who has never appealed to liberal democratic norms to authorise or legitimate his style of governance. By occupying what could be called the obscene illiberal gap between liberal democratic principles and the impossibility of their enactment, President Trump's grand strategy of illiberal hegemony pre-emptively takes the ground out from under his critics.

However, before he could install illiberal hegemony as a grand strategy within the global order, Trump needed to dismantle the domestic ideology of liberal internationalist globalism embraced by his predecessors in the Oval Office. The stratagem Trump devised to accomplish this aim led him to reanimate white settler-colonial dispositions and modes of governance.

Donald Trump's white settler-colonist state fantasy

> I play to people's fantasies. People may not always think big themselves, but they can still get very excited by those who do. That's why a little hyperbole never hurts. People want to believe that something is the biggest and the greatest and the most spectacular. I call it truthful hyperbole. It's an innocent form of exaggeration – and a very effective form of promotion.[29]

When Barry Posen ascribed the term 'grand strategy' to what many commentators and observers considered a hodge-podge of impromptu decisions and half-baked policies, he produced a conceptual framework for representing and ordering Trump's foreign policy objectives, identifying their rationale, designating the actual and potential resources necessary for their realisation, and articulating a realistic method to make use of resources to accomplish these objectives.

While Posen offers plentiful empirical evidence to warrant this explanation, I find the representation of the national interest warranting his account somewhat problematic. In his *Foreign Affairs* article Posen offers a definition of the nation's interest that appears indistinguishable from the cost–benefit calculations of Donald Trump. But what image of the United States do Posen and other foreign policy experts presuppose when they use the phrase 'in America's interest' to argue not merely the plausibility but the necessity of replacing liberal hegemony with Trump's illiberal alternative? The 'America' in whose name Donald Trump has inaugurated what Posen calls a grand strategy of illiberal hegemony is certainly different from the commonsensical image of the United States presupposed by the right- and left-thinking citizens who continue to use 'illiberal' to express their disapproval of President Trump's comportment and policies.

Trump may have violated the principles and institutions of the Liberal International Order for the purpose of inaugurating what Posen calls a 'grand strategy'. However, before such anomalous activities could be credibly taken to represent 'America's' interests President Trump needed a segment of the American electorate who consistently identified these illiberal acts as expressions of their sovereign will. Trump answered this need when, throughout his first thousand days in office, he held rallies at which he correlated his dismantling of the key institutions of the Liberal International Order to the sovereign will of the illiberal democratic movement that constituted his core support during his presidential campaign.

Barry Posen, Walter Russell Mead and the other foreign policy experts I cite depend primarily on realistic criteria to argue the urgent necessity to replace the grand strategy of liberal hegemony. But from the start Donald Trump used fantasy to generate American support for his illiberal political initiatives. Trump's presidential campaign officially began when he lent credence to a fabrication invented by alt-right ethno-nationalists that Barack Obama was a Kenya-born Muslim who lacked a valid United States birth certificate.[30] Trump went on to claim that immigrants across the global South shared the collective desire to render Obama's America their homeland because the Kenya-born president had remade America in the image of a Third World country. Such assertions would most certainly have abruptly terminated the political career of any other presidential candidate. But Trump would not back away from this racist fantasy no matter how much well-documented evidence was gathered to disprove it. Moreover, the enjoyment he took from the anger each repetition provoked among members of the liberal elite steadily increased his popularity with his populist base.

In proposing that Trump's populist movement traffics in fantasy, I do not mean that we need only expose its fantasmatic trappings to reveal the underlying truth. Following Slavoj Žižek, I would argue that far from offering an escape from reality, such fantasies actively construct social reality itself as an escape from some traumatic dimension.[31] Fantasy does not merely stage the fulfilment of the already constituted subject's wishes; it constructs the frame enabling us to desire something. It is through fantasy that the objects of desire are given, and it is through fantasy that we learn how to desire. The fantasy frame is constructed so that we experience our world as a wholly consistent and transparently meaningful order.[32]

Fantasies produce a figure, the subject who is supposed to believe in them, as the precondition of their credibility. Political theorists who believe they can dismantle the power of collective fantasy by exposing its factual inaccuracies believe that credibility rises and falls with the truth of a factual state of affairs. But the fetishism that lies at the heart of Trump's base is grounded on the active disavowal of knowledge. Fetishists are interested in facts as the occasion to display how their fantasies can reorganise these facts. Members of Trump's base might be described as having rephrased the fetishist's conventional formulation of 'I know this is not true but I believe it nonetheless' as 'I know this fantasy isn't true. But since I cannot otherwise make any sense of this crisis, I need to believe it just the same.'[33]

At the heart's core of Trump's populist movement there sits a fantasy in which only the restoration to power of white supervisory control of black lives can contain the trauma of its Real – the spectacle of a black man being in charge of the nation. This fantasy has cohered around Trump's populist supporters' response to Obama's bio-political contract. Trump's base considered the election of Barack Obama a breach of what the political philosopher Charles W. Mills has called the 'racial contract' that in the US political order distinguished (white) persons, who are full contractual parties to the social contract, from (non-white) subpersons, who are not.[34] According to Mills, race regulates the American social contract by dividing its contractees into two asymmetrical incompatible groups: the persons who comprise the full contractual parties to whom the social contract assigns its rights and liberties are white, unmarked citizens, while the subpersons who lack complete contractual identification with the rights and liberties of normal US citizens are racially marked. The election of Barack Obama meant that a subperson who lacked the full contractual rights and liberties of white US citizenship was now in charge of revising and enforcing the social contract.

In his monograph *White Nation* Ghassan Hage locates the origins of the racial contract in the inequivalent modes of 'national belonging' devised and sustained by the white inhabitants of Anglo-American settler-colonist nation-states like Australia and the United States. The (white) nationalist believes him- or herself to inhabit the nation at the level of what Hage calls 'active' governmental power inherent to the 'state's will'. Hage contrasts the active subjects of national belonging with those who belong passively to the nation. He describes the members of this latter category as populated by minoritised, non-white nationals who experience their presence as object-like and subject to the managerial will of those who actively belong to the nation.[35]

The members of Trump's populist movement believed that Obamacare in particular posed an existential threat to the white supremacist precondition to their national belonging. Obama's efforts to produce a new social contract with US citizens worked at the most intimate levels of the bio-political body. He wanted to change healthcare policies at a conjunctural moment when the US body politic had undergone a frightening depletion of its vital energies, and the white American middle class was undergoing the foreclosure of its customary forms of life. In his presidential campaign, Trump turned President Obama's changes in the provisions of the social contract related to healthcare into the occasion to repair the breach of the racial contract by promising to repeal and replace Obamacare.

To capitalise on the generalised insecurity surrounding Obamacare, Trump invested it in the belief that President Obama was a Kenya-born illegal immigrant. Describing Obama's presidency as a 'junta', Trump's speech writer and future security advisor Michael Anton cast the non-white immigrant population Obama celebrated as an invasion of Third World foreigners with no tradition of, taste for or experience in liberty.[36] Trump heightened his followers' agitation when he described the geographical territory over which Obama exercised rule as a retrograde nation from within which he intended to imprison and kill the descendants of white settler-colonists. The frontier site Trump restores at his rallies opens up an interval between the rally space and the normal political order where his followers collectively participate in the *fantasy* of their regression to the primal scene of their white settler ancestors' acts of dispossession and re-appropriation. Reduced to the political demand underwriting it, this fantasy can be restated as a collective desire to overthrow, usurp control over and re-settle the Third World colony to which Barack Obama has devolved the United States of America.

Whether or not this collective fantasy is factually true is of little importance, since such fantasies are structured at the site of the impossible demand that participants in Trump rallies act out. Political fantasies are always factually untrue, even as they reveal the truth of the participants' very *real* fears. What matters to the participants in Trump's movement is the way their demands are organised in response to the enframing anxiety over the Obama administration's imagined threat to the survival of their American way of life. Rather than becoming signatories to Obama's proposed changes in the social contract, the Affordable Care Act, members of Trump's base resituated the 'subject who is supposed to believe' within the provenance of the contract *from* the regressive settler-colonist America that Donald Trump would make great again.

Can illiberal democracy become hegemonic?; or, The passion for real settler-colonist state violence

As these observations attest, Donald Trump set the aspirations and aims of his presidential campaign within the contours of a fantasmatic narrative that projected the image of a meaningful and coherent social reality out of fragmented human experiences. Speaking and acting from the position of the inconsistency in Barack Obama's social order, Trump transmuted his supporters' heterogeneous and inconsistent motives and purposes into a singular fantasy. This fantasy possessed two vital dimensions. Firstly, Trump's signature injunction 'Make American Great Again!' offered his illiberal populist base a bellicose fantasy of the dispossession of the alien power that made them feel what the sociologist Arlie Russell Hochschild calls 'strangers in their own land'.[37] Secondly, the power of Trump's appeal was that he provided compelling explanations for America's decline by isolating the immigrant as the condensed signifier for everything that caused it.

President Obama deported more than five million undocumented immigrants in his eight years in office. He nonetheless characterised hospitality to immigrants as a trait intrinsic to the US national identity and associated American uniqueness with the nation's ability to foster a national identity that transcended tribe and sect.[38] Obama firmly believed that the United States' benevolent treatment of immigrants and political refugees sustained its image as the exemplary liberal democracy within the Liberal International Order. To preserve that image, Obama touted the Deferred Action for Childhood Arrivals (DACA) programme, which stopped deportations for undocumented minors brought to the country by their parents, one of the major accomplishments of his presidency.

Throughout his presidential campaign, Trump distinguished his strategies of governance from Obama's in that at his campaign rallies he instructed alienated working-class, predominantly white, voters to direct their hostilities against the immigrant as the figure responsible for the disappearance of their jobs and cause of the nation's global decline. The illegal immigrant became for Trump's acolytes the general equivalent for a whole range of socio-economic figures including political correctness, people of colour, radical Muslim extremists, feminists, Wall Street and the elite media. Identifying immigrants with the economic and social crises effected by globalisation, whose resolution requires their expulsion, Trump turned his rallies into settler-colonist liturgical ceremonies that cast immigrant populations as scapegoats within national rites of cathartic purification.[39]

However, following Trump's election into office, members of his movement demanded that he make good on his campaign promises by converting these strictly symbolic enactments into *real* state violence. Before he could meet this demand, Trump needed to construct a site within the domestic culture where the violence the state directed against immigrants would also foster the production and reproduction of the mindset of illiberal democracy. He created such a site at the southern border where the ongoing daily spectacle of border agents forcibly turning away political refugees, breaking up immigrant families, herding children into cages, and taunting and torturing deportees in their custody violated rules and laws of every institution within the national and global order established to protect the rights of stateless peoples.[40] Trump's encompassing strategy of illiberal hegemony acquires spectacular power each time these border patrol agents proffer no justification for the use of extra-legal force other than America's interest.

At the outset of this discussion I mentioned the monumental problems Trump faced in his effort to interconnect the domestic and global iterations of his grand strategy of illiberal hegemony. The problems he confronted can be formulated as interrelated questions. How can President Trump find a plausible way to persuade US citizens, who are, for the most part, accustomed to consider the principles and institutions of *liberal* democracy essential components of *American* democracy, to think and feel otherwise? If liberal democracy constitutes for the majority of Americans the hegemonic iteration of American democracy, why should they even want to decouple American democracy from the liberal principles and institutions to which it is inextricably linked? On the first day of his term in office, Trump discovered that the figure of the immigrant desirous of entry at America's southern border offered the most effective means of decoupling American citizens from their liberal attachments.

As a form of human life that has not yet been sutured to American democracy, the immigrant body offers a site whereon the distinction between liberal and alternative political iterations of national belonging become starkly visible. The immigrant has been the locus for the contestation between liberal and illiberal construals of US national identity throughout American history. Located at the border line separating the US national community and the Liberal International Order, the immigrant provides a figure of double-faced otherness through which the nation defines itself as an imagined community and against which the state affirms its sovereign power to secure and protect that community's borders. A self-differentiating figure, the immigrant can, on the one hand, confirm one of the foundational liberal myths of the United States as a tolerant, welcoming, political asylum for the oppressed; on the other hand, the immigrant can offer the illiberal settler-colonist state a threatening body upon which it can exert its sovereign nativist force.[41]

The United States liberal democratic imaginary conceptualises the immigrant as a necessary supplement to its procedures of national self-representation. The core liberal beliefs that the United States is a nation of immigrants, a refuge for the politically oppressed and a nation of nations all require the immigrant body for representation and perpetuation. For proponents of the liberal democratic imaginary, the immigrant figures as an embodiment of the political desire for the core liberal values – liberty, equality, social justice – upon which US liberal democracy was founded. The immigrant also necessitates the liberal institutions – equality under the law, impartial and independent courts and tribunals, separation of Church and state, the protection of basic liberties of speech, assembly, religion and property – to realise this political desire.

After World War II numerous multilateral institutions and agreements – the United Nations, Human Rights Watch, Amnesty International, the International Covenant on Civil and Political Rights – were established within the Liberal International Order with the express mandate to protect the human rights of immigrants, refugees, Indigenous tribes and other stateless peoples. It is precisely because the immigrant has solicited the protection of core liberal institutions within the domestic order and the attention as well of human rights commissions within the Liberal International Order that Trump regards the implementation of his inhumane, intolerant, cruel – in a word *illiberal* – immigration policies as the primary weapon in his campaign to render his illiberal grand strategy hegemonic.

Trump wants his immigration policies to attract the righteous indignation of the American Civil Liberties Union and Human

Rights Watch within US liberal democracy and the condemnation of the UN Human Rights Commission within the global order so that he can demonstrate his refusal to recognise the jurisdiction of any tribunal within the Liberal International Order.[42] He also views the state's horrific treatment of immigrants as the best way to break the back of President Obama's domestic ideology of liberal internationalist globalism.

While Trump may not want legal or juridical warrant for his immigration policies, he does need historical antecedents to verify their Americanness. Although it is not clear that Trump is acquainted with the specifics of Andrew Jackson's presidency (or any historical facts for that matter), his consultant and one-time national security advisor Steve Bannon has endorsed the claim, first proposed by Walter Russell Mead, that President Jackson's policies and populist constituency furnish useful historical precedents for understanding Trump's illiberal democracy.[43]

Andrew Jackson's comportment in office does bear an uncanny resemblance to Trump's. Like Trump, President Jackson, who famously remarked of a Supreme Court decision 'John Marshall has made his decision; now let him enforce it!', did not believe in the separation of powers; he refused to recognise the legal or civil rights of African-Americans, immigrants, indentured servants and other unprotected minorities; he used strictly political criteria in determining appointments to the Supreme Court; he attributed his 1824 loss to John Quincy Adams to a 'rigged' election; and he regularly issued legally binding acts of legislation by executive decree.

Holding President Jackson's strategies of governance alongside President Trump's also discloses the trans-historical applicability of anomalous extra-legal concepts that might otherwise seem utterly bizarre. Roger Taney, whom Jackson appointed to the Supreme Court in 1837, invented 'natal alienation' to describe a condition of existence that alienated the slave from all legally enforceable ties of kinship. This meant that in the eyes of the law a slave was radically kinless with no family relationships under the law's protection. Taney coined this term in handing down the notorious Dred Scott decision, which afforded the slave owner legal warrant for the violent separation of children from their enslaved parents in the antebellum period. The immigration officers empowered to carry out Donald Trump's executive orders at the nation's borders have reanimated this extra-legal fiction to forcibly break apart and cage the children of immigrant families in their custody.[44]

However, the deepest correlation between Jackson's presidency and Trump's is the uninterrupted and ongoing eventfulness of Jackson-era white settler-colonist violence. The Army Corps of Engineers enlisted to install the Dakota Access pipeline on the Standing Rock Sioux reservation, the participants in the 'Unite the Right' rally who chanted 'You will not replace us' in Charlottesville, Virginia on 11–12 August 2017, and the spectacular acts of violent dispossession that legal and extra-legal military patrols carry out each day at the nation's southern borders bring into stark visibility the ongoingness of white-settler colonist violence.

They also explain why the emblematic historical figure for Trump's settler-colonial nativism is President Andrew Jackson, who as a commander of a frontier militia demolished Native American tribes and drove the British and Spanish from the Deep South. As president, Jackson based his stratagems of governmental rule on the need to protect America from external and internal enemies. Trump's threats to build a wall to prevent illegal Mexican migration, and provisionally to bar all Muslims (later amended to Muslims from specific countries) from entering the United States, reanimate the settler-colonist disposition from the Jacksonian era.

Despite Jackson's defeat of the British in the War of 1812, the spectre of Britain's colonising power continued to exercise sway over Americans' political imagination, which did not let up until Jackson's stunning victory at the Battle of New Orleans. Jackson's victory also terminated the lingering fear that Americans might yet again become colonial subjects within the British Empire. The twinned policies of Indian removal and continental expansion that Jackson took up after routing the British also marked the historic moment of the shift in America's status from a colonial settlement to a New World imperial republic. The Jacksonian Americans who carried out both policies turned white settler-colonist violence against Indigenous peoples into the principal agency of the emergent American Empire.[45]

The revolutionary war may have overthrown British colonial subjection, yet the settler-*colonist* still felt obliged to carry out an imperial act of their own that would destroy the lingering British trace. The *American* settler-colonist who took possession of Indian tribal lands annulled the *British* colonial identity, and destroyed the identity traces of the Indians whose lands they appropriated. The white settler-colonists who were the agents and beneficiaries of Jackson's Indian removal crusades thereafter invented a fiction of their own that represented Indians' relationship to the territories they inhabited as theft, so as to justify the acts of forcible dispossession whereby the settlers 'recovered' ownership of their 'native' land. Since the Indigenous peoples did not understand what it meant to own property, as this nativist narrative states the matter, they never were in fact in possession of the land. It was because they occupied it as placeholders for the genuine owners that these squatters had to be ousted when the genuine owners took up residence.

The Jacksonian white settler-colonists who dispossessed Indigenous peoples from their lands also characterised this act of dispossession as that which entitled them to claim that, as the first inhabitants to legally own this land, they, and not the Indigenous tribes they removed, were the real Native Americans. These twinned acts of negation – severing the traces of British identity and the destruction of native peoples' ties to the land – also in effect constituted the precondition for white settler-colonists' production of the Nativist America that President Trump aspires to make great again.

However, Trump's latter-day white settler-colonists have replaced the Indian with the immigrant as the figure through whom they reactivate this nativist dialectic. The comparative literature scholar Ali Behdad has formulated a compelling rationale for this substitution in *A Forgetful Nation: On Immigration and Cultural Identity in the United States*.[46] According to Behdad, the immigrant reminds white settler-colonists of their disavowed archaic past as colonised subjects under British rule. In Behdad's account, Jacksonian settler-colonists became native Americans by aggressively dispossessing European immigrants of their claim to an American identity.

But under Trump's regime, the immigrant has also taken on a menacing demeanour. During his presidential campaign, Trump constructed an anxiogenic narrative of reverse colonialism that described President Obama as an illegal Muslim immigrant who had usurped power in a junta that turned America into a Third World country. Trump went on to represent Obama's America as itself having been overtaken by peoples who had been uprooted from their homelands by occupying forces of white American settler-colonists.[47] After the 2016 election, the Trump administration's policies of caging, deporting and killing immigrants gratified the desire of the descendants of Jacksonian era white settler-colonists to banish and 'disappear' the indigenous peoples they had dispossessed. Since, in Trump's view, the Indian removal policies of Jackson's settler-colonist state made America Great the first time, he aspired to make this relentlessly nativist American State Great Again.

As these remarks indicate, the white settler racism and entitlement embraced by Trump's populist supporters continue to manifest the ongoing, and intensely militant, cultural, political and economic attitudes sedimented in the matrix of Jackson-era white settler-colonist imperialism. It was Jackson's Indian removal policies which supplied the Trump administration with plentiful historical precedents for Trump's arrogation of the power to seize assets, lands, natural resources and fossil fuels around the world. The usurpation of Indigenous lands supplied the historical foundation of both wealth and power in Jackson's America; it continues to provide the context and primary driving force behind the uneven distributions and force of racial capitalism. The current dispossessive logics shaping financialisation and debt are founded on the racial regimes of transatlantic slavery and the colonial logics that justified the theft of Indigenous lands and death for Indigenous peoples. This reconfiguration of the stratagems and tactics of settler colonialism makes it clear that white settler colonialism should not be construed as an ephemeral historical event but the chronological template by whose means the present rewrites the past to cast the future.[48]

Trump's advisors may have selected the Jacksonian settler-colonist state to establish historical precedents for state policies that do not otherwise appear recognisably American. In so doing they have also resurrected a historical moment when the liberal strand had not yet become a seamless portion of the political fabric of American democracy. But the Jacksonian era was also a moment in which the widespread opposition to Jackson's Indian removal policies, the Southern slave power and predatory capitalism fostered activist political formations and literary movements whose members imagined political dispositions to discredit the democracy Jackson nurtured. The transcendentalists and abolitionists of the era also rendered imaginable the complete change in the political coordinates of the United States that seems more sorely needed now than ever before in the nation's history.

Notes

1. See John B. Judis, *The Populist Explosion: How the Great Recession Transformed American and European Politics* (New York: Columbia Global Reports, 2016); Jan-Werner Müller, *What Is Populism?* (Philadelphia: University of Pennsylvania Press, 2016). Unlike Müller, Judis draws a distinction between what he calls the 'triadic' structure of right-wing populism and the 'dyadic' structure of its left-wing iteration. Right-leaning populism is triadic in that it distinguishes 'the people' from those perceived as political elites as well as from those groups perceived to be at the bottom of the social order who are included in the national community in the form of excluded minorities. In so far as the 'dyadic' composition of left-wing populism merely distinguishes 'the people' from social and political elites, it can potentially include members of minority groups that right-wing populism constitutively excludes. Indeed by permitting the aggregation of demands of excluded minority groups, dyadic populism can also work as a corrective or what Ernesto Laclau calls a 'democratisation' of liberal democracy.
2. Fareed Zakaria, 'Illiberal Democracy in America', 29 December 2016, <https://fareedzakaria.com/columns/2016/12/30/illiberal-democracy-in-america> (accessed 16 January 2020). In this blog post, Zakaria builds on the insights he first proposed in his essay 'The Rise of Illiberal Democracy', *Foreign Affairs*, November/December 1997, 22–43.
3. See John J. Mearsheimer, *The Great Delusion: Liberal Dreams and International Realities* (New Haven, CT: Yale University Press, 2018).

4. Philippe C. Schmitter, 'Democracy's Future: More Liberal, Preliberal, or Postliberal?', *Journal of Democracy*, January 1995, 15–22.
5. Barry Posen, 'The Rise of Illiberal Hegemony: Trump's Surprising Grand Strategy', *Foreign Affairs*, March/April 2018, 20.
6. For a useful account of the history of the foreign policy elite's investment in perpetuating liberal hegemony, see G. John Ikenberry, *Liberal Leviathan: The Origins, Crisis, and Transformation of the American World Order* (Princeton: Princeton University Press, 2012). Also see Doug Stokes, 'Trump, American Hegemony and the Future of the Liberal International Order', *International Affairs* 94, no. 1 (2018), 133–50; Peter Dombrowski and Simon Reich, 'Does Donald Trump Have a Grand Strategy?', *International Affairs* 93, no. 5 (2017), 1013–37.
7. For a critique of these beliefs, see James Cardon, 'Why Liberal Hegemony?', *The Nation*, 12 November 2018, <https://www.thenation.com/article/liberal-hegemony-foreign-policy> (accessed 16 January 2020). Surprisingly, it is the revisionist historians, most of whom were critical of American imperial strategies, who have provided perspectives that Posen, Mearshimer and other scholars in the mostly conservative structural realist tradition draw upon. See, for example, William Appleman Williams, *The Tragedy of American Diplomacy* (New York: W. W. Norton, [1959] 2009); Christopher Layne, *The Peace of Illusions: American Grand Strategy from 1940 to the Present* (Ithaca, NY: Cornell University Press, 2006), who draws explicitly on Williams. See also Gabriel Kolko, *Century of War: Politics, Conflicts, and Society since 1914* (New York: New Press, 1995); Lloyd C. Gardner, *Imperial America: American Foreign Policy since 1898* (New York: Harcourt Brace Jovanovich, 1976).
8. Posen elaborates these claims in 'The Rise of Illiberal Hegemony'.
9. These statistics are drawn from Cardon, 'Why Liberal Hegemony?'.
10. 'Donald Trump Says China Won't Overtake US Economy under His Watch', *Economic Times*, 20 May 2019, <https://economictimes.indiatimes.com/news/international/world-news/donald-trump-says-china-wont-overtake-us-economy-under-his-watch/articleshow/69418379.cms> (accessed 16 January 2020).
11. Quoted in Posen, 'The Rise of Illiberal Hegemony'.
12. Posen cites these statistics ibid.
13. Francis Fukuyama, *The End of History and the Last Man* (New York: Free Press, 1992).
14. See Barry R. Posen, *Restraint: A New Foundation for US Grand Strategy* (Ithaca, NY: Cornell University Press, 2015).

15. Walter Russell Mead, 'Trump Brings Foreign Policy Back to Earth', *Wall Street Journal*, 29 November 2017, <https://www.wsj.com/articles/trump-brings-foreign-policy-back-to-earth-1511825878> (accessed 17 January 2020).
16. Adam Tooze substantiates this observation in 'Is This the End of the American Century?', *London Review of Books*, 4 April 2019, <https://www.lrb.co.uk/v41/n07/adam-tooze/is-this-the-end-of-the-american-century> (accessed 17 January 2020).
17. Heather Digby Parton, 'Donald Trump, Imperialist: Forget "Isolationism" – Trump Longs to Build Up Our Military and Then Use It', *Salon*, 24 January 2017, <https://www.salon.com/2017/01/24/donald-trump-imperialist-forget-isolationism-trump-longs-to-build-up-our-military-and-then-use-it> (accessed 17 January 2020).
18. Manfred Jonas, *Isolationism in America 1935–41* (Ithaca, NY: Cornell University Press, 1966), 41.
19. See Dennis Ross, 'What Trump Means by "America First"', *Wall Street Journal*, 8 January 2019, <https://www.wsj.com/articles/what-trump-means-by-america-first-11546992419> (accessed 17 January 2020).
20. Daniel Drezner, 'Donald Trump's Big Foreign Policy Speech, Explained', *Washington Post*, 27 April 2016, <https://www.washingtonpost.com/posteverything/wp/2016/04/27/donald-trumps-big-foreign-policy-speech-explained/> (accessed 17 January 2020).
21. Doyle McManus, 'Trump Says He Stands for "America First". What Does That Mean?', *Los Angeles Times*, 27 April 2016, <https://www.latimes.com/opinion/opinion-la/la-ol-trump-america-first-20160427-story.html> (accessed 17 January 2020).
22. Susan Rice, Barack Obama's national security advisor, has given this argument its most eloquent formulation: 'The world has long looked to the United States to lead with respect to our values, to lead with respect to our interests, to bring coalitions together – whether it's to fight ISIS, or to put pressure on Russia after its invasion of Ukraine, or to deal with the Ebola epidemic,' she said at the Women in the World summit in Manhattan. 'All of that has changed. Not only are we not leading, not only are we jettisoning our values, but we are actually modeling the opposite behavior.' Renae Reints, 'Susan Rice: The US Has Become an "Exporter of Instability" under Trump', *Fortune*, 12 April 2019, <https://fortune.com/2019/04/12/susan-rice-trump-foreign-policy/feed/atom> (accessed 17 January 2020).
23. Although the Trump administration did invoke 'democracy' to justify the coup it continues to sponsor in Venezuela, it defines

democracy to mean pursuing US-directed neoliberal privatisation of Venezuela's public infrastructure, demolishing the Venezuelan government's economic regulation policies and carrying out the dictates of US oil policy.

24. For a representative example of such criticism, see Michael Lewitt, 'Trump's China Policy: Simplistic, Inadequate and Harmful', *Forbes*, 6 June 2019, <https://www.forbes.com/sites/michaellewitt/2019/06/06/trumps-china-policy-simplistic-inadequate-and-harmful/#5246fdeb2dc8n> (accessed 17 January 2020).
25. See for example Gerald F. Seib, 'US Is Learning That China Likes Its Own Model', *Wall Street Journal*, 28 May 2019, <https://www.wsj.com/articles/u-s-is-learning-that-china-likes-its-own-model-11558964778> (accessed 17 January 2020).
26. For a superb elaboration of this point, see Tooze, 'Is This the End of the American Century?'.
27. Posen, 'The Rise of Illiberal Hegemony'.
28. As Adam Tooze points out in 'Is This the End of the American Century?', 'Europe was made to learn this lesson after the Second World War. It was the lesson that Japan was taught the hard way in the 1980s and early 1990s. It is because China refuses to learn this lesson that Trump has adopted a policy of truculent economic containment.'
29. Donald J. Trump, *Trump: The Art of the Deal* (New York: Ballantine, 2015), 58.
30. German Lopez, 'Trump Is Still Reportedly Pushing His Racist "Birther" Conspiracy Theory about Obama', *Vox*, 27 November 2019, <https://www.vox.com/policy-and-politics/2017/11/29/16713664/trump-obama-birth-certificate> (accessed 17 January 2020).
31. Throughout this analysis Žižek's Lacanian reading of state fantasy has supplied the interpretive context for my understanding of the role such a fantasy plays in the Tea Party movement. See Slavoj Žižek, *First as Tragedy, Then as Farce* (London: Verso, 2009), especially 43–56. I analyse the notion of state fantasy in *The New American Exceptionalism* (Minneapolis: University of Minnesota Press, 2009), 198–213.
32. I elaborate on the significance of a fantasy frame to the production of political desire in 'States of Fantasy: Barack Obama versus the Tea Party Movement', *boundary 2* 37, no. 2 (2011), 89–105.
33. I analyse this paradoxical knowledge-belief attitude more fully in 'States of Fantasy'. Theorists of ideology who restrict their focus to cognitive mistakes relative to economic interest fail to recognise

how emotional attachments have overridden what should have been seen as economic self-interest on the part of Trump's working-class and lower-income voters. Lauren Berlant has shrewdly remarked that 'all [affective] attachments are optimistic. When we talk about an object of desire, we are really talking about a cluster of promises we want someone or something to make to us and make possible for us. This cluster of promises could seem embedded in a person, a thing, an institution, a text, a norm, a bunch of cells, smells, a good idea – whatever.' Lauren Berlant, *Cruel Optimism* (Durham, NC: Duke University Press, 2011), 23. Thomas Frank offers an important corrective to this perspective in *What's the Matter with Kansas? How Conservatives Won the Heart of America* (New York: Henry Holt, 2004).

34. In *The Racial Contract* (Ithaca, NY: Cornell University Press, 1997), Mills defines the contract as that 'set of formal or informal agreements or meta-agreements (higher-level contracts about contracts, which set the limits of the contract's validity) between one subset of humans henceforth designated . . . as "white", and coextensive . . . with the class of full persons, to categorize the remaining subset of humans as "nonwhite" and of a different and inferior moral status, subpersons' (11). The 'full persons' referenced in this definition are contrapuntal ensembles that require their differentiation from subpersons to achieve self-identity. In other words, no matter how universal the applicability of this category, the figure of the person necessarily requires its distinction from the necessary and related category of the subperson. Although the racial contract that underwrites the modern social contract is constantly being rewritten, it invariably establishes epistemological norms of cognition along racial lines. It prescribes for its signatories an epistemology of ignorance, a resilient combination of disavowal and non-knowledge that guarantees that whites 'will in general be unable to understand the world they themselves have made' (45).

35. Ghassan Hage, *White Nation: Fantasies of White Supremacy in a Multicultural Society* (Sydney: Pluto Press, 1998). Hage further describes the way that white nationals inhabit, experience and conceive of their nation and of themselves as a fantasy in which they imagine themselves enacting the state's will (45–6).

36. Publius Decius Mus, 'The Flight 93 Election', *Claremont Review of Books*, 5 September 2016, <https://claremontreviewofbooks.com/digital/the-flight-93-election> (accessed 21 January 2020). Publius Decius Mus was Anton's pseudonym.

37. Arlie Russell Hochschild, *Strangers in Their Own Land: Anger and Mourning on the American Right* (New York: New Press, 2016).
38. Nathaniel Parrish Flannery, 'Who Stands to Benefit from Obama's Immigration Plan?', *Forbes*, 24 November 2014, <https://www.forbes.com/sites/nathanielparishflannery/2014/11/24/who-stands-to-benefit-from-obamas-immigration-plan> (accessed 17 January 2020).
39. For a thicker description of these rites of purification, see Donald E. Pease, 'Trump: Populist Usurper President', *REAL: Yearbook of Research in English and American Literature* 34 (2018), 145–75.
40. Angela Mitropoulos discusses these aspects of Trump's frontier settler capitalism in '"Post-Factual" Readings of Neoliberalism, before and after Trump', *Society and Space*, 5 December 2016, <http://societyandspace.org/2016/12/05/post-factual-readings-of-neoliberalism-before-and-after-trump> (accessed 17 January 2020).
41. I provide a more detailed analysis of the immigrant as a self-differentiating figure in 'Immigrant Nation/Nativist State: Remembering against an Archive of Forgetfulness', *boundary 2* 35, no. 1 (2008), 177–95.
42. For the tracking of Trump's ongoing violations of international law see 'Trump and International Law', Global Justice Center website, <http://globaljusticecenter.net/publications/advocacy-resources/law-and-trump> (accessed 17 January 2020).
43. Walter Russell Mead, 'The Jacksonian Tradition in American Foreign Policy', *National Interest*, Winter 1999/2000, 5–29. For an account of what Bannon made of Mead's claims, see Susan B. Glasser, 'The Man Who Put Andrew Jackson in Trump's Oval Office', *Politico*, 22 January 2018, <https://www.politico.com/magazine/story/2018/01/22/andrew-jackson-donald-trump-216493> (accessed 17 January 2020).
44. 'US: FOIA Suit on Border Guards' Rights Abuses', Human Rights Watch, 26 March 2018, <https://www.hrw.org/news/2018/03/26/us-foia-suit-border-guards-rights-abuses> (accessed 17 January 2020).
45. Patrick Wolfe, 'Settler Colonialism and the Elimination of the Native', *Journal of Genocide Research* 8, no. 4 (2006), 387–409.
46. Ali Behdad, *A Forgetful Nation: On Immigration and Cultural Identity in the United States* (Durham, NC: Duke University Press, 2005).
47. See Ian Schwartz, 'Trump: US a "Third World Country" in Many Cases, "It's an Embarrassment"', *Real Clear Politics*, 30 March 2018,

<https://www.realclearpolitics.com/video/2018/03/30/trump_us_a_third-world_country_in_many_cases_its_an_embarrassment.html> (accessed 20 January 2020).
48. Jodi A. Byrd, Alyosha Goldstein, Jodi Melamed and Chandan Reddy, 'Predatory Value: Economies of Dispossession and Disturbed Relationalities', *Social Text* 36, no. 2 (2018), 1–18.

2

Caesarism Revisited: Cultural Studies and the Question of Trumpism

Stephen Shapiro

Consider a failed New Jersey racketeer, whose angry bluster seeks to disguise his psychic damage and whose personal insecurity as a low-life, moral degenerate is balanced against leeching off gullible followers for his family's financial gain. This description of Tony Soprano might seem like an incongruous beginning to an essay that seeks to come to grips with American culture and society under Trump. In another sense, though, perhaps the roots to this moment's condition do harmonise with the changing media deployments that HBO's *The Sopranos* (1999–2007) is often taken as exemplifying. The neoliberal media deregulation exemplified by Clinton's Telecommunications Act of 1996 facilitated the expansion of cable television and the implementation of new communication technologies that created the industrial and material conditions for the rise of prestige television. In this new distribution ecology, television regained cultural status by screening narratives that focused on disreputable, but charismatic, men who abandoned consensual good-guy-ism in favour of often violent and routinely bullying behaviour. Brett Martin's *Difficult Men: Behind the Scenes of a Creative Revolution:* captures the turn when 'anger' became productive and 'creative', one in which, according to critic Alan Sepinwall, 'the revolution was televised'.[1] Although scripted life ('reality') television is typically excluded from these histories of cultural transformation, given their reliance on an older mode of network, rather than cable, television, Trump's role on *The Apprentice* from 2004 might retrospectively be interlaced within the new media narratives that acclimatised Americans throughout the first decades of the twenty-first century to a new common sense that was more comfortable with the representation of and rule by belligerent sociopaths.

It helps to consider the current moment of Trump's presidency in relation to a changing media environment, broadly configured, not least since nearly all accounts of the far right in the twentieth century have insisted on the constitutive nature of new media within a changing matrix of social (in)tolerance and political repression. Here I want primarily to revisit one influential approach that was noteworthy for deploying its reading of media within analyses of the New Right, that of Stuart Hall and the Centre for Contemporary Cultural Studies (the 'Birmingham School') in *Policing the Crisis: Mugging, the State, and Law and Order* (1978) and Hall's essays in the magazine *Marxism Today*, many of which were collected as *The Hard Road to Renewal: Thatcherism and the Crisis of the Left* (1988).[2] It was in 'The Great Moving Right Show', the first of the *Marxism Today* essays, where Hall coined the term 'Thatcherism' as a way of indicating a change beyond the quirks of a single individual, and towards a larger social trend, an '-ism'.[3] For Hall, Thatcherism was more than simply a right-wing response to 'the recession and crisis in capital accumulation'. It sought instead to dismantle the entire post-war compromise between capital and labour, a decomposition that was accompanied by 'the rise of the National Front as an open political force'.[4]

To understand Thatcherism, Hall insisted that we abandon the safety of automatic or prescribed responses. It was important to have a conversation 'on the Left without inhibition or built-in guarantees', especially as 'many of [the familiar positions] no longer provide an adequate or theoretical framework' to comprehend the rise of the right in the 1970s and 1980s, let alone provide a roadmap to a progressive replacement.[5] Here Hall was especially careful, in the first instance, to avoid a looseness of language and to fall back on 'fascism' as a clarifying term. Instead, he proposed understanding Thatcherism as an instance of 'authoritarian populism' to capture how Thatcher could rule while continuing to schedule elections, unlike mid-century fascism:

An exceptional form of the capitalist state – which, unlike classical fascism, has retained most (though not all) of the formal representative institutions in place, and which at the same time has been able to construct around itself an active popular consent. This undoubtedly represents a decisive shift in the balance of hegemony, and the National Front has played a 'walk-on' part in this drama. It has entailed a striking weakening of democratic forms and initiatives; but not their suspension. We may miss precisely what is specific to *this* exceptional form of the crisis of the capitalist state by mere name-calling.[6]

I want to recall Hall's arguments about the need to craft an analysis specific to the current moment to consider the continued efficacy of his account of Thatcherism for a discussion of Trump. Is there such a thing as 'Trumpism' in the same way as there was Thatcherism, or is there rather a *'trompe l'oeil'* effect, something that appears to be a comprehensive project, but which actually distracts us from seeing what is in fact before our eyes, no matter what the iconic brushstrokes may lead us to believe?

Given the mismatch between the tempo of contemporary events and the far slower pace of academic publishing, a delay that Hall escaped by writing for a monthly magazine, my comments mainly seek to consider the ways in which we might find Hall a usable resource (or not) in sketching out a general outline of *this* crisis. In retrospect, Hall considered *Policing the Crisis* (as forerunner to his work on Thatcherism) as among the first in Anglophone commentaries to stage a conjunctural analysis of his time.[7] Hall took the term 'conjunctural' from Antonio Gramsci's redefinition of *Konjunktur* from its more standard meaning in the German literature of the twentieth century. Gramsci knew the standard definition of 'conjuncture' was economic, 'as the set of [cyclical] circumstances which determine the market in a given phase', but he gave it a more political sense when he spoke of the conjunctural as that which 'appear[s] as occasional, immediate, almost accidental', in order to contrast it to the 'relatively permanent', the 'organic'.[8] The analysis of what may present itself as contingent and coincidental in contemporary politics and society is, however, for Gramsci linked to deeper, more intrinsic contradictions, so that he uses the conjunctural–organic opposition as a language to consider the balance between immediate tactics and long-term strategy. A conjunctural analysis is more than simply a presentist or journalistic description of the contemporary scene; it is an attempt to explain the present as conditioned by larger structuring forces and tensions in order to better ascertain the pattern within the noise. For Hall, a conjunctural analysis was meant as his attempt to avoid the mechanistic slogans of predicted historical transitions (from capitalism to communism) and to listen seriously to the sounds of today. In like fashion, this essay will end by charting out what features in the present may be analogous to those in the past, in order to argue that we may be post-Trump sooner than we imagine.

Thatcherism and authoritarian populism

Hall did not see Thatcher as simply a momentary note in the occasional transfer of office between political parties, but felt that 'Thatcherism' was a 'project,' an effort to change the basic social composition of Britain.

> Mrs Thatcher always aimed, not for a short electoral reversal, but for a long historical occupancy of power ... Thatcherism's project was to transform the state in order to restructure society: to decentre, to displace, the whole post-war formation; to reverse the political culture which had formed the basis of the political settlement – the [Keynesian welfare state] historic compromise between labour and capital – which had been in place from 1945 onwards.[9]

For Hall, Thatcherism was enabled by 'the recomposition and "fragmentation" of the historic relations of representation between classes and parties; the shifting boundaries between state and civil society' in a time when new contested social identities altered the balance and meaning of public and private.[10] Ideologically, it 'combines the resonant themes of organic Toryism – nation, family, duty, authority, standards, traditionalism – with the aggressive themes of a revived neoliberalism – self-interest, competitive individualism, anti-statism' alongside the creation of a punitive 'law and order' state.[11]

Culturally, Thatcherism was a form of what Hall called 'regressive modernization', a paradoxical attempt to tutor the populace in a revanchist syntax based on a regressive version of past imperial glories, but only for the purposes of restructuring Britain in ways that actually jettisoned the architecture of that past. The contradictions of this attempt to speak to two different kinds of Toryism, its backwards-looking landed element and its forwards-looking business one, were papered over by its ability to create mass consent and ensure electoral victory. Because Thatcherism had an 'unexpected ability to harness to its project certain popular discontents, to cut across and between the different divisions in society and to connect with certain aspects of popular experience', its success at the ballot box placated otherwise irreconcilable Tory factions.[12]

Thatcherism was more than an economic policy with an election attached (as it is often now seen). Instead it was an attempt to fashion an entire life perspective about what it meant to be English in the last quarter of the twentieth century. This partly involved a construction of 'others' and moral panics about racial minorities and gender/sexual dissidents for the purposes of replacing an internationally oriented class solidarity with an insular one of little England pulling itself together.

In this analysis, Hall made the distinction between a short-term crisis and a more significant one that broke 'across the social formation as a whole', so that it 'can no longer be reproduced on the basis of the pre-existing systems of social relations'.[13] This crisis of social reproduction was largely due to Britain's declining role in the post-war capitalist system, as a result of not having modernised its economy in the ways of Germany, Japan or the United States, and, as the Suez crisis had painfully revealed, Britain was not able to easily negotiate its loss of empire and acceptance of responsibility for its colonial legacy in the Caribbean and south Asia. These structural contradictions came to the surface with the failure throughout the mid-1960s and early 1970s to manage the above tensions through the dominant post-war apparatus of the Keynesian welfare state.

For Hall, Thatcherism was initially made possible by the space opened for it by the failures of the Labour Party to address its own internal contradictions as a social democrat formation. Labour may have been confronted by the economic crises of the 1970s, to which the normative model of Keynesian policy was felt incapable of forming a response, but it actually disintegrated due to the political equivalent of being seen swimming naked when the tide goes out, as it was caught within the contradiction of trying to satisfy both capital and labour. On the one hand, as a social democrat party, Labour sought to 'maximize its claims to be *the* political representative of the interests of the working class and organized labour [and] the party capable of (a) mastering the crisis, while (b) defending – within the constraints imposed by capitalist recession – working-class interests'.[14]

> But, once *in* government, social democracy is committed to finding solutions to the crisis which are capable of winning support from key sections of capital, since its solutions are framed within those limits. But this requires that the indissoluble link be used, not to advance but to *discipline* the class and organizations it represents. This is only possible if the link – class-to-party – is dismantled and if there can be substituted for it an alternative articulation: government-to-people. The rhetoric of 'national interest', which is the principal ideological form in which a succession of defeats has been imposed on the working class by social democracy in power, are exactly the sites where this contradiction shows through – and is being constantly reworked.[15]

By the 1970s, the social-democratic 'management of capitalist crisis by neo-Keynesian strategies, corporatist politics and the disciplining of working-class demands through incomes policy' had become discredited.[16] In hindsight, Labour's attempt to present a left version of Tory 'one-nationism' was always going to fail as it backed Labour into its own form of nostalgic reaction, where it held onto a core belief that the working class was to be dominantly configured as white, male, heterosexual and often in pre-war industries, like coal mining. Labour positioned itself as the party protecting the working class from the ongoing historical transformation of society and technology, rather than helping it to adapt to these changes. Thus, it pitched itself against nascent cultural energies, of which only some are adequately named by the slogan of the 'New Left'. Labour's inability to respond, not least, to changing industrial conditions and workforce composition, involving women and non-whites, meant that it fell into a form of intellectual rigidity that furthered its decline. For a left without cultural relevance is not a left that can ever truly win. As Hall said,

> Socialist ideas win only because they displace other not so good, not so powerful ideas. They only command a space because they grip people's imagination, or they connect with people's experience; or they make better sense of the world they live in; or they are better at analysing what is happening; or they provide a language of difference and resistance; or they capture and embody people's hopes. Apart from their effectivity there is no guarantee that socialist ideas must and will prevail over other ideas.[17]

Unable to respond to ongoing transformations, Labour gave up the 'battle for socialist ideas', like job security, fair wages and universal access to resources of social dignity, and consequently failed to magnetise working-class voters.

The right made no such mistake. While neoliberal (monetarist) economic policies had their own response to the 1970s downturn, these would not have been enough by themselves. Instead, Thatcherism represents the right taking ideas and the construction of a cultural common sense seriously. Furthermore, the right began to realise that there was no point in simply winning elections. The ground was instead prepared, in advance of electoral occupation, for a durable social transformation, even beyond the moment when the right was no longer in electoral office. This cultural project, for Hall, could be understood, in the most basic sense, as the goal of separating the concept of freedom from its historic association with democracy, so that liberty could be isolated from state-ensured equality and the 'fraternity' of collective rights and union organising. Here, as a hallmark of neoliberalism, freedom would be considered now as an economic, more than a socially embedded, concept. As Hall himself later acknowledged, his discussion was also a first salvo in attempting to comprehend the historic transition away from post-war Keynesianism and towards neoliberalism, which, at the time, Hall still called monetarism or monetarist realism.[18] But partly because of his desire to avoid economistic (and base–superstructure) claims, Hall approached Thatcherism more from its political aspects than its economic ones.

The use of Gramsci

Underscoring Hall's analysis of the crisis of the left in the 1970s and 1980s and the rise of the right was the importance of culture as the terrain over which the consent to rule, or hegemony, was fought. Though hegemony, as the force of otherwise explicitly non-coercive rule, is by now a more understood term, Hall's account of Thatcherism as a crisis of representation, in both its partisan and symbolic valences, also deployed a set of other key terms taken from Gramsci – revolution/restoration, passive revolution, transformism, and Caesarism – as a way of understanding how parties of order and reaction are able to seize the energies of historical and social transformation, in order to redirect their emancipatory tendencies.

Revolution/restoration is the study of how the old forces seem to change in times of rapid transformation, but only in ways that can recreate the social hierarchies before the period of seeming change.[19] 'By passive revolution Gramsci referred to historical occasions in which a "revolution" was installed from above, in order to forestall a threat from below, but in which the popular masses did not take or win the political initiative.'[20] Transformism was, for Gramsci, the method of 'gradual but continuous absorption' between 'antagonistic groups [that] seemed irreconcilably hostile' but began to converge in policies, especially as leaders of one side began to adopt the outlook of the other 'until there ceased to be any substantive difference between them'.[21]

These terms were useful to Hall as a way of understanding the exhaustion of social democrat parties and their increasing incorporation of the terms and assumptions of the (far) right, even after (formerly) social democratic parties regained political office in the 1990s, as with Blair and Clinton. The above concepts were used by Gramsci to then lead towards his term for when conventional political parties have stopped functioning as they were inaugurated: Caesarism.

> At a certain point in their historical lives, social classes become detached from their traditional parties. In other words, the traditional parties in that particular organisational form, with the particular men who constitute, represent and lead them, are no longer recognised by their class (or fraction of a class) as its expression. When such crises occur, the immediate situation becomes delicate and dangerous, because the field is open for violent solutions, for the activities of unknown forces, represented by charismatic 'men of destiny'.[22]

The Caesarist solution, though, is for Gramsci a symptom of impasse, not resolution. As Gramsci said,

> A crisis occurs, sometimes lasting for decades. This exceptional duration means that incurable structural contradictions have revealed themselves . . . and that, despite this, the political forces which are struggling to conserve and defend the existing structure itself are making every effort to cure them, within certain limits and to overcome them.[23]

Thus, Caesarism is a tracer of instability, rather than one of durable transformation, which can only come about through the reconsolidation of the populace with political (left-wing) parties who actually *do* represent and progress their interests. In this sense, *The Prison Notebooks* are less Gramsci's *Capital* than his 'Eighteenth Brumaire of Louis Bonaparte', his effort to explain the rise of dictatorial politics in 1920s and 1930s Italy and help prepare the left in exile for its own hard road to renewal.

Here Gramsci's account of his own time made for a good explanation to Hall for Labour's downfall. As Labour was unable, or unwilling, to pursue a class politics in government, it divorced itself from its electoral base, while also being unable to fashion an economic alternative. Thatcherism, conversely, looked to win the struggle over cultural power, the power to shape identities as way of ensuring that neoliberal tactics of privatisation and the rollback of union protections would become palatable to the working class through the orchestration of a deft combination of nationalism, claimed freedom from state bureaucracy and the whipping up of resentment against social groups portrayed as having done better than they ought to have deserved, especially given their 'new' status within England.

Stuart Hall today?

Hall's use of Gramsci for his own analysis of the rise of Thatcherism was both deft and prescient. Much of it seems immediately resonant for us today. Yet before resurrecting the analysis, a few caveats are necessary. The first comes from Hall himself.

Hall insisted that Gramsci's writings could not simply be extracted

> from his own specific and unique political formations ... [we cannot simply] ask him to solve our problems for us: especially since the whole thrust of his thinking was to refuse this easy transfer of generalization from one conjuncture, nation, or epoch to another.[24]

Hall did not assume 'the left in Britain is in exactly the same moment' as 1920s and 1930s Italy, but felt that there was enough of a similarity, nonetheless, so that 'Gramsci gives us, not the tools with which to solve the puzzle, but the means with which to ask the right kinds of questions about the politics of the 1980s and 1990s'.[25]

Consequently, we need to reflect if the (centre-)left in the United States is in exactly the same position as it was in Britain in the 1980s and 1990s. Three provisos are necessary. Firstly, for all his capacious intellect, Hall's framework remains provincial and nationalist, rather than world-systemic. He stands as a remarkable, but remarkably English, writer. Despite being among the chief redactors of Gramsci, and aware of the Scottish Tom Nairn's contemporaneous Gramscian study, *The Break-Up of Britain: Crisis and Neo-Nationalism*, Hall's writing has little reference to the condition of the other nations within the UK.[26] He continually, and problematically, uses 'British' to mean 'English'. Furthermore, Hall is almost never a comparative analyst. Continental Europe rarely gets a mention in his writing, let alone recognition of its constitutive feature in forming Englishness. Writing largely from within the Cold War's long winter, Hall is not unique among his contemporaries for lacking a European Union perspective, let alone identity, but clearly the study of nationalism today cannot be considered solely in terms of an unilinear metropolitan–(post-)colony relation, as was the case for much of Hall's work on Thatcherism.

Secondly, a host of historical features have intervened between Hall's writing and today. Perhaps most significant has been that Hall's work on Thatcherism was largely written before 1989, let alone September 11, 2001, the financial crash of 2008–11 or the ongoing ecological crisis. In multiple ways a new experience-system, or structure of feeling, has emerged in ways that cannot be easily ignored.

One such change is that Hall wrote as a member of the New Left generation, whose entire life experience was a lacerating sense of continual defeat and the ongoing containment of the utopian possibilities of the '1960s'.[27] For the current moment, it might be said that this sense of retrenchment is felt less sharply for generations who have not experienced its decay, given that they have been born and raised within neoliberalism as a dominant. Hall acknowledged that his writing was meant to waken up the Labour Party, but he underestimated Thatcherism's ability to conduct transformism to such an extent that Blair would be more Thatcher's protégé than her antagonist. Hall had wanted Labour to understand the power of Thatcherism in order to confront it, not to mimic and reinforce its direction.

Lastly, our conjuncture is not Hall's, given our different relation to post-war conditions in the West. Hall said that cultural studies began as an attempt to respond to a 'very concrete political problem and question: What happened to the working class under conditions of economic affluence?' represented by post-war Fordism and consumer prosperity.[28] The crisis of the 1970s, with its *stagflation*, the paradoxical combination of inflation and mass unemployment, was thus an existential challenge both to Keynesianism as well as its twin, the first formation of cultural studies. Thatcherism largely propelled a version of nationalism as a response to the decline in working-class relative affluence, the affluence that was the initial 'object' of cultural studies' inquiries. Consequently, the study of Thatcherism was also a self-investigation for cultural studies into its own formation. Today, neoliberalism has produced a different kind of crisis, one that might be called *stagployment*, a contradictory situation that gives mass employment, but without the conditions of consumer power that employment otherwise grants, even while that consumption continues via the systemic use of personal debt. In this sense, the machinery of Thatcherism might be as obsolete as Keynesianism was becoming in the 1970s.

Acknowledging Hall's category limits and historical location, then, let me return to the *Sopranos* question that began this essay. Is there such a thing as Trumpism, and is it Caesarist in Hall's and Gramsci's sense?

American Caesarism?

Taking up Hall's writing after nearly forty years, much of it, and Gramsci's terms, remains apposite for American politics. A renewed period of transformism occurred through the mid-1990s when the Democratic Party began to be embarrassed about the kinds of people who voted for it. Party elites adopted neoliberal perspectives for electoral victory. The second wave of Caesarist separation of political parties from the working and lower middle classes came with Bill Clinton's ensuing strategy of triangulation. This rightwards turn was papered over by the conditions of the long boom, which were substantively different from the grind of the 1970s and 1980s recession. Americans accepted the Caesarism of the 1990s as they were progressively won over with perceived increasing living standards, facilitated by the cheapening of commodities due to new pools of underpaid non-Western workforces, the onset of new technologies, and greater access to personal credit.

Between Hall's writing in the times of severe economic downturn in the 1970s and 1980s and the ensuing period that began in the mid-to-late 1990s came a series of structural rearrangements that seemed to empower the middle-class's 'entrepreneurial' agency in a situation much like Gramsci's description of revolution/restoration and passive revolution. The phase between the reunification of the Germanys (1989–90) and the fall of the Soviet Union (1991), on the one hand, and the handover of Hong Kong to the People's Republic of China (1997), on the other, substantively ended the Cold War's military Keynesianism and blockages of free movement, which had ensured Western job security, as Americans were protected from having to compete against eastern Europe and east Asia. While the first wave of working-class disempowerment came in the 1970s and 1980s through attacks on labour's power over *production* by undermining unions, this was still somewhat masked by the continuing presence of Cold War formations. A more serious second wave came through an attack that enabled (middle-class) *consumption*, via commodities produced by cheaper east European and Asian labour that facilitated a consumer revolution that broadened the spectrum of goods available to Americans throughout the class hierarchy. Many Americans throughout the 1990s began to feel as if they had 'never had it so good', especially with bank deregulation that vastly facilitated personal access to credit, which would enable non-staples purchasing.

Americans in the 1990s experienced something more liberating than freedom from government bureaucracy; they experienced freedom from a restricted palette of consumer options that was perceived as dull and limiting in choice. Neoliberal freedom was received not only by the removal of government regulation, but also by the new possibilities of retail therapy provided by the exploitation of a global workforce. Additionally, the middle class was encouraged to practise new management attitudes with the rise of personal computers and communication networks like mobile phones. One key moment in this transition was the 1995 introduction of Microsoft Office, which bundled word-processing, spreadsheets and presentation slide software into one easily available package. This software not only helped business-oriented information handling, but also allowed it to infiltrate the private sphere of personal life in ways as significant as new possibilities for personal computer purchasing.

However, like a thief in the night, the very structural readjustments welcomed by the broad (petite) bourgeoisie began to erode their own position *even while initially seeming to reward it*. From the mid-1990s, the American middle class saw what had previously been the mechanism and reward for middle-class status – home ownership, higher educational credentials, healthcare and pensions – become increasingly unaffordable. An asphyxiated middle class finds that it cannot breathe under the weight of debt and bourgeois fragility ('precarity'), even while the outward signs are ones of comfort. Thus, if the Democratic Party had incrementally dissociated itself from the role of protecting the labouring and lower middle classes throughout the 1990s, then it did likewise for the next higher strands of the class spectrum in the phase after the 2008–11 financial crisis. Hillary Clinton's loss was the cadenza of contradictions wherein the Democratic Party thought it could abandon the middle class and rule instead on a far more elite coalition of Wall Street, Silicon Valley and Hollywood. As Clinton discovered, this could not make for a winning, let alone durable, governing coalition.

The dynamics of the mid-1990s repeated what occurred in the 1970s and 1980s, but did so in a different score, at a higher class level. What differs, though, from the 1970s and 1980s is that the Caesarism of charismatic men from the mid-1990s onwards was produced not by politics but prestige television series, such as *The Sopranos*, which staged the moment's Caesarism better than did official party politics.[29] For despite Hall's resistance to older left accounts that he felt were still too mechanistic, his own writing incompletely freed itself from the sinking suspicion that national party politics *mattered* more to the recomposition of class relations than did global political economy and its effects on cultures of work and leisure.

Because the structural conditions of neoliberalism's crisis have already lasted for decades, Trump's election is significant less as a transformation than as a full-blown manifestation of effects that have been long percolating. As the appearance of Caesarism had already occurred before Trump, his arrival is merely the precipitant of long-endured effects. In this belatedness, Trump, more than anything else, seems to represent the state combination of greed and the manipulation of government for a handful of individuals or family gain that is otherwise associated with the weak state forms of recently decolonised nations. While one hesitates to be held hostage to fortune, the administration may itself be a harbinger of change as its success is the dead cat bounce or last gasp of an obsolete system. As Hall said of the Labour Party, the hard road to renewal is one that must begin by considering how actual social factions became demobilised, in order to reverse that trend and craft a new cultural symbolics that can pre-position groups to assume political power. Despite the momentary gloom, the green shoots for a (centre-)left renewal have already arrived, not least with the 2018 congressional midterm results, which delivered the House of Representatives to a Democratic Party that now contains younger members who are unwilling to continue a transformist strategy. What may a post-Caesarist formation look like?

A newer left?

In his book about the constitution of the Cultural Front in 1930s America, Michael Denning presents a case study for how classes can become reconnected with the politics of representation.[30] Denning argues that the groundwork for the post-war New Deal Consensus was initially cemented through the 1930s in a 'Popular Front social movement' that brought together 'three political forms: a social democratic electoral politics; politics of anti-fascist and anti-imperialist solidarity; and civil liberties campaigns against lynching and labour repression'.[31]

Herein three very different groups each had a particular crisis or concern that they wanted to overcome. One group, which Denning calls the plebeians, involved sections of the American population that had been marginalised, but now had their children seeking equality and incorporation within the social and institutional resources of class aspiration, largely involving access to education. These were the second-generation of (eastern and southern) European immigrants as well as northward-bound black Americans. With time, they championed a 'paradoxical synthesis of competing nationalisms – pride in ethnic heritage and identity along with an assertive Americanism – that might be called "ethnic Americanism"'.[32]

A second, smaller, group were the European refugees in flight from the rise of extreme right-wing (Nazi, fascist) governments. Composed of individuals who were able to overcome anti-immigration barriers, since they tended to have prior professional and educational credentials or considerable experience in the nascent cultural industries, many did not necessarily seek to remain within the United States longer than was necessary to defeat the far right, although several ultimately settled permanently. While in America, they sought to help Americans overcome their cultural and political isolationism by working with the arts to help 'transform the ways people imagine the globe'.[33] A third, even smaller, group consisted of those who were born in America, often coming from elite backgrounds and universities, and had considerable experience of the arts. This group embraced the aesthetics of modernism to convey their unhappiness about the lack of personal expression and available consumer choices in the United States.

In ways that were not to be expected, these three broad groups, different in size and relationship to the cultural industries, began slowly to converge. The particular concerns or problems of one group began to be championed by the others, so that over time they developed a sense of mutuality and shared dictionary of new key terms, like the 'American people'. These new terms did not belong to or emerge from any one group; instead they were crafted precisely as a means of registering the presence of and further constituting this social alliance or historic bloc.

These new keywords and narratives were disseminated to a wider public as members of the Cultural Front had access to the new mass cultural industries, like cinema, or were able to repurpose older ones, like radio. The Cultural Front had an influence greater than its relative numbers might suggest, since the broad American middle and working class were willing to follow the leadership of this social alliance precisely because the crisis of the Depression had delegitimised traditional leaderships and institutions.

Almost in passing, Denning suggests that an analogous kit of coalitional convergences occurred at an earlier moment of history, the antebellum America of the 1840s. In this time, a similar fusion of mixed-race social democracy, bourgeois dissidence and internationalism arose with abolition, feminism and interest in European strands of communitarian living, like those promoted by Charles Fourier. Similarly, older cultural forms, like ministerial itinerant circuits, became remade for secular lecturing and older textual forms repurposed into the 'American Renaissance' novel. If we take Denning's suggestion of how prior cultural formations appear in Caesarist phases of disconnect between political parties and classes, we might recognise the presence of a similar pattern within contemporary America, as Table 2.1 suggests.[34]

Table 2.1. The kit of social convergences at analogous crisis years/conjunctures

	1848	1930s	2010s
Mixed-race social democracy	Abolition	'Ethnic Americanism', anti-lynching, campaigns against labour repression	'Identitarian multitudes'
Bourgeois dissidence	Feminism	Radical modernism	Lesbian and gay marriage rights, student debt and precarity, trans and non-binary equality, anti-data surveillance
International awareness	Utopian socialisms	Émigré anti-fascism	Environmental concerns
New media and cultural forms	American Renaissance novel	Cinema	Blogosphere and social networks
Devalued media repurposed	Itinerant revival circuits	Radio	'Prestige' (cable) television

As with the 1930s, a version of 'ethnic Americanism' appears in 'identitarian multitudes', which combine a rhetoric of the under/commons alongside particularist concerns, like Black Lives Matter, and combine attention to racial and ethnic histories with a call for demotic assemblies. Aspects of middle-class-oriented reform appear with demands for non-systemic altering expansion of LGBT rights, student debt forgiveness and the right to an intimate life free from data surveillance and tracking. A new global awareness has come through the insistence on attention to ecological matters that transcend nation-state boundaries. Just as the Cultural Front rehabilitated older media, like radio, and strategically occupied new ones, like the studio system, today we have the restoration of status to television through prestige shows and the rise of social network communications that overcome the older journalistic medium of print and even other forms of broadcast communication.

This outline may be the foundation for overcoming the Caesarist impasse in America today. The proviso against such an optimistic reading is the rejoinder that neither the assemblages of the 1840s nor those in the 1930s were successful in foreclosing capitalism. Furthermore, these changes were unable to become instantiated without any ensuing cataclysmic event, such as the Civil War or the Second World War. In the desired absence of mass human loss, what might transform the situation? What further elements are necessary? For Gramsci it was the Communist Party. For Hall it was the Centre for Contemporary Cultural Studies, where 'organic intellectuals' could provide strategic analysis into Thatcherism. In our own moment, it will mean something else entirely. The challenge of forging a new intersectional form of left democratic institutionality is the task given to us today.

Notes

1. Brett Martin, *Difficult Men: Behind the Scenes of a Creative Revolution – From 'The Sopranos' and 'The Wire' to 'Mad Men' and 'Breaking Bad'* (London: Faber & Faber, 2013); Alan Sepinwall, *The Revolution was Televised: The Cops, Crooks, Slingers, and Slayers Who Changed TV Drama Forever* (New York: Gallery, 2013).
2. Stuart Hall, Chas Critcher, Tony Jefferson, John Clarke and Brian Roberts, *Policing the Crisis: Mugging, the State, and Law and Order* (London: Macmillan, 1978); Stuart Hall, *The Hard Road to Renewal: Thatcherism and the Crisis of the Left* (London: Verso, 1988).
3. Stuart Hall, 'The Great Moving Right Show', *Marxism Today*, January 1979, 14–20.
4. Ibid., 14.
5. Ibid., 14.
6. Ibid., 15.
7. Sut Jhally, 'Stuart Hall: The Last Interview', *Cultural Studies* 30, no. 2 (2016), 332–45.
8. Antonio Gramsci, *Selections from the Prison Notebooks*, trans. Quintin Hoare and Geoffrey Nowell Smith (New York: International Publishers, 1971), 177–8.
9. Hall, *The Hard Road to Renewal*, 163.
10. Ibid., 2.

11. Ibid., 48.
12. Ibid., 6.
13. Ibid., 96.
14. Hall, 'The Great Moving Right Show', 16.
15. Ibid., 17.
16. Hall, *The Hard Road to Renewal*, 59.
17. Ibid., 182.
18. Colin MacCabe, 'An Interview with Stuart Hall, December 2007', *Critical Quarterly* 50, no. 1–2 (2008), 12–42; Hall, 'The Great Moving Right Show'; Hall, *The Hard Road to Renewal*, 2.
19. Hall, *The Hard Road to Renewal*, 132; Gramsci, *Selections from the Prison Notebooks*, 219–20.
20. Hall, *The Hard Road to Renewal*, 114.
21. Gramsci, *Selections from the Prison Notebooks*, 58–9.
22. Ibid., 210, quoted in Hall, *The Hard Road to Renewal*, 100.
23. Gramsci, *Selections from the Prison Notebooks*, 178, quoted in Hall, *The Hard Road to Renewal*, 130.
24. Hall, *The Hard Road to Renewal*, 161.
25. Ibid., 162.
26. Tom Nairn, *The Break-Up of Britain: Crisis and Neo-Nationalism* (London: NLB, 1977).
27. MacCabe, 'An Interview with Stuart Hall', 26.
28. Stuart Hall, *Cultural Studies 1983: A Theoretical History* (Durham, NC: Duke University Press, 2016); MacCabe, 'An Interview with Stuart Hall', 19–20.
29. Stephen Shapiro, 'Zombie Health Care', in Edward P. Comentale and Aaron Jaffe (eds), *This Year's Work at the Zombie Research Center* (Bloomington: University of Illinois Press, 2014), 193–226.
30. Michael Denning, *The Cultural Front: The Laboring of American Culture in the Twentieth Century* (London: Verso, 1996).
31. Ibid., 37.
32. Ibid., 9.
33. Ibid., 12.
34. The table first appears in Stephen Shapiro, 'The Culture of Realignment: *Enlightened* and "I Can't Breathe"', in Doug Haynes and Tara Stubbs (eds), *Navigating the Transnational in Modern American Literature and Culture: Axes of Influence* (New York: Routledge, 2017), 144–61.

3

Hegemoronic Vistas: The Pseudo-Gramscian Right from the Powell Memorandum to the 'Flight 93 Election'

Frank Kelleter[1]

The hegemony you break may be your own

In the spring of 2016, I attended a conference in New York. It was primary season. Hillary Clinton was set to win the state's Democratic contest and Republican frontrunner Donald Trump was so far ahead in his party's delegate count that only a miracle could 'prevent' him from prevailing. This word kept coming up in op-eds, conversations and (it was rumoured) Republican strategy meetings at the time. There was a sense of clear and present danger. 'Keep Calm' posters and gift cards were being sold in all the stores I went to that spring, or so it seemed.

Trump was going to win the Republican nomination. But he would not be president. This was the unanimous consensus among the American attendees of our conference dinner. A colleague from India and two Europeans (one from Italy, me from Germany) were not so sure. We argued that demagoguery was a powerful force, unpredictable and feverishly self-reinforcing. We cited – perhaps not in these exact words – the fallout of decades of neoliberal governance by nominally centre-left governments. We pointed to the absence of progressive economic visions that could appeal to the losers in a global trade regime so perfectly embodied by Hillary Clinton. Our hosts would have none of it. A Trump win was *mathematically impossible*. The demographics were against him. It was a brilliantly straightforward argument:

There simply were too many women and minority voters in the electorate. This made a Republican victory not just unlikely but unthinkable.

At the time, this forecast was anything but idiosyncratic. It was, you might say, a fact, supported by numbers, pundits and political scientists. That it turned out to be wrong (even after the appearance of the *Access Hollywood* tape one month before the election, which, according to the logic of demographic blocs, should have secured an overwhelming majority of the women's vote for Clinton) threw an entire socio-political class into existential crisis – worldwide, as befits such global assurances. It was not just that an election was lost (or two, if you count Brexit, or three or four and more, if you widen your geographical horizons), but *reality* itself had come undone. The unthinkable had happened. The impossible had not only turned out to be possible but had established itself as an inescapable actuality.

Of course, the all-pervasive sense of disbelief and incomprehension among centrist voters after 8 November 2016 only strengthened the conviction of Trump supporters that they represented a 'movement': a heretofore invisible political force, repressed by out-of-touch liberal elites but now reasserting itself, literally, with a vengeance. Since then, the worrisome intellectual disingenuousness of this argument has repeatedly been outweighed by its even more worrisome intuitive adequacy. A media establishment proud of its professionalism may find it easy to mock Kellyanne Conway's bizarre proclamation of 'alternative facts'.[2] But such ridicule makes it difficult to acknowledge that our fact-checking news media have always been involved in constructing and safeguarding a rather peculiar sense of reality – one that excludes alternatives not simply because they lack veracity but because they are inconsistent with ruling assumptions of the political economy in place. Three years into Trump's presidency, it has become all but impossible to articulate this state of affairs without risking Trumpian associations. Put differently, the liberal order has lost – and keeps losing – a battle over public meaning and public affect: a battle over what feels normal and what can reasonably be expected to happen in civic life.

As so often, then, it was not reality that broke down in November 2016 but its liberal organisation. (There is an article to be written about how accurate many pre-election polls actually were, but how their raw data were spun into unambiguously confident predictions by reporters and commentators so predisposed. Or another one about the unending stream of competing post-election 'explanations', each working hard to align Trump's dissonant victory with whatever the writer in question had always held to be true.) What is being dismantled amid this ongoing irritation, when systems of thought are forced to find themselves validated by their very abrogation, is *hegemony*. But mainstream news sources – and yes, there is such a thing as mainstreaming media – refuse to recognise themselves in that term, preferring instead a fantastic but increasingly self-defeating image of neutrality. Similarly, many centre-left voters – among them, to be sure, actually existing liberal elites and globetrotting intellectuals – are reluctant to address the election of Donald Trump as a populist upheaval because they have learned to think of popular challenges to hegemony as something liberating and righteous, certainly not as the vicious and oppressive handling of public opinion that defines the Trump White House and its army of trolls.

Even so, my tiny sample of academics at the 2016 conference dinner who thought that Trump could be elected (two Europeans) and probably would be elected (one Indian) soon expanded into a larger group of American sceptics when I met with friends of more radical leanings, many of them socialist, many non-white. Well versed in political vocabularies outside the United States, none of them identifies as 'liberal' (as far as I know). All of them expected Trump to win, one black colleague going so far as to say that the ensuing madness was none of his business because this would now be a civil war among white people. And so it happened that for American liberals – a predominantly white, urban, well-educated and high-earning class – the *New York Times*, of all newspapers, and CNN, of all channels, turned into symbols of embattled civic discourse, brave strongholds of political reporting in an age of counter-hegemonic advances so malicious they defied white, urban, well-educated belief. CNN. The *New York Times*. Difficult times indeed.

Stress and boredom in the 'Age of Trump'

Next came hyperventilation. Trump earned his own 'age' in urgent think pieces and quickly rewritten conference papers even before he was inaugurated. This, too, indicated a rupture in the structures of reality. Even today, many liberals refuse to speak or write Trump's name, substituting it with silly synonyms or signs and numbers, as if the topmost task now were to preserve the integrity of a world of clean transactions temporarily disturbed by a vulgar visitor one better ignores. Can liberal politics save its composure by magical thinking, keeping itself pure from indecent annoyances by relegating them to another, semi-fictional realm of action? Shortly before the election, there was a theory floating around social media that Trump did not really want to win but that his candidacy was a marketing ploy for the one thing he truly desired: a television channel. As it turned out, he won and got all the channels.

We all live in Trump's reality now. Unpleasant as this situation is, there can be little doubt that Trump's presidency is already a 'transformative' one, as the coveted formula goes. Change, always touted in American election campaigns, has arrived at last – and it is not pretty. Nowhere is this clearer than in how the past itself has changed since November 2016. Suddenly, each history book, each art exhibition, each nineteenth-century Chinese novel is about the new American president or what he symbolises. If you doubt it, consult some post-election issues of the *New York Review of Books* – a flagship publication of American intellectualism – and count the articles that, no matter what their topic, felt a need to refer to the president-elect.

On the one hand, this feels like a genuine paradigm shift. On the other hand, the stressful spread of Trumpian realities, with their constant and contagious onslaught on established notions of political etiquette, oddly resembles liberalism's own triumphant march through the centuries. What Pankaj Mishra, referring to the history of Western expansion, calls 'the sheer velocity of a homogenizing globalization, which makes a settled ... politics impossible while making violence unpredictable and ubiquitous'[3] is intensified and accelerated, almost beyond recognition, by the spectacle of a rogue US president who wreaks havoc in the political imaginations of voters and office holders worldwide.

There is indeed an element of violence in the daily barrage of (typically aggressive) presidential tweets. Degree by degree, almost imperceptibly if not for their drastic results, these 'counterpunching' missives are pushing the limits of what can legitimately be said and legislated into a terrain of unregulated force, even brutality, while liberal institutions stand by helplessly, reduced to proclaiming that none of this is standard operating procedure. 'This is not normal!' has become a favourite meme among stressed-out onlookers, scandalised because nothing will produce a scandal anymore. Inciting public violence? Praising dictators? Apologising to neo-Nazis? Giving hush money to porn stars? Obstructing justice? Playing down the torture and dismemberment of a US-based journalist by Saudi security forces? We have reached a point where no conceivable misdemeanour or even crime by the president can be expected to have automatic or long-lasting consequences for his power or career. As the candidate himself put it in a statement that, by liberal standards, should have been enough to end his campaign but that really strengthened the very kind of 'loyalty' it was meant to illustrate, 'I could stand in the middle of Fifth Avenue and shoot somebody and I wouldn't lose any voters, okay?'[4]

No intellectual critique, no procedural complaint, appropriate or accurate as it may be, can ever hope to impinge on this crude and remarkably cruel insight. Historically, however, it is worth pointing out that Trump's appreciation of brute force is unusual for his office only in its lack of mannered propriety, not in its actual substance. This gives him a rhetorical advantage over his critics whenever he can point out – and often correctly so – that policies that cause outrage in liberal circles originated under President Obama. What is stressful about Trump's exhibitionistic display of American power is not so much that this power exists – or that it is grounded in military might and the will to use it – but how relentlessly it has taken over all available spaces of polite communication, where the nation used to be able to feel confident about itself even when addressing (or planning) its war crimes.

Perhaps the civil order of the Atlantic West encounters its own sinister double, its extreme but logical complement, in any such shameless display of authority by strength. In fact, the incessant repetition of shocking infringements – the steady increase in everyday acts of violence – is an old colonialist strategy, perfected by liberal powers in foreign countries to normalise the militarised rule of economic interest through sheer exhaustion. What Achille Mbembe has described as the 'cruel blunting'[5] of colonial subjectivities, who get habituated to ever higher body counts until their minds are bored into cynicism or made to break, is finally coming home, quite literally, to the centres of Western life.

Thus, when propagandists of the New Right gleefully diagnose a 'Trump derangement syndrome' among the old elites (sometimes followed by 'Trump emulation syndrome'), they are both correct and dishonest. They are correct because all kinds of respectable institutions are indeed struggling now for mental adaptation, and quite frequently, their anxious reactions reinforce the madness they are adapting to. But clearly there is also a good deal of dishonesty in Trumpian descriptions of centre-left insanity – made possible, in part, by the curious American history of the word 'liberalism' – because one thing the new nationalists usually prefer to gloss over is their own continuity with earlier forms of liberal rule, including the deep but affectively hidden links between right-wing populism and corporate capitalism (throwing into doubt the explanatory value of both terms and prompting many progressives, in turn, to proclaim Trump to be no populist at all but a puppet of invisible but strangely familiar forces).

This dialectic of stress and boredom – onslaught and exhaustion – threatens to turn interpretations of Trump into a symptom of Trumpism itself, and thus against one another. In this sense, the presidency of Donald Trump, as a phenomenon that appears to demand ever more innovative explanations, is perfectly aligned with the conditions of knowledge production in the age of neoliberalism. The humanities, in particular, run into all sorts of problems when they confront this presidency – not because they are beholden to 'symptomatic' readings, as some literary scholars would like to claim, but because their deepest professional desire is for conceptual supersession.[6] Of course, it is always advisable to avoid ideological automatisms in scholarship – all the more so when examining a political situation that defies common sense. But in most historical inquiries, the object of study is connected to its exegesis in telling ways.[7] In the present case, both activities – studying Trump and studying Trump studies – illuminate how conceptual boredom can arise as an effect of power. The exasperation with which the word 'neoliberalism' is greeted in some academic circles is a case in point.[8] Arguably, this term addresses a fairly precise historical constellation, rigorously reconstructed and differentiated in a number of reliable investigations from various fields – and then ever less so in a comet tail of trendy applications and nitpicky scholasticisms. Since this happens to all successful concepts, one could simply relax and appeal for good practice. But the boredom and annoyance elicited by 'neoliberalism' are special in this regard, because this word's repetitive career, its turn to an increasingly empty formula, indicates less a lack of originality on the part of those who use it than the stubborn persistence of the facts thus addressed. At issue here is not some deep epistemological flaw in critical thought but the frustrating futility of academic critique outside its own field of enunciation.

In this situation, one should be careful how one phrases one's disappointments. It is not that political economy, historical materialism or environmental sciences have run out of steam, like machines finally winding down after a good market run, but their practical utility is being exhausted by potent realities that refuse to yield to their reflection. The recent surge of illiberal extremism therefore invites us to honour the productive wear and tear of concepts that our professional boredom would have us abandon despite their relevance in the lives of so many people (say, capitalism, racism, sexism).[9] Anything else means shifting the burden of transformation from the sphere of social violence to the sphere of its description. Perhaps it is time to ask to what degree the current tedium with powerful abstractions is shaped by the real powers that gave rise to these labels in the first place – and to what degree scholarly desires for innovative 'post'-ness are motivated by the perseverance of those forces that all too flexibly refuse to truly change, to genuinely move 'post' themselves.

In other words, this is not a time for over-subtlety. Sometimes the most predictable explanations are the most plausible ones. Sometimes it is not in our interest to be interesting. This is an appeal neither for simplicity nor for common sense. Contemporary illiberalism's continuity with liberal governance requires us to think of the relationship between two conflicting positions as something other than an opposition. It also requires us to steer clear of quick formulas that declare Trump to be a mere distraction from deeper conspiracies, or a useful tool of neoliberal elites, or a non-ideological autocrat building his brand, or the lesser evil to Mike Pence, his most likely successor at the moment. There is probably a grain of truth in each of these statements, but their expressive clout overshadows their descriptive accuracy by far.

So what has befallen the body politic? If symptoms are active parts of a disease rather than passive signs of it – and if diseases never just pass through an organism but always change it – and if a disease is a disease only from the point of view of a body injured by it – then the challenge of analysing present political pathologies 'symptomatically', in a constructive sense of the term, is to shift focus away from Donald J. Trump's person and personality without losing sight of the unique agency exacted by both. The challenge is to depict structures and processes that can lay claim to objective existence while acknowledging their dependence on contingent subjects and constitutive subjectivities. The challenge is to reconstruct what we can call, for lack of a better term and without fetishising this one, Trumpism. Therefore, a bit of historical contextualisation is needed.

Of idiots and Gramscians

The most comforting liberal account of Trump's election sees it as the culmination of a larger 'backlash' against advances made in social policy since the late 1960s. According to this scenario, American conservatism (or what goes by this name) responds to the achievements of the civil rights and feminist movements with an ever more aggressive fantasy of socio-ethnic cohesion and stable gender norms. The relationship of left and right is cast here in terms of a reaction of the latter against the former. This way of seeing things is comforting precisely because it assumes that American liberalism (or what goes by this name) has history itself on its side. The future will be progressive because the nation is always moving forward, temporary setbacks notwithstanding. By contrast, the armies of reaction may be strong but, ultimately, theirs is a desperate struggle. They can win battles but never the war.

Trust in the beneficial effects of demographic change is closely linked to this backlash narrative. Both outlooks conceive of political antagonisms chiefly in terms of cultural allegiances, and less in terms of socio-economic constellations, because the former model is fully compatible with meritocratic notions of individual or collective empowerment, resilience and uplift – indispensable cornerstones of the current (neo)liberal order. This should give us pause, because the selfsame dispositions are valued by many of the actors and agencies typically subsumed under the backlash label, most prominently the Republican Party (before and after Trump). In fact, what is called conservatism in the United States would be called, regarding its economic policies, liberalism almost anywhere else in the world. This considerably complicates the American backlash narrative. Evidently, the dichotomy of 'progress' versus 'backlash' makes sense within – and to – the social system that produced it, but once we step out of this alluring frame of reference, we notice that the scenario's popularity (or its ostensible self-evidence) obscures deep alignments between opposing political forces in the United States. It also fails to account for the pace and comprehensiveness with which Trump has disrupted the spectrum of legitimate political standpoints within the Republican Party and elsewhere. This is not to say that Trump is an unprecedented innovator. On the contrary, his rise to power is inconceivable without his adopted party's recent history. The issue here, therefore, is not to declare Trump unique nor to claim some dubious equivalence between American left-wing and American right-wing organisations, but to recognise their systemic codependence.

In doing so, it becomes important that current right-wing political styles in the United States regularly act and understand themselves as anti-establishment styles, whether they rail against some diffuse 'liberal establishment' or the GOP's own 'party establishment'. The strictly pejorative function of the term 'establishment' in nominally conservative vocabularies is remarkable. It shows how deeply the American right is steeped in ideas of anti-centrism, anti-statism and the romance of the political outsider. Conservative storytelling is not much different from liberal storytelling in this regard. Both imaginaries are drawn to the figure of the marginalised provincial who fights an almost hopeless battle against the overwhelming force of entrenched interests. There is nothing surprising about the fact that Sarah Palin, in the first chapter of her 2010 memoir *America by Heart*, cites *Mr Smith Goes to Washington* as one of her favourite movies.[10] In the same year, Dick Armey and Matt Kibbe declared in the 'Tea Party Manifesto', 'Let us be clear about one thing: The Tea Party movement is not seeking a junior partnership with the Republican Party, but a hostile takeover of it.'[11] Trump's presidential campaign both built on and outbid such sensibilities, profitably aided by Steve Bannon's frequent self-stylisation as a 'street fighter' waging a 'war' against the Republican establishment – any establishment.[12]

While such self-descriptions and self-performances can always be contradicted by actual policies, they are no mere façade to conceal vested interests in the status quo. Progressive analysts who have understood this point therefore tend to argue that the New Right is 'appropriating' strategies invented on the left – remaining, in that sense, a reactive force. And true, as Alain de Benoist's use of Gramsci shows, there is a good deal of strategy involved in the right-wing embrace of select anarchist and Marxist concepts and techniques.[13] Nevertheless, these techniques and concepts shape thought, practice and feeling. They are not reducible to pure affect; nor are they passive intellectual containers that could be filled at will (as some leftist theorists have yet to learn in their attempts to 'make useful' Carl Schmitt or Martin Heidegger).[14] Since mental tools resemble their material counterparts in their lack of neutrality, they always have an impact on the when, if and how of their use.

The right's Gramscian moment, then, is less about an instrumental appropriation of strategies than it is about a competitive employment of commitments. Seen in this fashion, the performative origins of the New Right are really contemporaneous with the performative origins of its antagonist, the New Left. Quite genuinely, most conservative movements of the last fifty years have understood and experienced themselves as radical and rebellious movements. But while counter-hegemonic emotions on the left and on the right are organised by analogous habits of storytelling – such as the plot of the simple, sometimes simple-minded, maverick who takes on mighty hierarchies and evil empires – some narratives have been successfully branded as 'progressive' in the public mind. Hence the propensity of liberal discourses to recognise themselves in reassuring backlash and appropriation histories – and hence their inclination to keep a close watch over the ideological provenance of political keywords and explanatory frameworks.[15]

This is not to say that 'extremes meet' – or even that there are two such equivalent extremes that deviate from a healthy middle position of rational moderation. Rather, throughout the Western Atlantic world, multiple uprisings against globalised capitalist hegemony are currently taking place, and it is the hegemonic worldview itself, embattled but commanding, that channels them into self-aware and opposing factions. The ensuing conflicts and hostilities, though perhaps not inevitable, are certainly real. For example, a crucial difference between leftist and rightist dispositions concerns their respective understanding of defiant simplicity and anti-centrism. On the right, championship of 'the people' – that mythical subject of American politics – hardly ever takes the form of care or custodianship anymore, because these originally conservative attitudes have come to be associated with elite condescension. While left-wing populism tends to address socio-economic grievances through education (historical analysis, ideology critique, internationalism and so on) and organisation (collective bargaining, strikes, *operaismo* and the like), right-wing populism tends to communicate itself as the fierce self-expression of an identitarian will, often based in revanchism, vigilantism and conspiracy thinking. Thus, the naïve unpretentiousness of the provincial charmer who takes a moral case to Washington has been increasingly replaced in American conservative imaginaries by the belligerent determination of the no-nonsense avenger or, at long last, the spiteful stupidity of the reactionary simpleton who stages a deliberately trashy revolt against well-educated elitists and patronising experts. Trump's political appeal rests to a large degree on his ability to transform cartoonish inexperience and proud idiocy into the higher wisdom of gut feelings and sly intuition. Combining the hyperbolic willpower of the masculine fighter who always comes out on top with the punky DIY air of loser icons such as Pepe the Frog, Trump's persona taps into a large countercultural repertoire of anti-establishment attitudes while channelling their socio-economic concerns into increasingly explicit expressions of chauvinism and racism.[16]

On closer inspection, this is nothing new. As Pankaj Mishra has shown, angry masculinist *ressentiment* is modernity's constant companion. The current right-wing intellectual Jordan B. Peterson acknowledges as much by trying to provide a cure for it (albeit one that gets stuck in its own ideological obsessions, so that Peterson, himself a pretty tense guy underneath his sober attire of classical conservatism, doesn't quite know what to do with all those agitated far-right-wingers in his audience except to deny their existence). In the United States, such ultra-modern anti-modernity has a long history, reaching back at least to the nativist liberalism of Democratic president Andrew Jackson, whose portrait hangs in Trump's Oval Office. Because many of these supposedly reactive forces have been represented by consequential state actors and powerful national institutions, they are not easily filed under the 'backlash' label. Maybe the paranoid xenophobia of the Know Nothing Party or certain anti-immigration stances of the People's Party can be written off as infelicitous setbacks in an overall history of democratisation. But once we consider the long Southern tradition of amalgamating anti-capitalist sentiments with anti-black legislation, and its refusal to stay Southern, or Democratic president Woodrow Wilson's interpretation of the Civil War as a spiritual prelude to 'Reunion' ratified by white supremacy, it becomes difficult to subtract the nation's history of social anger from its official narrative of progress.

Against this background, it is not surprising that the blueprint for Trumpism was provided, as several commentators have noted, by earlier presidential bids: Barry Goldwater's Republican campaign in 1964, Democratic governor George Wallace's four runs for president in the 1960s and 1970s, Richard Nixon's 'Southern strategy' in 1968 and 1972, Ronald Reagan's victories in 1980 and 1984, and Pat Buchanan's challenges to President George H. W. Bush and Republican frontrunner Robert Dole in the 1992 and 1996 primaries.[17] Each of these campaigns was built on a platform that combined economic populism with racist invective, though in different degrees of explicitness and subtlety. George Wallace, in particular, translated the old Southern philosophy of states' rights into intense attacks on what he was among the first to call the 'Washington bureaucracy', adding to this bitter mix two more elements that have since become core ingredients of right-wing populism: protest against a totalitarian media establishment that manipulates public opinion (a typical countercultural theme) and strident calls for economic reforms for the working class (another standard concern of the 1960s and 1970s). Of course, what Wallace had in mind were measures that benefited 'hard-working Americans' while sidelining 'undeserving' elements. Without race being mentioned, this stuck close to the meritocratic consensus, but it was clear that Wallace's odd mixture of pro-labour and anti-New Deal sentiments was based on the assumption that workers were white and welfare recipients were not. It was President Reagan, then, who successfully nationalised this agenda, waging his war on (chiefly black) inner cities as a 'war on drugs' while defaming 'welfare queens' – thinly veiled code for single black mothers on state support who supposedly lived a luxurious life enabled by government programmes and taxes that redistributed money from the productive and labouring parts of society to its 'parasitical' members.[18] And according to meritocratic logic, these unproductive classes just happened to be predominantly non-white.

This is how 'the working class', both as a term and as a political force, was effectively neutralised, if not dismantled, through racialisation.[19] Ever since, the act of defining economic conditions as cultural conditions has become the preferred *divide-et-impera* strategy of neoliberal trade regimes.[20] In the American context, this intersection of right-wing populism and neoliberalism – confounding at first glance – is epitomised by Lewis F. Powell's notorious memorandum of 1971, 'Attack on [the] American Free Enterprise System', a corporate strategy paper with close ties to the Republican Party. (Powell wrote it shortly before accepting his nomination, by Richard Nixon, to the US Supreme Court.) Sometimes discussed as the secret master-plan that established conservative supremacy in American politics, the Powell memorandum was certainly no such thing. Its influence on policy making was comparatively small, and from today's perspective, many of its proposals look surprisingly statist, indicating the lingering force of Keynesian thought at the time, even in the Republican Party.[21]

Nevertheless, the memorandum perfectly expressed the right's desire for a new sense of ideological cohesion at the height of the countercultural movements. According to Powell, this could best be achieved through organised networks of public persuasion and influence. In this context, it is worth remembering that the political platform of neoliberalism had suffered recurring electoral defeats in American primaries and presidential campaigns before it triumphed spectacularly in the 1980s. This long history of setbacks, followed by a phoenix-like rise, attests to the ideological dedication of its supporters, kept alive through many a dry spell by interest groups, media agitators, corporate funding, think tanks and well-financed lobbyists.

The memorandum's rhetoric nicely exemplifies the New Right's emergent militancy and its counter-hegemonic self-understanding. Although Powell in 1971 still spoke in the respectable voice of a conservative mandarin – his language is a far cry from the demagogic fury of Donald Trump and his (social) media troops forty-five years later – the memorandum teems with excitingly rebellious keywords and provocative soundbites, asking for a 'political action program' and 'a more aggressive attitude' to promote the American 'enterprise system' (Powell's formula for neoliberal conservatism): 'Businessmen have not been trained or equipped to conduct guerrilla warfare with those who propagandize against the system, seeking insidiously and constantly to sabotage it . . . They have shown little stomach for hard-nose contest.'[22]

But businessmen should start with such combat tactics now, Powell holds, which is why they need to learn a lesson or two from the self-organised agitators of the New Left. In short, Powell suggests that radical activism must not be left to the civil rights movement. The memorandum dreams of a plan of action, a long-term campaign, which will create a vanguard of revolutionaries leading the way for the larger public to follow, in this case by forging a cadre of charismatic speakers who shall infiltrate television programmes and universities. We need our own ACLU, Powell says, which wins court cases for us. Corporate America needs its own lobbying organisations, its own propaganda officers, and altogether 'more direct political action'.[23] If this is conservatism, it sounds suspiciously like a revolutionary movement starting its long march through the institutions.[24]

Why is there no conservatism in the United States?

In 1971, Powell described his political position as anti-socialist and anti-totalitarian, but neoliberalism's goal at the time was really to roll back the social democratic welfare state, if need be by racial fear-mongering. After the triumph of this programme under Reagan, Bush and Clinton, the only political struggle left in national politics was between right-wing neoliberalism and left-wing neoliberalism. To understand how this spectacular flattening out of political options could be accompanied by an equally spectacular increase in partisan polarisation since the 1990s, it is useful to recognise the Gramscian dimension of the Powell memorandum and – indeed – the entire field of American 'conservatism' from Nixon to Trump.

Writing at the same time that Alain de Benoist assembled the philosophical foundations for *'la nouvelle droite'*, Powell was convinced that the coming struggle would be waged as a culture war. His memorandum was not overly troubled by the anti-business attitudes of a few far-left radicals; Powell's real grievance concerned the criticism coming 'from perfectly respectable elements of society: from the college campus, the pulpit, the media, the intellectual and literary journals, the arts and sciences, and from politicians'.[25] Looking upon politics as a fight for mainstream opinion, the memorandum identified three battlefields on which the American culture war would be waged over the following decades. It was a prophetic list, comprising public education, legal and legislative practice, and popular media culture. Of these, Powell saw the campus as 'the single most dynamic source' of 'ideological warfare against the enterprise system'.[26] The right's complaint about 'tenured radicals' starts here. Powell's recommendation on this matter was for corporations to do exactly what labour and civil rights activists had done, that is, influence the composition of textbooks.

Then there are the news media. The memorandum features some of the earliest examples of conservative protest against liberal bias in political reporting. As a corrective, Powell advocated an ethos of 'balanced viewpoints', 'equal time' and fair 'representation'.[27] This intervention actually had some justification in 1971, but it would soon turn political debate into a fight of mere opinions, culminating in a situation in which all types of speech, including scientific arguments, appear as equally valid belief systems.[28]

As for law making, one word: lobbying. In no uncertain terms, Powell reminded American entrepreneurs that they had the means to get the best government that money can buy:

> One should not postpone more direct political action, while awaiting the gradual change in public opinion to be effected through education and information. Business must learn the lesson, long ago learned by Labor and other self-interest groups. This is the lesson that political power is necessary; that such power must be assiduously [sic] cultivated; and that when necessary, it must be used aggressively and with determination – without embarrassment and without the reluctance which has been so characteristic of American business . . . There should not be the slightest hesitation to press vigorously in all political arenas for support of the enterprise system. Nor should there be reluctance to penalize politically those who oppose it.[29]

Needless to say, small government for big business is hardly a revolutionary programme, not in the most capitalist society on earth. Honouring the Marxist credentials of Gramsci's theory of hegemony, we might therefore want to speak of a *pseudo*-Gramscian right, keeping in mind that domination is always at its most compelling when it can pass for liberation. But it is also true that genuine anti-totalitarianism (many of neoliberalism's foundational thinkers in the United States were émigrés from European state tyrannies) and angry American populisms (merging political protest against bureaucratic elites, cultural protest against media elites, and socio-economic protest against progressive elites that supposedly subsidise non-white laziness) provided fuel to new ideological commitments that came to haunt the liberal trade order in much the same way that Donald Trump came to haunt the Republican Party.

Thus, while Trump is certainly a divisive force within the GOP, his rise to power was prepared by at least two – partly contradictory – trends in the party's recent history: its growing neoliberal fascination with 'disruption' as a political action programme and its increasingly explicit flirtation with select forms of populist anger since the 1960s. Three more specific features of Republican party politics since the 1990s need to be placed in this larger matrix: (1) a dynamic of ideological one-upmanship within the party, fuelled by outside money and new partisan media platforms; (2) a pervasive siege mentality, which has encouraged increasingly strident attitudes of revanchism; and (3) the belief that the republic is engaged in an existential war against the hegemony of 'political correctness' and 'cultural Marxism'.

The first of these developments – ideological radicalisation – is closely connected to the deregulation of financial campaign contributions after the 2010 Supreme Court decision in *Citizens United vs FEC*. As Jane Mayer has shown, the resulting influx of immense sums of private money into party politics and elections has streamlined legislative initiatives that favour corporate interests in aggressive ways.[30] Conservative politicians who care about climate change or support ecological reforms stand no chance against the financial power of corporate billionaires like the Koch brothers, who will sponsor and even groom Republican challengers supporting their agenda in the next primary. It is true that the Koch brothers did not back Donald Trump in the 2016 primaries – and that Trump prided himself on being independent of outside money, vowing to 'drain the swamp' of corruption in Washington – but *Citizens United* has legalised a system of ideological blackmail that has eliminated virtually all (traditionally conservative) concerns for preservation and moderation from the GOP's legislative platform. Add to this the emergence of new and often equally well-funded partisan media channels after the deregulation of telecommunication and the reorganisation of the

Federal Communications Commission under Ronald Reagan, and it becomes clear why the general political drift within the Republican Party has been ever more radically to the right rather than to some desired centre, however imaginary.

At the level of media politics, this development has been accelerated by a self-reinforcing dynamic of ideological one-upmanship, which cannot rest content with the strategic partisanship of Rupert Murdoch's Fox News but escalates almost logically into the conspiracy-driven alarmism of conservative talk radio. But then even extremists like radio host Rush Limbaugh can be outdone, as Alex Jones and others have demonstrated with the sheer craziness of Internet platforms like Infowars (a Gramscian name if ever there was one). What a few decades ago would have been considered a problem on the lunatic fringe of American politics has come to occupy a central place in GOP law making – and not simply because Donald Trump is highly susceptible to suggestions by commentators such as Ann Coulter, Laura Ingraham and even Alex Jones, but because the extremism of partisan narrowcasting is mirrored now in Congress itself by organisations like the Freedom Caucus, a dedicated band of hardliners trying to enforce ideological purity in the party's agenda. Aided by a noisy swarm of social media activists, the Freedom Caucus and similar groups have vowed to monitor Republican officials in their every action and statement. Whoever strays from the desired course risks being labelled a RINO ('Republican in Name Only') or worse. As a result, the jobs of speaker of the House and Senate majority leader have become virtually impossible to perform well (or for long) within the GOP.

This institutional atrophy naturally invites demagogues and shameless power players. It also explains why even before Trump's ascent, large parts of the Republican Party thought that they were engaged, not merely in political controversies with the Democratic Party, but in an existential battle over the survival of the nation. As the conservative blogger Publius Decius Mus (really Michael Anton, who served on President Trump's National Security Council (NSC) until April 2018) put it in his influential contribution to the 2016 campaign, an essay called 'The Flight 93 Election', 'The republic is dying.'[31] In making this claim and by choosing this title, 'The Flight 93 Election' deftly branded

Trump's candidacy as a make-or-break moment for conservative resistance against an otherwise perennial liberal supremacy. Asking establishment Republicans to swallow their mannered reservations about Trump and to join him in charging the cockpit of the hijacked nation (just like the passengers of Flight 93 had done on 9/11), Anton characterised the unloved candidate as a necessary evil, a suitably blunt instrument to save the republic from the power grip of a crushing enemy.

'The Flight 93 Election' thus warned against 'a tsunami of leftism' that 'engulfs our every – literal and figurative – shore'. Interestingly, such statements are in full accordance with the standard narrative of American progress, but they invert its optimism into fear: 'The whole trend of the West is ever-leftward', Anton notes, specifying that conservatism in the United States has been 'losing ground for at least a century'.[32] When Anton's follow-up piece 'Restatement on Flight 93' added that Obama 'was able to overwhelm us with sheer demographics',[33] white indignation finally revealed itself as the paranoid underside of liberal hope. As if conjuring some gloomy double of the nation's canonised tale of meritocratic multiculturalism, Anton declared, 'Every four years the electorate becomes more unfavorable to Republican candidates, owing above all to mass immigration.'[34]

According to Anton, it follows that 'the deck is stacked overwhelmingly against us'[35] and every true Republican knows it. But while 'the base' – another near-mythical entity in Republican thought – is hungering for a good fight, the party 'establishment' has accepted cultural defeat. Since the 1960s, Anton claims, GOP leaders have been playing 'by the self-sabotaging rules the Left sets for them', effectively installing a 'bipartisan junta' in Washington.[36] In this logic, Trump's outsider status, his refusal to play by the rules, his willingness to break with precedents, indeed his ignorance of precedents, are not lamentable shortcomings but powerful assets in a campaign that speaks to its followers' pervasive feeling of being besieged, their sense of occupying the dirty underdog position in a fight against omnipotent and omnipresent forces of cultural authority. As NSC staffer Richard Higgins wrote in 'POTUS & Political Warfare', his infamous White House memo in May 2017 (an over-the-top strategy paper that got Higgins fired at the request of the then national security advisor, General H. R. McMaster), 'This is not politics as usual but rather political *warfare* at an unprecedented level.'[37]

Recalling fascist theorist Carl Schmitt, Higgins defines politics here as a realm of existential and often fiercely territorial combat grounded in an elemental distinction between friend and enemy. In New Right circles, this Schmittian philosophy is regularly complemented – in Anton, in Higgins, in Bannon, in countless anecdotes and conspiracy theories circulating on alt-right platforms – by the idea that the ongoing struggle is a supremely cultural affair: a fight for endangered spaces and ways of living, a fight against the power of the distant and the foreign, a fight against hegemony.

Higgins's White House memo, for example, stresses that talk of 'political warfare' is anything but metaphoric. Rather, Higgins takes care to explain that he is using this term 'as understood by the Maoist insurgency model'.[38] Of course, militancy always goes well with a sense of victimisation, but what is remarkable about Trumpism – and what aligns this particular siege mentality with fascist examples – is how successfully the New American Right has managed to portray even positions of thoroughgoing power (most notably, commander-in-chief of the US military and highest executive office in the country) as oppositional, claiming that standpoints of undeniable privilege are beset by scheming and fanatical enemies. On the one hand, this is a self-fulfilling prophecy, drawing vindication from extreme reactions to the New Right's own extreme employment of force and intimidation. On the other hand, this is dangerous paranoia. 'POTUS & Political Warfare' imagines a broad cabal of anti-Trump forces, ranging from an illegitimate 'deep state' and the nation's own intelligence organisations to 'key international players' of 'the hard left', which are said to 'include the European Union, the UN, and the OSCE, the OIC and the International Muslim Brotherhood'.[39] In keeping with the pseudo-Gramscian impulses of right-wing populism, Higgins adds that the 'campaigns' of this unlikely group of allies 'operate through narratives'.[40]

Trumpism thus paints the picture of an American culture methodically infiltrated by what Higgins and others call 'Marxist memes'. These are said to undermine local lifestyles and even 'human nature' itself.[41] Television programmes, corporate advertisements, Hollywood movies, bestselling novels and the humanities departments of American universities: all these sites of cultural production are now being subjected to a right-wing hermeneutics of suspicion that is structurally saturated with the tools of left-wing critique. Arguably, identitarian concerns are strong in both discursive fields, but the Trumpian variety typically lacks commitment to the kind of historical or systemic analysis that would allow for a realistic assessment of power relations in the first place.[42] As if Fox News, talk radio or the president's Twitter account did not exist, Michael Anton claims in 'The Flight 93 Election' that '"conservative" media is a nullity, barely a whisper'. Given this conviction, it should not come as a surprise that American right-wingers remain completely unimpressed when film stars or media celebrities speak up against Trump. Rather than making them reconsider anything, this proves their worldview. As Higgins says about such 'attack narratives',

> [They] are pervasive, full spectrum and institutionalized at all levels. They inform the entertainment industry from late night monologues, to situation comedies, to television series memes, to movie themes ... The cultural Marxist narrative is fully deployed, pervasive, full spectrum and ongoing. Regarding the president, attacks have become a relentless 24/7 effort.[43]

Relying on such impressions of being marginalised, Trumpism channels all sorts of diffuse contrarian impulses – some of them justified, as anti-mainstream inclinations often are – into an attractively narrow but ultimately absurd political programme countering 'political correctness' and 'cultural Marxism'. While the first of these terms speaks to intuitions of paternalism that are then construed as acts of totalitarian censorship, the second term – a central component of current right-wing thought – comes with a fully fledged conspiracy theory attached. Coined by conservative publicist William Lind, 'cultural Marxism' claims rather concretely that the German immigrants of the Frankfurt School during and after World War II acted as intellectual double agents who systematically undermined American public institutions. In particular, they managed to instil Hollywood and other entertainment industries with 'nihilism'.⁴⁴ (This explains Higgins's bizarre, almost comical, reference in his 2017 White House Memo to a long-forgotten text by Herbert Marcuse. Obviously, alt-right ideologues have yet to learn that their hostility to Horkheimer and Adorno is all but matched by the dominant assessment of this critical theory in Anglophone media studies departments.)

It would be easy to write off such silliness as fringe politics, but Higgins's dismissal from the NSC – or Steve Bannon's departure from the White House in August 2017, after he miscalculated his position in the movement – should not detract from the fact that the political ideology and the political style of Trumpism have practically taken over the Republican Party, eclipsing not only any residual notions of traditional conservatism there but also, and more significantly, the party's neocon and neoliberal wings.

Neofascism versus/and neoliberalism

In the wake of 2016, numerous labelling anxieties have surfaced in the liberal blogosphere and some corners of academia. Trump's presidency must be unnerving for anyone who would like the world to correspond to the established (American) definitions of political keywords. One such keyword is 'populism'. Another is 'fascism'. Of course, anything can be compared to anything – and mere resemblance does not make an argument in political history. Let me stress, therefore, that when I use the term 'neofascism' to describe Trumpism, I do not mean to suggest – nor does anyone else who employs this term, as far as I can see – that 2016 was 1933 or that neoliberal America is Weimar Germany. Instead, I am following Karl Polanyi's argument that fascism is what happens when liberalism fails while no viable left-wing alternative is available.⁴⁵

But first things first: neoliberalism. Let us assume that this weary name refers to a socio-economic belief system based on the idea that market solutions to social problems are always more efficient than political solutions. Over the past four decades, this axiom has resulted in a systematic shrinking of the public sector in Western societies and elsewhere, subjecting schools, hospitals, public transport, welfare structures and entire nations to harsh austerity budgets that treat these institutions of communal life as if they were primarily run for profit – while corporate returns have exploded through deregulation. If we can agree that this describes, however roughly, our political economy since the late 1970s, we can immediately go on to say that neoliberalism – or 'the Washington consensus', as some have called it – is currently experiencing a most severe crisis. There is an undeniable sense of things going wrong. Of course, the fact that this realisation comes so late tells us something about neoliberalism's tacit entanglement with culturalist and racist structures of exploitation. Only now, when the fear of poverty has reached a section of the population that thought it was naturally immune to it – the proverbial 'middle class' – are we beginning to see significant signs of mainstream discontent. Only now that poverty can no longer be safely identified with minorities who are habitually held responsible for their own economic troubles does the crisis become visible as a crisis at all.[46]

Put differently, this crisis is also a crisis of legitimacy. Trickle-down-philosophies are difficult to uphold when social immobility ceases to be a cultural trait of non-white people in the inner cities. In fact, large parts of white America are even facing the humiliating spectre of *downward* mobility, including a rural working class that has learned to think of itself, against all odds, as middle class. Meanwhile, many metropolitan professionals, including academics, intellectuals and people working in creative industries (so beloved by the neoliberal economy), have been comparatively untouched by the current crisis, despite increasing job precariousness in the cognitive sectors of the labour market.

This is another way of saying that 'liberal elites' do in fact exist and that they do in fact dominate large parts of cultural production. There are social classes – and entire countries, like Germany – that continue to profit from the globalisation of markets, but also from the attendant economic inequalities, reaping disproportionate wealth through trade imbalances and the power to dictate reforms and austerity measures elsewhere. For the longest time, this crisis-prone system has been rendered socially acceptable by two fundamental ideas: the belief that economic globalisation constitutes a form of social progress (stressing a post-bourgeois pluralism of lifestyles and an often commodity-based multiculturalism over economic equity) and the widespread conviction that Western economies reward effort, talent and willpower with achievement and success (a ruling assumption of almost every American piece of entertainment). As David Graeber writes, 'Whole societies have come to represent themselves as giant credentialized meritocracies, rather than systems of arbitrary extraction.'[47]

In other words, if there is a hegemonic ideology in the United States and throughout the Western world, it is certainly not a Marxist one. Meritocratic narratives rule supreme in American popular and political culture. They organise neoliberal imaginaries on both the right and the left. But it was the neoliberalisation of left-wing governance, in particular, that provided the current political economy with its fatal air of inevitability in the 1990s. If the memorable claim that the system is 'without alternatives' still sounds forceful today, this is because plausible alternatives have indeed been expunged almost completely from centre-left party platforms, newspapers and public spheres. And this is not Marxism but the exact opposite: It is the abandonment by traditional organisations of the left (Democratic Party, Labour Party, SPD, Parti socialiste etc.) of any practical programme of non-corporate economic internationalism, favouring instead a type of society that is nominally progressive and symbolically diverse but in reality 'gentrified, overpriced, [and] under-resourced', as Keeanga-Yamahtta Taylor puts it.[48]

How, then, could Donald Trump get as far as he did, despite demographics and 'who we are'? When American liberals are struggling with this question, they would do well to look to more than the Electoral College or Russian interference (another reassuring tale: if the republic fails, it is because of foreign conspirators). They would do well to look to their own history. An important reason for Trump's victory was that his campaign provided something that Hillary Clinton's campaign could not provide without self-contradiction: a direct and stark response to the consequences of economic globalisation. It was a deeply reactionary response, channelling vague discontent and amorphous fears of loss into appeals to national entrenchment and racial animosity. But Trump's mobilisation of what sociologist Donald Warren (already in 1976) called 'middle American radicalism'[49] could not be countered by any credible leftist critique of existing economic arrangements, not after the Democratic Party had thoroughly neoliberalised itself from Bill Clinton to Barack Obama.

Famously, when Margaret Thatcher was asked in 2002 what she considered her biggest achievement, she replied, 'Tony Blair and New Labour.'[50] Ronald Reagan might have said the same thing about the Democratic Party. In the 2016 campaign, Hillary Clinton's routine invocations of small-business optimism and the American can-do spirit rang false because such noble platitudes all too obviously conflicted with her public record. Clinton's policies, much like her husband's and so many policies of her party, have shaped America's socio-economic (dis)order in fundamental ways, including its investment in mass incarceration and radical welfare cuts, both of which mostly harm minorities while metropolitan elites can continue to see themselves as open to the world, value-driven and, yes, self-confidently correct in their acts of consumption, which they deem acts of politics.

Thus, when Donald Trump pointed out that Bernie Sanders's 2016 and 2020 campaigns have been methodically undermined by the Democratic establishment, the glee with which he referred to this situation highlighted his dishonesty as much as the credibility of the underlying intuition that the system is 'rigged'. Since the 1990s, progressive institutions, discourses and media have gone out of their way to sideline, ridicule or declare obsolete exactly the types of structural critique that (could have) predicted the current crisis. The erosion of materialist politics in a number of intellectual and public arenas, whether by high-theoretical boredom, liberal triumphalism or professional pragmatism – but always in the name of some 'realism' – has opened the floodgates for a politics of racial scapegoating and cultural resentment that particularly appeals to those victims of free-market extremism who have no other means to explain their socio-economic failures. In much the same fashion in which the destruction of the Black Panther Party by state violence in the 1970s set large parts of American minority protest on a path of ontological confirmation, so it was only a matter of time before ever more American conservatives should come to explicitly embrace the white nationalism their party had tried to hold under strategic control while the Washington consensus still worked.

When the left goes neoliberal, the right goes neofascist. Of course, this is not an exclusively American phenomenon but part of a worldwide surge in embittered and often chauvinistic uprisings against neoliberal trade regimes. Some observers even speak of 'Global Trumpism' and an 'Authoritarian International'.[51] By contrast, President Obama epitomised his party's unacknowledged commitment to national exceptionalism when he characterised the results of the 2016 election in supremely American fashion as merely a 'zig' following a 'zag'.[52] However, Trump's victory is not some temporary aberration from one nation's regular course of history but rather the authentic face of something larger that Western liberalism has no plausible name for, because it concerns Western liberalism itself. Brexit – described by Jürgen Habermas as 'a victory for populism *over capitalism* in its country of origin'[53] – preceded the American election by only a few months. Since then, neofascist movements and parties have been gaining ground continuously within the very centres of globalised capitalism, staging unexpected revolts against the current economic order, but these are not the types of revolt that frequent-flyer progressives had in mind when they kept talking about social justice while marginalising trade unions and privatising public institutions.

Consider how Michael Anton's 'Restatement' inveighs against 'the Davoisie' and its 'rule by a transnational managerial class in conjunction with the administrative state'.[54] Behind the wild opportunism of Trumpian discourses there actually hides a remarkably coherent worldview, one of nonconformist provincialism and illiberal dissent. As Anton approvingly writes, 'On trade, globalization, and war, [Candidate] Trump is to the left (conventionally understood) not only of his own party, but of his Democratic opponent.'[55] Perhaps the same cannot be said about President Trump, but the fact remains that Trumpism, as a political philosophy, positions itself in diametric opposition to not just one but two core ideologies of the Republican Party. 'The Flight 93 Election' stresses this when Anton rhetorically asks whether it is 'just a coincidence' that Republican Never-Trumpers 'happen to favor Invade the World, Invite the World'.[56] The first of these slogans refers, of course, to the party's neocon wing, the second to its neoliberals. And true, similar to Pat Buchanan, who was no friend of foreign invasions or transnational corporations, Trump breaks with Republican neocon and neoliberal orthodoxies alike. He criticises the Iraq War, is unenthusiastic about NATO, and has announced the withdrawal of American troops from Syria. He rails against American businesses that invest overseas, favours reindustrialisation and tariffs, and opposes – as do many on the left – international trade agreements like NAFTA and TPP. Significantly, these are long-held beliefs with Trump, not mere expediencies for electioneering.

Despite its pronounced anti-intellectualism, then, Trumpism has attracted a number of intellectuals ('conventionally understood') who are hoping to organise their champion's rampant instincts and his orchestrations of popular fury into an avant-garde movement of political upheaval.[57] Doing so, these new masterminds of the far right tend to treat the president as a means to an end – a move that can be risky for their careers, as the case of Steve Bannon shows. Nevertheless, Bannon's speeches and interviews provide one of the most systematic accounts of Trumpism so far.[58] An enemy, like Michael Anton, of the neoliberal 'Davos class', Bannon insists that the 2016 campaign was all about a dedicated vanguard's 'takeover' of the Republican Party, followed by an even larger coup: the capture and dismantlement of 'the administrative state'. Thus, when Trump filled his administration with blatant non-experts – leaving liberals speechless – Bannon clarified that there was method to the madness: 'If you look at these Cabinet appointees, they were selected for a reason and that is . . . deconstruction.'[59]

On numerous occasions, Bannon has explained that the deconstruction of the administrative state is the first of three pillars of 'an entirely new political movement', which he labels 'economic nationalism' (a term meant to distance Trumpism from 'white nationalism', as if the movement's more unpalatable elements could be set aside as purely instrumental).[60] What Bannon has in mind is not so much the ongoing rollback of the New Deal welfare state – an orthodox principle of Republican governance since Ronald Reagan – but the steady hollowing out of constitutional checks and balances in favour of authoritarian decision making. From this perspective, Trumpism is really about the subversion of basic governmental norms and practices.

The second pillar of Bannon's revolutionary programme is 'anti-globalism', understood as unilateralism underwritten by unmatched military power, and economic strength through self-sufficiency. This includes welfare measures for an industrial working class that is tacitly racialised as white (although Bannon maintains this need not be the case). As a third pillar, Bannon lists 'national security and sovereignty'.[61] This translates into a harsh anti-immigration stance: not because certain types of immigration – especially those promoted by neoliberal elites – exacerbate global inequalities but because the American polity is imagined now as a rigorously circumscribed space of cultural identity that needs to be walled off, literally, against contamination. Trump's border wall is no vanity project in this regard, but really an expression of existential dread. In fact, Bannon's insistence that a nation is territorially defined by its borders – a truism elevated in far-right circles to the status of a spiritual profundity – is often impossible to tell apart from an anxious fantasy of ethnic purity. After all, Michael Anton defines Trumpism in exactly these terms as 'no more importing poverty, crime, and alien cultures' and then goes on to include the nation's own Black Lives Matter movement among the 'inanities' American patriots need to fight.[62]

There is a name for this type of insurrectionary populism and it is not conservatism. European history – which is in large part a history of capitalism dealing with its own consequences – provides some instructive examples of anti-establishment movements that have addressed national milieus worried about their socio-economic status and urged them to attribute their relative decline (actual or feared) to the advances supposedly made by other disadvantaged groups. One hundred years after Benito Mussolini founded the *Fasci italiani di combattimento* and one hundred years after the German November Revolution was smothered by the paramilitary *Freikorps*, it is a good time to remember that fascism has never simply been a failure of civic morality, or the result of strange rulers appearing with dark intentions like celestial supervillains, despite countless Hollywood movies telling us so. Outside of liberal narratives, fascism has always been a fiercely expressive force, a distorted articulation of popular fear and anger, the brutal protest of stressed communities believing themselves both privileged with identity and under life-threatening attack from foreign conspirators and traitors at home.

Conclusion

The election of Donald Trump and the concurrent rise of new styles of right-wing extremism are intertwined with self-aware but deliberately unsystematic and deeply affective revolts against transnational capitalism. Performing his campaign and his presidency as a 'movement', Trump has essentially promised to re-establish the lost primacy of the political over the economic, but the notion of 'the political' that underlies this promise seeks to subvert established norms and institutions of liberal democracy itself – while Trump's socio-economic policies maintain and intensify the worst effects of corporate-controlled governance. Thus, the slogan 'America First' can be understood by protest voters as declaring that the nation should 'have' an economy, not be run by one – but then its companion slogan, 'Make America Great Again', almost defiantly crude, appeals to notions of democracy obliquely grounded in white supremacy and male privilege.

The resulting (re)emergence and normalisation of fascist politics in the twenty-first century is not easily captured by the traditional explanatory models of leftist critique (describing fascism as an unadulterated form of capitalism) or by the strategic manoeuvres of established conservative institutions in the United States (hoping to functionalise the president and his constituency for evangelical, neoliberal or neoconservative policy missions). Both perspectives perceive something important about Trumpism – its entanglement with high finance and predator capitalism on the one hand, its continuity with a politics of felt dispossession and cultural revanchism on the other – but the distinctiveness of American neofascism only reveals itself when it is put in relation to, and simultaneously distinguished from, other and earlier forms of right-wing politics in the United States. Within this larger historical field, Trumpism has surfaced at the height of neoliberal crisis as an emphatically revolutionary and at the same time intensely resentful movement, offering a political vision of national fortification deceptively inspired by countercultural figures of thought such as anti-statism; the valuation of 'community' over 'society'; and the advocacy of long marches, deep campaigns and even political violence to combat an overpowering cultural hegemony.

To understand the logic of this erratic but highly targeted force, it helps to pay attention to the systemic codependence of opposing political positions in the United States today. To do so is not to claim moral equivalency between the New Left and the Newest Right. Rather, it is to highlight the derivative nature of contemporary right-wing revolutionism, which addresses complexity by performing simplicity and rashness. This paradoxical combination of insurrectionary victimology with unsubtle assertions of entitlement – encouraging counter-hegemonic disruptions while accelerating existing structures of exploitation – accounts for much of global Trumpism's current popular appeal, that is, its easy reproducibility, its international adaptability and its stressful speed and reach in a digital-capitalist media ecology.[63]

Notes

1. This essay is part of a larger project, possibly never to be finished, on brutality, triumphalism and liberal propriety.
2. 'Kellyanne Conway: Press Secretary Sean Spicer Gave "Alternative Facts"', *Meet the Press*, 22 January 2017, available at <https://www.youtube.com/watch?v=VSrEEDQgFc8> (accessed 20 January 2020).
3. Pankaj Mishra, *Age of Anger: A History of the Present* (New York: Picador, 2017), 293.
4. 'Trump: I Could Shoot Somebody and Not Lose Voters', CNN, 23 January 2016, available at <https://www.youtube.com/watch?v=iTACH1eVIaA> (accessed 20 January 2020).
5. Achille Mbembe, *Politiques de l'inimitié* (Paris: La Découverte, 2016), 53. My translation of Mbembe's '*cruelle hébétude*'.
6. See Frank Kelleter, 'DISCIPLINE COOL. Notes, Quotes, Tweets, and Facebook Postings on the Study of American Self-Studies

(Looking Forward Remix)', in Frank Kelleter and Alexander Starre (eds), *Projecting American Studies: Essays on Theory, Method, and Practice* (Heidelberg: Universitätsverlag Winter, 2018), 287–307.
7. See Frank Kelleter, *Serial Agencies: 'The Wire' and Its Readers* (Winchester: Zero, 2014).
8. See Daniel Rodgers, 'The Uses and Abuses of "Neoliberalism"', *Dissent*, Winter 2018, <https://www.dissentmagazine.org/article/uses-and-abuses-neoliberalism-debate> (accessed 20 January 2020).
9. The following sentences are adapted from Kelleter, 'DISCIPLINE COOL', 298–9.
10. Sarah Palin, *America by Heart: Reflections on Family, Faith, and Flag* (New York: Harper, 2010), 1.
11. Dick Armey and Matt Kibbe, 'A Tea Party Manifesto', *Wall Street Journal*, 17 August 2010, <https://www.wsj.com/articles/SB10001424052748704407804575425061553154540> (accessed 20 January 2020).
12. 'Breitbart's Bannon Declares War on the GOP', *60 Minutes*, 10 September 2017, <https://www.cbsnews.com/news/60-minutes-breitbart-steve-bannon-declares-war-on-the-gop> (accessed 20 January 2020).
13. See Alain de Benoist, *Les Idées à l'endroit* (Paris: Hallier, 1979).
14. See Chantal Mouffe (ed.), *The Challenge of Carl Schmitt* (London: Verso, 1999); Chantal Mouffe, *For a Left Populism* (London: Verso, 2018).
15. Consider all the think pieces explaining why the word 'populism' should not be used to describe Trumpian nationalism. Or consider all the poll-based articles trying to disprove economic accounts of Trump's election by pointing to the racial motives of well-to-do suburban voters. One of the most regrettable effects of Trump's election has been the wide acceptance and adoption by left-wing discourses of a typically right-wing strategy that contrasts class politics with identity politics. As a result, innumerable progressive debates after 2016 have been preoccupied with fruitless and misleading stand-offs between explanations highlighting 'neoliberalism' and explanations highlighting 'racism and sexism', as if these were competing alternatives.
16. See Dale Beran, '4chan: The Skeleton Key to the Rise of Trump', *Medium*, 14 February 2017, <https://www.medium.com/@DaleBeran/4chan-the-skeleton-key-to-the-rise-of-trump-624e7cb798cb> (accessed 20 January 2020). On the affective dimension of alt-right discourses, see Simon Strick, 'Alt-Right-Affekte: Provokationen und

Online-Taktiken', *Zeitschrift für Medienwissenschaft* 19 (2018), 113–25. For an extensive infrastructural account of the alt-right, see David Neiwert, *Alt-America: The Rise of the Radical Right in the Age of Trump* (London: Verso, 2017). A less reliable but widely cited study of the alt-right is Angela Nagle, *Kill All Normies: Online Culture Wars from 4chan and Tumblr to Trump and the Alt-Right* (Winchester: Zero, 2017). Nagle's book has been criticised for 'both-sides-ism', for reducing American leftist positions to a rigid dichotomy between class politics and identity politics, for turning alt-right discourses into a registry of everything she finds wrong with left-wing discourses, and for bad editing and plagiarism. By contrast, Strick's work stresses the performative 'atmospherics' of right-wing online culture, which is based in feelings (rather than convictions) of nonconformity. According to Strick, this non-intellectual spirit of defiance effectively insulates acts of trolling (online and offline) from critical questioning. In fact, alt-right provocations feed on critique; they typically anticipate their own political or moral condemnation since such reactions fuel the alt-right's constitutive feeling of hegemonic suppression. Placing these tactics in the context of a larger political economy, however, one should be careful not to fall into the trap of affective fundamentalism. Regardless of a standard axiom in Deleuzian affect theory, which posits that certain 'intensities' precede social interaction, there is no reason to disconnect feeling from structure (economies, networks, ideas, ideologies etc.) in the study of right-wing history. Moreover, the specific case of alt-right online polemics does not provide a general model for other – and quite different – communicative strategies of the New Right, ranging from the rhetoric of political philosophy all the way to conspiracy thought. Nevertheless, a purely 'intellectual' approach to Trumpism is obviously deficient; the New Right is not properly understood without considering its manifold affective dimensions.
17. See John B. Judis, *The Populist Explosion: How the Great Recession Transformed American and European Politics* (New York: Columbia Global Reports, 2016), 18–53. A pioneering study on this tradition, quoted by Judis, is Donald I. Warren, *The Radical Center: Middle Americans and the Politics of Alienation* (Notre Dame, IN: University of Notre Dame Press, 1976).
18. See Rick Perlstein, *The Invisible Bridge: The Fall of Nixon and the Rise of Reagan* (New York: Simon & Schuster, 2014).
19. See Jefferson R. Cowie, *Stayin' Alive: The 1970s and the Last Days of the Working Class* (New York: New Press, 2010).

20. On the culturalisation of poverty, see William J. Wilson, *When Work Disappears: The World of the New Urban Poor* (New York: Knopf, 1996).
21. For example, Powell proposed conducting his pro-business initiatives through the Chamber of Commerce. Movement Conservatism would soon follow a different path, more consistent with its philosophy of private initiative, enlisting think tanks and grassroots organisations. On Powell's memorandum as a central document of American neoliberalism, see David Harvey, *A Brief History of Neoliberalism* (Oxford: Oxford University Press, 2005), 43; Kevin Doogan, *New Capitalism? The Transformation of Work* (Cambridge: Polity, 2009), 34.
22. Lewis F. Powell Jr, 'Confidential Memorandum: Attack on American Free Enterprise System', 23 August 1971, 8, available at <https://scholarlycommons.law.wlu.edu/cgi/viewcontent.cgi?article=1000&context=powellmemo> (accessed 21 January 2020).
23. Ibid., 25.
24. For the 'long march' comparison, see Harvey, *A Brief History of Neoliberalism*, 40.
25. Powell, 'Confidential Memorandum', 2–3.
26. Ibid., 12, 5.
27. Ibid., 13, 17.
28. See Joan Walsh, 'The Right's Horrifying Edge: History Shows Surprising Pattern about Its Demise', *Salon*, 6 August 2014, <https://www.salon.com/2014/08/05/rick_perlstein_presents_ronald_reagan_exorcist> (accessed 21 January 2020).
29. Powell, 'Confidential Memorandum,' 25–26, 30.
30. Jane Mayer, *Dark Money: The Hidden History of the Billionaires behind the Rise of the Radical Right* (New York: Doubleday, 2016).
31. Publius Decius Mus, 'The Flight 93 Election', *Claremont Review of Books*, 5 September 2016, <https://claremontreviewofbooks.com/digital/the-flight-93-election> (accessed 21 January 2020).
32. Ibid.
33. Publius Decius Mus, 'Restatement on Flight 93', *Claremont Review of Books*, 13 September 2016, <https://claremontreviewofbooks.com/digital/restatement-on-flight-93> (last accessed 21 January 2020).
34. Ibid.
35. Decius, 'The Flight 93 Election'.
36. Ibid.
37. 'POTUS & Political Warfare', May 2017, available at <https://assets.documentcloud.org/documents/3922874/Political-Warfare.pdf> (accessed 21 January 2020); my italics.
38. Ibid.

39. Ibid.
40. Ibid.
41. Compare Anton, possibly channelling Jordan Peterson: 'Our liberal-left present reality and future direction is incompatible with human nature and must undermine society.' Concretely, Anton refers to 'the wars on "cis-genderism" – formerly known as "nature" – and on the supposed "white privilege" of broke hillbillies'. Decius, 'The Flight 93 Election'.
42. At present, the right's scientific field of choice seems to be evolutionary psychology, championed in its political implications most of all by Jordan Peterson (whose list of scientific questions that have been settled conclusively seems to exclude climate change).
43. 'POTUS & Political Warfare'.
44. William S. Lind, 'What Is Cultural Marxism?', Maryland Thursday Meeting (2008), <marylandthursdaymeeting.com/Archives/SpecialWeb Documents/Cultural.Marxism.htm> (accessed 21 January 2020).
45. Karl Polanyi, *The Great Transformation* (New York: Farrar & Rinehart, 1944).
46. Incidentally, this observation helps to dissolve the race-versus-class binary that has consumed so many liberal pundits since 2016. Voters do not have to experience real material decline to base their political decisions on (perceived or feared) socio-economic status threats. In fact, the expectation that people's economic politics are determined by their actual material situation presents a supremely neoliberal assumption to begin with, turning the individual voter into a *Homo oeconomicus*.
47. David Graeber, *The Utopia of Rules: On Technology, Stupidity, and the Secret Joys of Bureaucracy* (New York: Melville House, 2015), 28.
48. Keeanga-Yamahtta Taylor, *From #BlackLivesMatter to Black Liberation* (Chicago: Haymarket, 2016), 217.
49. Warren, *The Radical Center*, 1. See also Judis, *The Populist Explosion*, 21.
50. Quoted in Judis, *The Populist Explosion*, 95.
51. See Mark Blyth, 'Global Trumpism: Why Trump's Victory Was 30 Years in the Making and Why It Won't Stop Here', *Foreign Affairs*, 15 November 2016, <https://www/foreignaffairs.com/articles/2016-11-15/global-trumpism> (accessed 21 January 2020); Jürgen Habermas, 'Für eine demokratische Polarisierung: wie man dem Rechtspopulismus den Boden entzieht', *Blätter für deutsche und internationale Politik*, November 2016, 35–42; Christian Lammert and Boris Vormann, *Die Krise der Demokratie und wie wir sie überwinden* (Berlin: Aufbau, 2017).

52. 'Transcript: President Obama's Remarks on Donald Trump's Election', *Washington Post*, 9 November 2016, <https://www.washingtonpost.com/news/the-fix/wp/2016/11/09/transcript-president-obamas-remarks-on-donald-trumps-election> (accessed 21 January 2020).
53. Habermas, 'Für eine demokratische Polarisierung', 36; my italics.
54. Decius, 'Restatement on Flight 93'.
55. Decius, 'The Flight 93 Election'.
56. Ibid.
57. See new journals like Chris Buskirk's *American Greatness* (since summer 2016) and Julius Krein's quarterly *American Affairs* (since February 2017). However, one should not overestimate the philosophical ambitions of these more respectable outlets of contemporary right-wing thought – just as one should not divorce the affective activism of alt-right trolls from its constitutive ideas and ideological convictions. 'Intellectuals' like Ben Shapiro move easily from a register based in 'logic' (or performances thereof) to hyper-partisan social media agitation. Conversely, the demagogic opportunism of far-right gurus like Roger Stone – one of Trump's most colourful strategists and the missing link between the 2016 campaign and earlier Republican extremisms – is governed by deeply held political beliefs, many of which are shared, with local variations, by New Right movements across the globe.
58. See Joshua Green, *Devil's Bargain: Steve Bannon, Donald Trump, and the Storming of the Presidency* (New York: Penguin Press, 2017).
59. Tim Hains, 'Steve Bannon: Core of Trump's Platform is "Deconstruction of the Administrative State"', *RealClear Politics*, 23 February 2017, <https://www.realclearpolitics.com/video/2017/02/23/stephen_bannon_pillar_of_trumps_platform_is_deconstruction_of_the_administrative_state.html> (accessed 21 January 2020).
60. Quoted in Michael Wolff, 'Ringside with Steve Bannon at Trump Tower as the President-Elect's Strategist Plots "an Entirely New Political Movement"', *Hollywood Reporter*, 18 November 2016, <https://www.hollywoodreporter.com/news/stevebannon-trump-tower-interview-trumps-strategist-plots-new-political-movement-948747> (accessed 21 January 2020).
61. Hains, 'Steve Bannon'.
62. Decius, 'The Flight 93 Election'.
63. I would like to thank my readers Maxi Albrecht, Dustin Breitenwischer, Susanne Krugmann, Jenna Krumminga, Kathleen Loock, Martin Lüthe, Annelot Prins, Simon Schleusener, Joscha Spoellmink, Maximilian Stobbe, Simon Strick and Maria Sulimma.

4
Women Voters and Activists in Trump's America

Melissa Deckman and Kelley M. Gardner

Women's response to Donald Trump has been far more diverse than pundits and political observers often claim. The mainstream news media, for example, were shocked at how well Donald Trump performed in the 2016 presidential election with many women voters, particularly given his boorish, sexist behaviour, coupled with the leak of the infamous *Access Hollywood* tape in which Trump could be found bragging about his ability to sexually assault women because of his fame and wealth. At the same time, Trump's surprise victory also propelled many American women to engage in the politics of resistance, forming grassroots organisations to protest against his policies and inspiring a record number to run for political office for the first time in 2018.[1] A strong majority of women voters also helped the Democrats take back majority control of the US House of Representatives, with exit polls showing that roughly six out of ten women voters chose Democrats for Congress, nearly double the margin by which they voted Democrat in 2016.[2]

This chapter considers American women's response to Donald Trump and his presidency in three ways. First, it provides a brief overview of the women's vote in the 2016 presidential election, considering what sorts of women cast their ballots for Trump – and what sorts of women did not – highlighting how partisanship, race, class, religion and attitudes about gender, in particular, helped to shape women's voting choices. Second, it considers how American women rate Trump's performance as president two years into his term. Last, it considers how the Trump presidency has inspired a new cohort of activists and political candidates as part of the 'Resistance'. The chapter concludes by considering whether 'Trump's America' will more permanently alter the political behaviour of women during the 2020 presidential race and beyond – or if we can expect the same sorts of long-standing patterns to remain in effect.

The women's vote in 2016

Political scientists who study American politics have long known that women and men are politically different in notable ways, a concept referred to by scholars as the gender gap. American women consistently hold more liberal positions than men on a range of issues. They are more likely than men to support more government spending on social welfare programming,[3] and are more supportive of government regulation of the environment[4] and guns.[5] Women are also less likely than men to support the use of military force[6] and are more opposed to capital punishment.[7] Partly as a result of these attitudinal differences, American women are significantly more likely than men to identify as Democrats,[8] while men are more likely to identify as Republicans. This chasm has become wider in the past three decades, in large part because many men have left the Democratic Party.[9] Not surprisingly, then, women have been more likely than men to cast their ballots for Democrats for president since the election of Ronald Reagan in 1980.[10]

Exit polls show that the gender gap was alive and well in the 2016 presidential election. Men were significantly more likely to report voting for Donald Trump (52 per cent) compared with women (41 per cent) while women (54 per cent) were significantly more likely to report voting for Hillary Clinton compared with men (41 per cent).[11] When defined as the difference between the proportion of women voting for the winning candidate and the proportion of men voting for the winning candidate, the gap for 2016 was 11 per cent, which ties as the highest overall gender gap in the last ten presidential elections along with the 1996 presidential election, in which Bill Clinton was re-elected against Bob Dole.[12]

But this overall gender gap in presidential elections obfuscates certain features of the American electorate when it comes to gender, as women are far from monolithic in their voting decisions. Partisanship, age, race and religion explain far more about voting behaviour than does gender alone, as shown in Figure 4.1, in which we break down the women's vote by numerous categories using data collected by the Public Religion Research Institute (PRRI) and *The Atlantic* magazine in 2016 shortly after the election.[13] Party, naturally, is strongly linked to vote choice: Republican women overwhelmingly backed Donald Trump (86 per cent), while Democratic women almost uniformly cast their ballots for Hillary Clinton (96 per cent). Women who identify as Independents were split, although more reported voting for Clinton (49 per cent) than for Trump (33 per cent), with about one in five Independent women choosing a third-party candidate (data not reported).

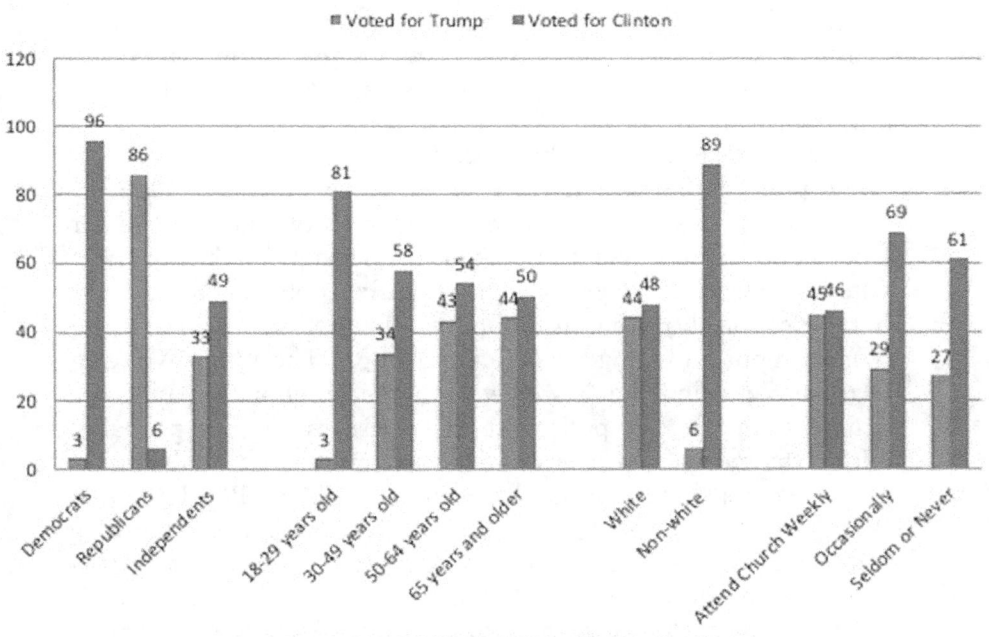

Source: 2016 PRRI/*Atlantic* White Working Class Survey

Figure 4.1. Vote (percentage) for Trump and Clinton in 2016: women only

There were important generational differences among women voters as well. Women less than thirty years old overwhelmingly backed Clinton (81 per cent). Although Trump failed to secure a majority of women voters in any age demographic, his support rose with each age cohort as displayed in Figure 4.1, doing best with women aged sixty-five and older. Religiosity, as measured by church attendance, shows that women who are regular church attenders split their vote between both candidates; however, those women who reported attending church occasionally (defined here as monthly or several times a year) or rarely, if ever, were far less likely to back Trump. These findings correspond with research that shows that secular voters – who represent the fastest growing 'religious' category in the United States, particularly among young people[14] – are far less likely to vote Republican.[15] Generally, Americans who are more religiously devout have been more likely to identify as and vote for Republicans,[16] although it is important to remember that people of colour, especially African-American women, are more religiously devout and are far more likely to identify as Democrats. That 46 per cent of regular church attenders report voting for Clinton is partially explained by the greater religiosity of women of colour.[17]

That women of colour historically and strongly prefer Democratic presidential candidates was borne out again in 2016, as Figure 4.1 shows that 89 per cent of women of colour voted for Clinton with just 6 per cent voting for Trump.[18] White women voters, however, largely split their vote. Exit polls taken the night of the election show that just more than half (52 per cent) of white women reported voting for Donald Trump.[19] The White Working Class surveys find that fewer white women reported voting for Trump than the exit polls, but that these results are probably within the margin of error and drawn from a much smaller sample of women voters. Notably, even in the 2016 PRRI/*Atlantic* White Working-Class Survey, Hillary Clinton failed to secure a majority of the white women's vote, and while this fact was shocking and disappointing to many political commentators,[20] it is very much in line with historical trends. As political scientist Jane Junn documents, a majority of white women have voted for the Democratic presidential nominee only twice since the 1950s, with the landslide election of Lyndon B. Johnson in 1964 and the re-election of Bill Clinton in 1996.[21]

Of course, not all white women voted for Donald Trump, and age, class and religion, in particular, heavily influenced the white women's vote. Figure 4.2 shows the breakdown of the white women's vote by these particular categories, although substituting particular religious affiliation with church attendance to gauge the impact of religion on vote choice. We find that younger white women, white women who attended college, and white women who are not Evangelical Protestants – especially the religiously unaffiliated – were the most likely to vote for Hillary Clinton. By contrast, nearly 70 per cent of white women voters who identify as Evangelical Protestants cast their ballot for Trump, which is not surprising given that white Evangelical Protestants have been among Trump's most ardent supporters during both his campaign and presidency. Much has been written about the economic factors that drove the white working class – those Americans who did not attend college – to vote for Donald Trump in larger numbers than

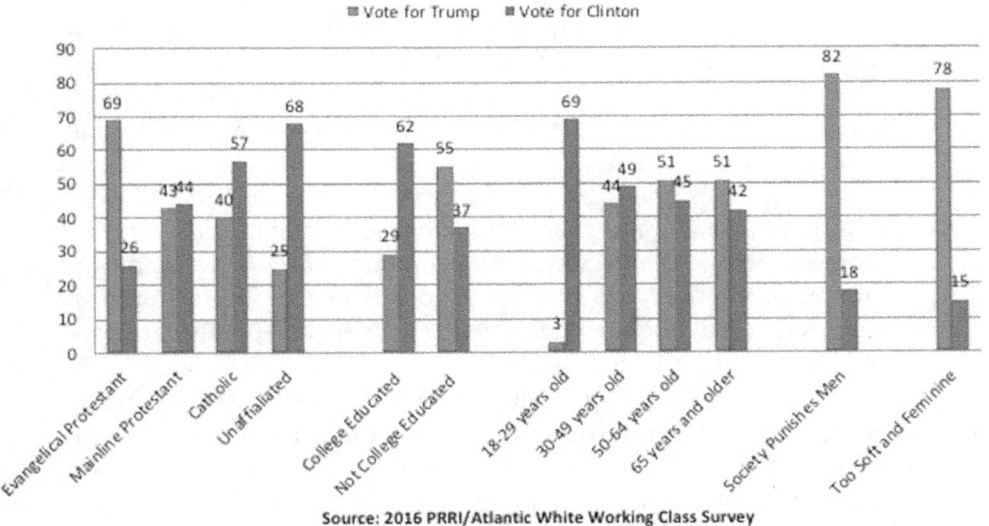

Source: 2016 PRRI/Atlantic White Working Class Survey

Figure 4.2. 2016 Presidential vote choice among white women by religion, education, age and gender attitudes

expected,²² although some scholarship finds that it was actually fears of cultural displacement rather than economic concerns that led them to do so.²³ This pattern also extends to white working-class women as shown in Figure 4.2, who were far more likely to vote for Donald Trump (55 per cent) than were white women who attended college (29 per cent). Indeed, some research shows that it was white working-class women's – not white working-class men's – greater attraction to candidate Donald Trump in 2016 than his immediate predecessor, Mitt Romney, that helped Trump do better overall among low-income white voters compared with 2012.²⁴

Still, many in the media, and many of Hillary Clinton's supporters, were all but certain that the nomination of the first woman presidential candidate for a major party would somehow unite more women voters together than in previous elections. Candidate Clinton embraced her gender as an asset while running for president in the 2016 campaign, which was a notable departure from her campaign for the presidency in 2008, in which she largely avoided mentioning her gender at all.²⁵ In her 2015 campaign kick-off, for instance, she told her supporters that while she would not be the youngest candidate in the race, she would become 'the youngest woman president in the history of the United States'.²⁶ Candidate Donald Trump famously mocked Clinton's appeal to women voters, telling *Vox* that 'the only thing she has going for her is the woman's card, and the beautiful thing is, women don't like her'.²⁷

Setting aside Trump's jab at Clinton – polls at the time showed that Trump was rated even less favourably than Clinton among women voters – the idea that women voters vote for women candidates merely because of their gender is not supported by past studies of voting behaviour. Instead, women voters rely far more on traditional cues and factors such as partisanship, incumbency and campaign spending when it comes to their decisions in the voting booth.²⁸ Moreover, gender consciousness, which is the notion that women have similar views and outlooks based on their shared experiences, has never united women voters in the same way that racial consciousness has brought voters of colour uniformly behind the Democratic Party, particularly when Barack Obama was running for president.²⁹

What about Trump's appalling, sexist behaviour on the campaign trail?[30] Wasn't his overtly sexist rhetoric and past misogynist behaviour, largely unprecedented in presidential campaign history, enough to inspire more women to vote for the other candidate, especially religiously devout women? As the data in Figure 4.2 show, white Evangelical Protestant women, who hold more socially conservative attitudes on a range of sexual topics than other American women, were among Trump's largest supporters. While some Evangelical women were uncomfortable electing a thrice-married, non-religious man who habitually lied and said degrading things about women in his past, many conservative Protestant women, much like their male counterparts, strongly supported Trump's policies with respect to abortion, immigration and religious liberty concerns, especially his pledge to appoint conservative jurists to the bench.[31] Moreover, many of these same white women were uniformly less bothered by Trump's sexist antics and, in fact, *endorse* sexist beliefs themselves. Compared with the 2012 presidential election, Erin Cassese and Tiffany Barnes find that Trump's campaign made sexist attitudes more salient as a predictor of vote choice, with white women who held sexist beliefs and who decried the prevalence of women's discrimination in society being significantly more likely to vote for Donald Trump – even while controlling for other factors such as partisanship, income and ideology.[32] They argue that such findings can be linked to system justification theory:

> Some white women are motivated to distance themselves from the disadvantage associated with their gender. As a result, their belief systems emphasize and privilege their relationships with white men while underscoring their racial advantage over poor and minority women. Not surprisingly, then, white women who harbored sexist attitudes were more likely to be tolerant of Trump's sexism and to cast their vote for him on Election Day.[33]

Although the PRRI/*Atlantic* survey did not ask respondents a question about sexism per se, it did ask voters the extent to which they agreed that society today 'seems to punish men for just acting like men'. As Figure 4.2 shows, an overwhelming majority of white women who agreed with this notion – 82 per cent – voted for Donald Trump, lending credence to the argument put forward by Cassese and Barnes. Moreover, support for Trump among white women is also linked to broader attitudes towards gender and nationalism.[34] As shown in Figure 4.2, more than three-quarters of white women voters who believe that society as a whole 'has become too soft and feminine' voted for him, which only reinforces a growing body of scholarly literature in political science that demonstrates that beliefs *about* gender, whether that includes attitudes on gender roles or gender stereotypes,[35] explain more about electoral behaviour than biological sex alone.

In sum, the women's vote in 2016 was as varied as women themselves. Although a majority of American women identify as Democrats or Independents, one in four identify as Republicans,[36] which represents millions of voters. Those Republican women turned out in force to support their nominee and overwhelmingly chose Donald Trump over Hillary Clinton in 2016 – despite any misgivings they might have had personally about Trump's character and misogynistic behaviour. Elections, of course, are largely binary events in American politics – the notion that Trump's appalling personal behaviour would cause Republican women en masse to cast their ballot for Hillary Clinton, whose policy views on abortion, gay rights, immigration and the size and scope of government were sharply different from their own, was really not realistic. At the same time, Clinton drew votes disproportionally from women of colour, young people and the religiously unaffiliated. Unfortunately for her, these same groups of people are less likely to be represented among Americans who turn out to vote. And while Clinton won the popular vote overall, her inability to secure enough votes – regardless of whether they came from women or men – in states that went for Barack Obama in both of his presidential races, such as Michigan, Wisconsin and Pennsylvania, resulted in Trump's election. Women voters in certain states, then, were pivotal to electing Donald Trump in 2016.

Women's support for Trump during his presidency

Trump's voting base consisted, in part, of conservative, Republican and working-class white women. Have these same women continued to support Donald Trump during his controversial presidency? There could be reasons to expect that Trump's support among conservative women has faltered, due to the ongoing drama surrounding the Mueller investigation into possible connections between the Trump campaign and the Russian government (and possible attempts by Trump to obstruct those investigations), his universally derided policy of separating migrant children from their parents seeking political asylum at the Mexican border as part of a 'zero tolerance' policy to stem illegal immigration, and his well-documented propensity toward dishonesty – among other issues. More allegations of Trump's sordid personal life have also come to light during his presidency. Roughly one year after his inauguration, the *Wall Street Journal* broke the Stormy Daniels story, detailing how Trump's personal lawyer, Michael Cohen, paid hush money to the adult film actress shortly before the election to prevent her from publicly sharing her story of an alleged affair with the president and thereby jeopardising his election chances. Shortly after, similar schemes to silence Karen McDougal, a Playboy model who alleged a longer-term affair with Trump in 2006, were revealed, involving Trump's personal friend David Pecker, the CEO of American Media, Inc., the publisher of the *National Enquirer* among other magazines, who paid for the rights for McDougal's story in order to bury it.[37] For the record, Trump continues to maintain that he did not have extramarital affairs with either woman. At the same time, has Trump been able to broaden his support with other sectors of American women? In general, the growth of the economy has been strong[38] and unemployment has been at near-record low levels during Trump's presidency,[39] although his critics point out that wage growth is slower to follow as the nation continues to endure massive income inequality. The United States, despite an increase in mass shootings and an alarming spike in organised activity carried out by white supremacists, enjoys a relatively low crime rate compared with previous decades and is not currently embroiled in a major war or foreign entanglement. Are these factors perhaps leading some women, especially political independents, to be more likely to change their opinion about Trump?

To answer these questions, we analysed data from the 2018 American Values Survey, taken in late September 2018 by PRRI at the height of the midterm elections. Specifically, we examined how the (mostly) same groups of women analysed in the first segment of the chapter rated Trump's performance as president in terms of job approval.[40] Overall, just 35 per cent of American women nationally, according to the PRRI poll, approved of Trump's job performance, compared with 48 per cent of men (data not reported). The gender gap apparent in voting in the 2016 presidential election is also present when it comes to Trump's approval rating. Isolating our analysis to American women only, Figure 4.3 shows the percentages of American women who expressed support for his job performance by party, race, age, class and religious tradition. There is no indication that Republican women are abandoning Donald Trump – 86 per cent of them approve of the job he is doing as president. Trump continues to struggle with women who are Democrats, not surprisingly, but his performance among

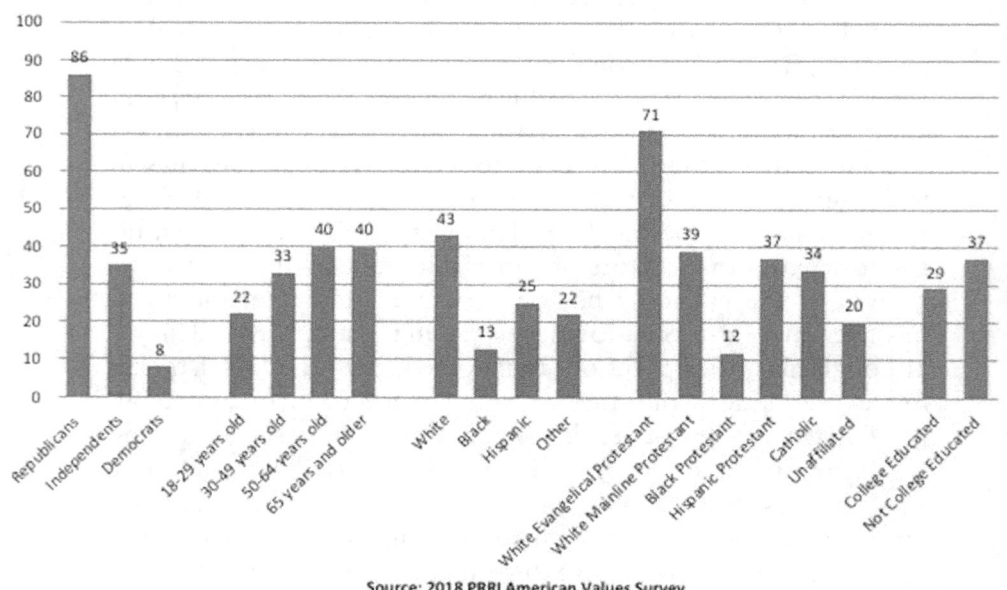

Source: 2018 PRRI American Values Survey

Figure 4.3. Percentage of women approving of Trump's job performance

women who identify as Independents is also far under water at 35 per cent. Trump's job approval is below 50 per cent with all age cohorts of women, although younger American women are especially critical of his performance, with only 22 per cent approving of his presidency.

Trump also fails to elicit the widespread support of any racial group of women, although his approval among white women is far higher than among the other three groups. Aside from Republicans, only white Evangelical women maintain steadfast support for Donald Trump, with more than 71 per cent approving of his job performance. When it comes to education, college-educated women are less likely to give Trump high marks for his presidency than those without a college degree. Although not shown in Figure 4.3, when considering just white women and education status, close to half (48 per cent) of white working-class women approve of Trump's job performance, compared with just 34 per cent of white women with a college degree. In essence, the overall picture is that views of Trump largely remain entrenched from his election in 2016 as he has failed to enlarge his base among American women, despite a booming economy.

Republicans continue to largely back the president, regardless of gender – the 2018 American Values Survey finds that 91 per cent of GOP men also approve of Trump's performance (data not reported). This is hardly surprising given the tribal nature of American politics, as studies show that Americans who are the most partisan are increasingly likely to view the opposition with deep scepticism and hostility. The Pew Research Center has found, for example, that from 1994 to 2016, the percentages of partisans who rank the opposition party as deeply negative, or even as a threat to the nation's wellbeing, increased precipitously.[41] In 2016, Pew found that 58 per cent of Democrats and 55 per cent of Republicans rated the other party as very unfavourable.[42] Negative partisanship also helps explain why Trump struggles to make inroads with Democratic women.

Yet why haven't more white Evangelicals – many of whom felt free to judge former president Bill Clinton's extramarital affair with White House intern Monica Lewinsky harshly – condemned Trump's behaviour while in the Oval Office? For instance, Reverend

Pat Robertson, founder of the Christian Coalition, called for Clinton's impeachment for turning the Oval Office into a 'playpen for the sexual freedom of the poster child of the 1960s'.[43] The relationship between many Evangelical leaders and this president has become more transactional, as prominent conservative Christians routinely praise Trump for his opposition to abortion, his appointment of conservative judges and his strong support for Israel. They also applaud his attempts to overturn the Affordable Care Act, including its controversial birth control mandate, which requires business owners who provide insurance to pay for birth control. In describing his actions towards Obamacare, Peggy Nance, the CEO and president of the Evangelical lobbying group Concerned Women for America, praised Trump as 'a president who is truly committed to liberty. He is committed to America, and he is working to keep his word to the American people. That is incredibly honorable and noble.'[44]

This is not to say that rank-and-file Evangelical women don't have some misgivings about the president's behaviour in office. While 71 per cent approve of his job as president, the 2018 American Values Survey finds that 55 per cent believe that Trump has damaged the dignity of the office (compared with just 39 per cent of white Evangelical men, notably; data not reported). Nonetheless, their support of Trump's policies overall has been enough to keep white Evangelical women firmly behind him.

At the same time, more progressive women, women of colour and younger women have not budged in their opposition to Donald Trump. If anything, Trump's presidency has spawned a backlash that began with the historic Women's March in Washington, DC, the day after Trump's inauguration and resulted, in part, in the election of a record number of women to Congress and to elected office more generally. We turn, lastly, to those efforts.

Women and the Resistance

The day after Donald Trump was inaugurated in 2017, millions of women marched in 'a massive show of resistance' in Washington, DC, and in cities around the world, in what was heralded by the *Washington Post* as probably the largest protest in US history.[45]

The Women's March featured women who were both angered by Trump's election and fearful about his administration's potential rollback of women's rights. At the Women's March, protesters focused on equal pay, reproductive freedom, criminal justice reform, immigrants' rights, opposition to sexual violence, LGBTQ rights and a living wage for domestic workers.[46] The organisers of the 2017 march received criticism from pro-life feminists who were excluded from the march,[47] and its leaders were urged to pay more attention to intersectionality and problems faced by non-white women, who have historically been neglected by the feminist movement.[48] But, as women protesters gathered in 2017, and again in 2018, the Women's March organisation 'became a powerful symbol of mass, unified opposition to the new Trump Administration'.[49]

Because Trump's unexpected victory alarmed progressive women and galvanised them to action,[50] women's political involvement following the first Women's March 'reinvigorated American politics at every level'.[51] Trump's misogynistic behaviour as a candidate and president has turned many women who previously had little political involvement into protesters, activists and candidates. The victory of Trump over Hillary Clinton, who would have been the nation's first female president, has resulted not only in high levels of attendance at these mass protests and an increase in participatory democracy/grassroots organising, but also in historic numbers of women running for office (and winning) and an unprecedented rise in political participation among young women.

Progressive and feminist groups have seen increased participation from women interested in resisting Trump, his administration and his policies. Women's organisations represent a wide range of issues, interests and ideological perspectives in contemporary politics,[52] but following Trump's election and the Women's March, many new progressive women's groups joined the growing Resistance to the Trump administration. One of the largest of these groups, Indivisible, was founded after the 2016 election with the goal of engaging in progressive advocacy and electoral work at the local, state and federal level to 'resist the Trump agenda'.[53] At least 70 per cent of Indivisible members are women, and most Indivisible groups have all-female leadership teams.[54]

Other prominent, more long-standing organisations such as the National Women's Law Center and the National Organization for Women have also seen increased support from women who oppose Trump and have become more politically engaged since his election in 2016, particularly with respect to the November midterm elections in 2018.[55]

Also leading up to the midterm elections, issues of sexual misconduct became a pressing social concern with the rapid rise of the #MeToo movement, which began after an explosive *New York Times* exposé detailed women's accounts of sexual assault and harassment at the hands of famed Hollywood producer Harvey Weinstein. Using the power of social media, women across the country who had experienced similar treatment at their workplaces posted their own stories under the #MeToo hashtag, a movement that was first developed more than a decade earlier by organiser Tarana Burke. As a result, the Time's Up movement began in January 2018 and focused on sexual assault, harassment and inequality in the workplace.[56] This heightened attention to the issue of sexual assault and harassment made Trump's nomination to the Supreme Court of Brett Kavanaugh, who later was accused of sexual misconduct by multiple women, most notably Dr Christine Blasey Ford, extremely controversial. Ford would go on to testify about the alleged sexual assault attempt by Kavanaugh when both were teenagers in front of the Senate Judiciary Committee in September 2018; Kavanaugh vehemently denied the charges. Despite Ford's compelling testimony, Kavanaugh was later confirmed largely along partisan lines, and the whole Kavanaugh spectacle was marked by widespread protests at the US Senate building in Washington and across the country, both by activists from the Resistance and by survivors of sexual assault and their allies. Many considered Kavanaugh's confirmation a failure in this era of #MeToo and Time's Up, and progressive women, again, were outraged by Trump's misogyny, the Republican Party, and Kavanaugh and Trump remaining in positions of power despite being credibly accused of sexual misconduct.

In addition to participation in social movements such as the Women's March, #MeToo and Time's Up, progressive women's response to Trump also resulted in a 'Pink Wave' of female candidates in the 2018 midterms. Research shows that women often underestimate their political abilities,[57] or need more encouragement to consider running for office,[58] but Trump's unusual candidacy and lack of political experience and credentials shifted previously held expectations of a candidate's desired qualifications.[59] One study of fifty-two women who ran for Congress – and ultimately lost their bids – found that two-thirds of them were running for office for the first time; moreover, twice as many of these candidates said that the election of Trump impacted their decision to run for office than said it did not.[60] Thousands of women also contacted women's candidate-training organisations for help in establishing their candidacies. For instance, Emily's List, one of the better-known candidate-training groups, which helps elect pro-choice Democratic women to office, reported that more than 46,000 women reached out to them about running for public office after the 2016 presidential race; prior to the 2016 elections, just 920 did.[61] Anger at Donald Trump's election, and the policies his administration proposed or enacted, such as attempts to overturn and weaken the Affordable Care Act, resulted in a record number of women filing to run for congressional seats (529) and gubernatorial elections (61).[62]

The Resistance to Trump and this wave of female candidates, not surprisingly, was largely Democratic. While these female candidates had different interests and ideologies – from the progressive firebrand Alexandria Ocasio-Cortez, who upset a long-term Democratic incumbent in the primary election in her liberal urban district in the Bronx, New York, to more moderate women such as Mikie Sherill in suburban New Jersey, who would go on to win in a large number of swing districts to tip the balance back to a Democratic majority in the House of Representatives – their shared opposition to Trump and his administration's policies united them. As female candidates ran in historic quantities in 2018, they also won at historic rates. The 116th Congress has more women serving in it than ever before, with a record 102 women serving in the House of Representatives and 25 women serving in the Senate.[63] The new Congress has 106 Democratic women, but only 21 Republican women, exhibiting a widening gap between female representation and partisanship. In fact, the overall number of Republican women serving in Congress dropped from twenty-eight in 2016 to twenty-seven in 2017, and after the 2018 midterms down to only twenty-one.[64] About 80 per cent of women now serving in Congress are Democrats, a big deviation from the 1980s, when Congress had roughly the same number of Democratic and Republican women.[65] At the state legislative level as well, a record number of women were elected in 2018, with 2,134 serving in state legislatures in 2019.[66] As in Congress, the proportion of Republican women in state legislatures also dropped, from 705 in 2018 to 662 in 2019.[67]

Not only did the Resistance to Trump drive a historic number of Democratic female candidacies and victories, the 2018 midterm elections were very much about voters' approval – or disapproval – of Donald Trump. According to CNN exit polls, two-thirds of voters said that their vote in the congressional election in November 2018 was about Trump, and more respondents said they were expressing opposition (39 per cent) than support (26 per cent) for him.[68] Voters turned out in support or opposition on a number of issues, including Trump's immigration policies, tax law, trade policies, healthcare, and their approval or disproval of Brett Kavanaugh's confirmation to the Supreme Court.[69] Moreover, women voters strongly backed Democratic candidates in the midterm elections. For instance, 59 per cent of women voted for Democrats, compared with 40 per cent of women who voted for Republicans, which was nearly double the margin from the 2016 vote for congressional candidates.[70] While women of colour once again overwhelmingly backed Democratic candidates for Congress, the exit polls show that white women split their vote equally, 49 per cent between both parties, which represents a significant shift leftward in their congressional voting patterns since 2014 and 2016.[71] The education gap among white women was especially pronounced – a strong majority of white working-class women voters chose Republican candidates for Congress (56 per cent) while an even larger majority of white college-educated women voters backed Democrats (59 per cent).[72]

Finally, one other notable trend to emerge with respect to women's engagement in politics in Trump's America concerns younger women. Women have historically expressed much less interest than their male counterparts in public affairs, and even in 2016, men were more likely than women to report that they paid attention to politics.[73] Data from a 2017 PRRI/MTV poll of Americans aged 15–24, however, demonstrated a shift in this gender gap, where young women expressed higher levels of political and civic engagement than young men.[74] The young women who were the *most* engaged were overwhelmingly Democratic, strongly preferred Hillary Clinton over Donald Trump in the 2016 election, and were personally committed to gender equality.[75] David Campbell and Christina Wolbrecht have also found that teenage girls who identified as Democrats and who were disillusioned with the American political system after Trump's election were more likely than other teens to indicate a willingness to become engaged in protest politics.[76] This is likely to be a direct reflection of the larger gender dynamics that emerged in wake of Trump's win that brought many Democratic women – of all ages – into the political sphere.

Conclusion: what the future holds

Clearly, women's political activism appears to be on the rise since Trump's election in 2016 – more progressive women are involved in social movements and grassroots organising, are running for office, and are participating in democracy at all levels. In some respects, their engagement in the political system, driven in response to the election of a president whose values and priorities are an affront to their own, echoes another recent political movement in American politics – the Tea Party. Following the election of the nation's first black president in 2008, the Tea Party movement galvanised conservative activists across the country – many of whom were engaged in politics for the first time – to protest against the policies advocated by President Obama during his first term in office, which included deficit spending to stimulate the economy and the overhaul of the nation's healthcare system through the Affordable Care Act. Subsequent studies found that racial resentment was a big driver of support for the Tea Party movement,[77] but another distinguishing feature of the Tea Party was the extent to which women were involved as activists and leaders, many of whom again were relatively new to politics.[78] While the heyday of the Tea Party movement has passed, with most of what's left of its supporters firmly behind Donald Trump, the tendency for activists at the grassroots level to mobilise as a reactionary response to national trends is not new. And in the past decade, many of these activists have been women.

The larger question is what happens with respect to women's political engagement once Trump is no longer president. Can we expect liberal or progressive women to keep running for office in record numbers and for them to remain involved in progressive causes at all levels of government? If recent history is any guide, it might be likely that the election of a Democrat to the White House in 2020 results in complacency among many newer activists and conservative women might be more motivated to become involved in organising. Or, perhaps this newer generation of younger women, who disproportionately lean to the political left and whose involvement in politics is due in no small part to Donald Trump, may be inculcating political habits that keep them engaged in social and political advocacy for the long haul. Only time will tell.

Notes

1. Lara Putnam and Theda Skocpol, 'Middle America Reboots Democracy', *Democracy*, 20 February 2018, <https://democracyjournal.org/arguments/middle-america-reboots-democracy> (accessed 21 January 2020).
2. Janie Valencia, 'The 2018 Gender Gap Was Huge', *FiveThirtyEight*, 9 November 2018, <https://fivethirtyeight.com/features/the-2018-gender-gap-was-huge> (accessed 21 January 2020).
3. Julie Dolan, Melissa M. Deckman and Michele L. Swers, *Women and Politics: Paths to Power and Political Influence* (Lanham, MD: Rowman & Littlefield, 2007); Leonie Huddy, Erin Cassese and Mary-Kate Lizotte, 'Gender, Public Opinion, and Political Reasoning', in Christina Wolbrecht, Karen Beckwith and Lisa Baldez (eds), *Political Women and American Democracy* (Cambridge: Cambridge University Press, 2008), 31–49.
4. Matthew Ballew, Jennifer Marlon, Anthony Leiserowitz and Edward Maibach, 'Gender Differences in Public Understanding of

Climate Change', Yale Program on Climate Change Communication, 20 November 2018, <http://climatecommunication.yale.edu/publications/gender-differences-in-public-understanding-of-climate-change> (accessed 21 January 2020).
5. Barbara Norrander, 'The History of the Gender Gaps', in Lois Duke Whitaker (ed.), *Voting the Gender Gap* (Urbana: University of Illinois Press, 2008), 9–32.
6. Dolan et al., *Women and Politics*.
7. Norrander, 'The History of the Gender Gaps'.
8. Heather Ondercin, 'Who Is Responsible for the Gender Gap? The Dynamics of Men's and Women's Democratic Macropartisanship 1950–2012', *Political Research Quarterly* 70, no. 4 (2017), 749–61.
9. Karen Kaufmann and John R. Petrocik, 'The Changing Politics of American Men: Understanding the Sources of the Gender Gap', *American Journal of Political Science* 43, no. 3 (1999), 864–87; Norrander, 'The History of the Gender Gaps'; Kristin Kanthak and Barbara Norrander, 'The Enduring Gender Gap', in Herbert F. Weisberg and Clyde Wilcox (eds.), *Models of Voting in Presidential Elections: The 2000 US Election* (Stanford: Stanford University Press, 2004), 141–60.
10. CAWP (Center for American Women and Politics), 'The Gender Gap: Voting Choices in Presidential Elections', Eagleton Institute of Politics, Rutgers University (2017), available at <https://cawp.rutgers.edu/sites/default/files/resources/ggpresvote.pdf> (accessed 21 January 2020).
11. 'Exit Polls', CNN, 23 November 2016, <https://edition.cnn.com/election/2016/results/exit-polls> (accessed 21 January 2020). The same exit polls show that 7 per cent of men and 5 per cent of women reported voting for a third candidate.
12. CAWP, 'The Gender Gap'.
13. Betsy Cooper, Daniel Cox, Rachel Lienesch and Robert P. Jones, 'Nearly One in Five Female Clinton Voters Say Husband or Partner Didn't Vote: PRRI/*The Atlantic* Post-Election Survey', PRRI, 1 December 2016, <https://www.prri.org/research/prri-atlantic-poll-post-election-white-working-class> (accessed 21 January 2020). These data come from the 2016 White Working-Class Survey, conducted by PRRI and *The Atlantic* jointly in November 2016. Though the name of the survey focuses on a particular demographic group, there was no oversample of white working-class respondents. N = 1,162 with a subsample of 969 voters (540 landline, 622 mobile; data collected 9–20 November 2016). The margin of

error with the subsample survey is ± 3.9 percentage points, but it is larger when the analysis focuses solely on women voters (N=417). For ease of interpretation, votes cast for third-party candidates by women are not included in the tables, so the figures do not round to 100 percent.

14. Betsy Cooper, Daniel Cox, Rachel Lienesch and Robert P. Jones, 'Exodus: Why Americans Are Leaving Religion – and Why They Are Unlikely to Come Back', PRRI, 22 September 2016, <https://www.prri.org/research/prri-rns-poll-nones-atheist-leaving-religion> (accessed 21 January 2020).

15. Jessica Martínez and Gregory A. Smith, 'How the Faithful Voted: A Preliminary 2016 Analysis', Pew Research Center, 9 November 2016, <https://www.pewresearch.org/fact-tank/2016/11/09/how-the-faithful-voted-a-preliminary-2016-analysis> (accessed 21 January 2020).

16. Robert Putnam and David E. Campbell, *American Grace: How Religion is Reshaping Our Civic and Public Lives* (New York: Simon & Schuster, 2010).

17. Though not reported in the figure, we found that 90 per cent of non-white women voters who attend church weekly voted for Clinton, compared with just 30 per cent of white women voters who attend church weekly.

18. Not shown in Figure 4.1 is that 0 per cent of African-American women reported voting for Donald Trump! We combined all women of colour into one category because their sample size in the survey was too small to yield reliable statistics.

19. Katie Rogers, 'White Women Helped Elect Donald Trump', *New York Times*, 9 November 2016, <https://www.nytimes.com/2016/12/01/us/politics/white-women-helped-elect-donald-trump.html> (accessed 21 January 2020).

20. See, for example, Sarah Ruiz-Grossman, 'Dear Fellow White Women: We F**ked This Up', *HuffPost*, 9 November 2016, <https://www.huffpost.com/entry/dear-white-women-we-messed-this-up-election-2016_n_582341c9e4b0aac62488970e> (accessed 21 January 2020).

21. Jane Junn, 'Hiding in Plain Sight: White Women Vote Republican', *Politics of Color*, 13 November 2016, <http://politicsofcolor.com/white-women-vote-republican> (accessed 21 January 2020).

22. Stephen L. Morgan and Jiwoon Lee, 'Trump Voters and the White Working Class', *Sociological Science* 5 (2018), 234–45, <https://www.sociologicalscience.com/download/vol-5/april/SocSci_v5_234to245.pdf> (accessed 21 January 2020).

23. Cooper et al., *Exodus*; Diana C. Mutz, 'Status Threat, Not Economic Hardship, Explains the 2016 Presidential Vote', *Proceedings of the National Academy of Sciences of the United States of America* 115, no. 19 (2018), E4330–E4339, <https://www.pnas.org/content/115/19/E4330> (accessed 21 January 2020).
24. Erin Cassese and Tiffany Barnes, 'Reconciling Sexism and Women's Support for Republican Candidates: A Look at Gender, Class, and Whiteness in the 2012 and 2016 Presidential Races', *Political Behavior* 41, no. 3 (2019), 677–700.
25. Kiana Scott, 'Madame President: Hillary Clinton, Gender, and the General Election', National Women's Political Caucus website (2016), <https://www.nwpcwa.org/madame_president_hillary_clinton_gender_and_the_general_election> (accessed 21 January 2020).
26. Quoted in Amy Chozick, 'Hillary Clinton, in Roosevelt Island Speech, Pledges to Close Income Gap', *New York Times*, 13 June 2015, <https://www.nytimes.com/2015/06/14/us/hillary-clinton-attacks-republican-economic-policies-in-roosevelt-island-speech.html> (accessed 21 January 2020).
27. Quoted in Libby Nelson, 'Donald Trump Says Women Don't Like Hillary Clinton. They Dislike Him Even More', *Vox*, 26 April 2016, <https://www.vox.com/2016/4/26/11514948/trump-clinton-women> (accessed 21 January 2020).
28. Kathleen Dolan, *When Does Gender Matter? Women Candidates and Gender Stereotypes in American Elections* (New York: Oxford University Press, 2014).
29. Nancy Burns and Donald Kinder, 'Categorical Politics: Gender, Race, and Public Opinion', in Adam Berinsky (ed.), *New Directions in Public Opinion* (New York: Routledge, 2012), 139–67; Michael Tesler, 'Why the Gender Gap Doomed Hillary Clinton', *Washington Post*, 9 November 2016, <https://www.washingtonpost.com/news/monkey-cage/wp/2016/11/09/why-the-gender-gap-doomed-hillary-clinton> (accessed 21 January 2020).
30. Jared Yates Sexton, 'Donald Trump's Toxic Masculinity', *New York Times*, 13 October 2016, <https://www.nytimes.com/2016/10/13/opinion/donald-trumps-toxic-masculinity.html> (accessed 21 January 2020).
31. Elizabeth Dias, '"I Pray for Him Daily." Why Socially Conservative Women Stand by Trump', *Time*, 20 February 2018, <http://time.com/5166765/donald-trump-evangelicals-religion-women> (accessed 21 January 2020).

32. Cassese and Barnes, 'Reconciling Sexism and Women's Support for Republican Candidates.'
33. Ibid., 20.
34. Melissa Deckman and Erin Cassese, 'Gendered Nationalism and the 2016 US Presidential Election: How Party, Class, and Beliefs about Masculinity Shaped Voting Behavior', *Politics & Gender* (2019), <https://doi.org/10.1017/S1743923X19000485> (accessed 21 January 2020).
35. Ana Bracic, Mackenzie Israel-Trummel and Allyson F. Shortle, 'Is Sexism for White People? Gender Stereotypes, Race, and the 2016 Presidential Election', *Political Behavior* 41, no. 2 (2019), 281–307; Erin Cassese and Mirya Holman, 'Playing the "Woman Card": Ambivalent Sexism in the 2016 US Presidential Race', *Political Psychology* 40, no. 1 (2019): 55–74; Brian F. Schaffner, Matthew MacWilliams and Tatishe Nteta, 'Understanding White Polarization in the 2016 Vote for President: The Sobering Role of Racism and Sexism', *Political Science Quarterly* 133, no. 1 (2018), 9–34.
36. Melissa Deckman, *Tea Party Women: Mama Grizzlies, Grassroots Activists and the Changing Face of the American Right* (New York: New York University Press, 2016).
37. Ronan Farrow, 'Donald Trump, a Playboy Model, and a System for Concealing Infidelity', *New Yorker*, 16 February 2018, <https://www.newyorker.com/news/news-desk/donald-trump-a-playboy-model-and-a-system-for-concealing-infidelity-national-enquirer-karen-mcdougal> (accessed 21 January 2020).
38. Steve Benen, 'Economy Shows Surprising Resilience in Early Months of 2019', MSNBC, 26 April 2019, <http://www.msnbc.com/rachel-maddow-show/economy-shows-surprising-resilience-early-months-2019> (accessed 21 January 2020).
39. Peter Eavis, 'US Adds 196,000 Jobs in March, a Return to Solid Growth', *New York Times*, 5 April 2019, <https://www.nytimes.com/2019/04/05/business/jobs-report-unemployment-march.html> (accessed 21 January 2020). At the time this volume went to press, however, economic fears sparked by the global outbreak of the coronavirus, or COVID-19, had only just begun.
40. The 2018 American Values Survey specifically asks a random sample of 2,509 Americans, 'Do you strongly approve, somewhat approve, somewhat disapprove, or strongly disapprove of the job Donald Trump is doing as President?' We have collapsed those four categories into two categories of approve and disapprove. N = 2,509

adults (age eighteen and up) living in all fifty states and the District of Columbia both by telephone and online. The data are weighted to create a representative sample of households in the United States with a margin of error of ± 2.8 percentage points at the 95% level of confidence. The margin of error for women only is larger.

41. 'Partisanship and Political Animosity in 2016', Pew Research Center, 22 June 2016, <https://www.people-press.org/2016/06/22/partisanship-and-political-animosity-in-2016> (accessed 22 January 2020).
42. Ibid.
43. Quoted in Associated Press, 'Pat Robertson Calls for Clinton's Impeachment', *Los Angeles Times*, 20 September 1998, <https://www.latimes.com/archives/la-xpm-1998-sep-20-mn-24574-story.html> (accessed 22 January 2020).
44. 'Donald J. Trump: Defender of Liberty', Concerned Women for America website, 6 October 2017, <https://concernedwomen.org/donald-j-trump-defender-of-liberty> (accessed 22 January 2020).
45. Danielle Kurtzleben, 'The Women's Wave: Backlash to Trump Persists, Reshaping Politics in 2018', NPR, 24 September 2018, <https://www.npr.org/2018/09/24/650447848/the-womens-wave-backlash-to-trump-persists-reshaping-politics-in-2018> (accessed 22 January 2020).
46. Christina Cauterucci, 'The Women's March on Washington Has Released an Unapologetically Progressive Platform', *Slate*, 12 January 2017, <https://slate.com/human-interest/2017/01/the-womens-march-on-washington-has-released-its-platform-and-it-is-unapologetically-progressive.html> (accessed 22 January 2020).
47. Melissa Deckman, 'Can Pro-Choice and Pro-Life Women Find Common Ground? It's Complicated', *Washington Post*, 20 January 2017, <https://www.washingtonpost.com/news/monkey-cage/wp/2017/01/20/can-pro-choice-and-pro-life-women-find-common-ground-its-complicated> (accessed 22 January 2020).
48. Karen Grigsby Bates, 'Race and Feminism: Women's March Recalls the Touchy History', NPR, 21 January 2017, <https://www.npr.org/sections/codeswitch/2017/01/21/510859909/race-and-feminism-womens-march-recalls-the-touchy-history> (accessed 22 January 2020).
49. Abby Vesoulis, 'Women First Marched to Challenge Trump. Now They Are Challenging Each Other', *Time*, 19 January 2019, <http://time.com/5505787/womens-march-washington-controversy> (accessed 22 January 2020).

50. Dolan et al., *Women and Politics*; Christina Wolbrecht, 'A Woman's Place is in the Resistance: Women, Gender, and American Democracy', memo prepared for 'A Republic, If We Can Keep It' conference, Cornell Center for the Study of Inequality and the New America Foundation, Washington, DC, 12–13 April 2018, available at <https://cornell.app.box.com/v/Memo-Wolbrecht> (accessed 22 January 2020).
51. Michelle Goldberg, 'The Women's Revolt: Can the Resistance Save America on Tuesday?', *New York Times*, 5 November 2018, <https://www.nytimes.com/2018/11/05/opinion/midterms-trump-women-liuba-grechen-shirley.html> (accessed 22 January 2020).
52. Dolan et al., *Women and Politics*.
53. 'About', Indivisible website, <https://indivisible.org/about> (accessed 22 January 2020).
54. Charlotte Alter, 'How the Anti-Trump Resistance Is Organizing Its Outrage', *Time*, 18 October 2018, <https://time.com/longform/democrat-midterm-strategy> (accessed 22 January 2020).
55. 'National Action Campaign', National Organization for Women website, <https://now.org/nap>; 'We the Resistance', National Women's Law Center website, <https://nwlc.org/we-the-resistance> (both accessed 22 January 2020).
56. 'Our Story: Time's Up Was Born When Women Said "Enough Is Enough"', Time's Up website, <https://www.timesupnow.com/about/our-story> (accessed 21 March 2020).
57. Jennifer Lawless and Richard Fox, *It Still Takes a Candidate: Why Women Don't Run for Office* (Cambridge: Cambridge University Press, 2010); Dolan et al., *Women and Politics*.
58. Richard L. Fox and Jennifer L. Lawless, 'Entering the Arena? Gender and the Decision to Run for Office', *American Journal of Political Science* 48, no. 2 (2004), 264–80.
59. Susan Chira, 'Banner Year for Female Candidates Doesn't Extend to Republican Women', *New York Times*, 15 November 2018, <https://www.nytimes.com/2018/11/15/us/politics/women-politics-republican.html> (accessed 22 January 2020).
60. Julie Dolan and Paru Shah, 'Missing the Wave? Women Congressional Candidates Who Lost in the 2018 Election', paper presented at the Midwest Political Science Association's annual meeting, Chicago, 4 April 2019.
61. Li Zhou, '12 Charts That Explain the Record-Breaking Year That Women Have Had in Politics', *Vox*, 6 November 2018, <https://www.vox.com/2018/11/6/18019234/women-record-breaking-midterms> (accessed 22 January 2020).

62. "2018: Women Primary for U.S. and Statewide Elected Executive', Center for American Women and Politics, 5 November 2018, <https://cawp.rutgers.edu/2018-primary-women-candidates-us-congress-and-statewide-elected-executive> (accessed 21 March 2020).
63. Drew Desilver, 'A Record Number of Women Will Be Serving in the New Congress', Pew Research Center, 18 December 2018, <https://www.pewresearch.org/fact-tank/2018/12/18/record-number-women-in-congress> (accessed 22 January 2020).
64. 'Results: Women Candidates in the 2018 Election', Center for American Women in Politics press release, 29 November 2018, available at <https://cawp.rutgers.edu/sites/default/files/resources/results_release_5bletterhead5d_1.pdf> (accessed 22 January 2020)
65. Elizabeth Herman, 'Redefining Representation: The Women of the 116th Congress', *New York Times*, 14 January 2019, <https://www.nytimes.com/interactive/2019/01/14/us/politics/women-of-the-116th-congress.html> (accessed 22 January 2020).
66. 'Women in State Legislatures in 2019', National Conference of State Legislatures website, 25 July 2019, <http://www.ncsl.org/legislators-staff/legislators/womens-legislative-network/women-in-state-legislatures-for-2019.aspx> (accessed 22 January 2020).
67. Ibid.
68. Jennifer Agiesta, Tami Luhby and Grace Sparks, 'Exit Polls: This Election Is about Donald Trump', CNN Politics, 7 November 2018, <https://edition.cnn.com/2018/11/06/politics/2018-exit-poll-results/index.html> (accessed 22 January 2020).
69. Ibid.
70. Valencia, 'The 2018 Gender Gap Was Huge.'
71. Ibid.
72. Ibid.
73. Melissa Deckman, 'A New Poll Shows How Younger Women Could Be a Democratic Wave in 2018', *Washington Post*, 5 March 2018, <https://www.washingtonpost.com/news/monkey-cage/wp/2018/03/05/a-new-poll-shows-how-younger-women-could-help-drive-a-democratic-wave-in-2018> (accessed 22 January 2020).
74. Alex Vandermaas-Peeler, Daniel Cox, Molly Fisch-Friedman and Robert P. Jones, 'Diversity, Division, Discrimination: The State of Young America – MTV/PRRI Report', PRRI, 10 January 2018, <https://www.prri.org/research/mtv-culture-and-religion> (accessed 22 January 2020).
75. Deckman, 'A New Poll'.

76. David E. Campbell and Christina Wolbrecht, 'The Resistance as Role Model: Disillusionment and Protest among American Adolescents After 2016', *Political Behavior* (2019), <https://doi.org/10.1007/s11109-019-09537-w> (accessed 22 January 2020).
77. Christopher S. Parker and Matt A. Barreto, *Change They Can't Believe In: The Tea Party and Reactionary Politics in America*, updated edition (Princeton: Princeton University Press, 2014).
78. Deckman, *Tea Party Women*.

Part Two

Foreign Policy and Global Relations

5

Angry at the World: Progressive Possibilities in Trump's Disruption of the Current Order

Patrick McGreevy

When Rabelais's noble giant Gargantua first entered Paris,

> the people so pestered him . . . that he was compelled to take a rest upon the towers of Notre-Dame; and when from there he saw so many, pressing all around him, he said in a clear voice: 'I think these clodhoppers want me to pay for my kind reception and offer them a solatium. They are quite justified, and I am going to give them some wine, to buy my welcome . . .' Then, with a smile, he undid his magnificent codpiece, and bringing out his john-thomas, pissed on them so fiercely that he drowned two hundred and sixty thousand, four hundred and eighteen, [with a] piss-flood.[1]

There is something Rabelaisian about the time that Donald Trump's ascendancy heralds, as if we have entered a festival where ordinary rhythms cease, hierarchies are inverted and a larger-than-life boy-bishop is elected to preside. At times Trump's approach to his presidential duties is reminiscent of a boy at play, and his language can be as lewd and scatological as Gargantua's, yet many people find all this tolerable, part of the fun, and even those who are appalled cannot avert their eyes from the spectacle. The global status quo has been interrupted. Many suspect that something fundamental is shifting. Others seem to crave it. In the spirit of Clifford Geertz's suggestion that 'every serious cultural analysis must start from a sheer beginning',[2] I propose to take an unblinking look at the bizarre texture of our time with its sense of rupture from the ordinary. Might it offer an opening to challenge the current order of things from other directions?

A festival, certain social theorists propose, is a liminal interlude during which ordinary life is suspended, a feature it shares with a rite of passage. The anthropologist Victor Turner began his study of liminality with west African puberty rituals in which initiates were removed to a liminal state to be transformed before returning to the everyday world in a new role. Later, Turner investigated pilgrimage traditions in the major religions, in which literally millions of believers leave behind the structures of everyday life to plunge into an intensely egalitarian experience they hope will transform them. In *Rabelais and His World*,[3] Mikhail Bakhtin examined early-Renaissance European festivals, which to him revealed the presence of an exuberant ongoing peasant *joie de vivre*. In these disruptive, bawdy interludes, Bakhtin saw a desire for an ideal egalitarian world. Trump is hardly a champion of social and economic levelling, but his supporters clearly see his attacks on global elites and trade agreements as promising a world fairer to non-elites. Moreover, his willingness to express positions rarely heard from mainstream politicians and to use 'common' uninhibited language performs a transgression that can seem levelling, even though it works to constitutes a 'we' in opposition to the presence of even less powerful groups.

The traditional festival is always defined in relation to the current order of things. Individuals and groups abandon the current order, experience something more free and equal, and then return to reintegrate into that order. But what if the experience of escaping structure awakens people to the possibilities of a better world? Stepping outside of structure creates a betwixt-and-between state that, conceivably, can contribute to two divergent political outcomes. The most likely outcome is a cathartic effect that, 'by allowing reversals and even apparent subversion', provides 'outlets for hostility and thus strengthen[s] the established order'.[4] The other possibility is that the disruption that accompanies the festival allows participants to glimpse and indeed experience what the current order excludes, and that this, in turn, may impel them to seek fundamental change. For Mikhail Bakhtin, the festival was not merely a respite from the current order: it was a wholesale rejection of it that reveals ordinary people's 'criticism, their deep distrust of official truth, and their highest hopes and aspirations'.[5] A liminal time is inherently a time of uncertainty, but one that is temporally circumscribed – no matter what its outcome, it comes to an end. The geographical scale of a festival or similar liminal event is always limited by the boundaries of the current order it disrupts. To the extent that there is now a global order, the urge to disrupt it may also be global. If the election of Donald Trump was, in part, a disruption of the so-called 'Liberal International Order', so was the Brexit vote in the UK, and perhaps the ascendency of authoritarian nationalism elsewhere.

People experience the current order not simply through the presence of a state, empire or even global system, but also outward from their own experience as it develops in relation to political, economic and cultural circumstances. Individual identity can interact with various group identities – including the national – in complex ways. Political scientist Elizabeth Anker argues that

> Trump promises to revive both individual and state sovereignty in a global era, when they might otherwise seem debilitated. He aims to do so by strengthening the most visible forces of state violence – including military, immigration and police power – and by himself performing a particularly white and masculinized American fantasy of individual domination.[6]

When you are powerful, you can do anything you like. To those who see themselves as outcasts, Trump invites a transference, proclaiming at his rallies, 'I am your voice.'[7] Some of his most transgressive gestures encourage supporters to connect, and even conflate, individual and national power. The global, or even the international, seems merely a backdrop, a screen on which to project fantasies and fears.

In spite of the size, power and wealth of the United States, the sense of the nation, in the consciousness of most Americans, has long been remarkably self-referential. When Canadian scholar Sacvan Bercovitch first encountered the American scene in the 1970s, he wondered how such diverse people could 'believe in something called the American mission, and could invest that patent fiction with all the emotional, spiritual, and intellectual appeal of a religious quest. I felt then', he concluded, 'like Sancho Panza in a land of Don Quixotes.'[8] Americans have long attempted to prop up individual and national identities with fantasies about what lay beyond the nation, but in reality, as W. E. B. Du Bois put it, 'the US was living not to itself, but as part of the strain and stress of the world'.[9] Although ordinary Americans' vision of the 'world' may be clouded in fantasy, the United States, in the century since Du Bois's time, has been arguably the single most important force shaping the world order. In fact, in much of the world, there is another word for the resented encroachments of the global: Americanisation. This fact sits uncomfortably and ironically beside the widespread obliviousness of most Americans to what Du Bois called the 'world' and many today call the global.[10]

Let us take an honest look at the reality of our current world order before attempting to understand how it is construed in the service of national identities. The most basic historical fact is that our current system is a descendant and close relative of European colonialism. In the past five centuries, European empires swarmed across the earth, bringing resources of all kinds to imperial centres and establishing a hierarchical political economy. After two world wars among these empires, two superpowers – the USA and the USSR – emerged and essentially divided hegemony across the globe, creating two orders. The Cold War was a period of ostensible decolonisation, but in the US-dominated part, colonialism was replaced by a similarly hierarchical political economy many labelled neo-colonialism. Since the founding of the United Nations, the US-led system has often been labelled the 'Liberal International Order'. US presidents Reagan to Obama pushed a neoliberal free-trade agenda that dominated the process known as globalisation. Those who characterise this order as Pax Americana often forget that this was a system of enforced inequality, just as Pax Romana was undergirded by slavery.

The world order associated with 1990s globalisation – with its intrusive IMF and World Bank actions, and its massive trade agreements – concentrated wealth and power in such a stark way that it spawned a global grassroots reaction. Although the anti-globalisation protesters who gathered at Seattle and other sites were silenced in the wake of the September 11 attacks, much of their anger concerning the inequalities of the world order continues to propel progressive politics in the US and elsewhere. Occupy Wall Street and the Arab Spring, in different ways, marked the continuation of this perspective. This fact remains underexamined in a time when the 'global' is more often critiqued as a threat to individual or national sovereignty than as a multiplier of economic inequality. If Trump supporters are willing to disrupt the current order in the name of fundamental change, so were the anti-globalisation activists and so are their contemporary allies.

In their writings on the evolution of the world order, the leftist scholars Immanuel Wallerstein and Giovanni Arrighi have criticised modernisation theory's assumption that regions without power and wealth are simply residuals that the global capitalist system will eventually uplift.[11] Instead, these scholars see systematic injustice as built into the system as well as increasing instability. Yet the consensus view in the mainstream US media is that the 'Liberal International Order' constructed under US leadership after World War II has spread peace, prosperity and maybe even democracy through a world finance and trade system undergirded by US military and economic supremacy. Through its network of about 800 military bases in about 70 countries,[12] the US kept the capital and commerce flowing – and when necessary punished 'rogue states' like Allende's Chile and Saddam's Iraq.

The September 11 attacks were an unmistakable impingement of the global into US domestic life. The target was the symbolic heart of the world capitalist system. The administration of George W. Bush responded by championing the neoconservative idea that the US should pursue global dominance in a more direct way. Bush claimed for the US the right to intervene anywhere to establish global order, to be so bold and powerful that all potential adversaries would be awed. Many of Bush's supporters even lost their aversion to naming this order 'empire'.[13] But this America-is-the-world endgame proved unattainable.[14] Since the start of the Cold War, US presidents have described their country as the leader of the free world but most have been reluctant to openly claim the imperial mantle. Although Obama continued Bush's strategy of assassinating perceived enemies anywhere and pursued economic agreements with both Europe and Asia, his 'smart power' approach to global power dynamics was a departure from the dream of full-spectrum US global dominance. In retrospect, Bush's post-9/11 attempts to shore up such dominance instead starkly revealed the limits of US power. The US engagement in the unwinnable wars in the Middle East and the 2007–8 financial crisis shook the foundations of the world financial and political order. Economic elites came out of the crisis with more wealth than ever. The tendency of this world order to concentrate wealth into fewer and fewer hands was accelerating. In fact, in terms of relative economic and political power, the United States reached its peak not after 9/11, but in the 1990s. The world order kept evolving and shifting. With apologies to Heraclitus, you can't go down to the same world order twice: it is not only the nature of the order that is shifting, but individuals and nations as well.

Arrighi and others argue that the globalisation that ratcheted up in the 1990s enhanced the power of transnational corporations and financial flows at the expense of nation-states. Financialised capitalism may be achieving a kind of escape velocity in which the state is no longer the primary site of its power. Neither Barack Obama, nor Hillary Clinton, nor Donald Trump, it seems, could resist the power of Citibank, Goldman Sachs, Exxon and the like. It is clear that certain corporations had the leverage during the crisis of 2007–8 to convince governments that they were too central to the global system to be allowed to fail. After September 11, perhaps there is no single centre of world power. If Trump supporters want to disrupt the current world order, one reason might be to rehabilitate a diminished United States – to make it 'great again'. The greatness they see for their country, however, is not about global leadership or responsibility for non-Americans. Trump's emphasis on the need for walls to protect the country from the outside world marks the extent to which many in the US have abandoned earlier dreams of a seamless Pax Americana. Trump's vision for US relations with the surrounding world seems to follow the pattern of its close ally Israel with its continuous wall, three-layered Iron Dome missile shield, and nuclear weapons at the ready. It boils down to a desire for absolute security and the absolute respect of adversaries.

Among the ways that the world order could develop is toward the emergence of a world state.[15] Had George W. Bush's push towards full-spectrum global dominance succeeded, the US itself might have become that world state. Now, though we all swim in a sea of capitalism, there are different forms: social market capitalism in Europe, neoliberal capitalism in the US, authoritarian capitalism in China, and populist capitalism in Latin America. In this multi-centred system, Bill Readings, Arjun Appadurai and others argue, the 'nation-state ceases to be the elemental unit of capitalism'.[16] But this does not mean there is no world order. 'The system of nation-states works', Appadurai reminds us, 'only because of its underlying assumption of a world order, guaranteed by a variety of norms, not least the norms of war itself.'[17]

Even at the apogee of US power in the 1990s, few Americans developed the sort of imperial consciousness that we presume elite Roman citizens embraced when the empire replaced the republic and expanded to encompass the entire Mediterranean world. Americans may think they live in 'the greatest country on earth', and they may be aware of its unrivalled power – military, economic and cultural – but few seem ready to embrace global leadership like the elites of first-century Rome or even nineteenth-century Britain. In general, Americans act as if they are not shaping the world but merely enduring it. Rather than a confident imperialism, many Americans display the same fear of the world that seems to be driving authoritarian nationalism in a growing number of countries. Perhaps the most common explanation for this, as well as the support for Trump and Brexit, is that these phenomena are reactions to perceived intrusions of a chaotic outside world. Gary Younge, for example, writes:

> Feeling under threat from a large world whose politics and economics we are unable to control, many resort instead to the defense of 'culture', the one thing people think they have a grip on. In short, they retreat into identities – often reinvented as the local, the known and, above all, the traditional – as a protective mechanism against the encroaching outside world. Quite what that identity might be – language, nation, race, religion – is down to context. More often than not, such retreats are reactionary.[18]

In a similar vein, Appadurai argues that the bodies of minorities become 'the flashpoint for a series of uncertainties that mediate between everyday life and its fast-changing global backdrop'.[19] Fear of and anger towards internal minorities become entangled with similar reactions to that turbulent global backdrop. But what do people mean when they say they are reacting to or resisting the global? Is it only reactionaries that resist? Are there possibilities for productive resistance of another kind, one that aims at a world with more economic and social justice? Historically, those marginalised because they were – for example – Indigenous, black or Shi'ite often organised their resistance around those very categories of their oppression. Was this a reactionary retreat into identity or an opportunistic attempt to resist with the tools at hand?

The relationship between identities – individual, group, national – and the perceived global backdrop is in flux, but changes to the international order are not just perceptions. We seem to be in the midst of a fundamental shift, creating a betwixt-and-between time of considerable uncertainty. The changes in the nature of capitalism that Appadurai, Arrighi and others highlight means that we are no longer certain about what political platform will be available to contain and support global capitalism. The rise of China, among other developments, has stressed the current international order based on a system of states. It might eventually be replaced by a new international system with a new set of norms, or even by some kind of world state.[20] But, for now, we are in an unmoored situation. While change in the global order is more than a perception, the ways people experience and perceive that order are indeed also in flux. And because identities emerge in relation to the experience of wider structures, both individual and national identities may well feel equally unmoored. We don't know how any of this will end.

A key characteristic of current global arrangements is that they are concentrating wealth[21] and, in the process, creating many losers, even in the United States. Some of them are very angry. Trump recognised this. So did Bernie Sanders. To the losers of the current global order, the prospect of a fundamental transformation may be a welcome development. Certainly, there are many who don't want a carnival or rupture of any kind: they support the current order, and in the US they supported people like Jeb Bush and Hillary Clinton in 2016. But among the others, we might say, there has developed a structure of feeling that suspects transformation is coming, expects it is coming, and even craves transformation. For such people, the uncertainty of our time is a palpable experience at multiple registers. Those who suspect, expect or crave transformation agree: the world order is rotten – sometimes in both senses of the word: it is evil and it is decayed. These include not only supporters of Trump and Sanders – and their polarised counterparts in other countries – but also the followers of ISIS and Al Qaeda.

Anger at the current global order certainly comes from different directions. While some are angry at an influx of people who they fear will reduce their own prosperity and status, others point to trade agreements and trade flows that seem to threaten domestic employment. Still others single out transnational corporations for prioritising profits above all else, leading to an increased concentration of wealth. Should we compare this situation to the Indian fable of the six blind men and the elephant? Each man encounters a different part of the elephant and they variously conclude that the elephant is like a tree, a wall, a spear, a fan, a rope and a snake. Each of the blind men believes that there is a whole elephant, but they each mistake the part for the whole. Because those who are angry at the world focus on different aspects of our global elephant, one might conclude that they are not describing a single creature. In blunt terms, is the world order identified by anti-globalisation activists the same one that Trump supporters believe can be addressed by a continuous border wall? Among those who welcome a disruption of the current order, there is, first of all, the common experience of uncertainty, of a shifting, unmoored world that seems threatening. There is also the common belief that they – as individuals, families and communities of various scales – are getting a bad deal. This implies that Trump himself is not the source of the disruption. The key disruption had already happened in the consciousness of diverse people who had weighed the costs of disruption against the costs of continuing to endure the current order and were increasingly open to its fundamental transformation. Trump was savvy enough to sense how many people were experiencing the current order as uncertain and unfair, but it was their own experience that eroded their acceptance of that order.

Because concentrating wealth, by definition, multiplies losers, it can never be in the economic interest of most. Perhaps that is why targeting the 1 per cent for protest is so threatening to mainstream defenders of the current order. In the US, the economic pain is widespread and tangible, increasingly in rural areas and in the old industrial heartland of the Midwest. In many rural and semi-rural counties, suicide, drug addition, poverty and incarceration rates have soared – in many cases surpassing those in what we used to think of as devastated inner-city areas. These and more urbanised counties lost industrial jobs in a series of waves; young and skilled people have been out-migrating for decades, leaving shells of towns and cities. The mostly white population of these places has seen an entire way of life disappear. Now they are reduced to what Wolfgang Streeck calls 'coping, hoping, doping, and shopping'.[22] Unlike the situation after the Great Depression and World War II, there was no GI Bill or other massive transfer of wealth downwards for retraining and re-stabilising those who had been harmed. They were cast aside like ploughed snow. Although Trump's strongest electoral base was among the 64 per cent of the population who earn more than $50,000 per year and among whites in general – even college-educated whites – the key to his electoral college victory was sweeping the core of the old manufacturing belt: Pennsylvania, Ohio, Indiana, Michigan and Wisconsin. These voters were ready for a rupture and a transformation. Hillary Clinton had little to offer them. In the Democratic primaries, Bernie Sanders had surprise victories in Michigan and Wisconsin. Had he been nominated, he might well have carried these and surrounding Rust Belt states rather than Trump.

Trump clearly broke from the argument Republicans had used since the time of Reagan: that individuals have responsibility – not for others, but only for their own choices. Trump was less patronising: he did not blame those struggling, exhorting them to work harder. Instead, he directed the blame at cosmopolitan elites, immigrants and minorities. As in Gary Younge's formulation, Trump's strategy was to conflate the global with cultural categories based on race, religion and language – and real Americans, he seemed to presume, shared his own race, religion and language. While progressives like Sanders were just as critical of the global order, they clearly parted company with Trump's supporters on the conflation of that order with minorities and immigrants.

One of the chief media criticisms of Trump is that his campaign openly attacked the so-called 'Liberal International Order'. The *New York Times* and the rest of the mainstream media, with their handful of corporate owners, absolutely support the current world order as if no alternative could be imagined, just as they earlier supported the Vietnam War, the invasion of Iraq and the large-scale free trade agreements. They also supported Hillary Clinton's campaign and relentlessly attacked Sanders. Then they turned on Trump and his apparent Russian abettors. Today, they favour maximum US hegemony but prefer what Joseph Nye calls a 'smart power' approach as the most effective way to achieve it. Trump is in the crosshairs of some of the most powerful defenders of the current global order. Is his unexpected ascension to power entirely unwelcome to those who criticise the global order for increasing economic and political inequality? Or might it signal an opening for a progressive alternative?

In spite of Trump's rhetoric, there is little doubt that he is betraying the least powerful of his supporters. The massive tax breaks he has secured for corporations and the wealthy prove that his least wealthy supporters will not get the transformation they sought. In fact, it appears that Trump will be exceedingly friendly to the forces of financial and corporate capitalism central to the current global order. If we are living through a liminal time in which the common-sense hegemony of that order has been ruptured, Trump may be attempting to revive it under a more bellicose and authoritarian US leadership. If successful, this festival of disruption will have functioned as a catharsis that ultimately strengthens that order.

Some are hoping that the wave of authoritarian nationalism appearing in many world regions will turn out to be a small bump on the road to a more liberal global order ushered in by a new generation of technical centrists like Justin Trudeau and Emmanuel Macron, but we would do well to recall how much they resemble another young centrist, Barack Obama, whose eight-year reign served as the antechamber to our current situation. More than perhaps anyone, Trump attempted to tar Obama as foreign, and he certainly exploited the substantial racism extant in the US – rendering his black body what Appadurai (quoted above) calls a 'flashpoint for a series of uncertainties that mediate between everyday life and its fast-changing global backdrop'.[23] But, in terms of soft or smart power, it is hard to imagine a US leader more effective at keeping their country at the centre of the current world order than Barack Obama. In today's world, that is the very definition of a centrist. Obama's view may be labelled centre-left, but it offers no fundamental critique of our inequality-generating global order. In the current Democratic Party debates about the 2020 presidential election, there is considerable sentiment to focus on electability – anyone but Trump. But, from the perspective of progressives with fundamental criticisms of the global order, is strengthening that order through a centrist US leader better than demanding a candidate who will challenge it, even if such a candidate should lose the election?

There is a great deal we do not know. It is quite possible that the 'Liberal International Order' might be shored up like a tree self-healing a gaping hole where a branch has broken off. The order may then continue to generate inequality indefinitely. The *New York Times* would welcome this. Critics on the left, however, might want to widen that gaping hole to create space for a fundamentally new global deal. If the current order prioritises making everyone and everything a means to the end of wealth generation for the few – and if enough people are angry about this because they themselves wish to be an end not a means – a thirst may develop for an even more fundamental disruption. But if this pervasive anger is not addressed, what might develop instead is an apocalyptic urge to bring down the temple, if necessary on our own heads. Some saw an element of this sentiment in the surge of support for Trump and Brexit.

Thomas Pynchon's 1970 novel, *Gravity's Rainbow*, an extended meditation on the missile as the ultimate show-stopper, concludes with a theatre full of people awaiting the missile's descent. They shout, 'Come-*on! Start*-the-*show!* Come-*on! Start*-the-*show!*'[24]

By 2016, many in the US were so exasperated by their daily experience – and in particular, by the ways global arrangements seemed to be affecting that experience – that they were ready to consider something completely different. Donald Trump appeared to offer exactly that. The same anger might have found a home in a progressive version of something completely different. It may still, and not only in the US. Ominously, an apocalyptic channel for that anger is ready in the wings.

The festival of disruption that Trump's rise and other events seem to signal might be compared to that brief time when a total solar eclipse interrupts the daylight to reveal the dome of distant stars. In this pellucid atmosphere, where the obscuring power of the daylight order is suspended, one can suddenly glimpse new possibilities that far exceed the spectrum of our daylight imaginations. This is a moment of danger. This is a moment of hope.

Notes

1. François Rabelais, *The Histories of Gargantua and Pantagruel*, tr. J. M. Cohen (Harmondsworth: Penguin, 1955), Book 1, ch. 17.
2. Clifford Geertz, 'Thick Description: Toward an Interpretive Theory of Culture', in *The Interpretation of Cultures: Selected Essays* (New York: Basic, 1973), 7.
3. Mikhail Bakhtin, *Rabelais and His World*, tr. Helene Iswolsky (Cambridge, MA: MIT Press, 1968).
4. Patrick McGreevy, 'Place in the American Christmas', *Geographical Review* 80, no. 1, 36; see also Max Gluckman, *Custom and Conflict in Africa* (Glencoe, IL: Free Press, 1959).
5. Bakhtin, *Rabelais and His World*, 269.
6. Elizabeth Anker, 'Longing for Sovereignty: Power and Violence in the Trump Era', a presentation sponsored by the Prince Alwaleed Bin Talal Bin Abdulaziz Alsaud Center for American Studies and Research (CASAR), American University of Beirut, 10 April 2017.
7. Carl M. Cannon and Emily Goodin, 'Trump to Disaffected Americans: "I Am Your Voice"', *RealClearPolitics*, 22 July 2016, <https://www.realclearpolitics.com/articles/2016/07/22/trump_to_disaffected_americans_i_am_your_voice_131285.html> (accessed 22 January 2020).
8. Sacvan Bercovitch, *The American Jeremiad* (Madison: University of Wisconsin Press, 1978), 11.

9. W. E. B. Du Bois, *Dusk of Dawn: An Essay toward an Autobiography of a Race Concept* (New York: Harcourt, Brace, 1940), 222.
10. Bijal P. Trivedi, 'Survey Reveals Geographic Illiteracy', *National Geographic*, 20 November 2002, <https://nationalgeographic.com/news/2002/11/geography-survey-illiteracy> (accessed 22 January 2020). See also Sahana Jayaraman, 'American Geographic Literacy Remains Problematic', *Jesuit News*, 4 May 2018, available at <https://wantnewsforteens.com/2018/05/19/american-geographic-literacy-remains-problematic> (accessed 22 January 2020).
11. Giovanni Arrighi, *The Long Twentieth Century: Money, Power and the Origins of Our Times* (New York: Verso, 1994); Giovanni Arrighi, Terence K. Hopkins and Immanuel Wallerstein, *Antisystemic Movements* (New York: Verso, 1989); Immanuel Wallerstein, *The Modern World-System I: Capitalist Agriculture and the Origins of the European World-Economy in the Sixteenth Century* (New York: Academic Press, 1974); Immanuel Wallerstein, *The Modern World-System II: Mercantilism and the Consolidation of the European World-Economy 1600–1750* (New York: Academic Press, 1980); Immanuel Wallerstein, *The Modern World-System III: The Second Era of Great Expansion of the Capitalist World-Economy 1730s–1840s* (San Diego: Academic Press, 1989).
12. David Vine, 'Where in the World Is the US Military?', *Politico*, July/August 2015, <https://www.politico.com/magazine/story/2015/06/us-military-bases-around-the-world-119321_full.html?print> (accessed 22 January 2020).
13. David Ray Griffin, 'The American Empire and 9/11', *Journal of 9/11 Studies*, May 2007, <http://www.journalof911studies.com/volume/200704/DavidRayGriffin911Empire.pdf> (accessed 22 January 2020); Andrew Bacevich, *American Empire: The Realities and Consequences of US Diplomacy* (Cambridge, MA: Harvard University Press, 2002).
14. Neil Smith, *The Endgame of Globalization* (New York: Routledge, 2005).
15. Giovanni Arrighi, 'Lineages of Empire', *Historical Materialism* 10, no. 3 (2002), 13.
16. Bill Readings, *The University in Ruins* (Cambridge, MA: Harvard University Press, 1996), 44.
17. Arjun Appadurai, *Fear of Small Numbers: An Essay on the Geography of Anger* (Durham, NC, and London: Duke University Press, 2006), 25.
18. Gary Younge, *Who We Are – And Should It Matter in the 21st Century?* (New York: Nation, 2011), 208.

19. Appadurai, *Fear of Small Numbers*, 25.
20. Arrighi, 'Lineages of Empire', 13.
21. Michael Savage, 'Richest 1% on Target to Own Two-Thirds of All Wealth by 2030', *The Guardian*, 7 April 2017, <https://www.theguardian.com/business/2018/apr/07/global-inequality-tipping-point-2030>; 'Part IV: Trends in Global Wealth Inequality', *World Inequality Report 2018* (World Inequality Lab, 2017), <https://wir2018.wid.world/part-4.html> (both accessed 22 January 2020).
22. Wolfgang Streeck, *How Will Capitalism End? Essays on a Failing System* (London: Verso, 2016).
23. Arrighi, 'Lineages of Empire', 13.
24. Thomas Pynchon, *Gravity's Rainbow* (New York: Viking Press, 1973), 670.

6

Trump or the Cultural Logic of 'Late' Democracy

David Ryan

'Late capitalism', the term Fredric Jameson used to describe the postwar economy that rose with the decline of formal empire and allowed for the thinking associated with an integrated global economy.[1]

... and his dream must have seemed so close that he could hardly fail to grasp it. He did not know that it was already behind him, somewhere back in that vast obscurity beyond the city, where the dark fields of the republic rolled on under the night.[2]

Trump is no exceptionalist. Presidential rhetoric, usually imbued with boundless US myth, is replaced by pugnacious fragments. Exceptionalism is dead; *Foreign Policy* noted it could 'rest in peace'. Some believed President Ulysses S. Grant's segregated narrative that US citizens were the 'freest of all nations', and 'Americans [a] favored "people struggling for liberty and self-government"'.[3] By the twenty-first century, that exclusive story of US liberty, self-determination and democracy was deeply compromised. Trump's campaign paraded US ills to disgruntled audiences eager to blame vacuous notions of the Other, in Iran or on the southern border, for their predicament. His inaugural promised recovery:

> We, the citizens of America, are now joined in a great national effort to rebuild our country and to restore its promise for all of our people. Together, we will determine the course of America and the world for years to come. We will face challenges. We will confront hardships.

But we will get the job done . . . January 20, 2017, will be remembered as the day the people became the rulers of this nation again. The forgotten men and women of our country will be forgotten no longer.[4]

The *forgotten* in American history cut many ways and Trump tapped into another 'forgotten': an echo of Nixon's 'forgotten Americans – the non-shouters; the non-demonstrators' – the 'good people', 'decent people' who work and pay taxes.[5] US exceptionalism insisted that the eyes of the world gazed on the proverbial city on the hill. It was *the* unique model, exemplar to the world; it would craft a world order with ideas, institutions, economic regimes, alliances and culture. Reagan exuded the exceptional language. Domestically, exceptionalism rested on the American Dream – anyone could make it from the humblest log cabin. Obama indulged the myth and himself: 'I will never forget that in no other country on Earth is my story even possible.'[6] The international intersected with the domestic through a history of immigration – of 'huddled masses' seeking opportunity. Obama tried to restore the 'hope' after Bush, just as Reagan polished the image of the elevated city as he dismantled its foundations. As the grounds collapsed Trump's 'city' rested 'in a valley'.[7] An already troubled political culture quickly transitioned from the fragmented to the ridiculous; the world's fear, loathing and jest rested upon him.

Americans are frustrated with government.[8] The Economist Intelligence Unit noted,

> The US fell below the threshold for a 'full democracy' in 2016 . . . primarily owing to a serious decline in public trust in US institutions that year. In 2018, the US fell further in the global ranking, to 25th place, from 21st in 2017 . . . It continues to be rated a 'flawed democracy'.[9]

Trump tapped into the acrimony and played on emotive issues, immigration and security, that fed his base. Not so much direct misery but an 'anxiety about the future' fuelled his election, nativist 'fears that in the white population were associated with hostility to Latinos and black Americans, and among men with hostility to upwardly mobile women', Adam Tooze notes.[10] Bluntly, 'Trump channelled rage'.[11]

Trump's fury feeds off the aggrieved. His ambition might be contained by institutional sclerosis, yet his manner and words signal malign intent. His bark might be worse than his bite, but 'diplomacy is about words, and many of Trump's words are profoundly toxic'.[12] They undercut the grand narrative of US liberalism and its world order.[13] Forty-fifth in a line of presidents from Washington, Jefferson, Lincoln and Roosevelt, to adopt the US iconic punctuation, James Fallows mourns,

> I view Trump's election as the most grievous blow that the American idea has suffered in my lifetime. The Kennedy and King assassinations and the 9/11 attacks were crimes and tragedies. The wars in Vietnam and Iraq were disastrous mistakes. But the country recovered. For a democratic process to elevate a man expressing total disregard for democratic norms and institutions is worse.[14]

Identity politics compound prejudice. Nativist sentiments, and dubious elections in 2000 and 2016, stoked distrust and a 'hate-mongering demagoguery, a popular backlash against "the establishment" and outsider minorities, and, above all, the transformation of democracy into an engine of zero-sum political tribalism'.[15]

This is not new. In the 1990s public life was 'rife with discontent'. Despite vast achievement in World War II and the Cold War, in economic affluence, in more inclusion and justice for women and minorities, 'our politics is beset with anxiety and frustration', Michael Sandel wrote. Americans felt they had lost control of their lives and 'from family to neighborhood to nation, the moral fabric of community is unraveling'.[16] In 1952 Reinhold Niebuhr identified the vectors in *The Irony of American History*: Alexis de Tocqueville encountered a 'troublesome and garrulous [US] patriotism'; the sentiment of American nationalism was built on the myth of the frontier, new beginnings and its rejection of Europe. Niebuhr wrote, 'when the frontier ceased to provide for the expansion of opportunities', technology provided new openings; the pursuit of happiness, understood as prosperity, drove economic expansion. Yet, 'this expansion cannot go on forever and ultimately we must face some vexatious issues of social justice' that Europeans confined by borders had to confront.[17]

Saturated American markets further engaged US business with Europe. Such integration, eventually globalisation, twisted the lens on US exceptionalism, which lost focus. It was difficult to remain particular in the universal.[18] Moreover, in the period of post-democratic globalisation the US entered relative decline and more Americans lost out. As domestic integration advanced with civil rights and feminism, the cultural logic of 'late' democracy amplified fragmentation. 'Separate but equal' was replaced by *conceptual* equality and vitriolic separation. Writing in 1998 John Gray argued that if US multiculturalism retained such 'separatism' unlike some of its peers, 'the fate of the United States will be to oscillate between an Enlightenment illusion of universality and the ugly realities of Balkanization'.[19]

In 2007 *The Atlantic* predicted Obama might heal the culture wars; they were wrong.[20] After then the US suffered more defeat in foreign wars; its economy 'crashed'; inequality, on the rise since the 1970s, accelerated; the 'American Dream' lost credibility as the political atmosphere degenerated. By 2016 for some the prospect of 'a woman following a black man into power did not represent progress; it represented another attack on their America'.[21] The backlash would be nasty, brutish and long. The verbal wars persist. Trump is a cornered rat in Jim Morin's syndicated cartoon for the *Miami Herald*; the caption reads, 'When cornered a frightened and desperate rat will. . . tweet.'[22]

Some Americans feel cornered. In the 1890s Frederick Jackson Turner noted the closing frontier's impact on US democracy.[23] In 1986 Allan Bloom bemoaned *The Closing of the American Mind;* its openness and multicultural histories subverted the big story.[24] The *pluribus* destabilised the *unum*. The 'forgotten' 'minorities' demanded inclusion domestically, and internationally endless war strained US credibility. The economy staggered and served fewer. Of the last four wars Washington lost three. Decisive victory in the 1991 Gulf War transitioned to a lost 'peace'; they had no post-war plan.[25] Postmodernity emerged from the culture of an earlier defeat and fragmented coherent US narratives.[26] Different voices told different stories. Feminists and black Americans challenged old 'national' stories on limitless progress, innovation, conflict and myth. Women began to vote 100 years ago, and the

Fifteenth Amendment was passed in 1870, yet obstacles prevented many African-Americans from voting until 1965; 'multiculturalism began to complicate and replace the traditional upbeat narrative of American history and culture'.[27] The vast payload of bombs dropped on Vietnam undermined US moral authority. The concept of 'late' democracy not only echoes Jameson's work on postmodernity and pluralism, but also the idea that the US only achieved full democracy *lately,* and then lost it in 2016.

The US sphere is constrained; its 'vaulting' economic ambition 'o'erleaps itself' and has rebounded to accelerate inequality and with it the politics of chauvinism, racism, nativism; it has lost numerous wars, compounding the impact of the Vietnam War. The 'era of reversals' in Tom Engelhardt's *The End of Victory Culture* has a new layer of sediment and malaise.[28] Under such weight the US story is untenable. The cultural logic of 'late' democracy has caught up with its exclusive edition. It will not revert to economic or military isolationism, as Gray suggested twenty years ago, for its vested interests are too deep; yet its political discourse exhibits a 'cognitive and cultural' isolationism.[29]

Spheres

Shortly after the Cold War, as a young academic I wrote the immortal lines (they sank without a trace): 'James Madison, unlike our generation, did not have to live through the 1980s to realise that enlightened states-people would not always be at the helm.' We can, with little concern, juxtapose Trump and Reagan, but Reagan had the ability to tell a story. After division he sought a calm and confidence which eluded his successors. Richard Hofstadter noted that the authors of the constitution 'did not believe in man' but in a 'good political constitution to control him'.[30] Internationally, there was no such 'social contract', yet the Cold War balance of power set the frontier at the Iron Curtain. As Madison

> went about his task of trying to make 'democracy safe for the world' by devising a new theory of republican government, in which selfish instincts would 'check and balance' each other, he initiated a system of expansion to mitigate the negative effects of factional interests,

thus preserving the liberty of those within the Union: 'Extend the sphere [he wrote] and you take in a greater variety of parties and interests...'[31]

The theory suggested that a competitive 'union' worked against a potential tyranny of the few. Constitutional powers were representative and separated, and though 'based on popular consent, [they] involved a serious diminution of popular participation'.[32] US 'happiness' was predicated on exclusion. But at least conceptually, liberty and expansion were planted in US discourse without any trace of irony. That liberty would facilitate expansion (as would slavery), there was little doubt. But ultimately by conquest and expansion across a continent, expansion through war and colonisation, through informal empire, in the Cold War and after 9/11, the 'security regimes' constrained liberty. No friend of liberal hegemony, John Mearsheimer argues, 'the state's militaristic behaviour is almost certain to end up threatening its own liberal values'.[33]

Yet the traditional discourse insists on US exceptionalism. The US is absent from the post-colonial critique of Empire. Extending William Appleman Williams's observation that 'there is no American Empire' in US historiography, Amy Kaplan and Donald Pease noted the 'absence of culture from the history of US imperialism; the absence of empire from the study of American culture; and the absence of the United States from the postcolonial study of imperialism'.[34] Some of these historiographical 'blank spaces' have been filled. That expansion might undermine liberty was lost on a culture intent on privileging certain 'truths'. Ironically, US imperialism informed the benign meta-narrative. The big histories written by George Bancroft, who served as secretary of war, subtitled *From the Discovery of the American Continent*, were closely associated with 'manifest destinies'.[35] For over a century it was not uncommon to see titles such as *The Epic of America*, by James Truslow Adams, or his *The March of Democracy: The Rise of the Union*.[36] Exclusive histories shaped a nation.[37] These were benign stories of small-'r' republicanism and the advance of exclusive democracy. Yet empire and liberty are central to US semiotic cognition. 'From George Washington's journey to the Monongahela

River in 1754 to George W. Bush's conquests in Mesopotamia in 2003, observers have puzzled over the relationship between our thirst for dominion and our attachment to freedom,' David Hendrickson observes.[38] But the histories, laid like telegraph wires to weave *the* story and the continent, focused on freedom, not domination. Yet now with all the division and decline the story is unsettled; the grand narrative is replaced by amorphous twitter – the springtime of sparrows.

Inveighed with O'Sullivan's 'manifest destiny' and images of Gast's *American Progress*, depicting westward expansion – the stagecoach, the wagons, the railroads, the oxen move across the continent beneath the watchful guidance of the allegorical angel stringing out cables, before retreating Native Americans, buffalo and a bear – out 'there' at the frontier and beyond there were few constraints on US-style liberty.[39] The violence of American conquest, Walter Hixon argues, 'fueled indiscriminate warfare, establishing a pattern of behavior that would play out continuously in subsequent American history'.[40] 'The true magnitude of the violent encounter . . . remains unacknowledged', Karl Jacoby contends, despite the 'outpouring of genocide studies'.[41] It continues on the southern border.[42]

The US failed to understand the importance of limits, Williams argued, which meant that it was 'plagued by the infinitely more subtle paradox of the failure of success'.[43] Ultimately, unbound, its expansion invited resistance. 'Open door' expansionism opened 'the door to the revolutions that can transform the material world and the quality of human relationships'. If Americans could not accept 'the existence of such limits without giving up democracy' and could not refine or enhance democracy within limits, the consequences were dire.[44] The tragedy decades after *The Tragedy of American Diplomacy* is that the message remains pertinent.

The US *overseas* empire was supposed to alleviate the frustrations of the 'closing frontier'. When US anti-imperialists railed against the acquisition of the Philippines as antithetical to the US republican tradition, in part they stood on nostalgic principle and in part on fictions; expansion, subjugation and slaughter were very much a part of the US tradition. Empire facilitated economic growth and eventually decolonisation gave way to economic integration; Soviet fragmentation enhanced globalisation and so the 'age of extremes'[45] moved to an 'age of anger'[46] for those who suffered under the illiberal order. Post-Cold War triumphal narratives elided the marginalised and oppressed voices that struggled against a US-centred 'West'. Domestically, the forgotten remained forgotten as History went on holiday. When Francis Fukuyama declared the 'end' of History,[47] as though the longitude of the frontier had wrapped around the global sphere, Isaiah Berlin observed that 'subjection to a single ideology, no matter how reasonable and imaginative, robs men of freedom and vitality'. It subdued new potential based on the 'experiments in living'.[48] Ralf Dahrendorf echoed the sentiment at the end of the Cold War:

> The battle of systems is an illiberal aberration. To drive the point home with the utmost force: if capitalism is a system, then it needs to be fought as hard as communism had to be fought. All systems mean serfdom.[49]

Ironically, those who did struggle against the US, nationalists, socialists and *the* communists, facilitated US cohesion and its national security regime. From the 1970s other industrial powers competed with the US from within the 'liberal' order; some hit 'beyond the boundaries' as German technology and Japanese cars came under US cultural indictment. Trump plays on the same fears of the 1970s and 1980s, the US urban crisis, cheap Japanese imports, defeat in Vietnam, but now 'transposed onto new enemies: China, Islam and undocumented Latino immigrants'.[50]

Historically, both domestically and internationally the US practised an exclusive liberalism and democracy, reinforced by 'national security' states engaged in 'low-intensity democracy'.[51] Limited participation was intentional. Jill Lepore writes that even if US stories provided 'an expansive, liberal account of the history of the American nation and the American people', the necessary 'blind spots' would ultimately find voice and Schlesinger's 'vital centre' would not hold.[52] The collective pronoun with the singular noun, 'We the people', was increasingly difficult to articulate.

Working against the 'collapse of comity' and the 'uncivil wars',[53] Reagan claimed he had done much to restore confidence, but lamented it still had to be institutionalised.[54] It was not to be.

Trump stoked the fear and loathing. He borrowed from Reagan's 'Make America Great Again', an 'earlier moment of reactionary nostalgia', Diane Roberts writes, but Reagan 'added sunshine to the rhetorical mix ("Morning in America"), with Trump there is no optimism about progress of any moral sort'.[55] There was little hope for unity within the fragments of verbiage.

As I recounted twenty years ago, Madison recognised potential dangers: 'In future times a great majority of the people will not only be without land but any other sort of property.' They would either 'combine', challenging the 'rights of property and public liberty', or more likely, 'they will become the tools of opulence and ambition', with its dangers. Madison wrote, 'The smaller the compass within which they are placed, the more easily will they concert and execute their plans of oppression.' The pursuit of happiness required expansion.[56] Greg Grandin observes, 'But today the frontier is closed. The country has lived past the end of that myth . . . Instead of peace, there is endless war. Instead of prosperity we have intractable inequality. Instead of a critical, resilient and open-minded citizenry, a conspiratorial nihilism, rejecting reason and dreading change' emerged.[57]

Illiberal economies

Trump does not share Reagan's innate confidence in teleological History. In pointed use of language that simultaneously took aim at Fukuyama, Obama and Martin Luther King Jr, Trump's 2017 National Security Strategy (NSS) asserted 'there is no arc of history that ensures that America's free political and economic system will automatically prevail'. The NSS asserted, 'We know how to grow economies so that individuals can achieve prosperity.' The words seemed to be drawn out of a liberal playbook that Trump frequently contradicted:

> The United States offers partnership to those who share our aspirations for freedom and prosperity. We lead by example. 'The world has its eye upon America,' Alexander Hamilton once observed. 'The noble struggle we have made in the cause of liberty, has occasioned a kind of revolution in human sentiment. The influence of our example

has penetrated the gloomy regions of despotism.' . . . We are not going to impose our values on others. Our alliances, partnerships, and coalitions are built on free will and shared interests. When the United States partners with other states, we develop policies that enable us to achieve our goals while our partners achieve theirs.[58]

But the sustenance of such stories requires optimism and wealth generation; the 'dream' needs to be fed. The 'world-system' Washington created tolerates inequality at home and abroad, the impact of which ultimately came home to roost.

Lepore's *These Truths* divides the period after the US Civil War into two 'contrasting arcs'. Sean Wilentz writes:

> After the overthrow of Reconstruction and with the coming of the Gilded Age, the principles of equality, natural rights, and popular rule rapidly receded, supplanted by a new industrial plutocracy and accompanied by vicious white supremacy. Progressive reformers for a time curbed the excesses, but the old order persisted until it collapsed in the Great Depression, clearing the way for FDR's New Deal, followed by America's emergence after World War II as the indispensable nation in the creation of a new liberal democratic order.[59]

There has been an outpouring of opinion on whether Trump is dismantling the liberal economic world order and with it the base that served the US grand strategy since 1945.

In 2017 it was difficult to place Trump among presidential traditions; after the election we did so in search of intellectual anchors. Trump upset everything. Jessica Mathews, in the *New York Review of Books*, argued that in 'this particularly dangerous moment' he has thrown a few US fundamentals out of the window. First, he failed to recognise that the US-designed system had brought stability and security. Second, the integrated global economy was mutually beneficial to the US and its allies. Third, 'dictators have to be tolerated, managed, or confronted, not admired'. Democratic values were important.[60]

Yet despite Trump's apparent instability, he displayed some consistency. In his 1987 open letter to the *New York Times* he advanced mercantilist economic views, held a complete disdain for allies and alliances, admired authoritarians and believed 'that the world economy is rigged against us'; the US was being 'spit on', 'kicked around' or 'laughed at' by the rest of the world.⁶¹ Gideon Rose, editor of *Foreign Affairs,* asked if we were 'present at the destruction'. Was this the omega to Secretary of State Dean Acheson's alpha, *Present at the Creation*? In presidential transitions, you get the 'the normal, the incompetent, and the dangerous'. But this time the 'danger is unique'.⁶²

The US made great gains over seventy years. Threats and challenges abounded, Nazi Germany, Soviet communism, revolutionaries and ultra-nationalists; they were all external. But Trump began 'to sabotage the order it created. A hostile revisionist power has indeed arrived on the scene, but it sits in the Oval Office, the beating heart of the free world. Across ancient and modern eras, orders built by great powers have come and gone – but they have usually ended in murder, not suicide,' John Ikenberry writes.⁶³ A year later and somewhat calmed, Ikenberry recognised the system's institutional resilience.⁶⁴

Yet Trump saw this period as one of 'national loss and decline'. The long arc of the liberal economy had benefited the US in uneven ways which became more obvious as decline set in after 1958, and more obvious still from the 1970s.⁶⁵ In recent decades, Ikenberry and Daniel Deudney concede, 'as free markets spread, problems began to crop up: economic inequality grew, old political bargains between capital and labour broke down, and social supports eroded. The benefits of globalization and economic expansion were distributed disproportionately to elites.'⁶⁶ Decades ago dependency theorists told similar stories of the Third World in the Cold War: macro-economic growth coupled with stark inequality. Modernisation theorists and liberals pointed to the macro, the revolutionaries pointed to the micro; the loaf expanded but there was insufficient bread on *each* table. The wrath is captured in Pankaj Mishra's *Age of Anger*.⁶⁷

The 'wider crisis across the liberal democratic world'⁶⁸ and the US sense of disappointment, envy and bewilderment⁶⁹ mix a dangerous cocktail of emotional force for establishment politicians. US strategists, intent on avoiding the 'ghosts of depression past',⁷⁰ promoted economic integration after 1945. The acrimony, violence, xenophobic racism and nationalism they feared are evident again.

Trump disdains the post-war system of multilateral integration instituted in part to dampen extremism. US commitments are contingent, deals adjusted, and allies must pay up.[71] The late-1940s global 'new deal' was premised on exclusion; without the Soviet 'threat' Congress would not have funded the Marshall Plan. The repressive 'Other' behind the Iron Curtain was essential to an expanding US sphere.[72] No such 'Other' exists today and the US does not quite know what to do.[73]

The West and its adjuncts held the majority share in global income in 1948; George Kennan, head of US Policy Planning, wrote, '[The] real task . . . is to devise a pattern of relationships which will permit us to maintain this position of disparity.'[74] But in recent decades 'for the first time in over a hundred years, its share of global GDP has fallen below half'. The National Intelligence Council posit the trends will continue.[75] Previously, the US elite profited and the global economic pie expanded but the relative share of the G7 (set up in 1976) contracted. In 1995 the G7 commanded 45.3 per cent of global GDP; the seven largest emerging powers (E7) commanded 22.6 per cent. By 2015 the G7 had shrunk to 31.5 per cent and the E7 had risen to 36.3 per cent.[76] 'This monumental shift of power away from the West' will challenge Western minds, Kishore Mahbubani contends.[77] Americans feel the frustrations of relative impoverishment and inadequate control over their lives, yet 'since 1970, Asia's per-capita incomes have increased fivefold'.[78] Still, the Liberal International Order is beset with problems because essentially, Inderjeet Parmar argues, the very system is Eurocentric, 'elitist and resistant to change'.[79] The US elite still benefit.

For Reagan, Clinton and Trump big government (associated with liberalism) was the problem; the swamp needed draining. Yet neither Reagan nor Trump blanched at big military spending. But government also stood squarely behind US trade expansion and Americanisation; it provided the not-quite-so hidden hand. The nineteenth century 'promotional state' was pivotal in 'selling the American dream'.[80] Washington allied with Wall Street in their global 'search for opportunity'.[81] After the Civil War the US became 'the largest and most advanced economy in the world'. It built a huge domestic market premised on immigration, population expansion, infrastructure and growing wealth;[82]

there was still elasticity in demand curves. Yet domestic markets were insufficient.

'Wilson made the revolutionary claim that the American national interest was inseparable from the larger *inter*national interest,' H. W. Brands writes.[83] US prosperity rested on multilateral integration. After the 1930s disintegration the US sphere expanded through the Marshall Plan and European integration. Transatlantic trade ushered in an unprecedented period of prosperity. Charles Maier described such elite understanding as a 'consensual hegemony';[84] the sovereignty of America's allies was somewhat compromised, but they had a good deal of latitude within the 'empire by invitation',[85] and after recovery played the game effectively. Perhaps too effectively. 'The Cold War is over', Senator Paul Tsongas exclaimed, 'and the Japanese won';[86] he might have added Germany. Yet Trump promised, 'We will never enter America into any agreement that reduces our ability to control our own affairs.' Deals had to be rearranged.[87]

Liberalism depended on the Cold War and after the Berlin Wall fell it was in trouble. In his 1995 State of the Union address Bill Clinton spoke of how a government that was once regarded as 'a champion of national purpose is now seen by many as simply a captive of narrow interests'. Clinton revelled in the number of government jobs he axed: 'We have to cut yesterday's Government to help solve tomorrow's problems.'[88] Older forms of liberalism were beyond resuscitation; the 'neo-' in 'neoliberalism' cared less about individuals, rights and liberties. Brands continues:

> Then the Cold War went bad in Vietnam, and suddenly the official wisdom of a quarter-century didn't seem so wise anymore. And just as popular confidence in government had previously extrapolated from foreign affairs to domestic, so now did popular distrust. Americans who discovered that their leaders had been tragically wrong about Vietnam began to wonder whether those same leaders could have been right about anything.

They were not just wrong, they were deceitful; Americans were disillusioned.[89] One immediately thinks of Iraq, WMD, the financial crash, ('the most severe synchronized contraction in international trade ever recorded'[90]), elite impunity from prosecution for immiserating so many lives, and the levels of distrust and acrimony that Bush and Obama generated. After 9/11 a brief period of conformity, not unity,[91] and silence in the culture wars was replaced by one of fear and anxiety. For Andrew Graham-Dixon the US was a changed country no longer confident and assured.[92] Soon after, 'as Baghdad burned, New Orleans flooded and high finance was laid low, America came to seem less like a chosen nation, than a country whose luck had run out', Diane Roberts concludes.[93]

Without prosperity, acrimony advanced. Prior to the downturn the politics of prosperity was intended to dampen extremist zeal. FDR implemented his programmes to lessen 'the hazards and vicissitudes of life'.[94] After the war, the price of utopia was too high and welfare reduced the costs of capitalism 'by narcotizing its members – they were sexually gratified, well fed, well housed and fashionably clothed, and they were taught to think no thoughts that would derail the society in which they lived,' Alan Ryan writes.[95] McCarthyism and security regimes helped. Yet this very vision eluded US policy makers after the 1970s. Widening inequality added pressures on the lower and middle classes.[96] Trump fuelled the flames: he exacerbated inequality with negative redistribution; with regard to racism, infamously, he saw 'blame on both sides' in Charlottesville; in certain ways he chimed with American history.[97] In 2017 David Rothkopf questioned whether the US was a failing state:

> We have a tin-pot leader whose vanity knows no bounds. We have the rapacious family feathering their nests without regard for the law or common decency. We have utter disregard for values at home and abroad, the disdain for democracy, the hunger for constraining a free press, the admiration of thugs and strongmen worldwide.[98]

Trump's assertive nationalism does not shy into isolationism, but rather a unilateralist engagement outside (at least in aspiration) an integrated world order. Madison's injunction is arrested. Expansionism, economic integration and globalisation eventually rebounded. By the late twentieth century the amorphous sphere offered lots of competition, and in part due to US domestic ideologies and policies associated with deregulation, redistribution and tax cuts, sections of American society lost out significantly. The United States had not learned to live within limits, nor had it perfected its democracy, within or outside those limits.

War

US military defeat exacerbated economic frustration; Washington was contained in the Middle East just decades after defeat in southeast Asia. Augmenting the effects of the economic crash, the US experience in Iraq, Afghanistan and elsewhere demonstrated that the 'greatest power' could not extend its strategic depth in unconventional wars of *choice*.[99] The US ended its wars with death, defeat and debt.

The US spent $604 billion on the military in 2016; China in second place spent $145 billion, Russia $58.9 billion, the UK $52.5 billion, India $51.1 billion. The US is no longer hegemonic.[100] It lost credibility through unnecessary overextension. Vietnam alienated many. When Reagan advanced incredible arguments on Central America, the UN and European Community moved in ushering in the 'last years of the Monroe doctrine'.[101] When George W. Bush invaded Iraq he sundered US normative power.[102] Obama's retrenchment, 'leading from behind', added perceptions of inhibition.[103] In short, if military power is situated at the top of Joseph Nye's power matrix, above economic, diplomatic or soft power, the Iraqis checked Washington on the battlefield, the liberal economy undermined the US dream, and Trump singlehandedly lost US diplomatic credibility.

In the 2017 NSS Trump writes, 'My Administration's National Security Strategy lays out a strategic vision for protecting the American people and preserving our way of life, promoting our prosperity, preserving peace through strength, and advancing American influence in the world.' Such concepts of 'peace through strength' provide balm to the bruised national ego, through the 'Pentagon's massive incursions against the federal budget'.[104] They echo Reagan.[105] But that profligate spending of the early 1980s provided the illusion of strength rather than its foundation.[106]

Trump revels in the trappings of US strength yet the 'failed experiments of the past 15 years have, for the moment at least, put Americans in a defensive crouch, if not isolationist mood'.[107] The culture of militaristic gesture and of supporting the troops, right or wrong, is one of the few areas of shared nationalism in this fractious period. 'Robust' military spending is an antidote to the national anguish which saddles future generations with a staggering debt burden and simultaneously limits liberal options and programmes.[108] Such spending will not restore hegemony or harmony but might make some feel good.

International liberal hegemony 'simply does not work. It was tried for twenty-five years and left a legacy of futile wars, failed diplomacy, and diminished prestige,' John Mearsheimer contends. The wars in Iraq and Afghanistan will cost some $5 trillion, money that could have been spent on the US infrastructure, they augmented the already huge US national debt, and they devastated peoples and regions. The costs of late liberal hegemony are also exhibited in 'the damage it does to the American political and social fabric. Individual rights and the rule of law will not fare well in a country addicted to fighting wars.'[109]

Story

Wars and economic distress eroded the American story; globalisation destabilised its exceptionalism. Prosperity was no longer a mythical given and disaffection compromised US democracy. After World War II Western democracies exhibited relative economic equality and comparative wealth with rising incomes from generation to generation. In the Western alliance 'no affluent member has experienced a breakdown of democratic rule',[110] albeit some were truly undemocratic. Success reinforces ideology, yet all this is changing. In the period from 1973 to 2015, under 'globalisation', the US outsourced many jobs, 'productivity rose 73.4 per cent while wages rose by only 11.1 per cent'.[111] Income inequality accelerated across the decades. Wages that roughly doubled between each generation 'have essentially remained flat' for the past thirty years.[112]

Despite the atrociously exclusive development of US democracy, income generation and moderate equality were recognised as important; democracy rested on the premise that everyone really did have the ability to pursue happiness and had some 'buy-in' to the system.

> Economic equality can no more be divorced from the functioning of democracy than the ballot. Jefferson, Brandeis, the Roosevelts all recognised this home truth. The American dream has to be the lived reality of the country, not just a pretty story we tell ourselves.[113]

That premise lost salience after the 1960s. Restoration of some equality is a strategic imperative. In 2018, Elizabeth Warren, candidate in the 2020 presidential race, called for a foreign policy made for the middle class,[114] echoing Bernie Sanders in 2015: 'We need to do everything possible to create millions of good-paying jobs and raise the wages of the American people.'[115] Pressures on the middle class are set to continue as millions will struggle for decades. It is not just automation, artificial intelligence, the information revolution; it is also transfers of jobs and the proverbial 'rise of the rest'. Edward Luce adds, '[The] past also tells us to beware of the West at times of stark and growing inequality. It rarely ends well.'[116]

Trump feeds off disenfranchisement. Families are down $4,000 per household since 2000; the middle class has seen its security slide since the 1970s. 'The widely shared income gains of the decades from 1946 to 1976 disappeared, replaced by dramatic increases for those citizens at the top,' according to Thomas Borstelmann.[117] The proportion of national income going to the richest 1 per cent of families grew from 9 per cent to 24 per cent between 1979 and 2007, a level not seen since 1928. The poorest 90 per cent of families had their share of income drop from 66 per cent to 50 per cent. The 2009 census recorded the widest gap between the richest and the poorest Americans. Under Bush Jr, the Republicans cut federal taxes, distributing 62 per cent of the benefits to the wealthiest 20 per cent by 2010. The federal (adjusted) minimum wage in 2006 had not been lower since the 1940s. The US has the most uneven income distribution among industrialised countries. Poverty reduced by half between 1959 and 1973, increased after that and rested at 13 per cent in 2008; 'the bottom 80 percent – four out of five citizens – shared just 15 percent of the nation's private assets'. Social mobility has been stagnant for three decades.[118] If the 'great' in Trump's America was the 1950s,[119] his tax legislation moves against restoration.

Reagan's revolution was modest, relatively speaking. He rolled back New Deal legislation. But his 'slow-release revolution' impacted after he left office. 'Quite simply, in his performance in office, Reagan was dramatically less Reagan-like than any of his successors, including . . . President Obama,' Doug McAdam and Karina Kloos argue. 'Or to paraphrase Jeb Bush, anyone advocating Reagan's policies today could never hope to secure the Republican presidential nomination.' Reagan unleashed the normative expectation on lower taxes and 'deep cuts in social spending'[120] justified by conservative ideologies.[121]

But when the 2008 crash hit those with real enfranchisement – 'those who actually go to the polls', Galbraith wrote earlier, 'in defence of their social and economic advantage'[122] – big government was there. When the 'systemic' interests are threatened, Adam Tooze argues, we clearly see that 'we lived in an age not of limited but of big government, of massive executive action, of intervention that had more in common with military operations . . . than with law-bound governance'.[123]

Cumulative change resulted in inevitable reaction. Globally, revolution, decolonisation and a centrifugal effect in the Western alliance unleashed postmodern, multicultural and post-colonial resistant narratives. In the US, feminism, civil rights and 'cultural pluralism' changed the society,[124] its institutions and the national discourse. The dramatic changes brought in a multitude of new voices, loosening the authority of traditional narrators. Borstelmann writes sardonically, 'Many citizens in the 1970s did not find the spread of egalitarian and inclusive practices in American public life to be completely inspiring.' Suddenly others had to be tolerated.[125]

America was born through a Declaration of Independence from the 'old world'. Trump wanted to declare independence from the US-created world-system; yet he was unsure where to dump the tea. Happiness was a nostalgic dream, 'men' were certainly not equal, poverty compromised liberty; the old 'truths' were no longer self-evident. In fact, it was no longer self-evident that truth of any sort had a role; if postmodernism 'relativised relativism', Trump absolutised it (to adapt Himmelfarb).[126] Trump practises an 'extraordinary uncouth variety of postfactual politics ... He doesn't tell the truth. He doesn't make sense. He doesn't speak coherently. Power appears to have become unmoored from the basic values of reason, logical consistency and factual evidence.'[127] Trump's imperious concept of news, facts, of what happened has liberated itself from the 'power of reasoning', which, Mahbubani posits, is one of the greatest gifts the West imparted. But he laments, the US is losing it.[128] Well before Trump, Michael Sandel questioned whether it was possible to maintain a civic strand of freedom or a sense of nation when the 'frenzied flow of money and goods, information and images, pays little heed to nations, much less neighbourhoods'.[129]

'In the realm of political economy, neoliberalism achieved quasi-theological status. As a result, some Americans got very rich, others managed to get by, and considerable numbers found themselves left behind,' Andrew Bacevich writes.[130] With such division it is difficult to hold onto 'an' American story. Through expansion, the US found and lost its happiness. Trump does not buy US exceptionalism. His story of America, in so far as one can follow the signals emitted by fireflies on a windy night, does not resonate with US ideals. Rather it is a bruised, nativist and pugnacious story.

It is not just that hubris undermined strategy;[131] the arc of US expansion to extend the sphere has been long and is central to *its* exclusive conception of democracy. It was extraordinary that it moved through continental conquest, slavery, racism, trans-oceanic colonialism, informal empire, economic integration and globalisation, and multiple military interventions, and managed to keep the story intact. Lepore recalls, 'Very often, histories of nation-states are little more than myths that hide the seams that stitch the nation to the state.' And, 'A nation born in contradiction will forever fight over the meaning of its history.'[132] It might be comforting for contemporary discourse to limit US ills to the post-Cold War period exacerbated by 9/11 and Iraq, and then blame Trump.

Notes

1. Gabrielle M. Spiegel, 'Revising the Past / Revisiting the Present: How Change Happens in Historiography', *History and Theory* 46, no. 4 (2007), 14.
2. F. Scott Fitzgerald, *The Great Gatsby* (Harmondsworth: Penguin, [1925] 1984), 171.
3. Daniel Sargent, 'RIP American Exceptionalism, 1776–2018', *Foreign Policy*, 23 July 2018, <https://foreignpolicy.com/2018/07/23/rip-american-exceptionalism-1776-2018> (accessed 22 January 2020).
4. 'The Inaugural Address', White House website, 20 January 2017, <https://www.whitehouse.gov/briefings-statements/the-inaugural-address> (accessed 22 January 2020).
5. Jill Lepore, *These Truths: A History of the United States* (New York: W. W. Norton, 2018), 632–3.
6. Diane Roberts, 'Death of an American Myth', *Prospect*, October 2017, 38.
7. Stephen Werteim, 'Policy Series: Donald Trump versus American Exceptionalism: Toward the Sources of Trumpian Conduct', *H-Diplo/ISSF*, 1 February 2017, <https://issforum.org/roundtables/policy/1-5K-Trump-exceptionalism> (accessed 22 January 2020).
8. Lepore, *These Truths*, 726.
9. 'Democracy Index 2018: Me Too?', Economist Intelligence Unit, 22 October 2019, <https://www.eiu.com/n/democracy-index-2018> (accessed 22 January 2020).
10. Adam Tooze, *Crashed: How a Decade of Financial Crises Changed the World* (London: Allen Lane, 2018), 576.
11. Edward Luce, *The Retreat of Western Liberalism* (London: Little, Brown, 2017), 97.
12. Eliot A. Cohen, 'How Trump Is Ending the American Era', *The Atlantic*, October 2017, <https://www.theatlantic.com/magazine/archive/2017/10/is-trump-ending-the-american-era/537888> (accessed 22 January 2020).
13. Luce, *The Retreat of Western Liberalism*, 28.
14. James Fallows, 'Despair and Hope in Trump's America', *The Atlantic*, January/February 2017, <https://www.theatlantic.com/magazine/archive/2017/01/despair-and-hope-in-the-age-of-trump/508799> (accessed 22 January 2020).
15. Amy Chua, 'Tribal World: Group Identity Is All', *Foreign Affairs*, July/August 2018, 30.

16. Michael J. Sandel, *Democracy's Discontent: America in Search of a Public Philosophy* (Cambridge, MA: Harvard University Press, 1996), 3.
17. Reinhold Niebuhr, *The Irony of American History* (New York: Charles Scribner's Sons, 1952), 28–9.
18. David Ryan, *US Foreign Policy in World History* (London: Routledge, 2000), 8; Serge Ricard, 'The Exceptionalist Syndrome in US Continental and Overseas Expansionism', in David K. Adams and Cornelius van Minnen (eds), *Reflections on American Exceptionalism* (Keele: Keele University Press, 1994), 73.
19. John Gray, *False Dawn: The Delusions of Global Capitalism* (London: Granta, 1998), 129.
20. Andrew Sullivan, 'Goodbye to All That: Why Obama Matters', *The Atlantic*, December 2007, <https://www.theatlantic.com/magazine/archive/2007/12/goodbye-to-all-that-why-obama-matters/306445> (accessed 22 January 2020). Sullivan wrote: 'Obama's candidacy in this sense is a potentially transformational one. Unlike any of the other candidates, he could take America – finally – past the debilitating, self-perpetuating family quarrel of the Baby Boom generation that has long engulfed all of us . . . A nonviolent civil war that has crippled America . . . It is a war about war – and about culture and about religion and about race. And in that war, Obama – and Obama alone – offers the possibility of a truce.'
21. Roberts, 'Death of an American Myth', 39.
22. Jim Morin (Toons Syndicate), 'Cornered Rat', 6 June 2018, available at <https://www.reddit.com/r/PoliticalHumor/comments/8p1f1o/cornered_rat> (accessed 22 January 2020).
23. Frederick Jackson Turner, *The Frontier in American History* (New York: Henry Holt, 1920).
24. Allan Bloom, *The Closing of the American Mind: How Higher Education Has Failed Democracy and Impoverished the Souls of Today's Students* (New York: Simon & Schuster, 1986).
25. David Ryan, 'The Ironies of Overwhelming "Victory": Exits and the Dislocation of the Gulf War', in David Fitzgerald, David Ryan and John M. Thompson (eds), *Not Even Past: How the United States Ends Wars* (New York: Berghahn, 2020).
26. Perry Anderson, *The Origins of Postmodernity* (London: Verso, 1998), 91.
27. Thomas Borstelmann, *The 1970s: A New Global History from Civil Rights to Economic Inequality* (Princeton: Princeton University Press, 2012), 114.

28. Tom Engelhardt, *The End of Victory Culture: Cold War America and the Disillusioning of a Generation* (Amherst: University of Massachusetts Press, 1998), 175–254.
29. Gray, *False Dawn*, 132.
30. Richard Hofstadter, *The American Political Tradition and the Men Who Made It* (New York: Vintage, [1948] 1989), 5.
31. David Ryan, 'US Expansionism: From the Monroe Doctrine to the Open Door', in John Philip Davies (ed.), *Representing and Imagining America* (Keele: Keele University Press, 1996), 181; James Madison, 'Federalist Paper No. 10', in Isaac Kramnick (ed.), *The Federalist Papers 1788* (Harmondsworth: Penguin, 1987), 122–8.
32. Martin Diamond, 'The Federalist', in Leo Strauss and Joseph Cropsey (eds), *History of Political Philosophy* (Chicago: University of Chicago, 1981), 638; Isaac Kramnick, 'Editor's Introduction', in Kramnick (ed.), *The Federalist Papers*, 41.
33. John J. Mearsheimer, *The Great Delusion: Liberal Dreams and International Realities* (New Haven, CT: Yale University Press, 2018), 2, 179–85.
34. Amy Kaplan, '"Left Alone with America": The Absence of Empire in the Study of American Culture', in Amy Kaplan and Donald E. Pease (eds), *Cultures of United States Imperialism* (Durham: Duke University Press, 1993), 11–14.
35. Jill Lepore, 'A New Americanism: Why a Nation Needs a National Story', *Foreign Affairs*, March/April 2019, 13.
36. James Truslow Adams, *The March of Democracy: The Rise of the Union* (New York: Charles Scribner's Sons, 1932); James Truslow Adams, *The Epic of America* (London: George Routledge, 1940).
37. Joyce Appleby, Lynn Hunt and Margaret Jacob, *Telling the Truth about History* (New York: W. W. Norton, 1994), 91–125.
38. David C. Hendrickson, *Republic in Peril: American Empire and the Liberal Tradition* (New York: Oxford University Press, 2018), 7, 10.
39. David Ryan, *US Foreign Policy in World History* (London: Routledge, 2000), 5–6.
40. Walter L. Hixon, '"No Savage Shall Inherit the Land": The Indian Enemy Other, Indiscriminate Warfare, and American National Identity 1607–1783', in Michael Patrick Cullinane and David Ryan (eds), *US Foreign Policy and the Other* (New York: Berghahn, 2015), 16.
41. Ibid., 16.
42. Greg Grandin, *The End of the Myth: From Frontier to the Border Wall in the Mind of America* (New York: Metropolitan, 2019), 253ff.

43. William Appleman Williams, *The Tragedy of American Diplomacy* (New York: Dell, 1962), 299.
44. Ibid., 308–9; David Ryan, 'Tragedy after Tragedy: The Failure to Recognise Limits in US Foreign Policy', paper delivered at the Conference of the 50th Anniversary of the Publication of William Appleman Williams's *Tragedy of American Diplomacy*, Rutgers University, 25 April 2009.
45. Eric Hobsbawm, *Age of Extremes: The Short Twentieth Century 1914–1991* (London: Michael Joseph, 1994).
46. Pankaj Mishra, *Age of Anger: A History of the Present* (London: Allen Lane, 2017).
47. Francis Fukuyama, 'The End of History?', *National Interest*, Summer 1989, 3–18.
48. Isaiah Berlin, *The Crooked Timber of Humanity: Chapters in the History of Ideas* (London: Fontana, 1991), 46.
49. Ralf Dahrendorf, *Reflections on the Revolution in Europe* (London: Chatto & Windus, 1990), 37.
50. Tooze, *Crashed*, 569.
51. Barry Gills and Joel Rocamora, 'Low Intensity Democracy', *Third World Quarterly* 13, no. 3 (1992), 501–23; Liam O'Brien and David Ryan, 'Democracy Promotion and US Foreign Policy', in Cameron G. Thies (ed.), *The Oxford Encyclopaedia of Foreign Policy Analysis* (New York: Oxford University Press, 2018).
52. Lepore, 'A New Americanism', 17–18.
53. Peter Novick, *That Noble Dream: The "Objectivity Question" and the American Historical Profession* (Cambridge: Cambridge University Press, 1988), 415–68; Mark Hamilton Lytle, *America's Uncivil Wars: The Sixties Era from Elvis to the Fall of Richard Nixon* (New York: Oxford University Press, 2006).
54. Ronald Reagan, 'Farewell Address to the Nation', Washington, DC, 11 January 1989, Ronald Reagan Presidential Library and Museum website, <https://www.reaganlibrary.gov/research/speeches/011189i> (accessed 23 January 2020).
55. Roberts, 'Death of an American Myth', 39.
56. Ryan, *US Foreign Policy in World History*, 32–3; Hofstadter, *The American Political Tradition*, 16–18; Madison, 'Federalist Paper No. 10', 124–8.
57. Greg Grandin, 'The Myth of the Border Wall', *New York Times*, 20 February 2019, <https://www.nytimes.com/2019/02/20/opinion/trump-border-wall.html> (accessed 23 January 2020); Grandin, *The End of the Myth*.

58. Donald J. Trump, 'National Security Strategy of the United States of America', White House, Washington, DC, December 2017, 37.
59. Sean Wilentz, 'The American Revolutions', *New York Review of Books*, 8 November 2018, 21.
60. Jessica T. Mathews, 'What Trump Is Throwing out the Window', *New York Review of Books*, 9 February 2017, 11.
61. Ibid., 11.
62. Gideon Rose, 'Present at the Destruction: What's Inside?', *Foreign Affairs*, May/June 2017, <https://www.foreignaffairs.com/articles/2017-04-17/present-destruction> (accessed 23 January 2020).
63. G. John Ikenberry, 'The Plot against American Foreign Policy: Can the Liberal Order Survive?', *Foreign Affairs*, May/June 2017, 2–9.
64. Daniel Deudney and G. John Ikenberry, 'Liberal World: The Resilient Order', *Foreign Affairs*, July/August 2018, 16.
65. Thomas J. McCormick, *America's Half-Century: United States Foreign Policy in the Cold War* (Baltimore: Johns Hopkins University Press, 1989), 125–54.
66. Deudney and Ikenberry, 'Liberal World', 18.
67. Mishra, *Age of Anger*.
68. Ikenberry, 'The Plot against American Foreign Policy'.
69. Franklin Foer, 'Apocalypse Now: What's behind the Volatile Mood of Today's American – and European – Voters', *New York Times*, 13 February 2017, <https://www.nytimes.com/2017/02/13/books/review/age-of-anger-pankaj-mishra.html> (accessed 23 January 2020).
70. Walter LaFeber, *America, Russia, and the Cold War 1945–2006* (Boston: McGraw-Hill, 2008), 11.
71. Ikenberry, 'The Plot against American Foreign Policy'.
72. Lloyd C. Gardner, *Spheres of Influence: The Partition of Europe, from Munich to Yalta* (London: John Murray, 1993), 263.
73. *Foreign Affairs*, May/June 2019.
74. 'Report by the Policy Planning Staff, PPS 23: Review of Current Trends in US Foreign Policy', in *Foreign Relations of the United States, 1948, General: The United Nations, Vol. I, Part 2* (Washington, DC: United States Government Printing Office, 1976), 510–29.
75. Yascha Mounk and Stefan Foa, 'The End of the Democratic Century: Autocracy's Global Ascendance', *Foreign Affairs*, May/June 2018, 30; National Intelligence Council, *Global Trends 2030: Alternative Worlds* (Washington, DC: Office of the Director of National Intelligence, 2012).

76. Kishore Mahbubani, *Has the West Lost It? A Provocation* (London: Allen Lane, 2018), 25.
77. Ibid., 26.
78. Luce, *The Retreat of Western Liberalism*, 21.
79. G. John Ikenberry, Inderjeet Parmar and Doug Stokes, 'Ordering the World? Liberal Internationalism in Theory and Practice', *International Affairs* 94, no. 1 (2018), 4.
80. Emily S. Rosenberg, *Spreading the American Dream: American Economic and Cultural Expansion 1890–1945* (New York: Hill & Wang, 1982).
81. Walter LaFeber, *The Cambridge History of American Foreign Relations, Vol. II: The American Search for Opportunity 1865–1913* (Cambridge: Cambridge University Press, 1993).
82. Walter Russell Mead, 'The Big Shift: How American Democracy Fails Its Way to Success', *Foreign Affairs*, May/June 2018, 10.
83. H. W. Brands, 'The Idea of the National Interest', *Diplomatic History* 23, no. 2 (1999), 243 (emphasis in original).
84. Charles S. Maier, 'Hegemony and Autonomy within the Western Alliance', in Melvyn P. Leffler and David S. Painter (eds), *Origins of the Cold War: An International History* (London: Routledge, 1994), 154–74.
85. Geir Lundestad, '"Empire by Invitation" in the American Century', *Diplomatic History* 23, no. 2 (1999), 189–217.
86. Tsongas quoted in Kishore Mahbubani, 'Japan Adrift', *Foreign Policy*, Autumn 1992, 126–44.
87. Charles A. Kupchan, 'The Clash of Exceptionalisms: A New Fight Over an Old Idea', *Foreign Affairs*, March/April 2018, 144.
88. H. W. Brands, *The Strange Death of American Liberalism* (New Haven, CT: Yale University Press, 2001), 166–7.
89. Ibid., xi–xii.
90. Adam Tooze, 'The Forgotten History of the Financial Crisis: What the World Should Have Learned in 2008', *Foreign Affairs*, September/October 2018, 200.
91. Lepore, *These Truths*, 722.
92. 'What Lies Beneath', *Art of America*, BBC Four, 29 January 2019.
93. Roberts, 'Death of an American Myth', 39.
94. David B. Woolner, *The Last 100 Days: FDR at War and at Peace* (New York: Basic, 2017), ix.
95. Alan Ryan, *After the End of History* (London: Collins & Brown, 1992), 2–3.
96. Hendrickson, *Republic in Peril*, 43.

97. Colin Kidd, 'Behold, America by Sarah Churchwell Review – the Underside of the "American Dream"', *The Guardian*, 14 July 2018, <https://www.theguardian.com/books/2018/jul/14/behold-america-history-of-american-dream-sarah-churchwell-review> (accessed 23 January 2020); Sarah Churchwell, *Behold, America: A History of America First and the American Dream* (London: Bloomsbury, 2018).
98. David Rothkopf, 'Is America a Failing State?', *Foreign Policy*, 10 May 2017, <https://foreignpolicy.com/2017/05/10/is-america-a-failing-state-trump-fires-comey-fbi> (accessed 23 January 2020).
99. Fredrik Logevall, *Choosing War: The Lost Chance for Peace and the Escalation of War in Vietnam* (Berkeley: University of California Press, 1999).
100. Christopher Fettweis, *Psychology of a Superpower: Security and Dominance in US Foreign Policy* (New York: Columbia University Press, 2018), 6–8.
101. Gaddis Smith, *The Last Years of the Monroe Doctrine 1945–1993* (New York: Hill & Wang, 1994).
102. Jürgen Habermas, *The Divided West* (Cambridge: Polity Press, 2006).
103. Cohen, 'How Trump Is Ending the American Era'.
104. Ellen Schrecker, 'Cold War Triumphalism and the Real Cold War', in Ellen Schrecker (ed.), *Cold War Triumphalism: The Misuse of History after the Fall of Communism* (New York: New Press, 2004).
105. Trevor McCrisken and Maxwell Downman, '"Peace through Strength": Europe and NATO Deterrence beyond the US Nuclear Posture Review', *International Affairs* 95, no. 2 (2019), 277–95.
106. John Kenneth Galbraith, *The Culture of Contentment* (London: Sinclair-Stevenson, 1992), 126.
107. David E. Sanger, 'A History of US Foreign Affairs in Which Grandiose Ambitions Trump Realism', *New York Times*, 27 December 2016, <https://www.nytimes.com/2016/12/27/books/review/tragedy-of-us-foreign-policy-walter-a-mcdougall.html> (accessed 23 January 2020).
108. Brands, *The Strange Death of American Liberalism*, 159.
109. Mearsheimer, *The Great Delusion*, 233.
110. Mounk and Foa, 'The End of the Democratic Century', 32–3.
111. R. W. Johnson, 'Trump: Some Numbers', *London Review of Books*, 3 November 2016, quoted in Mahbubani, *Has the West Lost It?*, 5.

112. Mounk and Foa, 'The End of the Democratic Century', 32–3.
113. Ben Fountain, 'Two American Dreams: How a Dumbed-Down Nation Lost Sight of a Great Idea', *The Guardian*, 17 September 2016.
114. Elizabeth Warren, 'A Foreign Policy for All: Strengthening Democracy – at Home and Abroad,' *Foreign Affairs*, January/February 2019, <https://www.foreignaffairs.com/articles/2018-11-29/foreign-policy-all> (accessed 23 January 2020).
115. Sanders quoted in Tooze, *Crashed*, 567.
116. Luce, *The Retreat of Western Liberalism*, 13.
117. Borstelmann, *The 1970s*, 306.
118. Ibid., 306–9.
119. Sanger, 'A History of US Foreign Affairs'.
120. Doug McAdam and Karina Kloos, *Deeply Divided: Racial Politics and Social Movements in Postwar America* (Oxford: Oxford University Press, 2014), 178–9, 207, 210.
121. Gray, *False Dawn*, 108.
122. Galbraith, *The Culture of Contentment*, 10.
123. Tooze, *Crashed*, 4, 10.
124. Rebecca Tillett, 'Cultural Pluralism and National Identity', in Martin Halliwell and Catherine Morley (eds), *American Thought and Culture in the 21st Century* (Edinburgh: Edinburgh University Press, 2008), 227–43.
125. Borstelmann, *The 1970s*, 114.
126. Gertrude Himmelfarb, *On Looking into the Abyss: Untimely Thoughts on Culture and Society* (New York: Alfred A. Knopf, 1994).
127. Tooze, *Crashed*, 21.
128. Mahbubani, *Has the West Lost It?*, 11.
129. Sandel, *Democracy's Discontent*, 317.
130. Andrew J. Bacevich, 'All Right We Are Two Nations', Moyers blog, 9 November 2016, <https://billmoyers.com/story/two-nations-election> (accessed 23 January 2020).
131. Mahbubani, *Has the West Lost It?*, 44.
132. Lepore, 'A New Americanism', 12, 19.

7

The End of the Age of Three Worlds and the Making of the Trump Presidency

Penny Von Eschen

In 1993, the Czech dissident poet-turned-president Václav Havel declared that 'the fate of the so-called West is today being decided in the so-called East'. Pushing back against US triumphalism, Havel warned that

> if the West does not find the key to us . . . or to those somewhere far away who have extricated themselves from communist domination, it will ultimately lose the key to itself. If, for instance, it looks on passively at 'Eastern' or Balkan nationalism, it will give the green light to its own potentially destructive nationalisms, which it was able to deal with so magnanimously in the era of the communist threat.[1]

At that moment, Havel's appeal for a vision of democratic freedom bridging old divides seemed to fall on deaf ears, as many in the West engaged in a giddy celebration of a supposed Western victory in the Cold War through military might and the purported superiority of free market capitalism. With the election of Donald Trump, a US president contemptuous of democracy and the rule of law, liberal ideals and norms that Havel and his fellow reformers risked their lives for, Havel's warning appears sadly prescient. The political conditions making Trump's election possible were long in the making. Trump's contempt for diplomacy, his fetish of militarism, his authoritarian disregard for rules and norms, and his xenophobic white nationalism – all of these can be traced, as Havel suggested, to developments after the collapse of the Eastern Bloc.

In keeping with Havel's 1993 warning that the US was susceptible to giving 'the green light' to its own nationalisms, in order to understand Trump's overt nods to white supremacy, Islamophobia and anti-Semitism, and xenophobia, which found fertile ground among a significant number of US citizens, we need to return to the dynamics that so disturbed Havel in the immediate aftermath of the fall of communism.

The rise of xenophobic ethnic nationalisms within and beyond US borders has roots that long preceded the end of the Cold War, but ideas of nationalism tied to race were powerfully rearticulated in the geopolitical shift accompanying the collapse of the Soviet Union. By the end of the 1980s, US politicians and pundits were making the triumphalist assertion that the United States had won the Cold War through military strength, while simultaneously casting it as a *victim*, vulnerable to external and internal threats. This immediate recasting of Cold War bipolar conflict – once directed against subversion by Soviets and their agents – deployed a reinvented and racialised global imaginary of Islamophobia – the clash of civilisations.

The death of George H. W. Bush on 30 November 2018 prompted an outpouring of nostalgia from Americans who remembered him as a 'consummate public servant and statesman who helped guide the nation and the world out of a four-decade Cold War that had carried the threat of nuclear annihilation'.[2] Against a backdrop of Trump's insults toward US allies, his open disdain for his own State Department and intelligence community, and his admiration of authoritarian leaders from Vladimir Putin to Kim Jong-Un, Trump's critics basked in the nostalgic glow of tributes to Bush as a 'steadfast force on the international stage for decades'.[3]

Much of the commentary occasioned by Bush's passing viewed Trump's rejection of the post-war multilateral order of liberal democracies as the antithesis of all that George H. W. Bush had stood for. Here, post-Cold War memory proved selective; in fact, the Bush administration's wariness of multilateral institutions and Bush's eagerness to assume the mantle of unipolar status signalled the limits of US international cooperation. In what came to be known as the Wolfowitz Doctrine (named after its author, aide Paul Wolfowitz), leaked to the press in February 1992, US policy makers resolved to ensure that 'no rival superpower is allowed to emerge in Western Europe, Asia, or the former Soviet Union'.[4]

By the time the US-led military coalition invaded Iraq in Operation Desert Storm in January 1991, US hegemonic objectives had won out over rival visions of multilateral cooperation and disarmament. George H. W. Bush's conception of American leadership of a 'new world order' self-consciously appropriated Mikhail Gorbachev's earlier formulation of a demilitarised 'new world order'. In their pursuit of a unipolar world undergirded by US-led military force, US policy makers spurned Gorbachev's vision of multinational cooperation for the nationalism of Boris Yeltsin's post-Soviet Russia. Relying on political scientist Samuel Huntington's 'clash of civilisations' concept to justify military spending and interventions, and constructing new enemies at home, US officials in Congress and the national defence establishment wittingly and unwittingly fuelled the short- and long-term development of xenophobic right-wing ethnic nationalisms within and beyond US borders.

Trump's demonisation of his political opponents, his wanton lying, and the authoritarian posturing of his campaign rallies and tweets represented a rupture in US political norms, but they were not without precedent. Rather they were the outcome of a global process long underway, where electorates in Western industrial democracies, frustrated with governments unable and often unwilling to protect citizens/workers from the economic dislocations of globalisation, have increasingly turned to right-wing authoritarian leaders. It is worth underscoring the point that this process was not inevitable, not driven by supposedly inexorable market forces. Rather, the way that global economic integration occurred, accelerating in the 1970s, then assuming new forms after the collapse of the Soviet Bloc, was the outcome of the deliberate decisions and deregulatory policies of US and Western politicians, bankers and financiers. And their highly profitable actions dramatically increased economic inequality within their societies and globally.

In the early 1990s, triumphalists across the political spectrum assumed that liberal capitalist democracy had survived the collapse of communism. But to echo Havel, the end of the East portended the end of the West. In the Cold War competition over which system could best deliver the good life to the masses, if the East was found wanting in most regards, it had arguably obliged the West to deliver on the social compact of affordable consumer goods, cheap gasoline and a social safety net. In 1993, as Havel cautioned, liberal capitalist institutions may have appeared robust, even if they were imposed on the global South and were required as the precondition for aid to the former Soviet Bloc. But as market fundamentalism conflated democratic governance and capitalism, undermining the former, it changed the rules of politics. In the wake of the collapse of the Soviet Union, US policy makers searched frantically for a new enemy. Academic and political big thinkers proposed new internal as well as external targets, and in the ensuing years bipartisan political norms rapidly eroded.

Republican Party politics embraced anti-government partisan warfare predicated on scapegoating enemies within. The litany of post-Cold War attacks on internal enemies includes Republican vice-presidential candidate Dan Quayle's targeting of poor African Americans and single women in his 'family values' and law-and-order speech of May 1992. That same year, Republican presidential candidate Pat Buchanan declared that the 'culture wars' had replaced the Cold War. Following the hyperbolic attacks on Bill Clinton's 1993 healthcare proposal, with critics likening it to communism and 'cradle-to-grave slavery', Republican House speaker Newt Gingrich's scorched-earth partisanship culminated in his 1995 and 1996 shutdown of the government over GOP attempts to slash government spending. Even Democrats embraced the scapegoating logic as Clinton capitulated to welfare reform and harsh sentencing laws.

The weakening of the US welfare and distributive state has gone hand in hand with rise of the carceral and surveillance state. As state governance shifted from regulatory to carceral functions, deregulation and privatisation, in tandem with accelerating economic inequality, fuelled disinvestment in public infrastructure and the institutions vital to a healthy democracy, including public education, daily newspapers and independent media. The social safety net has deteriorated with the decline of accountable nation-state power.

Moreover, in a neoliberal global order defined by weakened state sovereignty, foreign policy making defaults to unconventional actors, whose influence stems from their unaccountability to nation-states. Foreign policy makers, as described in the conception of empire advanced by Michel Hardt and Antonio Negri, are everywhere and nowhere, a congeries of non-governmental organisations (NGOs), popular culture producers, corporations, and social media corporations and sites – all rivalling the influence of nation-states.[5] First visible in crises involving failed states but echoing throughout the developed world, private actors and NGOs increasingly provide relief and social services that governments are no longer able or willing to provide. But at the same time, as Jan Eckel has argued, what many human rights activists consider an 'ethical imperative of intervention' often entails working for 'profound changes in the political systems and even social practices of foreign countries'.[6]

The assertion of US power abroad has historically worked through a partnership between corporations and private citizens on the one hand, and foreign policy officials and the State Department on the other, with no dearth of examples of direct US interference in the affairs of sovereign nations whether by coups or other means. The neoliberal post-Soviet order, however, has allowed new tools for the intervention of US 'soft power', including involvement in elections in the post-Soviet sphere of US politicians, NGOs and human rights groups.

More recently, the US state has become vulnerable to external destabilisation as well as internal capture by authoritarian figures such as Donald Trump, who hacked American democracy by manipulating corporate media (24-hour cable news) and exploited weaknesses inherent in partisan politics and the electoral system. Russian interference in the 2016 US presidential campaign, Trump's unwavering praise of Putin, and the Kremlin's influence over Trump's campaign and subsequent actions are but a twist in a broader drama involving new techniques of intelligence and information warfare in an era of weakened states, rising economic inequality, fragmented publics and polarised public constituencies.

Trump's penchant for deception, disinformation and the propagation of 'alternate realities' has clear precedents. Long before the 2016 election, a host of actors unsettled the terrain of public discourse and power relations by conjuring a new public constituency, eager for geopolitical intervention based not on facts, but on a socially constructed 'tabloid geopolitical imaginary'.[7] A contempt for diplomacy – the rejection of political resolutions to conflict in favour of military ones – was fully evident in the 2008 Republican presidential campaign. That campaign also served as a dress rehearsal for the conflation of fact and fiction that may have proved decisive in the 2016 campaign and the early days of the Trump administration. The 2008 John McCain–Sarah Palin Republican ticket anticipated the victorious Trump campaign with the angry populism of Palin's rallies, the Islamophobic smears against Democratic candidate Barack Obama, and the mocking disregard for facts, expertise and the very idea of the truth among McCain–Palin supporters and surrogates.

Even the flagrant Republican Party denial of the overwhelming evidence for human-caused climate change has roots in the squandered opportunities of the late 1980s. In November 1989, after running as an environmentalist, the Bush administration acquiesced to climate change denialism, reinvigorating corporate resistance to environmental regulations and undermining the authority of science and the very notion of truth.

As the Eastern Bloc unravelled, many on both sides of the former divide confronted the environmental damage and refuse in towering landfills, incinerated garbage and nuclear waste. The sense that the race for superiority in weapons and consumption was unsustainable called for a radical rethinking of the good life, including a growing scientific consensus on climate change. Ronald Reagan had fought environmental protections; in one of the first acts of his presidency he removed thirty-two solar panels Jimmy Carter had installed on the White House roof, calling them a 'joke'. But in his 1988 campaign, during the hottest summer yet recorded, George H. W. Bush declared himself an environmentalist. Embarking on a five-state environmental campaign tour, he argued that 'those who think we are powerless to do anything about the greenhouse effect are forgetting about the White House effect'.⁸ Once in office, Bush and a bipartisan group in Congress moved to immediately cut emissions in the United States. While the Soviet Union and eastern European countries were slow to acknowledge the environmental damage wrought by their arms and development race, by 1989, a 'public awakening about environmental problems' was taking hold there 'comparable to that triggered by Earth Day in the United States in 1970'.⁹

On 6 November 1989, three days before the astonishing breaching of the Berlin Wall, an international group of scientists and diplomats met in Noordwijk in the western Netherlands, intending to pass a comprehensive treaty enforcing strict emissions restrictions. The meeting marked the culmination of a decade of scientific and diplomatic cooperation. But unexpectedly at the last minute, at the urging of Bush's political advisor John Sununu, the US withdrew from the treaty, and with the acquiescence of Britain, Japan and the Soviet Union forced the conference to abandon the commitment to freeze emissions.¹⁰

The Noordwijk convention reversed the perestroika-era resolve of the major superpowers to clean up their Cold War mess. In addition, Sununu's dismissal of the international scientific consensus as 'technical poppycock' signalled a new attack on science that would soon manifest itself in climate change denial. While Sununu's particular position undoubtedly reflected oil and gas executives' will to protect their enormous profits, the fateful choice to side with extractive energy industries over the scientific community had unintended and far-reaching consequences. Conspiracy theories had long existed at the fringes of American culture, but in the 1990s, as politicians and CEOs impugned the integrity of environmental scientists, widespread scepticism and paranoia about the status of truth itself entered the American mainstream.¹¹

Re-racialising global disorder

George H. W. Bush announced his Strategic Doctrine before Congress on 11 September 1990, in a speech originally scheduled for 2 August, the day Iraq invaded Kuwait. In the interval between the invasion and Bush's address, the US had launched Operation Desert Shield, with US troops and F-15 fighters landing in Saudi

Arabia on 7 August. Beyond signalling the intention to liberate Kuwait, the mission sought to deter Iraq from invading Saudi Arabia to seize control of the Hama oil field near the countries' shared border.

The Persian Gulf crisis, Bush told his audience, provided 'a rare opportunity to advance toward a historic period of cooperation'. Linking the crisis to his idea of an American-led new world order, Bush argued that out of these 'confused times' could emerge a 'new world order, a time freer of threat and terror'. Just as critically, in doing so he yoked his unipolar new world order to emergent 'clash of civilisation' ideas. 'Today,' Bush told his audience, 'this new world is fighting to be born . . . a world where the rule of law is taking the place of the rule of the jungle.'[12] In the armed conflict with Iraq, a very recent strategic ally whom the US had supported by supplying weapons, aid and strategic advice during its long and costly war with Iran from 1980 to 1988, after the Iranian revolution, Bush's reference to the law of the jungle – suggesting a force of primitive tribalism that must be subdued – is telling.[13] At pains to justify a costly deployment in the Persian Gulf at a moment when many Americans expected that the end of the Cold War would bring a 'peace dividend', Bush employed a phrase from the heyday of European imperialism. Bush's 'jungle' highlighted the idea of cultural conflict as a threat to global stability, and an urgent call to arms. Bush's framing of cultural conflict was animated by, if not borrowed from, Bernard Lewis's article 'The Roots of Muslim Rage', published just a week earlier in *The Atlantic* magazine. In that article, Lewis put forth the phrase 'clash of civilisations' – a concept famously elaborated by political scientist Samuel Huntington, first in a 1993 *Foreign Affairs* article, and then in his 1996 book of that title. Lewis's 1990 essay alerted readers to a 'surge of hatred' rising in the Islamic world that constituted 'a rejection of Western civilization as such', portending inevitable conflict with the West.[14]

Lewis's essay provoked outrage and incisive critique, the latter owing to its outsized influence on policy makers and on popular opinion. Critics have dissected Lewis's sweeping assumption that 'all of Islam is, by nature, based on a religious obligation to slay the infidel', an assumption that made him unable to 'distinguish

Wahhabi extremism from other forms of Islam'.[15] Though appallingly wrongheaded, the essentialising essay was instrumental in Bush's appeal for domestic and international support for military intervention in the Gulf. Bush did not traffic in Islamophobia, but his naming of inscrutable threats to shore up his regional defence strategy resonated with Lewis's ominous portrayal of an irrational and threatening Muslim world, as well as with Huntington's 1989 dire forecast of increased instability and violence in international affairs.[16] In invoking a fight of the rule of law against the law of the jungle, Bush did not need to consciously embrace a clash-of-civilisations frame as his words reverberated through media and popular culture.

From the time of the Gulf War, the Bush administration's vague but unrelenting suggestions of new shadowy threats that required a stronger military despite victory in the Cold War helped set the terms for a popular Islamophobia that would take root in popular culture. From the late-1980s conception of outlaw, rogue states to the post-9/11 formulation of the 'Axis of Evil', Republican (and sometimes Democratic) foreign policy rhetoric resorted to a similar Manichaeism, a parallel re-articulation of external enemies that questioned the legitimacy of diplomacy when employed with those judged as being hostile to US interests. In part, the rejection of diplomacy drew on the triumphalist story of the US supposedly having won the Cold War through the assertion of military might. But conceiving of outlaw states as existing 'beyond the family of nations'[17] also placed them beyond the pale; once deemed illegitimate, the only acceptable goal for these states was destruction or regime change.[18] Years later, some American politicians would argue, as did Newt Gingrich in 2010, that Islamic Sharia law was 'a mortal threat to the survival of freedom in the United States'.[19]

As the US constructed a world of irrational outlaw states, the studied indifference and unwillingness to work with international organisations to stop the slaughter of hundreds of thousands in Bosnia and Rwanda depended on racialised clash-of-civilisation ideas as well as on effacements of the history of the final decades of the Cold War. More than simply forgetting or erasing the memory of past actions, new frameworks rendered invisible Western culpability in the making of conditions for foreign policy crises, including genocide. As Mahmood Mamdani has argued, 'the most intractable internal conflicts in contemporary Africa', as well as those in other places such as Afghanistan and Iraq, 'are driven by regional tensions, which are in turn a by-product of the Cold War that led to a regionalisation of proxy wars and internal conflicts'.[20] Eliding a far more intertwined colonial and Cold War history, and refusing to examine political and historical causes, the Bush and Clinton administrations fell back on popular notions of 'primordial' hatreds articulated by Bernard Lewis, Samuel Huntington and last but not least, the travel-writer-turned-policy-influencer Robert Kaplan. Such atavisms, the argument went, were timeless, recurring and intractable, a view informing reluctance to intervene. The clash-of-civilisations theory racialises disorder created by Cold War policies while attributing that disorder to the victims of the Cold War.[21]

In a saturnine portrait based on travels in the region, Kaplan depicted the Balkans as seething with ancient and timeless hatreds, at once incomprehensible and uncontrollable. Kaplan insists that *Balkan Ghosts*, published in 1993, has been misunderstood. But one could go to nearly any page of the book to find examples of how Kaplan's purported inquiries and conclusions represent a doubling back on his initial assumption that the people of the Balkans live in a world predetermined by ancient conflict, outside of history, untouched and unchanged through the years. While Kaplan claims to have intimate knowledge of many countries and communities, in his world, every person encountered, every story told, is simply another illustration of a homogenised foil to an assumed Western modernity.

Elizabeth Drew and Richard Reeves have argued that Bill Clinton read *Balkan Ghosts* and concluded that 'these people have been killing each other for 10 centuries', leading him to shift away from campaign promises to intervene.[22] Indeed, by Clinton's own accounts, Kaplan's books shaped his view of global conflict.[23] Clinton enthusiastically recommended the work of Kaplan, as well as Huntington, to members of his administration.

Kaplan closed his *Balkan Ghosts* with a loaded question: 'Had the poison of eastern despotism and decline, seeping from Byzantium, to the Sultan's Palace, to the Kremlin, finally expended itself?' Assuming a poison-saturated 'East', Kaplan answered his own question – had the poison expelled itself? – with a bizarre paradox of hope emerging only through apocalyptic violence:

> I felt it had. Here at the world's end, at a place whose very collapse gave the twentieth century its horrifying direction . . . As I observed the violent disintegration of Yugoslavia and the turmoil that was bound to continue in other Balkan states, I was reminded of a line from Shakespeare's *Life and Death of King John*: 'So foul a sky clears not without a storm.'

Recalling Shakespeare prompts Kaplan to conclude that 'conflicting ethnic histories, inflamed by the living death of communism, had made the Balkan sky so foul that now, sadly, a storm was required to clear it'. For Kaplan, writing at the moment that 'ethnic cleansing' had been instigated in Bosnia, it was only with the cleansing storm of violence that 'the Enlightenment was, at last, breaching the gates of these downtrodden nations. A better age would have to follow.'[24] Kaplan's disturbing denouement goes beyond hand wringing over the purported inevitability of violence to imbue the policy of 'ethnic cleansing' with positive necessity, the storm that is required for 'a better age'.

While Kaplan's assumptions about unbridgeable difference and inevitable violence have long precedents in Western thought, rather than repeat his mistake and see such concepts as timeless, it is important to stress how such tropes were remade and reinvigorated in a profound moment of geopolitical shift, as the ideas of Kaplan, Lewis and Huntington moved across multiple registers throughout politics and the media. As Tom Bissell has argued, 'Not many authors can expect blurbs from senators, former Department of Defense secretaries, the Director of Central Intelligence or Tom Brokaw, but Kaplan can.'[25]

In February 1994, as US officials received warnings of Rwandan government-led plans to carry out genocide, Bill Clinton read another Kaplan essay, 'The Coming Anarchy', published in the *Atlantic Monthly*. Painting a bleak portrait of 'tyranny' and 'lawlessness' ravaging African cities, where 'criminal anarchy emerges as the real strategic danger', Kaplan raised the sensationalist bar on his earlier portrait of the Balkans.[26] Comparing Africa with the Balkans, Kaplan argued that in the latter 'the threat was the collapse of empires and the rise of nations based solely on tribe'. Now, he continued, 'the threat is more elemental: nature unchecked'. Kaplan had depicted strife in the Balkans through the lens of an invented history; Africa was presented as 'elemental'. In 'the coming upheaval', he warned, 'foreign embassies are shut down, states collapse, and contact with the outside world takes place through dangerous, disease ridden, coastal trading posts'.[27] Clinton praised Kaplan's essay as 'stunning', pushing it on White House aides. Vice-President Al Gore spearheaded a task force on 'countries at risk'. The issue became one of the highest selling in the magazine's history.[28]

One might easily move from Kaplan's hysterics to Donald Trump's January 2018 question, in discussions with law makers about immigration for people from Haiti, El Salvador and a homogenised African continent, 'Why are we having people from all of these shithole countries come here?'[29] But the conditions for Trump's crude racism were laid in the widespread acceptance of Kaplan's portrait of anarchy by the very politicians and thinkers many now find themselves nostalgic for.

Kaplan's depiction of a world of anarchy had a popular parallel in the bestselling novels of Tom Clancy. Clancy's unique relationship with the Republican and military establishment made him a conservative icon and a critical bridge between Cold War and clash-of-civilisation views of the world. Clancy had once figured the Soviets as the prime deceivers but the Cold War victory brought new paranoia. His 1990s novels veer between a clash-of-civilisations frame with Middle Eastern and Muslim threats to the US and a rebooting of older Asian enemies, as Clancy became a major architect of popular Islamophobia and racialised xenophobia. *The Sum of All Fears*, released on 14 August 1991 and debuting at number one on the *New York Times* bestseller list, imagines Palestinian and East German terrorists conspiring to carry out a nuclear attack on US soil. The 1994 *Debt of Honor* reinvented a Japanese enemy who, seeking revenge for their defeat in World War II, had secretly developed a nuclear weapon. While some critics found Clancy's depictions of Japanese people racist, others thought he was onto something. One praised Clancy for his clear warning 'that recent downsizing in the defense establishment has so depleted our military resources that the country is vulnerable to aggression that can arise anywhere anytime'.[30] In full-blown clash-of-civilisations paranoia, Clancy's 1996 *Executive Order*, which sold 2.3 million copies, opened with the US president and nearly all the Cabinet killed by a vengeful Japanese pilot. The new threats? Iran assassinates the leader of Iraq with the assistance of India and China, then forms a United Islamic Republic that initiates a full air, land and sea attack on the US, complete with a weaponised release of the Ebola virus into the US and an attempted kidnapping of the new president's daughter.[31]

Like Clancy and Kaplan, George W. Bush conjured a world of ubiquitous and menacing threats to Americans well before 9/11. In his 2000 presidential campaign, Bush told a group of students:

> When I was coming up, it was a dangerous world, and you knew exactly who 'they' were. It was us versus them and you knew who 'them' was. Today we're not so sure who the 'they' are, but we know they're there.[32]

Bush punctuated his Cold War nostalgia – growing up with danger in an 'us versus them' world but at least knowing 'who "them" was' – with dire warnings about the present.[33]

In the wake of the 9/11 terrorist attacks, the rapid congressional approval of the Patriot Act in October 2001 sanctioned a far-reaching apparatus of internal security and surveillance not seen since the McCarthy era. The Patriot Act and the establishment of the Homeland Security Administration enabled the simultaneous *extension and privatisation* of government security and surveillance on an unprecedented scale, on the pretext of fears of terrorism and threats from perceived internal and external enemies.[34] The only alternative to further catastrophe, suggested Bush, was expanded mobilisation for permanent warfare. Arguing for an enlarged security state, Bush promised to 'improve intelligence collection and sharing, increase the number of patrols at our borders, strengthen the security of air travel, and use technology to track the arrivals and departures of visitors to the United States'.[35]

Trump's horribly effective summoning of a white public under siege from within and without, mobilising his base to see the country as a warzone, has antecedents in Bush's war on terror. The Patriot Act vastly expanded the security state, with provisions undermining civil liberties and resulting in indefinite detentions of enemy combatants, summary deportations of immigrants, and government searches of homes and businesses without the consent of the occupant or owner. Indeed, Trump's insistence that he has the right to build a wall on the Mexican border and his cruel separation of children from their families, built on the structural changes prompted by the Patriot Act as well as its ideological underpinnings.

Moreover, the lies of the Bush administration's fabricated weapons of mass destruction in Iraq, and the international lawlessness of US detainment of prisoners and torture at Guantánamo and in CIA prisons, eroded not just US credibility but transparency and accountability within the government. The continued production and reproduction of absolute enemies by the Bush administration and within popular culture spun a thick web of fear and hatred.

Bush's 'Axis of Evil' speech named Iraq, Iran and North Korea as sources of threats of weapons of mass destruction, laying the ground to justify his administration's invasion of Iraq.[36] Vowing to 'shut down terrorist camps', Bush quickly departed from references to Afghanistan and the actual locales where 9/11 hijackers had trained, to a sweeping and ambiguously defined goal of preventing 'regimes that sponsor terror from threatening America or our friends and allies with weapons of mass destruction'. Critically, Bush's argument for a broader war against an 'Axis of Evil' was based not on current actions or threats but, in his words, on the 'true nature' of 'these regimes'. Indeed, he acknowledged, 'some of these regimes have been pretty quiet since September 11', but, he continued, 'we know their true nature'. Bush punctuated Iraq's supposedly existential flaws: 'This is a regime that has something to hide from the civilized world.'[37]

In the 2008 presidential campaign, with his own pet project of expanding NATO, John McCain drew on assumptions of existentially flawed regimes to argue that any discussion with such regimes constituted appeasement. McCain claimed that his rival,

Barack Obama, would 'condone the positions of our enemies' and 'legitimize illegal behavior by sitting down for negotiations without preconditions'. Perhaps deliberately misunderstanding the word 'negotiation', he lamented that Obama 'thinks that he can negotiate with Iran and get anything he wants'.[38] Despite the sharp tension between McCain's ambitions to expand NATO and Trump's desire to destroy it, both share a common view of Iran and a common view of US power as able to unilaterally remake the world, even if McCain sought to do so through internationalist institutions like NATO.

Dismissing the very notion of diplomacy by activating inherently unbridgeable us-versus-them dichotomies, McCain's 2008 campaign unveiled the renunciation of political expertise and procedures in yet another way. In putting forward an inexperienced, charismatic vice-presidential candidate in Alaskan governor Sarah Palin, the campaign rejected knowledge, facts and logic as basic qualifications for a 'leader of the free world'. In her 'authentic' demeanour and syntax, Palin's evident weaknesses, combined with her evangelical fervour, only enhanced her appeal to many Republicans. To the astonishment of political observers, Palin's deficiencies and skewed sense of reality resonated with a broad swathe of the Republican base. There would be more astonishment to come, as Palin was in important ways a precursor to Donald Trump, stumping for the Tea Party as she led the charge that the GOP establishment had abandoned its base.[39]

In this world of 'knowledge', there is no room for politics, for negotiation or for considering the possibility that any interests of one's opponent might be legitimate. The dissolution of boundary between fact and performance was dramatically documented in the 2008 US presidential elections and in the fierce partisan battles that have followed. 'Women warrior' politicians such as Palin and Minnesota congresswoman Michele Bachmann simply made things up, such as the claim that Barack Obama is not a US citizen, or that he is a Muslim, with no repercussions. Following the 2008 campaign, when Palin argued that humans have not influenced changes in climate, she stepped up her role as a climate change denier. Confusing climate with weather, she posted on Facebook, 'Global warming my gluteus maximus,' pointing to a picture of her daughter Piper in the snow after her May graduation.[40] Palin helped to mainstream reactionary gibberish as a legitimate mode of Republican rhetoric. When she and Trump say things that are syntactically nonsensical and factually wrong, they are doing more than displaying their ignorance. They are making ignorance and the refusal to defer to expertise a central feature of what it means to be a Republican.

Internationalising pay-to-play politics

Russian interference in the 2016 US presidential election was unprecedented in many ways, but worked through an ongoing breakdown of corporate, national and international boundaries. Much has been made in the US media of Trump's affinity to Russia and Putin, and how this seems to represent a break in the historic US position towards an often-conflated Russia/Soviet Union. But US influence peddling in the post-Soviet republics and post-Soviet Russian influence peddling in the United States highlight continuity rather than rupture between Trump and earlier US post-Soviet relations with Russia. By the mid-1990s, different factions of the GOP (and Democrats to a lesser extent) were solidly in league with different groups of Russian oligarchs and/or anti-Russian Ukrainians and Georgians. The most visible group advocated containing Russian influence and expanding NATO. But other US politicians and lobbyists further transnationalised US pay-to-play lobbying practices by pursuing cushy relations with the very Russian oligarchs their colleagues sought to contain.

US pursuit of vast pipeline projects depended on a grand containment of Russia – a containment that required severing Russian ties with regions long part of the Soviet Union and the Tsarist empire that preceded it. The quest to control oil supplies in the Caspian by re-routing a pipeline away from Russia lured corporate and government officials into covert relationships with the Taliban. The Faustian pursuit of Caspian oil provides an important context for the Republican Congress's push to expand NATO and declared intentions to contain Russia outlined in the GOP's 1994 'Contract with America'.

In 1995 for example, the US oil company Unocal was among several companies that formed a cartel in Washington to further their interests in the Caspian, seeking to build oil and gas pipelines from Turkmenistan through Afghanistan to Pakistani ports.[41] After the Taliban seized power in Afghanistan in 1996, oil insiders invited Taliban leaders to Houston.[42] Dick Cheney told a gaggle of industry executives in 1998, 'I can't think of a time when we've had a region emerge as suddenly to become as strategically significant as the Caspian.'[43] This view continued to inform cooperation with the Taliban in Pakistan and Afghanistan at least up to two weeks before the 9/11 attacks, all at enormous cost to the Pakistani, Afghani and later American people. The thirst for Caspian oil would guide the George W. Bush administration's approach to the war on terror as well as its relation to Russia from beginning to end. Towards the end of his vice-presidency, in September 2008 Cheney travelled to Azerbaijan, where in 'the shadow of the Russian invasion of Georgia' he met with Azerbaijani president Ilham Aliyev at his residence on the Caspian Sea, followed by talks with executives from BP and Chevron.[44]

Yet while one group of politicians attempted to isolate Russia, others sought lucrative relationships with Russian oligarchs. In the late 1990s, Tom DeLay, a Republican representative from Texas, visited Moscow several times along with the lobbyist Jack Abramoff. Organised by Russian oil and gas executives who wanted to lobby the US government for more foreign aid, the trips were paid for by a Bahama-based group associated with Abramoff and suspected of being financed by Russians. DeLay 'subsequently voted for the bill the Russians were pushing'.[45] The Russians had also given a million dollars to a group called the US Family Network, an 'advocacy' group that was part of DeLay's 'political money carousel' and had also received half a million dollars from the Republican National Campaign Committee.[46] Investigated in 2005, DeLay's spokesman claimed that the main propose of DeLay's 1997 trip was 'to meet with religious leaders'. The Family Network acknowledged that its payment was intended 'to influence DeLay's vote in 1998 on legislation' to help Russia, but DeLay insisted that the group, which raised $2.5 million during its five years of existence but kept its list of donors secret, was 'a grassroots organization'.[47]

Private actors and the Georgian and Ukrainian crises

A display of NGOs and politicians running their own foreign policy surfaced in the 'going rogue' foreign policy celebrated by Sarah Palin and advanced by Republican candidate and Arizona senator John McCain during his presidential campaign. As Palin announced her willingness to attack Russia if she were in the Oval Office, McCain's involvement in the 2008 Georgia crisis prompted questions of propriety from the media, the Obama campaign and even President Bush.

Randy (Randall James) Scheunemann, the McCain campaign's principal foreign policy advisor and a board member of the neoconservative Project for the New American Century (PNAC), also worked for the Georgian regime of Mikheil Saakashvili. Scheunemann's two-man lobbying firm had received $730,000 since 2001 to get Georgia into the NATO alliance, and 'he had been paid by Romania and Latvia to do the same'. In the fifteen months Scheunemann worked for McCain, his Orion Strategies received $290,000 from Saakashvili.[48]

The Georgia crisis erupted into war on 7 August 2008 when the Georgian government launched an attack on a rebel group based in the city of Tskhinvali, South Ossetia, a province that had been part of Georgia within the USSR. South Ossetia had declared its independence from the Soviet Union in 1991 as a sovereign state. Georgia had attempted to establish control, leading to the 1991–2 war, which ended in the de facto secession of South Ossetia as well as Abkhazia.

To this day, US press accounts of the 2008 conflict nearly always omit the fact that Georgia attacked before Russia, narrating the war as a simple act of Russian aggression. And indeed, Russians look back at the Georgia crisis as the time they lost the information war – with international media showing Georgian tanks invading but attributing them to Russia – a lesson that they would not forget as they vowed to step up their efforts in this arena.[49] In fact, in response to the Georgian attack, Russian troops repulsed the Georgian military in Tskhinvali and occupied part of Georgia including the city of Gori until 23 August. A European Union commission ruled a year later that Georgia had initiated the conflict by invading South Ossetia in violation of international law. Finding fault with all three parties, the EU report categorically rejected the claim by Mikheil Saakashvili that Russia had launched an attack before the Georgian attack and also found no evidence that a Russian attack was pending. At the same time, the report branded the secession of South Ossetia and Abkhazia from Georgia 'illegal and Russian recognition of the two "states" in violation of international law'.[50]

In the midst of the 2008 crisis, on 12 August McCain told Saakashvili, 'I know I speak for every American when I say ... today we are all Georgians.'[51] McCain's statement prompted critical rejoinders including, 'Spare me. You couldn't find one American in a thousand who could find Georgia on a map.' Undeterred, McCain reported that had he reassured Saakashvili that 'the thoughts and prayers and support of the American people are with that brave little nation as they struggle for their freedom and independence'.[52] As McCain ridiculed Obama's call for diplomacy to resolve the crisis, he emphasised his past trips and experience in the region. At the same time, Saakashvili reported speaking with McCain several times a day.[53]

McCain's close ties with Saakashvili proved only a harbinger of the accelerating dissolution between state and foreign state and non-state actors' involvement in purportedly national elections. The 2009 reset of US–Russian relations announced by Dmitry Medvedev and Barack Obama was undone by a similar cast of characters in the crisis in Ukraine, albeit with a twist.[54] From promoting the failed Orange Revolution of 2004 to the 2014 crisis, US politicians, lobbyists and NGOs were deeply involved in internal politics in Ukraine. In November 2013, with the US actively pushing the integration of Ukraine into the EU, the government of Viktor Yanukovych backed away from signing an EU association agreement that would have 'driven a deep wedge' between Russia and Ukraine. With the opposition leader, Vitaly Klichko, close to the State Department as well as German chancellor Angela Merkel, protests ensued that drove Yanukovych from power on 22 February 2014, prompting Russia's intervention and its annexation of Crimea on 18 March. Critics charged that US money had funded anti-Yanukovych protests through the Belgrade-based group CANVAS.⁵⁵ This group had received significant money from the US State Department to stage the first successful 'colour revolution' against Slobodan Milošević in then-Yugoslavia. Since then they have been transformed into a full-time 'revolution consultancy' for the US, posing as a Serbian grassroots group backing 'democracy'. Klichko was backed by US assistant secretary of state Victoria Nuland, formerly ambassador to NATO and advisor to Dick Cheney, and a neoconservative married to leading neoconservative hawk Robert Kagan.⁵⁶

Human rights groups, citing abuses by pro-Russian factions, argued for intervention on humanitarian grounds. Indeed, the human rights logic of the 'imperative to intervene' presents a justification and moral responsibility for intervention as sweeping in scope as the Cold War-era Truman Doctrine of 1947 and the National Security Council's Document 68 of 1950. But here, Ukrainians were offered two profoundly non-democratic choices: Putin-style authoritarianism on the one hand, or policies protecting global corporate interests on the other.

Experts on the region such as the historian Tarik Amar pleaded in February 2014 for diplomacy, for the US 'to decode the sabre-rattling of Putin – and help prevent Ukraine from turning into a proxy battlefield', further cautioning that warnings to Putin 'without any face-saving offers would be more than useless' and needed to be accompanied by appeals for restraint on the part of the Ukrainian leadership.⁵⁷ Instead, the next month Senator John McCain pronounced that 'Russia is a gas station masquerading as a country', undermining such diplomatic efforts and goading Putin.⁵⁸

As the major face-off between Russia and the US over Ukraine emboldened hawks in the US government, the 2016 presidential campaign brought another twist with the revelation that Paul Manafort, Trump's first campaign manager, had been working for the pro-Russian Yanukovych for years. A long-time Republican operative and lobbyist from the time of the Reagan administration, Manafort had worked as a lawyer for such brutal US Cold War clients as Jonas Savimbi, president of UNITA in Angola, Sese Seko Mobutu, president of Zaire (Democratic Republic of Congo), and Ferdinand Marcos of the Philippines.⁵⁹ Manafort had first butted heads with the State Department in 2006, when 'the American ambassador to Ukraine asked Manafort to ask his client to stop bad-mouthing NATO. Manafort flatly refused.' According to his friends, Manafort had always been primarily motivated by cash but that was 'the moment that he crossed over.'[60] In supporting US-backed dictators in the Cold War, Manafort could see his work as supporting American interests, but in blocking NATO expansion, Manafort answered to a different master.

Manafort laid low until he resurfaced in the Trump campaign. But he had essentially been doing what McCain's top advisor and other US lobbyists had been doing all along, aggressively promoting the interests of his clients in the US Congress. The problem was not that Manafort acted as an agent of a foreign government; the problem was that his client was on the wrong side in the eyes of the US foreign policy establishment.

While increasing revelations of Manafort's financial ties to Russia and his pro-Russian, pro-Putin stance led to his resignation as Trump's campaign advisor, by December 2016 he was back advising the president-elect. Two years later he would be tried and convicted of two counts of conspiracy to violate foreign lobbying law, commit money laundering and obstruct justice (in addition to bank and tax fraud convictions).

Hacking democracy

Fighting back from what Russians view as aggressive US attempts to isolate Russia diplomatically and economically, in the 2016 US election, active measures deployed by Russian intelligence hacked Democratic Party emails, attempted to break into the election websites of at least thirty-nine states, and sought influence by circulating false news stories through phony and legitimate Facebook and Twitter accounts.[61] Rebooting the Cold War with a combination of old KGB methods and new Internet technologies, Russians showed that they too have mastered cyber war and the projection of alternative realities.

If a bizarre set of circumstances led to Trump's election, the conditions for Trump's autocratic rejection of norms of diplomacy abroad and compromise at home were long in the making and well established. Trump has exploited a political system with an electoral college set up to protect slave owners and already riven with partisanship, racial polarisation, a contempt for democratic participation and economic inequality. He has claimed unlimited executive powers, rejecting any pretence of democratic accountability, laying waste to regulatory agencies, and attacking the free press, the rule of law and the independence of the judiciary. He gleefully incites violence by stoking or condoning racial, Islamophobic and anti-Semitic hatreds. And if the Cold War national-security state once offered a carrot-and-stick social wage, Trump presides over a brave new neoliberal order that offers the abandoned citizen/subject the false promise that they will be protected by an authority figure, reducing governance to 'deal making' among kleptocrats.

Notes

1. Václav Havel, 'The Co-responsibility of the West', in *The Art of the Impossible: Politics as Morality in Practice* (New York: Knopf, 1997), 141. Originally written for *Foreign Affairs*, 22 December 1993.
2. Karen Tumulty, 'George H. W. Bush, 41st President of the United States, Dies at 94', *Washington Post*, 30 November 2018.
3. Ibid.
4. Patrick E. Tyler, 'US Strategy Plans Calls for Insuring No Rivals Develop a One-Superpower World: Pentagon's Document Outlines Ways to Thwart Challenges to Primacy of America', *New York Times*, 8 March 1992.
5. Michael Hardt and Antonio Negri, *Empire* (Cambridge, MA: Harvard University Press, 2001).
6. Jan Eckel, 'The Rebirth of Politics from the Spirit of Morality', in Jan Eckel and Samuel Moyn (eds), *The Breakthrough: Human Rights in the 1970s* (Philadelphia: University of Pennsylvania Press, 2014), 257.
7. Frédérick Gagnon, 'Invading your Hearts and Minds: *Call of Duty®* and the (Re)Writing of Militarism in US Digital Games and Popular Culture', *European Journal of American Studies 5*, no. 3 (2010).
8. Nathaniel Rich, 'Losing Earth: The Decade We Almost Stopped Climate Change', *New York Times*, 1 August 2018, <https://www.nytimes.com/interactive/2018/08/01/magazine/climate-change-losing-earth.html> (accessed 23 January 2020).
9. Anthony Cortese, 'Regulatory Focus: Glasnost, Perestroika, and the Environment', *Environmental Science and Technology* 23, no. 10 (1989), 1212–13.

10. Rich, 'Losing Earth'.
11. Rob Nixon, *Slow Violence and the Environmentalism of the Poor* (Cambridge, MA: Harvard University Press, 2011), 39–40.
12. Speech available at 'September 11, 1990: Address before a Joint Session of Congress', Miller Center website, <http://millercenter.org/president/bush/speeches/speech-3425> (accessed 24 January 2020). On US aid to Iraq, see, Shane Harris and Matthew M. Aid, 'Exclusive: CIA Files Prove America Helped Saddam as he Gasses Iran', *Foreign Policy*, 26 August 2013, <https://foreignpolicy.com/2013/08/26/exclusive-cia-files-prove-america-helped-saddam-as-he-gassed-iran> (accessed 24 January 2020).
13. Seymour M. Hersh, 'US Secretly Gave Aid to Iraq Early in Its War with Iran', *New York Times*, 26 January 1992, <https://www.nytimes.com/1992/01/26/world/us-secretly-gave-aid-to-iraq-early-in-its-war-against-iran.html> (accessed 24 January 2020).
14. Bernard Lewis, 'The Roots of Muslim Rage', *The Atlantic*, September 1990, <https://www.theatlantic.com/magazine/archive/1990/09/the-roots-of-muslim-rage/304643> (accessed 24 January 2020).
15. Emran Qureshi and Michael A. Sells (eds), *The New Crusades: Constructing the Muslim Enemy* (New York: Columbia University Press, 2003), 16.
16. Samuel P. Huntington, 'Repent! The End Is Not Near', *Washington Post*, 24 September 1989, <https://www.washingtonpost.com/archive/opinions/1989/09/24/repent-the-end-is-not-near/cdadb244-5e61-4828-8650-4532471b4458> (accessed 24 January 2020).
17. Charles K. Armstrong, *Tyranny of the Weak: North Korea and the World 1950–1992* (Ithaca, NY: Cornell University Press, 2013), 292.
18. Anthony Lake, 'Confronting Backlash States', *Foreign Affairs*, March/April 1994, <https://www.foreignaffairs.com/articles/iran/1994-03-01/confronting-backlash-states> (accessed 24 January 2020).
19. Peter Beinart, 'The New Enemy Within', *The Atlantic,* May 2015, <https://www.theatlantic.com/magazine/archive/2015/05/the-new-enemy-within/389573> (accessed 24 January 2020).
20. Mahmood Mamdani, *Saviors and Survivors: Darfur, Politics, and the War on Terror* (New York: Pantheon, 2009), 227.
21. Susan L. Woodward, *Balkan Tragedy: Chaos and Dissolution after the Cold War* (Washington, DC: Brookings Institution Press, 1995). Paul Hockenos, *Homeland Calling, Exile Patriotism and the Balkan Wars* (Ithaca, NY: Cornell University Press, 2003) examines the roll of émigré and exile communities in fanning the violence.
22. Richard Reeves, *Running in Place: How Bill Clinton Disappointed America* (Kansas City, MO: Andrews McMeel, 1996); Elizabeth

Drew, *On the Edge: The Clinton Presidency* (New York: Simon & Schuster, 1994); Michael T. Kaufmann, 'The Dangers of Letting a President Read', *New York Times*, 22 May 1999, <http://www.nytimes.com/1999/05/22/books/the-dangers-of-letting-a-president-read.html> (accessed 24 January 2020)

23. See 'Bill Clinton's World', *Foreign Policy*, 30 November 2009, <https://foreignpolicy.com/2009/11/30/bill-clintons-world> (accessed 24 January 2020).
24. Robert D. Kaplan, *Balkan Ghosts: A Journey through History* (New York: St Martin's Press, 1993), 286–7.
25. Tom Bissell, 'Euphorias of Perrier: The Case Against Robert D. Kaplan, *VQR*, Summer 2006, <https://www.vqronline.org/euphorias-perrier-case-aganist-robert-d-kaplan> (accessed 24 January 2020).
26. Robert Kaplan, 'The Coming Anarchy', *Atlantic Monthly*, February 1994.
27. Ibid.
28. Toby Lester, 'Beyond "The Coming Anarchy"', *Atlantic Monthly*, August 1996, <https://www.theatlantic.com/past/docs/issues/96aug/proport/kapsid.htm> (accessed 24 January 2020)
29. Josh Dawsey, 'Trump Derides Protections for Immigrants from "Shithole" Countries', *Washington Post*, 12 January 2018, <https://www.washingtonpost.com/politics/trump-attacks-protections-for-immigrants-from-shithole-countries-in-oval-office-meeting/2018/01/11/bfc0725c-f711-11e7-91af-31ac729add94_story.html> (accessed 24 January 2020).
30. Review of Tom Clancy, *Debt of Honor*, *Publishers Weekly*, 15 August 1994, <https://www.publishersweekly.com/9780399139543> (accessed 24 January 2020).
31. On Clancy's post-9/11 novels, see Bradley J. Birzer, 'Who Wrote Tom Clancy's Last Novels?', *Imaginative Conservative*, 25 November 2016, <http://www.theimaginativeconservative.org/2016/02/who-wrote-tom-clancys-last-novels.html> (accessed 24 January 2020).
32. George W. Bush, Iowa Western Community College, 21 January 2000.
33. Ibid.
34. State of the Union address, White House, 29 January 2002, <https://georgewbush-whitehouse.archives.gov/stateoftheunion/2002/index.html> (accessed 24 January 2020); see Amy Kaplan, 'Homeland Insecurities: Reflections on Language and Space', *Radical History Review* 85 (2003), 82–93.
35. State of the Union address, White House, 29 January 2002.
36. Ibid.

37. Ibid.
38. 'Transcript of First Presidential Debate', CNN, 26 September 2008, <https://edition.cnn.com/2008/POLITICS/09/26/debate.mississippi.transcript> (accessed 24 January 2020).
39. John Hayward, 'Sarah Palin: Trump Movement Began with the GOP's "Shocking Betrayals" of Tea Party Voters', *Breitbart*, 25 November 2016, <http://www.breitbart.com/radio/2016/11/25/sarah-palin-trump-movement-began-with-the-gop-establishments-shocking-betrayals-of-tea-party-voters> (accessed 24 January 2020).
40. Nick Wing, 'Sarah Palin: It Snowed in Alaska in May, So There Is No Global Warming', *Huffington Post*, 20 May 2013, <http://www.huffingtonpost.com/2013/05/20/sarah-palin-global-warming_n_3306867.html> (accessed 24 January 2020).
41. Ahmed Rashid, *Taliban: Militant Islam, Oil, and Fundamentalism in Central Asia* (New Haven, CT: Yale University Press, 2000), 162.
42. Ibid., 162–9; George Monbiot, 'America's Pipe Dream: A Pro-Western Regime in Kabul Should Give the US an Afghan Route for Caspian Oil', *The Guardian*, 23 October 2001, <https://www.theguardian.com/world/2001/oct/23/afghanistan.terrorism11> (accessed 27 January 2020).
43. Marjorie Cohn, 'Cheney's Black Gold: Oil Interests May Drive US Foreign Policy', *Chicago Tribune*, 10 August 2000, <https://webcache.googleusercontent.com/search?q=cache:xtjky3BMgXEJ:https://www.chicagotribune.com/news/ct-xpm-2000-08-10-0008100507-story.html+&cd=1&hl=en&ct=clnk&gl=uk&lr=lang_en%7Clang_fr> (accessed 30 January 2020).
44. 'Cheney Pays Visit to Russia's Neighbors', NBC News, 3 September 2008, <www.nbcnews.com/id/26522284/ns/world_news-europe/t/cheney-pays-visit-russias-neighbors> (accessed 27 January 2020).
45. Heather Digby Parton, 'Why White House Counsel Don McGahn Has Donald Trump Extremely Worried', *Salon*, 20 August 2018, <https://www.salon.com/2018/08/20/why-white-house-counsel-don-mcgahn-has-donald-trump-extremely-worried> (accessed 27 January 2020).
46. Ibid.
47. R. Jeffrey Smith, 'The DeLay–Abramoff Money Trail', *Washington Post*, 31 December 2005, <https://www.washingtonpost.com/archive/politics/2005/12/31/the-delay-abramoff-money-trail/262aebb2-0c1f-46de-aa81-98a203e2a0ad> (accessed 27 January 2020).
48. Pat Buchanan, 'Georgia's Man in the McCain Camp', *Toronto Star*, 2 September 2008, AA06. PNAC was headed by William Kristol

and he had called for a US invasion of Iraq four years before 9/11, with Scheunemann serving as president of PNAC's Committee for the Liberation of Iraq.
49. On Russian lessons from Georgia, see, Evan Osnos, David Remnick and Joshua Yaffa, 'Trump, Putin, and the New Cold War', *New Yorker*, 6 March 2017, <https://www.newyorker.com/magazine/2017/03/06/trump-putin-and-the-new-cold-war> (accessed 27 January 2020).
50. Ian Traynor, 'Georgia Blamed for Starting Russia War; Tbilisi Launched Assault on South Ossetia – EU Inquiry', *The Guardian*, 1 October 2009, 23.
51. 'McCain: "We Are All Georgians"', NBC News, 12 August 2008, <http://firstread.nbcnews.com/_news/2008/08/12/4431528-mccain-we-are-all-georgians> (accessed 27 January 2020).
52. Ibid.
53. Dan Eggen and Robert Barnes, 'McCain's Focus on Georgia Raises Question of Propriety', *Washington Post*, 15 August 2008, <https://www.washingtonpost.com/wp-dyn/content/article/2008/08/14/AR2008081403332.html>; Rod Dreher, 'We Are Not All Georgians Now', *Real Clear Politics*, 26 August 2008, <https://www.realclearpolitics.com/articles/2008/08/we_are_not_all_georgians_now.html> (both accessed 27 January 2020).
54. See James L. Goldgeiger, 'A Realistic Reset with Russia', *Policy Review*, August/September 2009, available at <https://www.hoover.org/research/realistic-reset-russia>; and 'US–Russia Relations: "Reset" Fact Sheet', White House, 24 June 2010, <https://obamawhitehouse.archives.gov/the-press-office/us-russia-relations-reset-fact-sheet> (both accessed 27 January 2020).
55. William Engdahl, 'Ukraine Protests Carefully Orchestrated: The Role of CANVAS, US-Financed "Color Revolution Training Group"', Global Research, 14 March 2014, <https://www.globalresearch.ca/ukraine-protests-carefully-orchestrated-the-role-of-canvas-us-financed-color-revolution-training-group/5369906> (accessed 27 January 2020).
56. Ibid.
57. Tarik Cyril Amar, 'This Is No Second Cold War: Ukraine's Territorial Integrity Must Remain Intact', *The Guardian*, 28 February 2014, <https://www.theguardian.com/commentisfree/2014/feb/28/ukraine-this-is-no-second-cold-war> (accessed 27 January 2020).
58. 'John McCain: Russia "Is a Gas Station Masquerading as a Country"', *The Week*, 14 March 2014, <https://theweek.com/speedreads/456437/

john-mccain-russia-gas-station-masquerading-country> (accessed 27 January 2020).

59. Adam Rawnsley, 'How Manafort's Work for the "Torturer's Lobby" Came Back to Haunt Him', *Daily Beast*, 23 February 2019, <https://www.thedailybeast.com/how-manaforts-work-for-the-torturers-lobby-came-back-to-haunt-him> (accessed 27 January 2020); Franklin Foer, 'Paul Manafort, American Hustler', *The Atlantic*, March 2018, <https://www.theatlantic.com/magazine/archive/2018/03/paul-manafort-american-hustler/550925/> (accessed 27 May 2020).

60. Robert Kolker, 'Paul Manafort Is Back: The King of K Street Is Ready for the New Washington', *Bloomberg Businessweek*, 28 November 2016, <https://www.bloomberg.com/news/articles/2016-11-28/paul-manafort-is-back> (accessed 27 January 2020).

61. Timothy Snyder, *The Road to Unfreedom: Russia, Europe, America* (New York: Vintage, 2019), 30.

8

Trumpism and the Future of US Grand Strategy

Jack (John M.) Thompson

When Donald Trump announced his 2016 presidential campaign slogan, 'Make America Great Again', many journalists and pundits sniggered. Trump had not even bothered to coin something original; he was obviously copying Ronald Reagan's 1980 campaign slogan, 'Let's Make America Great Again'. What was more, many (especially liberal) critics complained, he was obviously appealing to a specific type of nostalgia – common among culturally conservative, white Americans – that would have no appeal to most of the (increasingly diverse) modern US electorate. There was no way that such a tone-deaf, disconnected approach could succeed.

In retrospect, the joke was on the naysayers. Trump's slogan was easily the catchiest of the campaign. More importantly, it captured something profound about the nation's mood. Most voters, including Democrats, were worried about the future and believed that reform was in order. Americans did not agree on much, but there was near unanimity that change was needed, at home and abroad.

As a result, a significant portion of the electorate was open to at least some of Trump's diagnosis: that the world was becoming more dangerous; that policy makers should focus less on the stability of the international system and more on making the United States safe and prosperous; that previous presidents had done a poor job of protecting Americans from the vicissitudes of the globalised economy and allowed the United States to be taken advantage of by other nations; and that the system was rigged on behalf of members of the political and economic elite, who used their influence to get richer while everyone else got poorer. To fix these problems, Trump promised to get tough with the nation's allies, forcing them to pay more for US protection, which would allow the United States to spend more on problems at home. He would extract concessions from trading partners, thereby reviving US industry. He would restrict immigration to prevent foreigners undercutting the wages of US workers.[1]

To the surprise of many, including reportedly Trump himself, this message appealed to just enough voters to get him elected, and is currently the dominant influence in US foreign and economic policy. Trumpism melds populist rhetoric about the downsides of global political and economic engagement with overt appeals to white nationalism and a promise to restore the nation to an imagined former greatness. Appalling though it may be, Trumpism resonates with many and its appeal necessitates rethinking the future of the nation's relationship with the world. Certainly, the president's weaponisation of racial fears is anathema to many voters, his nationalism worries the tens of millions of Americans who have benefited from the globalised economy, and he appears to be at least as corrupt as the elites he bashes. However, in an era of relative US decline, characterised by intensifying geopolitical competition and rapid technological change, the urge to embrace unilateralism and partial withdrawal – an impulse that has been present in debates about foreign policy since the Revolutionary War – will remain powerful. Thinking about the future of US grand strategy will need to reckon with it.

US grand strategy and its discontents, 1992–2016

There was significant variation between the presidencies of William J. Clinton, George W. Bush and Barack Obama, but several commonalities linked US grand strategy between the end of the Cold War and the election of Donald Trump.[2] Each administration pursued a version of muscular liberal internationalism. This entailed military predominance, albeit within the framework of security alliances and robust participation in international organisations, the lowering of trade barriers via multilateral negotiations, the promotion of democracy, at least in theory, and the acceptance of legal immigration as economically beneficial and culturally acceptable.[3] On the whole, this agenda contributed to the maintenance of what is often referred to as the liberal world order (LWO) – the web of institutions, alliances and norms that the United States led the way in creating in the decades following World War II – even if some episodes, such as the 2003 invasion of Iraq, were counterproductive.

In spite of this bipartisan consensus about the chief parameters of US strategy, there were noteworthy dissenting voices on both sides of the US political divide.[4] On the right, Pat Buchanan fashioned a version of conservative populism that echoed Joseph McCarthy and George Wallace, among other fringe figures.[5] The former Richard Nixon speech writer ran for president as a Republican in 1992 and 1996, and at the heart of his campaigns was a critique of key aspects of the internationalist consensus. He castigated the financial and political elite for pursuing a globalist agenda that enriched a few at the expense of the working and middle classes, and promised that there would be 'no more NAFTA sellouts of American workers' on his watch. He called for an aggressively unilateralist foreign policy that put 'America first', and he criticised policy makers for accepting 'the burden of defending rich and prosperous allies who take America's generosity for granted as they invade our markets'.[6]

On the left, activist Ralph Nader – drawing, in part, on the legacy of the 1960s and early 1970s New Left – ran for president several times, most notably on the Green Party ticket in 1996 and 2000. Nader expressed scepticism about global engagement, calling for massive cuts to the military budget, complete nuclear disarmament, the closing of all foreign military bases and rethinking trade deals such as NAFTA. Like Buchanan, he portrayed partial withdrawal from the international system as a way to fix many of the country's problems, and accused members of the political and economic elite of profiting from a disastrous trade policy.[7]

Neither Buchanan nor Nader came close to winning a presidential election. However, in retrospect, the enthusiasm with which large minorities – especially in the case of Buchanan – greeted their candidacies, and responded to their calls for making Americans safer and more prosperous by partially withdrawing from international politics and trade, should have served as a warning that many were unhappy with the internationalist consensus. Even though the 1990s US economy appeared to be robust, seemingly vindicating Bill Clinton's centrist, neoliberal agenda, storm clouds were gathering. These included the emergence of China as an economic powerhouse, stagnating real income levels for most Americans, the withering of large portions of the manufacturing sector, and increasing anxiety among culturally conservative whites about the nation's growing diversity. It was only in the wake of the Great Recession, in the early 2010s, that these problems became pressing enough to reshape the mainstream political parties, in the form of the presidential candidacies of Senator Bernie Sanders and Donald Trump.

US foreign policy: key challenges

The United States confronts an international environment that is more challenging than at any point since the end of the Cold War. Geopolitical competition has intensified in recent years, and the United States no longer oversees a unipolar system in which it predominates as a lone superpower. Instead, it is now the world's foremost power, but confronts a complicated and fragmented global landscape.[8]

China has discarded its previous 'peaceful rise' strategy, which was designed to assuage other countries' concerns about its growing economic and political strength, and has begun to challenge the United States across the globe. President Xi Jinping, in parallel with a dramatic consolidation of power at home, has signalled that China's long-term strategy is to fracture the existing security structure in east Asia in order to facilitate Chinese predominance in the region. He is using a mixture of sticks and carrots to do so. Beijing has become much more assertive in pursuing claims to disputed territory and regularly challenges US military craft navigating the region. Though it still trails the United States in overall military power, and in vital areas such as weapons technology, the gap is closing, and Beijing has accelerated this process through an aggressive espionage programme. China has also sought to consolidate ties with other countries through development projects and political organisations that exclude the United States. The Belt and Road Initiative and the Asian Infrastructure Investment Bank potentially offer participating countries billions in investment. The Shanghai Cooperation Organisation, though still limited in its overall influence, includes member countries that account for nearly half the world's population and provides a forum for Chinese–Russian cooperation. China is also expanding its economic and political footprint in Africa, South America and eastern Europe.[9]

Like China, Russia also seeks to overturn central components of the prevailing order and views the United States as the foremost obstacle in this regard. It cannot match China's economic power and lacks the overall military strength of the Soviet Union, but Moscow retains considerable diplomatic and military heft. It has utilised its limited assets intelligently, and has thwarted US goals in eastern Europe and the Middle East. In addition, though its attempts to form a closer relationship with China have only partially succeeded, and the relationship increasingly appears to be weighted in Beijing's favour, collaboration between the world's foremost illiberal powers poses a significant problem for US policy makers.[10]

At the regional level, Iran has capitalised on the post-Iraq War chaos. It has much more influence in Iraq than before the war, is playing a leading role in the denouement of the Syrian Civil War, and in general has increased its influence in the Middle East. In the majority of these activities, Tehran is acting in opposition to US interests. Another troublesome regional challenger is North Korea. The communist regime, with its large military and paranoid worldview, threatens two US allies, Japan and South Korea. To make matters worse, Pyongyang probably possesses intercontinental ballistic missiles capable of reaching the US mainland.

Washington's struggles to develop an effective strategy for the changing geopolitical landscape highlight an unavoidable long-term problem – that it is probably in decline relative to other powers, especially China. To be sure, the United States remains the world's most influential nation, with the most powerful military, the most important economy and considerable diplomatic sway. However, US power has receded from its post-Cold War apex.[11]

Washington's waning power has constrained its ability to influence the trajectory of vital geopolitical developments, including Russia's interference in Ukraine, the Syrian Civil War and Beijing's launch of the Asian Infrastructure Investment Bank (AIIB), a potential rival to the World Bank and IMF.

One consequence of US decline is the extent to which it has struggled to take advantage of the new technologies that are transforming international politics. The United States retains an advantage over China and other competitors when it comes to military technology.[12] However, that edge is slowly eroding. The share of economic output of non-Western economies has risen dramatically in recent decades. The corresponding drop in Western economic power is reducing its technological dominance. In addition, the ways in which military technology is developed have shifted. In the 1970s, the US federal government played a central role in research and development of technologies that had potential military applications; today, the action has moved to the private sector. This means it is more difficult for national governments to prevent the diffusion of sensitive information. The internationalisation of higher education has further contributed to this process, as have massive espionage efforts by countries such as China.[13]

The most vital area of competition in emerging technologies is artificial intelligence (AI). The United States and China have emerged as the world leaders in AI. Though AI has many potential applications, and should not be reduced to a question of national security, there is no doubt that each country views itself as being in a race with the other to develop its AI sector and to take advantage of the potential economic, military and social benefits. Beijing has an ambitious and coherent long-term strategy for growth in the AI sector, which seeks to harness the fruits of private sector AI research for military applications. Meanwhile, Washington has failed to implement a strategy to harness the rich AI activity in the United States, a problem that is compounded by the open nature of the US economy – which has allowed China to invest in the US's AI sector while preventing US firms from doing the same – and complicated immigration policies that make it difficult for US firms to attract the top researchers in the field.[14]

Another challenge posed by the open nature of the US political and economic system is the weaponisation of information by illiberal states. Russian interference in the 2016 presidential election is only the most dramatic example of a deeper challenge that the United States and its allies face – how to maintain the key elements of a democratic society while preventing illiberal adversaries, which effectively control information in their own countries, from sowing distrust and confusion. In the United States, there is an especially rich target environment for countries such as Russia, given the extreme polarisation in the United States and the significant role played by extremist sources in the nation's political culture.[15]

The most pressing challenges facing the United States and the rest of the world are climate change and environmental degradation. National security experts and military officials comprehend the scale of the threat. They recognise that rising sea levels, increasingly extreme weather patterns, food shortages and significant levels of population displacement are already causing significant economic and political problems. However, this specialist knowledge about the problem, and widespread public discussion, mostly remains disconnected from discussions about US grand strategy.[16]

All of these challenges abroad are linked to domestic economic, cultural and political problems. The United States is experiencing historically high levels of income inequality, a problem that has numerous negative cultural and political consequences. Inequality is driven partly by changes in policy since the 1970s. This includes the partial unravelling of the social safety net, as well as the evolution of the international economic system. The so-called China shock, for instance, has profoundly affected parts of the United States. There have been significant job losses in parts of the Midwest and southeast, for instance, and unemployed workers have found it difficult to secure new jobs and face lower lifetime income levels. Not surprisingly, public attitudes towards China have hardened in recent years, as have the views of experts and academics.[17]

Cultural changes in the United States are also affecting the nation's foreign policy. Regions with more exposure to international trade competition are more likely to elect politicians that support policies such as higher barriers to trade and immigration restrictions. However, rising nationalism is more than just a response to trade policies – it is also the product of a broader shift among cultural conservatives. These Americans are worried that multiculturalism and the nation's growing diversity are a threat to the values that, in their view, made the nation great. Alongside protectionism and nativism, there has been a growth of illiberal attitudes among these voters – a development which has implications for democracy promotion, participation in international institutions, and relations with non-democratic regimes.[18]

Does this mean that the United States has turned decisively against the long-standing consensus in favour of global engagement? No, it does not. Public opinion analysts have noted that, Trump's election notwithstanding, a majority of Americans favour most aspects of internationalism. What these commentators overlook, however, is that a formerly fringe set of ideas has moved to the political mainstream. In the Republican Party (GOP), a majority of voters are now wary of key aspects of internationalism, including trade, participation in alliances and international organisations, immigration, and the need to fight climate change – and among core Trump supporters, the numbers are even starker. Though Democrats overall are much more supportive of an internationalist stance, much of the grassroots left is also sceptical of trade and alliances. In short, a higher percentage of the electorate is receptive to partial withdrawal from the international system than at any point since the early years of the Cold War.[19]

Trumpism and foreign policy

For a time after he took office, in January 2017, Trump seemed to restrain some of his more extreme instincts (with notable exceptions). His national security team included a number of relative moderates, as did his team of economic advisors. However, over the following two years, the president slowly but surely shed most of his mainstream advisors and embraced ever more nationalist policies. Though he has faced considerable criticism at home and abroad, Trump remains committed to his agenda, not least because it seems to be working, at least in the short term.

One issue on which the president immediately took an extreme position, from which he has not retreated, is immigration. Trump wants to reduce immigration levels of all types, but his priority is immigrants from the Muslim world and Latin America.[20] After several revisions in response to legal challenges, the president's order banning visitors from a number of mainly Muslim countries was upheld by the US Supreme Court. The administration has also taken steps to dramatically reduce the number of refugees admitted and to discourage potential asylum seekers. Meanwhile, his declaration of a national emergency has allowed him to transfer billions of dollars in funding from other parts of the federal government to begin construction of a wall on the southern US border – one of his chief campaign pledges.

Trump also promised to use his alleged negotiating prowess to extract better deals from allies and trading partners and he has put considerable effort into this objective. In Trump's mind, trade and national security are interconnected – with two types of partners of particular importance. For years, he has criticised allies such as Germany, Japan and South Korea for low levels of defence spending, an offence which, he claims, has given them an advantage in domestic investment and export promotion. Meanwhile, they remain dependent upon the United States to protect them. In order to force these countries to change their behaviour, Trump has threatened that, if significant defence spending increases are not forthcoming, the United States might not honour its security commitments. Simultaneously, he has imposed, or threatened to impose, punitive tariffs. In addition to 25 per cent tariffs on steel imports from almost every country, Trump has threatened to impose additional tariffs of 25 per cent on automobile imports, which would especially affect Germany, Japan and South Korea. Trump also used the threat of punitive tariffs to force Canada and Mexico to renegotiate NAFTA, though the new deal, the United States–Mexico–Canada Agreement (USMCA), included only modest concessions and may never be ratified by the US Senate.

The other target for Trump's overlapping trade–national security strategy is China, which the administration portrays as the foremost threat to US interests.[21] In order to force Beijing to the negotiating table, the administration imposed 25 per cent tariffs on more than $50 billion of Chinese goods. When the Chinese retaliated in kind, the president imposed 10 per cent tariffs on another $200 billion of Chinese goods, with a threat to raise the tariff levels to 25 per cent, though this threat is currently suspended. The administration is also seeking to formulate a series of bilateral deals that discourage other countries from trading with China, with the USMCA serving as a model for future agreements.

It is not a coincidence that the administration is mainly pursuing bilateral trade agreements. Its belief that such deals give them more leverage dovetails with a broader conclusion that multilateral action has historically constrained the United States. As a result, Trump has withdrawn the United States from a series of international agreements and institutions. This includes the Trans-Pacific Partnership (TPP) trade deal; the Paris climate accords; the nuclear deal with Iran; the United Nations Educational, Scientific, and Cultural Organisation (UNESCO); the United Nations High Commissioner for Refugees (UNHCR); and the United Nations Relief and Works Agency (UNRWA). Washington has begun the process of withdrawing from the Universal Postal Union and threatened to pull out of numerous other agreements.

The problems with Trumpism

At first glance, there appears to be method in the madness of Trump's approach. Immigration numbers are down in most categories. Allies in NATO and in east Asia are scrambling to increase their defence spending. All of the United States' major trading partners have offered concessions. Trump is also correct in arguing that China's trade policies and increasingly aggressive foreign policy need to be tackled. Despite fierce criticism, the president is happy with the political results of his policies. His core supporters remain loyal, and a large majority – about 90 per cent – of Republican voters approve of his performance.

Though these factors have been enough to convince the president to stay the course, they cannot outweigh the damage Trumpism is doing to the United States. The president's drive to lower all forms of immigration is a key part of his appeal to culturally conservative white voters, but it will harm the country. The evidence is indisputable: immigration boosts the economy in a number of respects, has little or no effect on the wages of working-class citizens, and does not increase crime rates. By reducing immigration, the president is not only unfairly demonising millions of people – and in the process exacerbating cultural and political divisions – he is ensuring that the economy will grow more slowly.[22]

The president's treatment of allies and trading partners is another area in which he mistakes modest concessions abroad, and applause from his base at home, for real progress. Trump may succeed in accelerating the rate at which Germany increases its defence spending, or in convincing Japan to become a more active partner. However, Berlin and Tokyo already acknowledge the need to take these steps. Furthermore, getting NATO members to spend slightly more, or convincing Japan to develop a more robust defence strategy, will not fix the real problems facing these alliances. NATO needs to address numerous internal divisions and interoperability shortcomings, and decide upon the future of its relationship with the United States and how to tackle a resurgent Russia. Meanwhile, in east Asia, the biggest problem is that Trump has weakened the long-standing web of regional alliances, and embarked upon a confrontational approach with China, without a broader strategy. The Obama administration's approach, though imperfect, had the virtue of preparing to confront Beijing where necessary, albeit in concert with allies, and provided scope for cooperation where possible.[23]

Trump's approach to allies presents long-term problems for the current international order. The president's preference for working with authoritarian strongmen, and dislike for other democratic leaders – his appalling treatment of Angela Merkel has been especially counterproductive[24] – has done much to facilitate a more illiberal world order. This is not an abstract concern. After 1945, in spite of many missteps, the United States led the way in developing institutions and norms that made the international system better than at any point in human history. This was good for the world, and it was good for the United States, and a key component of US power was its alliances, especially with democratic nations such as Germany. By treating Berlin as a competitor, and reducing US support for, and participation in, international institutions, the president is weakening the current order. After holding their noses and attempting to work with Trump, European policy makers have largely given up and are now planning for a future in which the United States is not a reliable ally. Some European independence is a good thing for both sides of the transatlantic relationship, but not if it comes as a result of alienation.

Meanwhile, the Trump administration's attempts to dismantle the multilateral framework for international trade, painstakingly developed in the decades after 1945, will make the world more dangerous and poorer. When countries consider trade from a mercantilist perspective, negotiations are viewed in zero-sum terms and inevitably become entangled with geopolitical problems. This is a formula for an international system based mainly on power relations, where democratic values recede and war is more likely.

Certainly, the United States needs to reform its economic policies. Communities in the Midwest and southeast who have been harmed by trade with China, for instance, should not be left to fend for themselves. However, a more effective approach would combine working in concert with allies – who are also troubled by China's trade policies and expansionism – to confront Beijing, with domestic initiatives such as developing a more robust social safety net and public education system.

The future of US grand strategy

The current ascendancy of Trumpism does not guarantee that US foreign policy will be more unilateralist and more nationalist in the long run. However, it is also not an anomaly. It reflects long-term trends in US political culture that will not soon change and which will have a significant, perhaps even decisive, influence on the nation's role in world affairs.

US grand strategy in the twenty-first century will need to account for an international order that is becoming more competitive for the gradually declining United States, and more complicated. Great-power competition is once again a key feature of the international order, but, paradoxically, the state is, in some ways, less important than at any point in modern history. Non-state actors such as corporations, non-governmental organisations

(NGOs) and terrorist groups, new technologies, and global problems such as climate change will all play a role in shaping international politics. US strategy will also need to account for daunting domestic problems, including disastrous levels of inequality, a political system that is more responsive to the needs of the political and economic elite than to the wishes of most of the electorate, and the large minority of voters uncomfortable with the nation's growing diversity.[25]

Broadly speaking, there are two ways that the United States can respond to this complex international and domestic landscape. Trumpism embodies one way forward, which leverages the worst impulses in US political culture – nativism, protectionism and unilateralism. To the extent that Trumpism includes a conscious strategy, it seeks a partial deglobalisation of the current system and a dismantling of the LWO framework. In its place would be a world where states are motivated by realpolitik and where international institutions and democratic norms have little or no role in shaping state behaviour.

Even though this would represent a departure from recent prevailing strategy, it is in many ways an easier option. It draws on long-standing historical impulses and offers seemingly simple answers to an impossibly complex set of challenges. Republicans, in particular, are becoming older, whiter, more rural and less educated, and Trumpism appeals to the anxieties and prejudices of many in this demographic. It is here to stay and is poised to become the dominant tendency in the GOP (and will probably amplify concerns about international engagement on the left). That it will not solve any of the problems facing the United States – indeed, it will exacerbate them – has not affected its political impact.

The other approach to the changing global order is more challenging and will require more imagination from policy makers and the US public. Instead of viewing the rest of the world with fear and cynicism, Americans can recognise what this moment represents – an opportunity to reboot US grand strategy in a way that will keep the nation relatively safe and prosperous. This would not simply represent a continuation of the status quo. Instead, it would blend the best aspects of the LWO – democratic values, international institutions, strong alliances and a multilateral framework for trade liberalisation – with updated policies that reflect the nation's new role in world affairs. This would mean a more intelligent and humble form of leadership: less interventionism, better cooperation with allies, and readiness to work through international institutions and to compromise. Competition with China, Russia and other illiberal challengers will be unavoidable, but the United States should adopt an intelligent approach to these relationships. It should stand firm as often as necessary, but encourage reform where possible and be ready to work together on problems such as climate change, establishing cyber norms and creating a framework for AI governance. At home, this approach would necessitate a stronger social safety net to help those harmed by the vicissitudes of the globalised economy, and a smarter, more compassionate approach to immigration, which welcomes immigrants and refugees but does a better job of integrating them into US society.

Unfortunately, such an approach to grand strategy is unlikely. More probable, given the nature of the US system, is oscillation between Trumpism and the current version of internationalism. The best we can realistically hope for is less of the first option, and more of the second.

Notes

1. 'Here's Donald Trump's Presidential Announcement Speech', *Time*, 16 June 2015, <https://time.com/3923128/donald-trump-announcement-speech>; Ryan Teague Beckwith, 'Read Donald Trump's "America First" Foreign Policy Speech', *Time*, 27 April 2016, <https://time.com/4309786/read-donald-trumps-america-first-foreign-policy-speech>; 'Read Donald Trump's Speech on Trade', *Time*, 28 June 2016, <https://time.com/4386335/donald-trump-trade-speech-transcript> (all accessed 27 January 2020).
2. In brief, grand strategy can be understood as a nation's attempt to coordinate all aspects of its foreign policy – diplomatic, economic and military – in order to achieve short- and long-term objectives. For a more detailed explanation, see Hal Brands, *What Good Is Grand Strategy? Power and Purpose in American Statecraft from Harry S. Truman to George W. Bush* (Ithaca, NY: Cornell University Press, 2014), 3–6.

3. Admittedly an imperfect guide to the way in which US foreign policy operates in practice, US National Security Strategies nevertheless provide a reasonable overview of the overarching thinking and goals of each administration. See the National Security Strategies published 1994–2000, 2002, 2006, 2010 and 2015.
4. Ross Perot also ran for president in the 1990s, garnering 18 per cent of the vote in 1992. His themes were ideologically heterogeneous, but he also expressed scepticism about key aspects of international engagement, including NAFTA and alliances in Europe and east Asia.
5. Jack Thompson, 'Donald Trump's Foreign Policy: McCarthyism as a Cautionary Tale', *Policy Perspectives* 4, no. 10 (2016).
6. '1996 Announcement Speech', Patrick J. Buchanan website, 20 March 1995, <https://buchanan.org/blog/1996-announcement-speech-171>; 'A Crossroads in Our Country's History', speech in Concord, New Hampshire, 10 December 1991, transcript available at <http://www.4president.org/speeches/buchanan1992announcement.htm> (both accessed 27 January 2020).
7. Ralph Nader, announcement speech in Washington, DC, 21 February 2000, transcript available at <http://www.4president.org/speeches/nader2000announcement.htm>; James Dao, 'Nader Fades in Polls but Draws Crowds', *New York Times*. 24 September 2000, <https://www.nytimes.com/2000/09/24/us/the-2000-campaign-the-green-party-nader-fades-in-polls-but-draws-crowds.html>; Ruth Conniff, 'On the Road with Ralph Nader', *The Nation*, 29 June 2000, <https://www.thenation.com/article/road-ralph-nader> (all accessed 27 January 2020).
8. Walter Russell Mead, 'The Return of Geopolitics: The Revenge of the Revisionist Powers', *Foreign Affairs*, May/June 2014, 69–79.
9. Kevin Rudd, 'How Xi Jinping Views the World: The Core Interests That Shape China's Behavior', *Foreign Affairs*, 10 May 2018, <https://www.foreignaffairs.com/articles/china/2018-05-10/how-xi-jinping-views-world>; Robert D. Blackwill and Kurt M. Campbell, *Xi Jinping on the Global Stage: Chinese Foreign Policy under a Powerful but Exposed Leader*, Council on Foreign Relations, February 2016, available at <https://cdn.cfr.org/sites/default/files/pdf/2016/02/CSR74_Blackwill_Campbell_Xi_Jinping.pdf>; Linda Maduz, *Flexibility by Design: The Shanghai Cooperation Organisation and the Future of Eurasian Cooperation*, Center for Security Studies, May 2018, available at <https://css.ethz.ch/content/dam/ethz/special-interest/gess/cis/center-for-securities-studies/

pdfs/Maduz-080618-ShanghaiCooperation.pdf> (all accessed 27 January 2020).
10. Brian G. Carlson, 'Room for Maneuver: China and Russia Strengthen Their Relations', in Oliver Thränert and Martin Zapfe (eds), *Strategic Trends 2018: Key Developments in Global Affairs*, (Zurich: Center for Security Studies, 2018), 29–44.
11. There is a large and growing body of literature on the decline debate. For two of the best contributions on either side, see Stephen G. Brooks, G. John Ikenberry and William C. Wohlforth, 'Don't Come Home, America: The Case against Retrenchment', *International Security* 37, no. 3 (2012/13), 7–51; Christopher Layne, 'The US–Chinese Power Shift and the End of the Pax Americana', *International Affairs* 94, no. 1 (2018), 89–111.
12. Andrea Gilli and Mauro Gilli, 'Why China Has Not Caught Up Yet: Military-Technological Superiority and the Limits of Imitation, Reverse Engineering, and Cyber Espionage', *International Security* 43, no. 3 (2018/19), 141–89.
13. Michael Haas, 'The Eclipse of Western Military-Technological Superiority', in Jack Thompson and Oliver Thränert (eds), *Strategic Trends 2019: Key Developments in Global Affairs* (Zurich: Center for Security Studies, 2019), 27–44.
14. Ryan Hass and Zach Balin, 'US–China Relations in the Age of Artificial Intelligence', Brookings Institution website, 10 January 2019, <https://www.brookings.edu/research/us-china-relations-in-the-age-of-artificial-intelligence> (accessed 27 January 2020); Sophie-Charlotte Fischer, 'Artificial Intelligence: China's High-Tech Ambitions', *CSS Analyses in Security Policy* 220 (2018), <https://css.ethz.ch/en/center/CSS-news/2018/02/artificial-intelligence-chinas-high-tech-ambitions.html> (accessed 27 May 2020).
15. Eric Rosenbach and Katherine Mansted, 'Can Democracy Survive in the Information Age?', Belfer Center for Science and International Affairs, Harvard Kennedy School, October 2018, <https://www.belfercenter.org/publication/can-democracy-survive-information-age> (accessed 27 January 2020).
16. Office of the Under Secretary of Defense for Acquisition and Sustainment, 'Report on Effects of a Changing Climate to the Department of Defense', US Department of Defense, January 2019, available at <https://media.defense.gov/2019/Jan/29/2002084200/-1/-1/1/CLIMATE-CHANGE-REPORT-2019.PDF> (accessed 27 January 2020).

17. David H. Autor, David Dorn and Gordon H. Hanson, 'The China Shock: Learning from Labor Market Adjustment to Large Changes in Trade', National Bureau of Economic Research, January 2016 <https://www.nber.org/papers/w21906>; Richard Wike and Kat Devline, 'As Trade Tensions Rise, Fewer Americans See China Favorably', Pew Research Center, 28 August 2018, <https://www.pewresearch.org/global/2018/08/28/as-trade-tensions-rise-fewer-americans-see-china-favorably> (both accessed 27 January 2020).
18. David Autor, David Dorn, Gordon Hanson and Kaveh Majlesi, 'Importing Political Polarization? The Electoral Consequences of Rising Trade Exposure', National Bureau of Economic Research, December 2017, <https://www.nber.org/papers/w22637>; Christopher Weber, Christopher Federico and Stanley Feldman, 'How Authoritarianism Is Shaping American Politics (and It's Not Just about Trump)', *Washington Post*, 10 May 2017, <https://www.washingtonpost.com/news/monkey-cage/wp/2017/05/10/how-authoritarianism-is-shaping-american-politics-and-its-not-just-about-trump> (both accessed 27 January 2020).
19. Dina Smeltz, Ivo Daalder, Karl Friedhoff and Craig Kafura, 'What Americans Think about America First', Chicago Council on Global Affairs, October 2017, 2, available at <https://www.thechicagocouncil.org/sites/default/files/ccgasurvey2017_what_americans_think_about_america_first.pdf> (accessed 27 January 2020).
20. The administration has dramatically slowed the rate of approval of applications for legal immigration.
21. 'Remarks by Vice President Pence on the Administration's Policy Toward China', White House, 4 October 2018, <https://www.whitehouse.gov/briefings-statements/remarks-vice-president-pence-administrations-policy-toward-china>; 'National Security Strategy of the United States of America', December 2017, <https://www.whitehouse.gov/wp-content/uploads/2017/12/NSS-Final-12-18-2017-0905.pdf> (both accessed 3 February 2020).
22. Ryan Nunn, Jimmy O'Donnell and Jay Shambaugh, 'A Dozen Facts about Immigration', Hamilton Project, October 2018, available at <https://www.hamiltonproject.org/assets/files/ImmigrationFacts_Web_1008_540pm.pdf> (accessed 27 January 2020).
23. Jonathan Eyal, 'The Real Problems with NATO: What Trump Gets Right, and Wrong', *Foreign Affairs*, 2 March 2017, <https://www.foreignaffairs.com/articles/europe/2017-03-02/real-problems-nato>; Jeffrey A. Bader, 'Obama's China and Asia Policy: A Solid Double', Brookings Institution website, 29 August 2016, <https://www.

brookings.edu/blog/order-from-chaos/2016/08/29/obamas-china-and-asia-policy-a-solid-double> (both accessed 27 January 2020).
24. Susan B. Glasser, 'How Trump Made War on Angela Merkel and Europe', *New Yorker*, 24 December 2018, <https://www.newyorker.com/magazine/2018/12/24/how-trump-made-war-on-angela-merkel-and-europe> (accessed 27 January 2020).
25. Martin Gilens and Benjamin I. Page, 'Testing Theories of American Politics: Elites, Interest Groups, and Average Citizens', *Perspectives on Politics* 12, no. 3 (2014), 564–81.

9

From George W. Bush to Donald Trump: Understanding the Exceptional Resilience of Democracy Promotion in US Political Discourse

Eugenio Lilli

Throughout the 2016 US presidential campaign and during his first months in office, Donald Trump made public statements that showed little regard for liberal democratic values and their promotion abroad. More broadly, many of Trump's statements were at odds with the tradition of liberal internationalism in foreign policy. In the context of the United States, liberal internationalism has generally been referred to as Wilsonianism, defined as

> a view that insists that the United States has the right and the duty to change the rest of the world's behavior, and that the United States can and should concern itself not only with the way other countries conduct their international affairs, but with their domestic policies as well.'[1]

More to the point, Wilsonianism is the approach to US foreign policy that attaches the greatest importance to spreading liberal democratic values to other countries.

To begin with, Trump openly questioned the long-standing narrative of US 'innocence' in foreign policy. In brief, this popular national narrative maintains that the United States intervenes on the international stage always in reaction to external events or threats, is constantly committed to just causes, and acts invariably with good intentions and for the noblest purposes.[2] Trump's departure from the narrative of innocence could have hardly been sharper. During a February 2017 interview with *Fox News*, when the host Bill O'Reilly bluntly called Russian president Vladimir Putin 'a killer', Trump interjected and said, 'There are a lot of killers. We have got a lot of killers. What do you think – our country's so innocent?' Trump then continued, 'We made a lot of mistakes [. . .] a lot of people were killed. A lot of killers around, believe me.'[3] In an earlier occasion, candidate Trump had also disputed the international role of the United States as the prime exemplar of a liberal democracy. In a July 2016 interview with the *New York Times*, he stated, 'I think right now when it comes to civil liberties, our country has a lot of problems, and I think it is very hard for us to get involved in other countries when we do not know what we are doing and we cannot see straight in our own country.'[4]

These arguments formed the basis of Trump's rejection of a core idea of Wilsonianism, the right and duty of the United States to concern itself with the domestic policies of foreign countries. In this regard, Trump was particularly consistent. In his first State of the Union address, the US president acknowledged that 'America respects the right of all nations to chart their own path. My job is not to represent the world. My job is to represent the United States of America.'[5] Similarly, during a May 2017 visit to Saudi Arabia, one of the countries with the worst human rights record in the world, Trump declared, 'America will not seek to impose our way of life on others,' and added, 'We are not here to lecture – we are not here to tell other people how to live, what to do, who to be or how to worship. Instead, we are here to offer partnership.'[6] The US president's candid scepticism about his country's right to lecture others went hand in hand with a strong critique of US efforts at democratic nation building abroad, that is, US policies aimed at helping foreign peoples to establish a stable and functioning state ideally featuring liberal democratic norms and institutions.[7] At the July 2016 Republican National Convention, Trump described as 'failed policy' past US attempts at nation building. Moreover, soon after winning the presidential contest, he reaffirmed his opposition to this particular policy: 'We are going to stop trying to build new nations in far-off lands. You have never even heard of these places.'[8] By questioning the moral higher ground of US foreign policy, doubting the role of the United States as a beacon of freedom for other peoples to emulate, and criticising past US attempts to promote liberal democratic values abroad, Trump challenged some of the traditional ideas at the very basis of Wilsonianism.

The full budget proposal for the fiscal year 2018 shed some light on the Trump administration's foreign policy priorities. The proposed major cuts, roughly 30 per cent, affected the funding of the State Department, the United States Agency for International Development (USAID) and the Treasury International Program.[9] That is, the offices of the federal government arguably most involved in policies aimed at advancing liberal democratic values abroad. In what could be interpreted as a symbolic move against the idea of Wilsonianism itself, the budget also proposed to eliminate the activities funded through federal appropriations at the Woodrow Wilson International Center for Scholars.[10]

Unsurprisingly, the Trump administration's un-Wilsonian rhetoric elicited strong reactions. Mainstream publications discussing US politics featured articles expressing their deep alarm for the future of democracy promotion in US foreign policy. Headlines from a small but illustrative sample of these publications include 'Democracy, You're Fired!' (*Huffington Post*), 'Donald Trump: Making the World Safe for Dictators' (*Foreign Policy*), 'Democracy on the Brink' (*Foreign Affairs*), 'Is Trump Ready to Abandon the Democracies?' (*Newsweek*), 'Trump Could Undermine Democracy outside the US' (*Bloomberg*) and 'Down with Democracy' (*New Republic*).[11] Even members of the president's own party expressed unease with the un-Wilsonian aspects of the administration's rhetoric. Randy Hultgren, a Republican representative from Illinois and co-chair of the Tom Lantos Human Rights Commission, made public his concern 'at the muted attention the administration has given so far on human rights'.[12]

There is merit in saying that Trump's ascent to the US presidency was exceptional. His personality, background and ideas surely made him an unorthodox pick for the office of US president. However, as far as the topic of this article is concerned, Trump's behaviour was less exceptional than one would have thought after reading the reactions it elicited. In fact, the history of the United

States shows that democracy promotion in US political discourse has gone through repeated cycles of decline and popularity. This has been especially evident in the twenty-first century, when the elections of President Trump's two immediate predecessors were also followed by announcements of democracy promotion's impending demise. Nevertheless, each time democracy promotion managed to survive, hence demonstrating impressive resilience.

Democracy promotion under Bush and Obama

The election of George W. Bush to the White House in 2000 was also accompanied by claims of a retreat from Wilsonianism in US foreign policy. During the presidential campaign the Bush team conveyed their clear preference for realist power politics over the Wilsonian notion of advancing liberal democracy abroad. Tellingly, candidate Bush maintained that the United States must be 'humble in how we treat nations that are figuring out how to chart their own course'.[13] Bush went on, 'I just do not think it is the role of the United States to walk into a country and say, we do it this way, so should you.'[14] Moreover, he strongly criticised the previous administration's initiatives at building democratic nations abroad. Discussing Operation Restore Hope in Somalia, Bush stated, 'I do not think our troops ought to be used for what is called nation building. I think our troops ought to be used to fight and win war.'[15] Similarly, referring to Operation Uphold Democracy in Haiti: 'I would not have sent troops to Haiti. I did not think it was a mission worthwhile. It was a nation-building mission, and it was not very successful. It cost us billions, a couple billions of dollars, and I am not so sure democracy is any better off in Haiti than it was before.'[16]

Political commentators interpreted these early statements as evidence that the Bush administration was going to backpedal on democracy promotion.[17] Popular publications in the United States began to feature headlines such as 'Bush "Realists" Say Goodbye to Democracy Promotion', 'The Return of Realpolitik?' and 'Dewy-Eyed about Democracy? Hardly'.[18] However, the 9/11 terrorist attacks against the Pentagon and the World Trade Center radically altered this picture. In his response to the attacks, Bush fully embraced the rhetoric of democracy promotion. His second Inaugural Address was especially indicative of this shift:

> The survival of liberty in our land increasingly depends on the success of liberty in other lands. The best hope for peace in our world is the expansion of freedom in all the world ... So it is the policy of the United States to seek and support the growth of democratic movements and institutions in every nation and culture, with the ultimate goal of ending tyranny in our world.[19]

Likewise, the 2002 National Security Strategy document maintained that the United States would 'make freedom and the development of democratic institutions key themes in our bilateral relations' and 'use our foreign aid to promote freedom and support those who struggle non-violently for it, ensuring that nations moving toward democracy are rewarded for the steps they take'.[20] After 9/11, the rhetoric of promoting democracy abroad undoubtedly regained its prominent status in US foreign policy.

A similar dynamic played out during President Barack Obama's first term in office. Soon after the election, political analysts argued that the new administration would herald a break with the US tradition of democracy promotion.[21] Representative headlines included 'Obama's Foreign Policy: Abandon Democracy', 'Obama the Realist' and 'The Abandonment of Democracy'.[22] These analyses were commonly based on four pieces of evidence: first, Obama's willingness to engage diplomatically with the non-democratic governments of Iran, Syria, Russia and China; second, the US's quasi-silent criticism of the Iranian government's crackdown on pro-democracy protests in the summer of 2009; third, Obama's decision not to mention even once the word 'democracy' in his Inaugural Address – the first US president to do so since Ronald Reagan in 1981;[23] fourth, the fact that democracy promotion did not rank high on the list of foreign policy priorities presented by the US president during his renowned Cairo speech. In addition to that, public statements like 'America does not presume to know what is best for everyone'[24] and 'No system of government can or should be imposed upon one nation by any other'[25] further increased the general perception that President

Obama had no intention to make democracy promotion a pillar of his foreign policy.

However, the outbreak of the Arab Awakening unequivocally returned the rhetoric of democracy promotion to the forefront of US foreign policy. After the first popular demonstrations erupted in late 2010, the world witnessed a crescendo of Wilsonianism in the Obama administration's public rhetoric. Addressing the continued upheaval in the Middle East and north Africa in May 2011, President Obama stated:

> Our support for these [Wilsonian] principles is not a secondary interest – today I am making it clear that it is a top priority that must be translated into concrete actions, and supported by all of the diplomatic, economic and strategic tools at our disposal.[26]

A month later, Obama reaffirmed his strong commitment to advancing liberal democratic values abroad:

> We protect our own freedom and prosperity by extending it to others. We stand not for empire, but for self-determination. That is why we have a stake in the democratic aspirations that are now washing across the Arab world. We will support those revolutions with fidelity to our ideals, with the power of our example, and with an unwavering belief that all human beings deserve to live with freedom and dignity.[27]

As had been the case with the George W. Bush administration, after an objectively slow start democracy promotion was restored to its traditional place in US political discourse. The examples of the Bush and Obama administrations shed light onto the instrumental use made by US leaders of the rhetoric of democracy promotion: that is, onto those instances when advancing liberal democratic values is not necessarily a goal in itself but rather a means to a different political end.

First, US presidents regularly resort to the rhetoric of democracy promotion as a mobilisation tool. This analysis shows a clear pattern whereby US presidents faced with a serious international crisis tend to frame their response in distinctly Wilsonian terms.

This is especially true in the case of a response that requires the deployment of US military power. After the 9/11 terrorist attacks, President Bush resorted also to Wilsonianism to legitimise his decisions to go to war in Afghanistan and Iraq. Likewise, in the context of the Arab Awakening, President Obama put forward traditional Wilsonian themes to justify US participation in the 2011 military intervention in Libya. US presidents seem to agree that the argument of championing the spread of liberal democratic values is particularly effective in marshalling public support for US interventions abroad.

Second, this analysis demonstrates that US presidential candidates consistently rely on the rhetoric of democracy promotion as part of their campaign strategy. In particular, they utilise democracy promotion for the double purpose of criticising their predecessor's policies while presenting themselves as bearers of change. In 2000, Bush ostensibly campaigned on an ABC ('Anything but Clinton') platform. Since the enlargement of the community of democracies was a foreign policy priority for President Clinton, Bush's critique of Clinton's interventions to advance democracy in Somalia and Haiti could have been part and parcel of this ABC campaign strategy. Similarly, candidate Obama won the 2008 presidential election on a political platform promising change. Once in office, to live up to his campaign promises, Obama took steps aimed at putting some distance between himself and some of the most controversial policies of his predecessor. This was especially evident regarding championing liberal democracy abroad, a concept that had been highly compromised by President Bush's 2003 invasion of Iraq and other policies related to the wider global war on terror. Alternatively, one could argue that Bush's and Obama's initial toning down of Wilsonian rhetoric was not campaign strategy but rather a reflection of a deeply held scepticism towards democracy promotion. Nevertheless, this alternative interpretation is undermined by the fact that neither president's rejection of democracy promotion was ever total. Noticeably, in November 1999 Bush delivered a speech at the Ronald Reagan Presidential Library laying out his vision for 'A Distinctly American Internationalism'. On that occasion, Bush's words sounded unequivocally Wilsonian:

> Some have tried to pose a choice between American ideals and American interests – between who we are and how we act. But the choice is false. America, by decision and destiny, promotes political freedom – and gains the most when democracy advances ... Our advocacy of human freedom is not a formality of diplomacy, it is a fundamental commitment of our country.[28]

Likewise, early in his tenure, Obama also espoused traditional Wilsonian rhetoric:

> I do have an unyielding belief that all people yearn for certain things: the ability to speak your mind and have a say in how you are governed, confidence in the rule of law and the equal administration of justice, government that is transparent and does not steal from the people, the freedom to live as you choose. These are not just American ideas, they are human rights. And that is why we will support them everywhere.[29]

Statements like these are clearly at odds with the interpretation maintaining that Bush and Obama were inherently opposed to championing liberal democratic values abroad. This evidence suggests that criticism aimed at their predecessors' policies rather than a wholehearted opposition to Wilsonianism as such characterised Bush's and Obama's early views on democracy promotion.

As a third example, US presidents commonly use the rhetoric of democracy promotion as an ideological weapon. There is ample evidence showing that compliance with liberal democratic practices and norms is one of the favourite rhetorical tools employed by US leaders to criticise their international foes. US–Venezuelan relations after the election of President Hugo Chávez and the implementation of his Bolivarian Revolution are a case in point. Referring to Venezuela, Bush stated that 'elected leaders have resorted to shallow populism to dismantle democratic institutions and tighten their grip on power'.[30] Bush's 2006 National Security Strategy document reinforced this view: 'In Venezuela, a demagogue awash in oil money is undermining democracy and seeking to destabilize the region.'[31] Obama sounded very similar chords when he announced his support for 'struggling democrats as they denounce elections that are not free or fair and fight those who seek to undermine the democratic process, so that flawed elections can no longer be used to legitimize rule in places like Venezuela'.[32] Concern for Venezuela's perceived democratic deficit was also expressed in Obama's 2015 National Security Strategy document: 'We stand by the citizens of countries where the full exercise of democracy is at risk, such as Venezuela.'[33]

The political expediency of the rhetoric of democracy promotion in marshalling domestic support, winning votes and criticising foreign enemies makes it a continuing attractive tool to US politicians, even to those who would not identify themselves as Wilsonian. Nevertheless, some US presidents may have used the rhetoric of advancing liberal democracy because they genuinely shared its underlying Wilsonian rationale: the idea that the spread of liberal democratic values results in increased US security and more peaceful international relations. This Wilsonian idea draws upon Immanuel Kant's argument that peace is a natural by-product of cooperation among market democracies,[34] upon the writings of liberal scholars maintaining that democracies possess normative and/or institutional characteristics which make them almost incapable of waging war against each other,[35] and upon a form of neo-Hegelian teleology that identifies liberal democracy as the evolutionary pinnacle of human socio-political development.[36] The influence of this idea on US leaders cannot be completely dismissed, especially given the long-standing and distinguished philosophical tradition advancing it.

The precedents of George W. Bush and Barack Obama suggest that the above dynamics could also play out under a Trump presidency. In other words, the election of Donald Trump could mark the start of yet another cycle of decline and resurgence in the popularity of democracy promotion in US political discourse. During the 2016 presidential campaign, Trump presented himself as the anti-establishment candidate. If Bush campaigned on an ABC platform, Trump took the concept to another level and campaigned on what could be described as an ABW ('Anything but Washington') platform. As part of this ABW campaign strategy, Trump frequently referred to the political establishment in Washington as 'failed and discredited politicians'[37] who had neglected the needs of the American people for too long. He also promised 'to reverse these failures, and create a new American future'.[38] Unsurprisingly, one of Trump's targets of choice was his Democratic opponent, and long-time politician, Hillary Clinton. At one of his campaign rallies, in Miami, Trump said, 'Clinton has been there in Washington for thirty years – her disastrous record speaks for itself.'[39] Specifically attacking Clinton's attempts at democracy promotion during her tenure as Obama's secretary of state, Trump declared, 'We must abandon the failed policy of nation building and regime change that Hillary Clinton pushed in Iraq, Libya, Egypt and Syria.'[40] Once more, a US presidential candidate was instrumentally exploiting Wilsonian themes to distance himself from the 'wrongheaded policies' of his predecessors. The argument that Trump's public demotion of democracy promotion is at least partly instrumental is backed up by those instances when Trump has in fact resorted to Wilsonian themes in his remarks. Again, Venezuela offers a good example. Reacting to popular unrest in the country in late 2016, Trump stated that 'the next president of the United States must stand in solidarity with all people oppressed in our hemisphere, and I will stand with the oppressed people of Venezuela yearning to be free'.[41] President Trump has also sounded very Wilsonian while discussing the future direction of US–Cuban relations: 'We will not lift sanctions on the Cuban regime until all political prisoners are freed, freedoms of assembly and expression are respected, all political parties are legalized, and free and internationally supervised elections are scheduled.'[42] These examples demonstrate that Trump has been willing to espouse the championing of liberal democratic values when he thinks this will serve his broader political agenda. The fact that Trump readily abandoned his un-Wilsonian stance to pursue the uncontroversial goal of criticising two governments hostile to the United States suggests that he would not hesitate to turn himself into a champion of liberal democracy if he had to justify to Congress and the US public a more difficult decision, such as, for example, one concerning the use of US military force. In other words, there is reason to believe that, if faced by a serious international crisis, Trump could follow in the steps of his predecessors and revert to Wilsonian rhetoric to legitimise his response.

Democracy promotion's resilience in US political discourse

Above, I showed *how* US presidents have been instrumentally using the rhetoric of democracy promotion to pursue political goals regardless of their personal adherence to Wilsonianism. In this section, I turn to the explanation of *why* democracy promotion has been an effective rhetorical means to pursue such goals. I argue that the effectiveness of the rhetoric of democracy promotion in helping US leaders to advance their political agenda can explain democracy promotion's enduring presence within US political discourse in the face of repeated announcements of its imminent demise.

First, the rhetoric of democracy promotion has been effective because it conforms with the image that the United States holds of itself and of its role in the world. In other words, liberal democracy represents a deeply cherished and time-honoured feature of US national identity. The identification between the United States and liberal democratic values is as old as the Republic itself. In his first inaugural address on 30 April 1789, President George Washington said, 'The preservation of the sacred fire of liberty, and the destiny of the republican model of government, are justly considered as deeply, perhaps as finally staked, on the experiment entrusted to the hands of the American people.'[43] This identification has continued remarkably unaltered to the present time. A recent USAID strategy document states that the 'promotion of democracy, human rights and governance is a reflection of fundamental American values and identity'.[44] The United States' association with liberal democracy is a legacy of the Age of Enlightenment and draws largely on the influential work of the liberal philosopher John Locke, particularly on his *Two Treatises of Government* (1689). It also finds expression in the American Creed and in the special status that the Creed recognises with respect to liberal democratic values within US society. The relationship between liberal democratic values and US national identity has been long documented.[45] Lincoln Mitchell maintains that 'democracy promotion is, among other things, the foreign policy extension of this identity' and that 'democracy promotion is deeply and unavoidably tied to America's view of itself'.⁴⁶ Similarly, Nicolas Bouchet speaks of the 'identification' of the United States with 'democratic political principles and their spread'.⁴⁷ This identification is especially entrenched in the worldview of the US foreign policy establishment.⁴⁸ Other studies have described the US policy of promoting liberal democratic values abroad in terms of national mission. Samuel Huntington calls the United States 'a missionary nation' driven by the belief that 'the non-Western peoples should commit themselves to the Western values . . . and should embody these values in their institutions'.⁴⁹ Likewise, James Traub writes that 'democracy has always been our [US] national credo, and the ambition to spread it abroad, our missionary impulse'.⁵⁰

The rhetoric of democracy promotion not only conforms with US identity but also reinforces the country's self-image of an exceptional nation. A foreign policy approach framed in Wilsonian terms fits better into the idea of US exceptionalism than one based on realism – arguably Wilsonianism's main competitor among US approaches to foreign policy. According to realism, great powers behave in a similar fashion regardless of their internal characteristics, such as their form of government or their system of values. Consequently, pursuing a realist foreign policy would inevitably make the United States a less exceptional nation. As noted by Frank Ninkovich,

> realpolitik as a statesman's creed [has] never been congenial to a country in which values, in one form or another, [have] always played a central role in foreign policy and in which the amoral pursuit of power as the core necessity of national existence tend[s] to be viewed as an un-American activity.⁵¹

Wilsonianism, on the other hand, holds that domestic features do matter. Thus, a Wilsonian foreign policy stressing the role of promoting democracy (at least at the rhetorical level) strengthens the US self-image of national exceptionalism. As pointed out by David Forsythe, Richard Nixon and Henry Kissinger (two quintessential realist US leaders) 'failed to achieve a domestic consensus in support of a realist foreign policy because in general such a policy failed to draw enough on American exceptionalism'.⁵²

The second reason explaining democracy promotion's enduring resilience is that the endeavour of spreading liberal democratic values abroad is an expression of US national power. Mitchell correctly maintains that 'at its core, democracy promotion is a policy pursued by powerful countries in less powerful countries'.[53] For example, through the National Endowment for Democracy (NED), the United States has repeatedly provided substantial funding to political parties in other countries in order to influence foreign elections. Venezuela is a case in point. There is large evidence showing that the NED in the early 2000s funded Venezuelan opposition groups in their attempts to topple the democratically elected President Chávez.[54] In a harsh critique of the NED, Barbara Conry states that 'through the endowment, the American taxpayer has paid for special-interest groups to harass the duly elected governments of friendly countries, interfere in foreign elections, and foster the corruption of democratic movements'.[55] Regardless of one's opinion, the NED's activities clearly demonstrate the US's willingness and ability to sway democratic elections abroad – even by controversial means. Meanwhile, Americans have proved very sensitive to foreign meddling in their own politics, as evidenced by the huge scandal following allegations of Russian interference in the 2016 US presidential election.

Similarly, every year the US Department of State releases a report that assesses foreign countries' records on human rights. However, as noted by Forsythe, 'no body of foreigners has the moral stature to pass judgement on the American human rights record at home'.[56] The United States can arguably get away with these contradictions while retaining the mantle of the champion of democratisation because of US power. In other words, the United States has the right to perform democracy promotion activities abroad, whereas other countries are generally not allowed to do so on US soil (or at least not in any meaningful way), not because US democracy is flawless but rather because the United States is a very powerful country. These power dynamics closely resemble the classical realist argument put forward by Thucydides, according to which the strong do what they can and the weak suffer what they must.[57] In light of these considerations, promoting democracy looks less like what Michael Mandelbaum referred to as a form of 'social work'[58] and more like what Arthur Link described as a form of 'higher realism'.[59] As long as Americans perceive the United States as a powerful country, the rhetoric of democracy promotion will continue to feature prominently in US politics.

Understanding change

In this article, I have explained the reasons for the enduring presence of democracy promotion within US political discourse. These reasons have mostly to do with the instrumental value of using the rhetoric of democracy promotion to advance distinct political goals. Moreover, I have argued that the rhetoric of democracy promotion remains an effective political tool because it continues to be associated with both US national identity and US national power. In this final section, I turn my attention to the factors that could markedly alter the prominent status of democracy promotion within US politics.

A first factor is the overall health of liberal democracy in the United States. I maintain that the corruption of democracy at home could significantly change the way Americans see themselves. The long-standing identification of US national identity with liberal democratic values could weaken, as could Americans' commitment to their 'special mission' to spread those values abroad. The election of Donald Trump to the US presidency has been followed by numerous expressions of concern for the future of democracy in the United States.[60] Some people have even warned about the imminent risk of the country descending into fascism.[61] However exaggerated these concerns might be, they express real discomfort with the current state of US democracy. Tellingly, in its 2016 Democracy Index (released in January 2017) the Intelligence Unit of *The Economist* demoted the United States from the status of full democracy to that of flawed democracy.[62] Along with substantial domestic challenges, including extreme political polarisation, increasing income inequality and a divided society, US democracy is also challenged from the outside. In recent years, forms of state capitalism in undemocratic countries like China have cast doubts on the US model of free-market liberal democracy as the most successful way to sustain development. In a society that no longer identifies itself with liberal democracy, a rhetoric based on democracy promotion will probably be less effective in advancing US leaders' political agendas and, consequently, be less likely to remain a prominent element of US politics.

A second factor is the relative decline of US national power. A realignment of the international distribution of power capabilities that significantly penalises the United States could affect democracy promotion in at least two ways. First, a less powerful United States would be less able to advance policies of democracy promotion in foreign countries. It is no accident that one of the largest expansions and consolidations of democracy in the world occurred during the first decade after the end of the Cold War, when the United States was at the apex of its power – the so-called US unipolar moment. In contrast, US engagement in democracy promotion was less enthusiastic and effective, for example, during the nineteenth century when the United States was weaker than many other world powers. Second, as Americans' perception of US power changes so does their idea about the importance of spreading liberal democracy abroad. As it is true that ideas somewhat influence the exercise of national power, it is also true that ideas do not develop in complete isolation from material realities. In other words, while ideas help shape material reality (including the use of power), they are themselves shaped by such a reality. In particular, citizens of a less powerful country may start questioning the rationale for an assertive foreign engagement. Therefore, a considerable decline in US national power could have tangible implications for the way Americans will continue to think and talk about democracy promotion.

A last factor is the arrival of a new leadership at the White House. How important is the election of a new president for the future of democracy promotion in US political discourse? As the examples of Bush, Obama and Trump show, the election of a new president generates widespread expectations for change, including in the area of democracy promotion. This is a consequence of what other scholars have described as the 'fairly self-evident fact that American presidents matter a great deal when it comes to determining the country's foreign policy'.[63] However, the same examples also demonstrate that there are limits to a president's ability to bring about significant change in foreign policy. In fact, initial presidential views on promoting democracy abroad can change. Presidents can either end up genuinely espousing Wilsonianism or learn the instrumental benefits of using democracy promotion to pursue their broader political agenda. Moreover, the concept of path dependency in public policy suggests that attempting significant change to cherished assumptions about foreign policy may be costlier for a leader than maintaining things the way they have traditionally been.[64] This is especially true in the case of the US policy of democracy promotion since, as noted by Thomas Carothers, 'over the last few decades, Congress has built a record of strong support for US democracy policies'.[65] In addition to bipartisan backing in US Congress, a number of influential domestic and foreign stakeholders have a vested interest in the continuation of such policies. Lincoln Mitchell describes these groups and individuals as

> well-connected, with strong relationships in Congress and throughout the foreign policy establishment. In addition, the network of scholars and others working in support of democracy promotion have access to opinion pages, influential websites, and other media that can help to shape public opinion.[66]

This is not to say that the election of a new leadership is irrelevant to the future of democracy promotion in US foreign policy. The agency of a new president, in fact, could be an important factor in facilitating change that is already taking place in the structures of the US domestic system of values and/or of the international distribution of power. For instance, President Trump's personal disregard for liberal democratic norms and practices may contribute to the larger and ongoing process of democratic decline in the United States. Although important, however, the election of a new leadership alone is unlikely to drastically alter the status of democracy promotion within US political discourse. US leaders will continue to resort to the rhetoric of democracy promotion for as long as they perceive it to be an effective political tool. Therefore, to experience substantial change, there needs to be a sharp decline in US leaders' belief in the instrumental value of using democracy promotion in US politics. I suggest that such a decline is more likely to occur because of significant shifts in the values associated with US national identity and/or in US relative power than as a result of the election of a new leadership to the White House.

Notes

1. Walter Russell Mead, *Special Providence: American Foreign Policy and How It Changed the World* (New York: Routledge, 2002), 138.
2. Eugenio Lilli, *New Beginning in US–Muslim Relations: President Obama and the Arab Awakening* (New York: Palgrave Macmillan, 2016).
3. 'Donald Trump Super Bowl Interview Transcript with Fox News' Bill O'Reilly,' SBNATION, 5 February 2017, <https://www.sbnation.com/2017/2/5/14516156/donald-trump-interview-transcript-bill-oreilly-super-bowl-2017> (accessed 27 January 2020).
4. 'Transcript: Donald Trump on NATO, Turkey's Coup Attempt and the World', *New York Times*, 22 July 2016, <https://www.nytimes.com/2016/07/22/us/politics/donald-trump-foreign-policy-interview.html> (accessed 27 January 2020).
5. 'Remarks by President Trump in Joint Address to Congress', White House, 28 February 2017, <https://www.whitehouse.gov/briefings-statements/remarks-president-trump-joint-address-congress> (accessed 27 January 2020).
6. 'President Trump's Speech to the Arab Islamic American Summit', White House, 21 May 2017, <https://www.whitehouse.gov/briefings-statements/president-trumps-speech-arab-islamic-american-summit> (accessed Monday, 27 January 2020).
7. Francis Fukuyama, 'Nation-Building 101', *The Atlantic*, January/February 2004, <https://www.theatlantic.com/magazine/archive/2004/01/nation-building-101/302862> (accessed 27 January 2020).
8. Thomas Carothers, 'Prospects for US Democracy Promotion under Trump', Carnegie Endowment for International Peace, 5 January 2017, <https://carnegieendowment.org/2017/01/05/prospects-for-u.s.-democracy-promotion-under-trump-pub-66588> (accessed 27 January 2020).
9. Kim Soffen and Denise Lu, 'What Trump Cut in His Agency Budgets', *Washington Post*, 23 May 2017, <https://www.washingtonpost.com/graphics/politics/trump-presidential-budget-2018-proposal/?utm_term=.83ef5bdfcf66> (accessed 27 January 2020).

10. Gregory Krieg and Will Mullery, 'Trump's Budget by the Numbers: What Gets Cut and Why', CNN, 23 May 2017, <https://edition.cnn.com/2017/05/23/politics/trump-budget-cuts-programs/index.html> (accessed 27 January 2020).
11. Michael Goldfien, 'Democracy, You're Fired!', *Huffington Post*, 4 September 2017, <https://www.huffpost.com/entry/democracy-youre-fired_b_11847022>; James Traub, 'Donald Trump: Making the World Safe for Dictators', *Foreign Policy*, 3 January 2017, <https://foreignpolicy.com/2017/01/03/donald-trump-is-making-the-world-safe-for-dictators>; Suzanne Mettler, 'Democracy on the Brink: Protecting the Republic in Trump's America', *Foreign Affairs*, May/June 2017, <https://www.foreignaffairs.com/reviews/review-essay/2017-04-17/democracy-brink>; Jeffrey Gedmin, 'Is Trump Ready to Abandon the Democracies?', *Newsweek*, 26 November 2016, <https://www.newsweek.com/trump-ready-abandon-democracies-524148>; Francis Wilkinson, 'Trump Could Undermine Democracy outside the US', *Bloomberg*, 3 March 2017, <https://www.bloomberg.com/opinion/articles/2017-03-03/trump-could-undermine-democracy-outside-the-u-s>; Jeet Heer, 'Down with Democracy,' *New Republic*, 14 September 2016, <https://newrepublic.com/article/136784/trump-embrace-putin-return-traditional-conservative-values> (all accessed 27 January 2020).
12. Peter Baker, 'For Trump, a Focus on US Interests and a Disdain for Moralizing', *New York Times*, 4 April 2017, <https://www.nytimes.com/2017/04/04/us/politics/syria-bashar-al-assad-trump.html> (accessed 27 January 2020).
13. 'The 2000 Campaign; 2nd Presidential Debate between Gov. Bush and Vice President Gore', *New York Times*, 12 October 2000, <https://www.nytimes.com/2000/10/12/us/2000-campaign-2nd-presidential-debate-between-gov-bush-vice-president-gore.html>/ (accessed 21 March 2020).
14. Ibid.
15. Ibid.
16. Ibid.
17. Thomas Carothers, 'Promoting Democracy and Fighting Terror', *Foreign Affairs*, January/February 2003, <https://www.foreignaffairs.com/articles/2003-01-01/promoting-democracy-and-fighting-terror> (accessed 27 January 2020); Barbara Ann J. Rieffer and Kristan Mercer, 'US Democracy Promotion: The Clinton and Bush Administrations', *Global Society*, 19, no. 4 (2005), 385–408.

18. Elizabeth Cohn, 'Bush 'Realists' Say Goodbye to Democracy Promotion,' *NACLA*, 25 September 2007, <https://nacla.org/article/bush-realists-say-goodbye-democracy-promotion>; Jim Lobe, 'Politics-US: The Return of Realpolitik?', *IPS North America*, 14 December 2000, <https://www.ipsnews.net/2000/12/politics-us-the-return-of-realpolitik>; Thomas Carothers, 'Dewy-Eyed about Democracy? Hardly', *Washington Post*, 23 January 2000, available at <https://carnegieendowment.org/2000/01/23/dewy-eyed-about-democracy-hardly-pub-429> (all accessed 27 January 2020).
19. 'Inaugural Address by George W. Bush', *New York Times*, 20 January 2005, <https://www.nytimes.com/2005/01/20/politics/inaugural-address-by-george-w-bush.html> (accessed 27 January 2020).
20. 'The National Security Strategy of the United States', White House, September 2002, <https://georgewbush-whitehouse.archives.gov/nsc/nss/2002> (accessed 27 January 2020).
21. Nicolas Bouchet, 'The Democracy Tradition in US Foreign Policy and the Obama Presidency', *International Affairs* 89, no. 1 (2013), 31–51; Tony Smith, 'Democracy Promotion from Wilson to Obama', in Michael Cox, Timothy J. Lynch and Nicolas Bouchet (eds), *US Foreign Policy and Democracy Promotion: From Theodore Roosevelt to Barack Obama* (Abingdon: Routledge, 2013).
22. 'Obama's Foreign Policy: Abandon Democracy', Fox News, 1 September 2009, <https://www.foxnews.com/opinion/obamas-foreign-policy-abandon-democracy>; Ross Douthat, 'Obama the Realist', *New York Times*, 6 February 2011, <https://www.nytimes.com/2011/02/07/opinion/07douthat.html>; Joshua Muravchik, 'The Abandonment of Democracy', *Wall Street Journal*, 29 June 2009, <https://www.wsj.com/articles/SB124631424805570521> (all accessed 27 January 2020).
23. Nicolas Bouchet, 'Barack Obama's Democracy Promotion after One Year', *E-International Relations*, 25 February 2010, <https://www.e-ir.info/2010/02/25/barack-obama's-democracy-promotion-after-one-year> (accessed 27 January 2020).
24. 'Text: Obama's Speech in Cairo', *New York Times*, 4 June 2009, <https://www.nytimes.com/2009/06/04/us/politics/04obama.text.html> (accessed 27 January 2020).
25. Ibid.
26. 'Remarks by the President on the Middle East and North Africa', White House, 19 May 2011, <https://obamawhitehouse.archives.gov/the-press-office/2011/05/19/remarks-president-middle-east-and-north-africa> (accessed 28 January 2020).

27. 'Remarks by the President on the Way Forward in Afghanistan', White House, 22 June 2011, <https://obamawhitehouse.archives.gov/the-press-office/2011/06/22/remarks-president-way-forward-Afghanistan> (accessed 28 January 2020).
28. 'A Distinctly American Internationalism', speech delivered at Ronald Reagan Presidential Library, 19 November 1999, transcript available at <https://www.mtholyoke.edu/acad/intrel/bush/wspeech.htm> (accessed 28 January 2020).
29. 'Text: Obama's Speech in Cairo'.
30. 'Remarks to the Democracy and Security Conference in Prague', *GPO*, 5 June 2007.
31. 'The National Security Strategy', White House, March 2006, <https://georgewbush-whitehouse.archives.gov/nsc/nss/2006> (accessed 28 January 2020).
32. 'A New Partnership for the Americas', 23 May 2008, https://obama.3cdn.net/ef480f743f9286aea9_k0tmvyt7h.pdf (accessed 25 August 2019).
33. 'National Security Strategy', White House, February 2015, <https://obamawhitehouse.archives.gov/sites/default/files/docs/2015_national_security_strategy_2.pdf> (accessed 28 January 2020).
34. Immanuel Kant, *Perpetual Peace: A Philosophical Sketch* (1795).
35. Michael Doyle, *Ways of War and Peace: Realism, Liberalism, and Socialism* (New York: Norton, 1997).
36. Mark J. L. McClelland, 'Exporting Virtue: Neoconservatism, Democracy Promotion and the End of History', *International Journal of Human Rights* 15, no. 4 (2011), 520–31.
37. 'Remarks at a Rally at the James L. Knight Center in Miami, Florida', American Presidency Project, 16 September 2016, <https://www.presidency.ucsb.edu/documents/remarks-rally-the-james-l-knight-center-miami-florida> (accessed 28 January 2020).
38. Ibid.
39. Ibid.
40. 'Address Accepting the Presidential Nomination at the Republican National Convention in Cleveland, Ohio', American Presidency Project, 21 July 2016, <https://www.presidency.ucsb.edu/documents/address-accepting-the-presidential-nomination-the-republican-national-convention-cleveland> (accessed 28 January 2020).
41. 'Remarks at a Rally at the James L. Knight Center'.
42. 'Remarks by President Trump on the Policy of the United States towards Cuba', White House, 16 June 2017, <https://www.whitehouse.gov/briefings-statements/remarks-president-trump-policy-united-states-towards-cuba> (accessed 28 January 2020).

43. 'Washington's Inaugural Address of 1789', National Archives and Records Administration, <https://www.archives.gov/exhibits/american_originals/inaugtxt.html> (accessed 28 January 2020).
44. 'USAID Strategy on Democracy, Human Rights and Governance', USAID, June 2013, 4, available at < https://www.usaid.gov/sites/default/files/documents/1866/USAID-DRG_fina-_6-24-31.pdf> (accessed 28 January 2020).
45. Louis Hartz, *The Liberal Tradition in America: An Interpretation of American Political Thought since the Revolution* (New York: Harcourt, Brace & World, 1955).
46. Lincoln A. Mitchell, *The Democracy Promotion Paradox* (Washington, DC: Brookings Institution Press, 2016), 106, 131.
47. Bouchet, 'The Democracy Tradition in US Foreign Policy and the Obama Presidency', 35.
48. Stephen M. Walt, 'The Broken Policy Promises of W. Bush, Clinton, and Obama', *Foreign Policy*, 18 September 2016, <https://foreignpolicy.com/2016/09/18/broken-foreign-policy-promises-bush-clinton-obama-iraq-syria> (accessed 28 January 2020).
49. Samuel P. Huntington, *The Clash of Civilizations and the Remaking of World Order* (New York: Simon & Schuster, 1996), 184.
50. James Traub, 'The Freedom Agenda', *New York Times*, 11 October 2008, <http://www.nytimes.com/2008/10/11/books/chapters/chap-freedom-agenda.html> (accessed 28 January 2020).
51. Frank Ninkovich, *The Wilsonian Century: US Foreign Policy since 1900* (Chicago: Chicago University Press, 1999), 234.
52. David Forsythe, 'US Foreign Policy and Human Rights', *Journal of Human Rights* 1, no. 4 (2002), 517.
53. Mitchell, *The Democracy Promotion Paradox*, 154.
54. Rieffer and Mercer, 'US Democracy Promotion'.
55. Barbara Conry, 'Loose Cannon: The National Endowment for Democracy', Cato Institute, 8 November 1993, <https://www.cato.org/publications/foreign-policy-briefing/loose-cannon-national-endowment-democracy> (accessed 28 January 2020).
56. Forsythe, 'US Foreign Policy and Human Rights', 503.
57. Thucydides, 'The Melian Dialogue', in *History of the Peloponnesian War*, Book 5 (422–415 BC), 84–16, <http://www.perseus.tufts.edu/hopper/text?doc=Perseus%3Atext%3A1999.01.0200%3Abook%3D5%3Achapter%3D89%3Asection%3D1> (accessed 21 March 2020).
58. Michael Mandelbaum, 'Foreign Policy as Social Work', *Foreign Affairs*, January/February 1996, 18.

59. Arthur Link, 'The Higher Realism of Woodrow Wilson', *Journal of Presbyterian History* 76, no. 2 (1998), 153.
60. Mettler, 'Democracy on the Brink'; Robert Mickey, Steven Levitsky and Lucan Ahmad Way, 'Is America Still Safe for Democracy? Why the United States Is in Danger of Backsliding', *Foreign Affairs*, May/June 2017, 20–9.
61. Robert Kagan, 'This Is How Fascism Comes to America', *Washington Post*, 18 May 2016, <https://www.washingtonpost.com/opinions/this-is-how-fascism-comes-to-america/2016/05/17/c4e32c58-1c47-11e6-8c7b-6931e66333e7_story.html> (accessed 28 January 2020).
62. 'The Economist Intelligence Unit's Democracy Index', <https://infographics.economist.com/2017/DemocracyIndex> (accessed 28 January 2020).
63. Michael Cox, Timothy J. Lynch and Nicolas Bouchet, 'Introduction: Presidents, American Democracy Promotion and World Order', in Cox et al. (eds), *US Foreign Policy and Democracy Promotion*, 4.
64. David A. Welch, *Painful Choices: A Theory of Foreign Policy Change* (Princeton: Princeton University Press, 2005).
65. Thomas Carothers, 'Democracy Promotion under Trump: What Has Been Lost? What Remains?', Carnegie Endowment for International Peace, 6 September 2017, <https://carnegieendowment.org/2017/09/06/democracy-promotion-under-trump-what-has-been-lost-what-remains-pub-73021> (accessed 28 January 2020).
66. Mitchell, *The Democracy Promotion Paradox*, 150.

Part Three

Identity Politics and the Politics of Spectacle

10

'If You Want to Know Why 2016 Happened, Read This Book': Class, Race and the Literature of Disinvestment (the Case of *Hillbilly Elegy*)

Hamilton Carroll

In the aftermath of Donald J. Trump's election to the presidency of the United States of America in November 2016, publishers were keen to provide the reading public with the means to understand Trump's elevation and the social, cultural, political and economic reasons for it. While a handful of hastily published books such as Jonathan Allen and Amie Parnes's *Shattered: Inside Hillary Clinton's Doomed Campaign*[1] and Susan Bordo's *The Destruction of Hillary Clinton*[2] set out the putatively self-inflicted reasons for Hillary Clinton's failure to secure the presidency in what most commentators had previously imagined was the most likely outcome of the election, the dominant trend was a turn to the right – and to the travails of the white working classes in particular – as the major topic of sociological and journalistic analysis. Alongside a veritable avalanche of newspaper and magazine accounts, book-length works of non-fiction such as J. D. Vance's *Hillbilly Elegy: A Memoir of a Family and Culture in Crisis*,[3] Tara Westover's *Educated: A Memoir*[4] and Monica Hesse's *American Fire: Love, Arson, and Life in a Vanishing Land*[5] were all cited as offering deep insight into the transformations of American social, political, cultural and economic life that propelled Trump to the presidency.

Of all of these books, none was more widely read and praised than *Hillbilly Elegy*. Writing for the *New York Times*, Jennifer

Senior referred to it as 'a compassionate, discerning sociological analysis of the white underclass that has helped drive the politics of rebellion, particularly the ascent of Donald J. Trump'. 'Essential reading for this moment in history,' she concluded.[6] On an episode of the *Times*' pre-election podcast series *The Run-Up* entitled 'Understanding the Trump Voter', Vance's memoir was called 'a cultural anthropology of the white underclass that has flocked to the Republican presidential nominee's candidacy'.[7] Further, after the election the memoir was high on two separate lists published in the paper of books that could help bemused liberals understand Trump's victory.[8] On the other side of the Atlantic, Sarah Baxter claimed in her review for the *Sunday Times* that Vance's memoir was the 'political book of the year'[9] and, in a somewhat implausible claim quoted on the cover of the UK hardback edition of the book, Ian Birrell wrote for the *i* that it was 'a great insight into Trump and Brexit'.[10] The book was also an astounding commercial success: it was ranked twice at number one on the *New York Times* bestseller list (in August 2016 and January 2017), and spent a full year after its initial publication in hardback in the Amazon.com top-ten bestseller list. Moreover, while Vance already was a frequent and long-time contributor to conservative organs such as the *National Review*, after the election he also became a regular contributor to left-leaning media outlets. In the year following the publication of *Hillbilly Elegy*, for example, he wrote opinion pieces for the *New York Times* with titles such as 'Barack Obama and Me', 'The Bad Faith of the White Working Class' and 'Why I'm Moving Home', and, for *The Guardian*, 'How Donald Trump Seduced America's White Working Class'.[11] So high were the book and its author in the cultural firmament of post-election America that the film rights were bought by Ron Howard, who in partnership with Netflix is producing and directing the cinematic adaptation. Suffice it to say that *Hillbilly Elegy* was nothing short of a critical and commercial juggernaut, Vance was ordained with the authority to explain to America (and to the rest of the English-speaking world) why Trump happened, and he quickly became the liberal media's native informant *du jour*.[12]

In this chapter, I examine Vance's memoir in relation to the perceived transformations in American social, political and cultural life that subtended the election of Donald J. Trump, and that have most typically been explained through the lens of white working-class disinvestment. Given the book's extraordinary critical and commercial success (and particularly its uptake by the left as a window into the world of the right), I ask why its particular representations of working-class disaffection – and in particular its representations of the white, rural poor – have resonated so powerfully with readers and critics alike. I ask not only what those representations have to tell us about Trump's election but also what their reception says about the fault lines of class and race in contemporary America that still dominate so much of the country's understanding of citizenship and identity. In particular, I chart these representations in Vance's memoir through the intersectional identity categories of whiteness and masculinity. I argue that *Hillbilly Elegy* offers little new but, instead, conforms to long-standing beliefs not only about the rural poor but also about the 'common sense' understanding of the United States as a meritocratic society in which inherited categories of class, race and gender should not and do not hold back the hard-working and the ambitious. As such, the focused analysis of *Hillbilly Elegy* that I provide in these pages serves as evidence for a broader set of social, cultural and political conditions; it is one example that helps to explain the whole. *Hillbilly Elegy*, I argue, rejects and mobilises in equal measure powerful dynamics of race and gender that have returned to the fore in the renewed era of identity politics that Trump rode to the presidency. Without a proper understanding of how those dynamics work, it is all but impossible to fully account for the current political moment in the United States.

'I may be white, but . . .': class as a racial identity

Hillbilly Elegy is a non-fiction *Bildungsroman* in which the narrator describes his life as a teleological progression towards normality. In the opening pages of the book, Vance claims that he has 'accomplished nothing great in [his] life' (he's thirty-one at the time of writing) and that he wrote the book because, even though he has only achieved 'something quite ordinary', it is something that rarely happens to 'most kids who grow up like me'.[13] Leaving aside the fact that as a graduate of Yale Law School (which has an annual graduating class of about 200 people) he has achieved something that rarely happens to anyone, regardless of their socio-economic background, 'ordinary' is something that Vance claims he has had to become. As such, the memoir describes its author's ascent to this cultural position, which he claims he has had to earn by overcoming the pitfalls of his 'hillbilly' roots. This is not a straightforward story, however, for Vance refers to himself at different times in the memoir both as a 'tall, white, straight male [who has] never felt out of place in [his] entire life' and – in a complete negation of that normality – as part of a 'persecuted minority'.[14] *Hillbilly Elegy* is above all else, then, a book about becoming white; or, more specifically, about attaining the privileges typically invested in whiteness that its author believes kids like him have lost, if they ever had them in the first place. As an elegy for privilege lost (or never held but always believed to be just around the corner), Vance's memoir is a revanchist text that seeks to reclaim the investments of whiteness by recasting it as a minority identity.[15]

Race appears almost immediately in Vance's memoir. 'There is an ethnic component lurking in the background of my story,' he states on the second page, going on to explain that

> in our race-conscious society, our vocabulary often extends no further than the color of someone's skin – 'black people', 'Asians', 'white privilege'. Sometimes these broad categories are useful, but to understand my story, you have to delve into the details. I may be white, but I don't identify with the WASPs of the Northeast. Instead, I identify with the millions of working-class white Americans of Scots-Irish descent who have no college degree. To these folks, poverty is a family tradition – their ancestors were day laborers in the Southern slave economy, sharecroppers after that, coal miners after that, and machinists and millworkers during more recent times. Americans call them hillbillies, rednecks, or white trash. I call them neighbours, friends, and family.[16]

There is a powerful repudiation at work in this passage, one that is routed through an equally powerful investment in the disaggregation of whiteness from privilege through the mobilisation of both class and subaltern forms of white ethnicity. Whiteness here is cast in terms of historical class formations, running alongside the racial logic of plantation slavery and Jim Crow, of religion and region, and of educational attainment. The whiteness Vance describes here is divorced from privilege and transformed into a race-based form of prejudiced identity.

Some thirty pages later, Vance turns again to the problematic racialisation of working-class whites. Quoting from a historical study on the mass migration of poor whites from the South to the Midwest that his own grandparents were a part of, Vance states, 'These migrants disrupted a broad set of assumptions held by northern whites about how white people appeared, spoke, and behaved . . . the disturbing aspect of *hillbillies* was their racialness.'[17] As such, Vance's grandparents and their fellow migrants had to deal not only with the fact of being uprooted from familiar kinship structures but also with the harsh realities of being relegated to a lower rung on the ladder of American racial identities. Yet the narrative Vance provides is one of uplift and of a slow and turbulent but ultimately successful transition into mainstream whiteness, of which he himself is the apotheosis. It is a teleological narrative that relies heavily on a belief in the United States as a meritocratic society untroubled by the sorts of race- and class-based disenfranchisement that Vance himself has claimed his immediate ancestors were victims of.

While white working-class marginality is in no way unique or without historical precedent – and in fact is the continuation of a centuries-old problem of the racialisation of poor whites in the United States – its contemporary structures are inseparable from current transformations in national politics. In *Strangers in Their Own Land*, Arlie Russell Hochschild identifies a profound distrust of the federal government on the part of lower-middle- and working-class whites that she observes is typically routed through one or more of three main hot-button issues: religious faith, taxes and a perceived loss of honour.[18] It is precisely these issues that spawned the Tea Party movement in 2009 and produced a profound national swing to the right of centre. Even if it is often cast in terms of economic dissatisfaction, this swing is nevertheless intertwined with a narrative of national decline in which 'typical American values' are understood to have been eroded. As Theda Skocpol and Vanessa Williamson point out in *The Tea Party and the Remaking of Republican Conservatism*, the 'authentic patriotism' of the Tea Party's dominant symbolism had 'visceral meaning to people who [felt] that the United States as they [knew] it was slipping away'.[19] Furthermore, according to Hochschild, the gulf between the right and the left has widened markedly in recent years. In 1960, she claims, only 5 per cent of respondents to a national survey said that a child marrying a member of the other party would disturb them. In 2010 the same question yielded responses of 'yes' from 33 per cent of Democrats and 40 per cent of Republicans.[20] At the same time (and as these statistics suggest), this widening of the gulf between the left and the right has come about not because the left has moved left but because the right has moved much further right. So much so, in fact, that previously mainstream Republican policy platforms are now viewed with suspicion by many in the party.[21] This increased partyism, Hochschild claims, now is a more divisive source of prejudice than race.[22] Moreover, as Hochschild points out, this trend to the right has a strong racial component, with whites making up a declining majority of registered Democrats but an increasing majority of Republicans.[23]

That stable forms of long-term, full-time employment with wages high enough to support a family are harder to come by than ever before is undeniable. Robert Reich makes the point in *Saving Capitalism: For the Many, Not the Few* that

> fifty years ago, when General Motors was the largest employer in America, the typical GM worker earned $35 an hour in today's dollars. By 2014, America's largest employer was Walmart, and the typical entry-level Walmart worker earned about $9 an hour . . . In the 1950s, a third of all private-sector workers in America belonged to a union; now, fewer than 7 percent do.'[24]

Such a radical shift in the employment landscape of the country has profound effects not only on lived experience but also on perceived injustice. For, while the economy was a motivating factor for many who turned to Trump as either a figure of salvation or a protest against the status quo, a profound sense of cultural dissatisfaction was also a significant motivating factor for many. As Yuval Levin claims in *The Fractured Republic: Renewing America's Social Contract in the Age of Individualism*:

> Especially important for Trump and his voters, was a melancholy sense of what had been lost on other fronts, too: social, cultural, and moral. His support reflected a profound dissatisfaction with how modern life had turned out for many in our country.[25]

This 'profound dissatisfaction' was often targeted at minorities, immigrants and other groups that have come to stand as symbols of the disenfranchisement of white Americans. Many working-class whites believe, as Hochschild puts it, that 'the federal government was taking money from the workers and giving it to the idle. It was taking from people of good character and giving to people of bad character.'[26] Because of the racial identities of those perceived to be on the receiving end of this equation, race is cast in moral terms. It is this turn towards an identitarian logic of class- and race-based white disenfranchisement into which Vance's memoir was released, and which accounts for much of its appeal. As an elegy, Vance's memoir is a lament for the putatively lost security of white privilege produced through the mobilisation of the hillbilly as a figure of cultural nostalgia. But the memoir is equally reliant on an understanding of middle-class stability.

As such, Vance does much to establish his status as a member of the white middle class. For example, in spite of the historical racialisation Vance describes, his uncle Jimmy tells him that the transplanted family led a 'typically middle-class life' and that 'we were just a happy, normal middle-class family. I remember watching *Leave It to Beaver* on TV and thinking that looked like us.'[27] While there are numerous examples given in the book of the absolute failure of Vance's grandparents (and particularly of his mother) to live up to the expectations of white middle-class life, it is also the case that of seven maternal aunts and uncles, three 'owned ... successful business[es] and earned considerable wealth in the process'.[28] Vance reads these stories of success against the struggles of those uncles and aunts who stayed in Kentucky but he also admits that all but one of those who chose to stay behind nevertheless 'managed a life of relative comfort by the standards of their community'.[29] Of his own maternal grandfather he states, 'Papaw had retired only a few years earlier, owned stock in Armco, and had a lucrative pension.'[30] Of the eight siblings in his grandparents' generation, three achieved 'considerable wealth,' four lived in 'relative comfort' and only one failed by the standards Vance himself sets for prosperity. The members of Vance's own family must be seen, then, not only as hillbillies but also as examples of the relative socio-economic mobility available to many whites.

By his own account, Vance was a member of a solidly middle-class family largely removed from the travails of marginalised identity that his memoir claims to eulogise. As an identity formation, hillbilly recasts whiteness as a minoritised identity that denies white racial investment and masks Vance's own cashing in of that investment. In Vance's memoir, moreover, the term 'hillbilly' names a nostalgic cultural formation.[31] Not only does Vance provide ample evidence of his family's overall stability and security, but a significant portion of the evidence he gives for the failure of his family to assimilate in the North because of their hillbilly roots stems from family lore and stories told about a time long before he was born. Unsullied by either structural impediments or racial investments, Vance is able to promulgate a strong belief in the meritocratic character of the United States that resonates across the political spectrum and crosses class lines – in large part by claiming that they don't exist. As T. R. C. Hutton puts it, '*Hillbilly Elegy* staunchly defends the up-by-your-own-bootstraps fairy tale that capitalism has always used to win support from the underclass.'[32] Vance uses the nostalgic formation of the hillbilly to make claims for his own racialised identity in order to disown the privileges of whiteness that were afforded to him by his own middle-class upbringing.

'A peculiar crisis of masculinity': mainstream marginality

More often than not – and perhaps unsurprisingly – the sense of dissatisfaction at the socio-political-cultural status quo evidenced by Trump's elevation has produced a renewed investment in the reclamation of obsolete forms of masculine identification. As one of Hochschild's subjects proclaims, 'These days, American men are an endangered species too.'[33] There is, of course, a degree of truth to this lament. Vance, likewise, points to the increasing mortality rates in working-class communities, saying, 'A recent study found that unique among all ethnic groups in the United States, the life expectancy of working-class white folks is going down.'[34] As Justin Gest points out, 'Whether white people's working class status is defined according to education-, occupation-, or income-based standards, a 30% to 50% decline in the relative size of this group from the World War II era to today in the United States has transpired.'[35] 'Recent research suggests', he continues, 'that these trends may be intensified by an extraordinary 22% rise in the mortality rate of white working class people since 1999 – which has taken place in an era during which the death rates among all other groups decline.'[36] Moreover, as mortality rates among working-class whites have risen more sharply than those of any other group, they have risen higher still for men. In America today, as Hochschild tells us, older white men have statistically higher death rates from drugs, alcohol and suicide than any other demographic.[37] However, while there are a myriad of structural and historical reasons for this transformation, Vance positions the reduced opportunities available to white men such as himself as a question of choice. Of the current plight of men in his community, Vance states:

> Many of us have dropped out of the labor force or have chosen not to relocate for better opportunities. Our men suffer from a peculiar crisis of masculinity in which some of the very traits that our culture inculcates make it difficult to succeed in a changing world.[38]

For Vance, this 'peculiar crisis' is a symptom of a deeper socio-cultural malaise that manifests itself most clearly in what he sees as a generational shift in values and expectations. 'Not all of the white working-class struggles,' he admits. 'I knew even as a child that there were two separate sets of mores and social pressures. My grandparents embodied one type: old-fashioned, quietly faithful, self-reliant, hardworking. My mother and, increasingly, the entire neighborhood embodied another: consumerist, isolated, angry, distrustful.'[39] What his community has lost, Vance explains here, is the opportunity to dream. No longer able to rely on the traditional tenets of hard work and self-reliance, or on a teleology of national prosperity, the community has lost its faith in the viability of what Vance unsurprisingly refers to as a putative birth right: the American Dream. What his neighbours have lost faith in is the United States as a meritocracy.

Later in the memoir, Vance turns again to the topic of a generational socio-cultural decay. Returning home from college the summer before starting law school, he observes a radical difference between his own outlook and that of many around him. As he puts it, 'The incredible optimism I felt about my own life contrasted starkly with the pessimism of so many of my neighbors.'[40] While Vance again offers the familiar narrative about how 'years of decline in the blue-collar economy manifested themselves in the material prospects of Middletown's residents', he also paints a broader picture of disinvestment born of a deeper sense of cultural malaise.[41] 'As a culture,' he claims, 'we have no heroes.'[42] Barack Obama, George W. Bush and Bill Clinton are all despised or distrusted figures, he states, while Ronald Reagan is 'long dead'.[43] This 'cultural detachment', to use Vance's phrasing, is linked to a profound sense of loss in which the belief in America as 'the best and greatest country on earth' is radically divorced from everyday lived experience and, therefore, no longer produces a common patriotism born of perceived opportunity.[44] As he explains:

> We loved the military but had no George S. Patton figure in the modern army. I doubt my neighbors could even name a high-ranking military officer. The space program, long a source of pride, had gone the way of the dodo, and with it the celebrity astronauts. Nothing united us with the core fabric of American society. We felt trapped in two seemingly unwinnable wars, in which a disproportionate share of the fighters came from our neighborhood, and in an economy that failed to deliver the most basic promise of the American Dream – a steady wage.[45]

Citing the profound distrust of the mainstream media that accompanies this disunity, Vance states, 'This is deep scepticism of the very institutions of our society. And it's becoming more and more mainstream.'[46]

It should come as no surprise that the pantheon of fallen and inadequate heroes Vance provides are all men and all white, for while the malaise he diagnoses affects women's ability to serve as wives and mothers, it is perceived primarily here as an impediment to masculine self-fulfilment, and the transformations of white male opportunity and experience in the contemporary United States are a core subject of Vance's memoir. However, he again rejects the dominant understanding of this phenomenon, in which (to quote his formulation of it), 'as the manufacturing center of the industrial Midwest has hollowed out, the white working class has lost both its economic security and the stable home life that comes with it'.[47] For Vance, this narrative of economic insecurity tells only part of the story. As evidence he describes a year of summer work he undertook between graduating from Ohio State and moving to New Haven to begin law school. Needing money to finance his move, he took a job working at a floor tile distribution business run by a family friend. A small business with a largely reliable and long-term workforce, the business provided relatively high wages for unskilled labour, good health insurance and stable employment. Despite this, Vance claims, the managers found it difficult to find employees to permanently fill the warehouse positions such as the one he himself had taken up on a temporary basis. One fellow employee, whom Vance calls Bob, serves for the author as a representative example of all that is wrong with white working-class men today: he routinely skipped work, took frequent and excessively long bathroom breaks and, when he was fired, complained, 'How could you do this to me? Don't you know I've got a pregnant girlfriend?'[48] Adding grist to Vance's mill, during the same period Bob's pregnant girlfriend was also hired by the company but was soon let go because of her own persistent absenteeism and unreliability. It is not that there isn't work available, Vance believes, but that people are unwilling to do it. As Lisa R. Pruitt observes, 'Vance acknowledges the tough knocks people like his grandparents took in relation to globalisation, but he generally downplays ... the structural factors that led to the decline of the Rust Belt and the diminution of worker wages and protections.'[49]

The idleness of men is a particular problem for Vance, whose social conservatism expects different roles of men and women. In a later chapter of the book in which he charts the rapid decline of his hometown following the collapse of the steel industry, he states:

> People talk about hard work all the time in places like Middletown. You can walk through a town where 30 per cent of the young men work fewer than twenty hours a week and find not a single person aware of his own laziness.[50]

Vance uses these examples to advance the following argument:

> You can't ignore stories like this when you talk about equal opportunity. Nobel-winning economists worry about the decline of the industrial Midwest and the hollowing out of the economic core of working whites. What they mean is that manufacturing jobs have gone overseas and middle-class jobs are harder to come by for people without college degrees. Fair enough – I worry about those things, too. But this book is about something else: what goes on in the lives of real people when the industrial economy goes south. It's about reacting to bad circumstances in the worst way possible. It's about a culture that increasingly encourages social decay instead of countering it.
>
> The problems that I saw at the tile warehouse run far deeper than macroeconomic trends and policy. Too many young men immune to hard work. Good jobs impossible to fill for any length of time. And a young man with every reason to work – a wife-to-be to support and a baby on the way – carelessly tossing aside a good job with excellent health insurance. More troubling, when it was all over, he thought something had been done *to him*. There is a lack of agency here – a feeling that you have little control over your life and a willingness to blame everyone but yourself. This is distinct from the larger economic landscape of modern America.[51]

This is not, he goes on to insist, a story about race. 'I'm not arguing that we deserve more sympathy than other folks. This is not a story about why white people deserve more sympathy than other folks,' he states, concluding, 'I have known many welfare queens; some were my neighbors and all were white.'[52]

'IF YOU WANT TO KNOW WHY 2016 HAPPENED, READ THIS BOOK'

Nancy Isenberg cites a profound dissatisfaction on the part of the white working poor with those believed to be lazy, idle or gaming the system. As she states in the preface to the paperback edition of *White Trash: The 400-Year Untold Story of Class in America* (published in early 2017):

> Trump perceived a world of winners and losers, and many of his supporters want to reinforce the old stigmas that separated the productive worker from the idle. They wanted the boundaries between the unemployed and employed to be firmly enforced, not weakened. 'Make America Great Again' is another way of saying that hard work is no longer automatically rewarded as a virtue. It tapped into the anxieties of all who resented government for handing over the country to supposedly less deserving classes: new immigrants, protesting African Americans, lazy welfare freeloaders, and Obamacare recipients asking for handouts.[53]

Likewise, as Justin Gest points out, 'white working class people sense that they have been demoted from the center of their country's consciousness to its fringe. And many feel powerless in their attempts to do anything about it . . . Many white working class people', he suggests, 'feel like the victims of discrimination.'[54]

At another point in the memoir, Vance describes the sense of class-based resentment he developed working part time as a cashier at a local grocery store during his final years of high school. The experience, he states, 'turned [him] into an amateur sociologist'.[55] What Vance's 'amateur sociology' taught him was a deep distrust in government assistance or welfare programmes. As he describes it:

> As my job taught me a little more about America's class divide, it also imbued me with a bit of resentment, directed toward both the wealthy and my own kind. The owners of Dillman's were old-fashioned, so they allowed people with good credit to run up grocery tabs, some of which surpassed a thousand dollars. I knew that if any of my relatives walked in and ran up a bill of over a thousand dollars, they'd be asked to pay immediately. I hated the feeling that my boss counted my people as less trustworthy than those who took their groceries home in a Cadillac. But I got over it: One day, I told myself, I'd have my own damned tab.

> I also learned how my own people gamed the welfare system. They'd buy two dozen-packs of soda with food stamps and then sell them at a discount for cash. They'd ring up their orders separately, buying food with food stamps, and beer, wine, and cigarettes with cash. They'd regularly go through the checkout line speaking on their cellphones. I could never understand why our lives felt like a struggle while those living off of government largesse enjoyed trinkets that I only dreamed about.[56]

In his descriptions of the moral failings of poor whites who game the welfare system, Vance shares a great deal with *National Review* reporter Kevin D. Williamson, who in the essay 'The White Ghetto' makes similar claims about the inability of poor whites to get out from under because they have it too good, and about the region as an undifferentiated location of moral failure. 'Welfare', Williamson alleges, 'has made Appalachia into a big and sparsely populated housing project – too backward to thrive, but just comfortable enough to keep the underclass in place', or, as it is put in the strap line of Williamson's article, 'in Appalachia the country is beautiful and the society is broken'.[57] Because it marks a liminal identity – white but racialised both as something less and (in Vance's telling at least) as something more – the term 'hillbilly' carries with it a moral indictment. As such, Vance's understanding of the failings of his fellow hillbillies as the self-imposed consequence of bad choices offers little useful analysis but conforms to long-standing beliefs about white identity. The 'moral unworthiness of poor whites' has deep roots in American culture, as Matt Wray asserts, and it is these that Vance calls upon as he celebrates and defends his own family's cultural history while negating the lived experiences of his former neighbours, whom he holds responsible for their failure to overcome their own dire circumstances.[58] In the words of John Hartigan Jr, the racialisation of poor whites 'involves a reaction to bodily conditions and behaviors that offend certain class decorums'.[59] As a newly confirmed member of the meritocracy, Vance frequently finds himself offended by the reactions of others to circumstances that he cannot see in anything but moral and absolute terms.

For Vance, as for others, the rightward turn of the working classes can be explained by their proximity to this perceived rot at the heart of the welfare system. Following his description of welfare recipients gaming the system at Dillman's, Vance goes on to explain how 'Appalachia and the South went from staunchly Democratic to staunchly Republican in less than a generation', and places the blame for this shift squarely on the shoulders of feckless welfare recipients.[60] The explanation lies, he states, 'in the fact that many in the white working class saw precisely what I did, working at Dillman's'.[61] This is a resentment born of proximity: 'despite our efforts to draw bright lines between the working and nonworking poor, Mamaw and I recognised that we shared a lot in common with those whom we thought gave our people a bad name'.[62] And the research bears him out on this point: those most resentful of government assistance programmes are those who stand most precariously close to needing them; and, as Alec MacGillis has shown, those who benefit directly from them are disproportionately unlikely to vote. 'In eastern Kentucky and other former Democratic bastions that have swung Republican in the past several decades,' MacGillis points out, 'the people who most rely on the safety-net programs secured by Democrats are, by and large, not voting against their own interests by electing Republicans. Rather, they are not voting, period. They have ... become profoundly disconnected from the political process.'[63] Correspondingly, as Isenberg puts it in *White Trash*,

> angry Trump voters were convinced that these classes (the 'takers') were not playing by the rules (i.e., working their way up the ladder) and that government entitlement programs were allowing some to advance past more deserving (white, native-born) Americans. This was how many came to feel 'disinherited'.[64]

Understood in this way, Vance's condemnation of his fellow shoppers can be seen as part of a long-standing tradition of the condemnation of the rural white poor that serves, in part, to police the boundaries of identity. Proximity breeds contempt and the structural reasons for the underemployment and reliance on welfare that he sees can be denied by a turn to morality mobilised in the name of meritocracy.

Conclusion

Deeply conservative both in its appraisals of the current plight of the white working classes and in its prescriptions, Vance's memoir nevertheless produces a powerful account of the current trials and tribulations of this broad socio-economic group that is often understood to be – and, crucially, sees itself as – America's newest minority. *Hillbilly Elegy* mourns a culture that it believes to have been lost and prescribes a typically American route to emancipation that nevertheless is thoroughly underpinned by the ideological tenets of neoliberalism: a commitment to the shrinking of the state and federal welfare programmes, a belief in the self-regulatory capacities of both corporations and individuals, and a demonisation of the feckless poor (who are deemed incapable of self-regulation and unworthy of assistance). From the vantage point of his 'quite ordinary' position as a graduate of Yale Law School and the meritocratic comforts of Silicon Valley, where he currently resides, J. D. Vance has written a memoir that appeals strongly to readers at both poles of the political spectrum because in the contemporary travails of the white working class it identifies a reason for the election of Donald J. Trump that liberals can understand and a solution to those travails that the right can get behind. Isenberg points out that Trump 'tapped into a rich vein of identity politics: the embrace of the common man, the working stiff, the forgotten rural American';[65] or, as Hochschild puts it, Trump 'was the identity politics candidate for white men'.[66] Vance's memoir offers another category of white male identity that, like Trump, is enshrined in a narrative of self making that repudiates both individual privilege and deep-rooted historical and structural inequalities.

If the representations of a marginalised and stigmatised white working class minority offered in *Hillbilly Elegy* cast contemporary forms of class- and race-based inequality in an identitarian conceptual framework that the left can understand (if not always sympathise with), the book likewise offers solutions to that inequality that are thoroughly steeped in the small-government, self-enfranchisement policies of the rightmost wing of the Republican Party. The party of Lincoln has become the party of

Trump in part because he speaks to white working-class anxieties about the vexed relationship between the American Dream and the American reality, and gives those anxieties expression in the most pernicious forms of populist xenophobia. Despite the intentions of its author, what *Hillbilly Elegy* tells is the story of whiteness come good through the frame of class gone bad; what Vance claims is that he succeeded *despite* his class, the unstated (and disavowed) corollary of which is that he succeeded *because* of his race. As Gest argues, 'Divorced by upwardly mobile white co-ethnics and relegated to an increasingly entrenched economic underclass where they are segregated from the solidarities of ethno-religious affinities, white working class communities are disempowered in a very unconventional sense.'[67]

A self-described 'persecuted minority' who has 'never felt out of place in [his] entire life', J. D. Vance embodies – both literally and metaphorically – the contradictory position of the white working-class disinvested subject. That he also stands as the poster boy for the myth of American meritocracy, however, shows how powerful the legacies of that myth are. By denying both the privileges of skin colour and the structural inequalities that affect the working poor regardless of race, Vance is able to present himself as a self-made recipient (by individual virtue) of everything but the beneficiary (by accident of race, class or gender) of nothing. That *Hillbilly Elegy* was taken up so readily by both the right and the left to explain the elevation of Trump suggests just how far there is to go in the nation's understanding of its still-shifting political landscape and its age-old problems of race- and class-based inequalities. Understanding how narratives of individual self-making such as those offered up by Vance remain part of the problem is essential if we are to come any way towards finding a solution. What Ron Howard will make of it all is a subject for another day.

Notes

1. Jonathan Allen and Amie Parnes, *Shattered: Inside Hillary Clinton's Doomed Campaign* (New York: Crown, 2017).
2. Susan Bordo, *The Destruction of Hillary Clinton* (New York: Melville House Press, 2017).

3. J. D. Vance, *Hillbilly Elegy: A Memoir of a Family and Culture in Crisis* (New York: Harper, 2016).
4. Tara Westover, *Educated: A Memoir* (New York: Random House, 2017).
5. Monica Hesse, *American Fire: Love, Arson, and Life in a Vanishing Land* (New York: Liveright, 2017).
6. Jennifer Senior, 'In "Hillbilly Elegy", a Tough Love Analysis of the Poor Who Back Trump', *New York Times*, 10 August 2016, <https://www.nytimes.com/2016/08/11/books/review-in-hillbilly-elegy-a-compassionate-analysis-of-the-poor-who-love-trump.html> (accessed 28 January 2020).
7. Michael Barbaro, 'Understanding the Trump Voter', *New York Times*, 19 August 2016, <https://www.nytimes.com/2016/08/19/podcasts/understanding-the-trump-voter.html?_r=0> (accessed 28 January 2020).
8. See Ross Douthat, 'Books for the Trump Era', *New York Times*, 21 December 2016, <https://www.nytimes.com/2016/12/21/opinion/books-for-the-trump-era.html>; '6 Books to Help Understand Trump's Win', *New York Times*, 9 November 2016, <https://www.nytimes.com/2016/11/10/books/6-books-to-help-understand-trumps-win.html> (both accessed 28 January 2020).
9. Sarah Baxter, 'Books: *Hillbilly Elegy: A Memoir of a Family and Culture in Crisis* by J. D. Vance', *Sunday Times*, 18 September 2016, <https://www.thetimes.co.uk/article/books-hillbilly-elegy-a-memoir-of-a-family-and-culture-in-crisis-by-jd-vance-lv2hh06tx> (accessed 28 January 2020).
10. Ian Birrell, 'What J. D. Vance's Hillbilly Memoir Tells Us about the People Who Support Trump – and Brexit', *i*, 2 October 2016, <https://inews.co.uk/opinion/jd-vances-hillbilly-memoir-tells-us-people-vote-trump-brexit/> (accessed 28 January 2020). The relationship between Trump's election, Brexit and the rise of national populism across Europe has been much discussed and, while there are clear links, there are also often overlooked differences. For a detailed and meaningful account of such transatlantic affinities, see Justin Gest, *The New Minority: White Working Class Politics in an Age of Immigration and Inequality* (New York: Oxford University Press, 2016).
11. J. D. Vance, 'Barack Obama and Me', *New York Times*, 2 January 2017, <https://www.nytimes.com/2017/01/02/opinion/barack-obama-and-me.html>; J. D. Vance, 'The Bad Faith of the White Working Class', *New York Times*, 25 June 2016, <https://www

.nytimes.com/2016/06/26/opinion/sunday/the-bad-faith-of-the-white-working-class.html>; J. D. Vance, 'Why I'm Moving Home', *New York Times*, 16 March 2017, <https://www.nytimes.com/2017/03/16/opinion/why-im-moving-home.html>; J. D. Vance, 'How Donald Trump Seduced America's White Working Class', *The Guardian*, 11 September 2016, <https://www.theguardian.com/commentisfree/2016/sep/10/jd-vance-hillbilly-elegy-donald-trump-us-white-poor-working-class> (all accessed 28 January 2020).
12. This is not to say that the book and its author didn't receive criticism. See, for example, Sarah Jones, 'J. D. Vance, the False Prophet of Blue America', *New Republic*, 17 November 2016, <https://newrepublic.com/article/138717/jd-vance-false-prophet-blue-america> (accessed 28 January 2020); Anthony Harkins and Meredith McCarroll (eds), *Appalachian Reckoning: A Region Responds to 'Hillbilly Elegy'* (Morgantown: West Virginia University Press, 2019).
13. Vance, *Hillbilly Elegy*, 1.
14. Ibid., 202, 98.
15. For a broader study of the use of identity politics as a tool for the maintenance of white male privilege, see Hamilton Carroll, *Affirmative Reaction: New Formations of White Masculinity* (Durham, NC; Duke University Press, 2012).
16. Vance, *Hillbilly Elegy*, 3.
17. Ibid., 31 (original emphasis).
18. Arlie Russell Hochschild, *Strangers in Their Own Land: Anger and Mourning on the American Right* (New York: New Press, 2016), 35, 47.
19. Theda Skocpol and Vanessa Williamson, *The Tea Party and the Remaking of Republican Conservatism*, rev. ed. (New York: Oxford University Press, 2016), 7.
20. Hochschild, *Strangers in Their Own Land*, 6.
21. Ibid., 7.
22. Ibid., 6.
23. Ibid., 12.
24. Robert Reich, *Saving Capitalism: For the Many, Not the Few* (New York: Alfred A. Knopf, 2015), xiii.
25. Yuval Levin, *The Fractured Republic: Renewing America's Social Contract in the Age of Individualism* (New York: Basic, 2016), 222.
26. Hochschild, *Strangers in Their Own Land*, 114.
27. Vance, *Hillbilly Elegy*, 33, 39.
28. Ibid., 29.
29. Ibid., 29.

30. Ibid., 54.
31. For an account of the historical transformation in the imaginary of the nation undergone by the residents of Appalachia, see Steven Stoll, *Ramp Hollow: The Ordeal of Appalachia* (New York: Hill & Wang, 2017).
32. T. R. C. Hutton, 'Hillbilly Elitism', in Harkins and McCarroll (eds), *Appalachian Reckoning*, 23.
33. Hochschild, *Strangers in Their Own Land*, 61.
34. Vance, *Hillbilly Elegy*, 148.
35. Gest, *The New Minority*, 6.
36. Ibid., 6.
37. Hochschild, *Strangers in Their Own Land*, 125.
38. Vance, *Hillbilly Elegy*, 5.
39. Ibid., 148.
40. Ibid., 188.
41. Ibid., 188.
42. Ibid., 188.
43. Ibid., 188.
44. Ibid., 188, 189.
45. Ibid., 188–9.
46. Ibid., 193.
47. Ibid., 5.
48. Ibid., 6.
49. Lisa R. Pruitt, 'What *Hillbilly Elegy* Reveals about Race in Twenty-First-Century America', in Harkins and McCarroll (eds), *Appalachian Reckoning*, 117.
50. Vance, *Hillbilly Elegy*, 47.
51. Ibid., 7.
52. Ibid., 7.
53. Nancy Isenberg, *White Trash: The 400-Year Untold History of Class in America* (New York: Penguin, 2017), xxii.
54. Gest, *The New Minority*, 15.
55. Vance, *Hillbilly Elegy*, 138.
56. Ibid., 139.
57. Kevin D. Williamson, 'The White Ghetto', *National Review*, 16 December 2013, <http://www.nationalreview.com/2014/01/white-ghetto-kevin-d-williamson> (accessed 28 January 2020).
58. Matt Wray, *Not Quite White: White Trash and the Boundaries of Whiteness* (Durham, NC: Duke University Press, 2006), 16.
59. John Hartigan Jr, *Odd Tribes: Toward a Cultural Analysis of White People* (Durham, NC: Duke University Press, 2005), 24.

60. Vance, *Hillbilly Elegy*, 140.
61. Ibid., 140.
62. Ibid., 140.
63. Alec MacGillis, 'Who Turned My Blue State Red?', *New York Times*, 20 November 2015, <https://www.nytimes.com/2015/11/22/opinion/sunday/who-turned-my-blue-state-red.html> (accessed 28 January 2020).
64. Isenberg, *White Trash*, xxii.
65. Ibid., xv.
66. Hochschild, *Strangers in Their Own Land*, 230.
67. Gest, *The New Minority*, 36–7.

11
Ivanka Trump and the New Plutocratic (Post)feminism

Diane Negra

The current climate is frequently characterised as being marked by a mix of residual postfeminist formations and proliferating new feminisms. But complicating the picture further is the emergence of a high-profile plutocratic (post)feminism associated with figures ranging from Sheryl Sandberg to Beyoncé to Ivanka Trump. The new (faux) feminism of privilege dissociates itself from notions of social justice except in the most cursory and rhetorical fashion, cleaving to neoliberal individualism and global capitalism. This intensely market-based form of feminism joins together female affective composure as a hallmark with safe performances of empowerment and displays of family capital; in so doing it works to soothe cultural tensions in regard to race, class and technology. Using Ivanka Trump as a case study I want to investigate the nature and functions of this new style of feminism and assess its value to current hegemonies of class and capital, particularly the regressive adulation of the wealthy.[1]

Noting feminism's public revival, Rosalind Gill has observed that 'while a few years ago it sometimes felt difficult to make *any* feminist arguments 'stick' in the media, today it seems as if *everything* is a feminist issue. Feminism has a new luminosity in popular culture.'[2] Likewise, Nancy Fraser observes that 'increasingly, it is liberal feminist thinking that supplies the charisma, the aura of emancipation, on which neoliberalism draws to legitimate its vast upward redistribution of wealth'.[3] The field of feminist commentary has notably broadened of late, with some of the most high-profile bestsellers of recent years having a comedic bent (work by Caitlin Moran, Tina Fey, Mindy Kaling, Amy Schumer and Amy Poehler) or a business self-help bent (*Lean In, You Are a Badass, #girlboss, Girl Code: Unlocking the Secrets to Success, Sanity and Happiness for the Female Entrepreneur*). Both modes of (post)feminist discourse are strongly allied to what Nathan Heller has called the 'organisation celebrity', a type defined by proficient multitasking that he points out 'tends to be emphasized in its female form'. For Heller 'female celebrity . . . is moving toward a work and achievement culture, and such re-narrativization requires active reinforcement in the public eye.'[4] Twitter and other social media forms have served as vital resources for the organisation celebrity, helping to communicate constant productivity. In this way such celebrity documents a vacillation between a (post)feminism that accedes to and takes full part in neoliberal capitalism and one which is devoted to fantasy corrections of it. Ivanka Trump, in my estimation, personifies the organisation celebrity, and her claims to feminism resonate within the new gendered affective landscape of neoliberal capitalism. The exploitative production conditions associated with her branded goods, moreover, offer a stark illustration of the way in which 'the postfeminist rhetoric of triumphalism not only makes race disappear . . . but it also uses the global capitalist hierarchy of the Global North and Global South to make multinationals' exploitation of female workers disappear'.[5]

As her father's political status accrued in 2016 and into 2017, Ivanka Trump's adept performance of moral thoughtfulness indirectly gratified a fantasy that the presidency would compel civility and decency from Donald Trump. The highly touted bond between the two served initially as a key part of his political mythology, helping to repair the president's amply documented misogyny, his track record of divorce and the public limitations of his current wife, whose use of English as a second language, flagrant plagiarism in her speech to the 2016 Republican National Convention and seeming reticence to inhabit the role of first lady are notable liabilities.[6] In Donald Trump's symbolic re-activation of the American Dream he fills the role of the crude cretin capable of producing progeny who are polished elites with (potential) altruistic intent. This is one reason why Trump's eldest daughter is so key to his mythology since his other children conspicuously fail to fill that role.[7] As Amy Davidson Sorkin has noted, Ivanka Trump continuously asks us to accept that nepotism is 'one of her father's virtues, and proof of his good character'.[8] What I want to examine is the question of what kinds of fantasies she focalises and her use value to a political administration seeking to effect a separation from democratic habits, norms and values.

'The unprecedented nature of my role': a template for branded first daughterhood

The irrational hopefulness that was sometimes attached to Trump in the lead-up to her father's presidency and in its first six months is hard to source. Trump's pre-casting for an idealised role may be attributed in part to twenty years of princess-oriented popular culture which normalised elite intergenerationalism and dynastic privilege. Media coverage of Chelsea Clinton, the Bush twins and the Obama daughters stoked interest in the figure of the first daughter, as did films like *Chasing Liberty* and *First Daughter* (both 2004).[9] Nevertheless, the intense media interest in Ivanka Trump has no real precedent in the annals of presidential daughterhood. A preoccupation of the high-end press and particularly female commentators, Trump was frequently imagined to be a mitigator of her father's worst inclinations, a moral check on his heedless disregard for constituencies other than the privileged.[10] (Such hopes were based on very flimsy suppositions such as the fact that because Trump had studied ballet as a child she would be an arts advocate in the administration).[11] In a *New York Times* article that sought to explain Donald Trump's astonishing success with women voters, nearly every woman profiled expressed a strong antipathy towards Hillary Clinton and several noted their preference for Donald Trump's daughter over Clinton in explaining their decision making, taking for granted the nepotistic involvement in any Trump administration of a person whose name was not listed on any ballot. For instance, a 49-year-old from Virginia noted:

Look at how much Trump hires women, how much he does rely on women, how much he relies on his own daughter. I'm sort of amazed by her. She may pull him more into the middle. She'll be a good voice for women.[12]

The affective contrast, of course, between Ivanka Trump and the Democratic candidate was all in the former's favour. Where Clinton was often categorised using the old misogynist descriptor 'shrill', Trump was serene; where Clinton was sometimes cast as too old to be president, Trump seemed young to have attained her influence and profile outside of a nepotistic context. Where Clinton was indelibly associated with a difficult marriage, Trump appeared in warmly lit campaign ads glorifying her family life. Serenity, transcendence and composure are Trump's performative keynotes; these are to be experienced as a relief from precarity and she is exonerated from appearing to be simply a rich dilettante because she combines the appearance of these qualities with entrepreneurial 'hustle'. Moreover, Ivanka Trump's initial public appeal might well be linked to her presentation as the affective antithesis of her father. Karin Wahl-Jorgensen has highlighted 'the importance of anger to [Donald] Trump's appeal and rhetoric' and his daughter's relentlessly calm and pleasant demeanour serves as a counterweight.[13]

In the persona of Ivanka Trump dynastic privilege is re-written as exemplary achieved confidence. 'Confidence chic', as identified by Laura Favaro, is part of a cultural turn whereby 'negative affect is rapidly silenced and with that goes the transformative force of collective anger at structural realms of injury and injustice'.[14] Yet Trump's display of confidence chic is hazardous and at times only narrowly avoids problematic excess, as when she took her father's place at the table at the G20 summit in Hamburg in July 2017. Trump is an iconic figure for an era in which 'the promotion of self-confidence has surfaced as the site for expanded, heightened and more insidious modes of regulation often spearheaded by those very institutions invested in women's insecurities'.[15]

Ivanka Trump's anodyne positioning as wife and daughter is bound up with insistent cultural messaging that the (marketised) family is the only safe space for American women. She strikingly illustrates Catherine Rottenberg's claim that, 'no longer deeply interested in the struggle for equal rights or for an end to gender discrimination, neoliberal feminism focuses principally on the notion of work–family balance'.[16] In an era in which marriage and motherhood operate as markers of personal success and (increasingly) socio-economic security, Trump's status marriage to Jared Kushner can usefully be understood as a form of assortative mating and elite social behaviour that has long existed but that has become more conspicuous in the era of renewed wealth triumphalism. Noting that 'the wife has morphed into postfeminist media culture's most favoured icon', Suzanne Leonard observes that 'marriage occupies new ground as a cultural status symbol'. As she puts it, 'wifedom is newly professionalized as an occupation in its own right and the regulatory and affective investments that characterize contemporary labor relations also ground American wifedom'.[17]

Ivanka Trump's (projected) role as a foil to her father stands in contrast to her actual role as his accessory and business partner. It runs the risk of suppressing her earlier positioning as a junior version of him, which is certainly how she was cast during her period of participation on the NBC reality series *The Apprentice*. In 2003, in an earlier and substantially reduced phase of her celebrity, Trump was profiled in the documentary *Born Rich* in a manner that strikingly differs from her present-day media representation (not least because in several segments she appears as a brunette). Showing off her perfectly preserved childhood bedroom at one point, she gestures towards the window overlooking an expansive vista of Central Park and says with satisfaction, 'Not a bad view.' Trump's appearance in *Born Rich* is a reminder that her celebrity emerges in significant ways out of the millennial socialite culture, a fact that her current persona seeks to occlude. The thriving socialite culture of those years also gave rise to Paris Hilton and the Kardashians, as well as reality franchises like *The Hills* and other vigorous efforts to consolidate and commercialise second- and third-generation celebrity and launch women in female-focused commercial endeavours.[18] Trump and Kushner's joint 2010 cameo in the CW series *Gossip Girl* cements these sorts of associations with

IVANKA TRUMP AND THE NEW PLUTOCRATIC (POST)FEMINISM

Figure 11.1. In their cameo appearance in an episode of teen drama *Gossip Girl*, Ivanka Trump and Jared Kushner are presented as an exemplary 'power couple' on the rise

female-centred commercial concerns in the lifestyle and fashion industries alongside dynastic privilege.

A television show about young women's efforts to build capital to secure their place in the social order, *Gossip Girl* sets itself in a very Trumpian milieu. It flourished in the era of reality series such as *My Super Sweet Sixteen*, which chronicled the opulent coming-of-age parties of the progeny of the super-rich, and Adam (son of novelist Saul) Bellow's publication of a book entitled *In Praise of Nepotism*, defending what he perceived as the flourishing force of a 'new nepotism' in contemporary society.[19] The culture of celebrity nepotism might have slightly abated after the global financial crisis but aspirationally driven representational agendas and media consumption of the super-rich have flourished and taken on new forms.

In an appearance on *The Late Show with David Letterman* in 2007, Trump repeatedly emphasised filial likeness, saying, for instance, 'Not unlike my father, I have a tendency to fight back' while the host commented, 'Your manner of speech is very much like your father's.' In conjunction with the logic of *The Apprentice* Ivanka Trump speaks here in a crass and triumphalist fashion about her profit motivation and enthusiasm for leveraging the family brand name. Near the close of the interview there is the following exchange:

Trump: [*Speaking of her father*] One of the principles he's always espoused – whether it's good or bad, I personally have adopted it myself – but if somebody comes after you, you have to go after them. Because it will teach anyone else that wants to do it, it will at least let them know you're gonna respond to it.
Letterman: What about turning the other cheek? What about turning the other cheek? What about rising above the fray? Taking the high road?
Trump: [*With a sceptical shrug to the audience*] I guess that's one approach. I don't know. I'm not well studied in that. I did go to a finance school as well.

The appearance, in which Trump is amusingly played in to Hall & Oates's 'Rich Girl,' is notable also as a showcase of a rather different speech style and comportment than Trump presently uses, offering evidence of the extent of her affective and physical makeover over the past decade. Present-day Ivanka Trump has been smoothed over; the diminishment of her New York accent, the slowing and softening of her speech and her gravitation away from declarative or emphatic statements bring her in line with codes of non-threatening, low-affect femininity in a fashion that is almost caricatural.[20] And indeed her demeanour (which verges on the stilted) has given rise to a rich corpus of critiques and parodies, not least *Saturday Night Live*'s 2017 parody ad for 'Complicit' perfume.[21] In this regard I would observe that Ivanka Trump's relentless poise is important as a contrast to the bloviating, choleric style of Donald Trump and those around him (notably Sean Spicer and Rudy Giuliani) and the disingenuous double-talk of Trump advisor Kellyanne Conway. She helps to secure a retro gender order in which elite femininity holds itself at a composed remove.

Trump's position as her father's character witness signals an ideological reversion to a nineteenth-century conception of gendered capitalism in which women's public activities were frequently tied to their attributed role as agents of moral uplift whose influence kept men functional and incentivised within the prevailing economic order. Trump's bid for public recognition as a feminist, concretised and commercialised in her book *Women Who Work: Rewriting the Rules for Success* (2017), marked a break with the earlier discourses of aggressive capitalism showcased in her earlier *The Trump Card: Playing to Win in Work and Life* (2009). The alteration of focus from the family name in the first book to 'women' in the second illustrates Trump's shifting target of identification and affiliation. Moreover, the 'women who work' tag, as the *New York Times* has reported, originated in a 2013 strategy session held by Trump, her husband and several of her employees designed to generate a quasi-feminist motto that could follow the surging popularity of Sheryl Sandberg's 'Lean In'.[22]

As she came into her father's administration, Trump noted 'the unprecedented nature of my role'.[23] The function often attributed to her has been to act as a moral check on unfettered capitalism yet there are no signs of the social benevolence so often ascribed to her. In interviews Trump herself regularly insists that though it's publicly invisible it does exist. Speaking with Gayle King, for instance, she maintained that when she disagrees with her father she 'expresses [herself] with total candor' yet rhetorically echoed Sandberg when she stated, 'Where I agree I fully lean in and support the agenda.'[24]

It is beyond my scope to fully analyse Trump's maternal persona but I would briefly note that her performance of the sort of privileged postfeminist mothering I have previously characterised as 'bravura' stands in contrast and as an implicit reproach to the kinds of mothers whose ranks are likely to swell under this administration, those who in Julie Wilson and Emily Chivers Yochim's vivid phrasing are 'mothering through precarity'. In profiling this population Wilson and Yochim track a maternal 'resilient subject who must cultivate capacities to cope with the shrivelling resources and broken promises that neoliberalism brings to social life'.[25] As they write:

> Mothers are the ones who ultimately come to compensate for lost jobs, underfunded public schools, decimated state budgets, and the volatilities all these bring to family life, as mothers constantly retool and expand their women's work – taking on more and more social responsibility with less and less social support.[26]

With fantasies and enmities swirling around Ivanka Trump so intensely, the question of why she rivets so many people deserves complicating. At a prosaic level it's worth reiterating the sheer conspicuousness of her gender difference in a political administration that regularly and unapologetically releases photos of clusters of white men ostensibly doing the nation's business as if it were the nineteenth century.[27] Illustrating the ways that women's proximity to power must be carefully managed, high levels of opprobrium were directed at Kellyanne Conway for a February 2017 photo in the Oval Office in which just such a group gathered in the middle and background while she was pictured in the foreground, barefoot and with her legs drawn up under her on a sofa, a pose that many deemed disrespectful and symptomatic of the casualisation and crudity of the office under Donald Trump. Like Conway, Ivanka Trump is continually placed as the female figure of exception and she stands out for that very simple reason. Another attribute that Conway and Trump hold in common is blondeness and its visual signification should also not be underestimated. Scholars including Joanna Pitman have dedicated themselves to analyses of its functions as a sign of female allure and power.[28]

However, I want to suggest that the public absorption and fascination with Ivanka Trump is importantly tied to the pressing question of what women's relationship to crony capitalism is. In an era in which capitalism is increasingly in disrepute, should women be moral counterweights and figures of opposition to it or full and enthusiastic participants, 'leaning in' to get their piece of the pie? Trump, it seems to me, is trying to be both. She personifies on the one hand women's traditional moral obligation to stand apart from markets – to segregate themselves from the most aggressive forms of capitalism. Simultaneously, though, and with great meticulousness about how she is presented, she also epitomises dynastic privilege and capitalist zeal.

Multiplatforming dilemmas and the depreciation of Ivanka Trump's celebrity

Much contemporary discourse about/around feminism has come to be concerned with the limitations, political vacuity and ideologically misguided or disingenuous nature of contemporary feminist claims as they are articulated in mainstream spheres of celebrity culture and popular media and embodied by figureheads like Emma Watson, Lena Dunham or Sheryl Sandberg. Against this backdrop, Ivanka Trump's paradoxical positioning, her polished, coached and careful affect, and her commercial and political brand building constitute for some an extraordinary provocation. An icon of cruel optimism, she has proved adept at rhetoricising postfeminist self-interest as feminist commitment. Her positioning tellingly illustrates Sarah Banet-Weiser's observation that 'postfeminism in practice is often individualised and constructed as personal choice rather than collective action; its ideal manifestation, in turn, is not struggle for social change but rather capacity for entrepreneurship'.[29]

Trump's role as what I have called a character witness for her father is read by many as strategic calculation, an expression of the boundaries that still circumscribe female power and discursive authority. Trump's seeming mastery of the balancing act incessantly ascribed to women involving raising children and playing a public role is without doubt one of her signature features. As the exemplary female figure of the Trump administration (especially after the departure of Hope Hicks and the relative lowering of Conway's profile), it is clear that Ivanka Trump plays a pivotal role in what Catherine Rottenberg has characterised as a neoliberal colonisation of feminism that is 'producing a very clear distinction between female subjects who are worthy because they are aspirational and thus convertible and the majority of female subjects, who are deemed irredeemable due to their insufficient aspirations and responsibilization'.[30] In this sense Trump has come to embody a shift charted by Rottenberg in which women are converted to neoliberal human capital, a shift which in its most fully realised form will entail 'a complete splitting of female subjecthood: [into] the worthy, capital-enhancing female few and the disavowed rest'.[31]

I have focused to this point on what now reads as the peak period of Ivanka Trump's political capital but I want to offer a brief assessment of her significantly diminished profile since the failure of *Women Who Work*, in which much of the optimism and feminist political ambition of the earlier phase of her celebrity has drained away. In this context a landmark event was the closure in July 2018 of Trump's fashion brand after it had been dropped by

DIANE NEGRA

Figure 11.2. The failure of Ivanka Trump's 2017 self-help book *Women Who Work: Rewriting the Rules for Success* augured a shift in her marketability

a number of large US and Canadian retailers and at a time when her father's administration was threatening to escalate its trade dispute with China, where many of the products associated with the brand were manufactured.[32]

By the latter part of 2017 Trump was increasingly being cast as a Marie Antoinette figure, as could be starkly seen in the scornful reporting of her website's promotion of a costly Thanksgiving 'tablescape' in November and in caustic press coverage in outlets such as *Marie Claire*, which in September of that year published an article by Jessica Valenti entitled 'The Eternal Uselessness of Ivanka Trump'.[33] In this phase, Trump becomes increasingly the subject of mockery, as in a piece by Lindy West in which West observed that

> Ivanka Trump is never going to come through. Coming through isn't her function. She is more a logo than a person, a scarecrow stuffed with branding, an heiress-turned-model-turned-multimillionaire's-wife playacting as an authority on the challenges facing working women so that she can sell more pastel sheath dresses.[34]

An autumn 2017 article in *Vanity Fair* offered a bleak account of Trump and Jared Kushner's political effectiveness, noting that if Trump's 'main value in Washington is her access to her father and she is unable to sway him, then she is simply a 35-year-old former real-estate and retail executive in over her head'.[35] A prominent piece in the *New York Times* saw the paper's editorial board pointing to Trump's conspicuous lack of public policy successes and concluding bluntly that 'Ivanka Trump isn't serving America'.[36]

The hazards of Trump's position were strikingly illustrated in a cruel and clumsy 2017 controversy. On 22 August Louise Linton posted on Instagram a photo of herself and her husband, Treasury secretary Steven Mnuchin, descending from a government plane in Kentucky and detailed the high-fashion clothing and accessories she was wearing. In response to criticism from a woman who deemed the post 'deplorable', Linton lashed out, calling the woman 'adorably out of touch' and advising her to relax and watch *Game of Thrones*. Linton was then compelled to apologise. Linton's itemisation of the elements of her high-fashion wardrobe on Instagram while on a trip paid for by taxpayers was a step too far but it prompted numerous comparisons to Trump. The shift in public perception of the 'first daughter' was tellingly revealed in December 2017 when she made a surprise visit to a school in Connecticut and a number of parents pulled their children from class as a result.[37]

By 2018 it began to seem that Ivanka Trump could do no right. Her efforts to display her vaunted ties to Chinese culture (a cover, it would seem, for her commercial interests in China) subsided or misfired as when in June she tweeted a 'Chinese proverb' that was quickly exposed as having no Chinese origin.[38] Press coverage and social media discourse in relation to her turned consistently sceptical and critical; in March on a visit to Iowa in which she donned a lab jacket, goggles, gloves and other accoutrements for a photo op Trump was accused of 'cosplaying' as a scientist.[39] A steady series of revelations regarding Trump and Kushner's accumulation of vast profits from various commercial interests cast doubt on their professed commitment to public service and prompted the most critical press coverage yet.[40] One article devoted itself to pondering the question of whether Ivanka was 'the worst Trump'.[41]

The Linton incident had exposed the risks of female self-promotion via social media and those risks would become apparent to Trump in May 2018 when her effort to celebrate herself as a loving mother backfired as the image of her cuddling her son Theodore was read in relation to her father's government's policy of separating immigrant children from their families at the border. The conjunction of Trump's self-representation with the cruelty against asylum-seeking families reached a crescendo when late-night television host Samantha Bee called out Trump as a 'feckless cunt' and was herself vilified for her crudity and disrespect. The outcry over Bee's characterisation points to the affective contrast between a TV host whose anger and outrage form the basis of her comedy and low-affect figures like Trump. Long anathematised as 'unwomanly', female rage has become a subject of interest, with recent books on it by Rebecca Traister and Soraya Chemaly and of course its centralisation in the confirmation hearings for Brett Kavanaugh, which among other things showcased the need for women to suppress anger if they are to be deemed credible while the performance of male anger by a Supreme Court nominee underscored its political usefulness. Ivanka Trump's postfeminist affective composure is thus in line with a gendered emotional landscape that contrasts the anger of the many with the decorum of the few.

IVANKA TRUMP AND THE NEW PLUTOCRATIC (POST)FEMINISM

Figure 11.3. Ivanka Trump's tweeted photo with son Theodore gained notoriety as a display of triumphalist privilege in 2018 when Donald Trump's government was separating asylum seekers at the US border from their children (Source: Ivanka Trump (@IvankaTrump), Twitter, 27 May 2018, https://twitter.com/ivankatrump/status/1000770717628104710, accessed 29 January 2020)

Most recently, as the Trump administration has come to be increasingly understood as a chaotic, corrupt and careening enterprise, Ivanka Trump's role in it has become even less clear. The ambiguity and awkwardness of her positioning was on display for instance in her attendance with her husband at the funeral of Senator John McCain in August 2018, an event staged largely as a public repudiation of Trumpism and in which the celebrity of another blonde political daughter, Meghan McCain, was consolidated in a grief-stricken, passionate eulogy. When an anonymous 2018 editorial appeared in the *New York Times* declaring that administration insiders were acting to mitigate Donald Trump's worst inclinations there was speculation that the editorial's author was Ivanka Trump. After the resignation of Nikki Haley as UN ambassador, Trump's name was bandied about as someone who might fill the role (though her father petulantly complained that if he were to appoint her the move would be seen as cronyism). In January 2019 Trump was satirised in an episode of the sitcom *Family Guy* that took aim at her scrupulous self-presentation with a song, 'Ivanka Trump Has a Gentle Breeze Indoors'. Meanwhile a Washington, DC, art installation, *Ivanka Vacuuming*, by Jennifer

Figure 11.4. Meghan McCain drew plaudits for her speech at John McCain's funeral in which she repudiated Donald Trump's 'Make America Great Again' slogan

Rubell, had a model dressed in Trump-branded clothing vacuuming a carpet onto which spectators threw panko breadcrumbs.

Ivanka Trump may be seen as a key participant in what Anand Giridharadas has deemed 'the elite charade of changing the world'.[42] In this account I have sought to chart some of the elements and incidents that have most decisively impacted her signification as one of the highest-profile women in American politics. The cycling of her business persona through her roles as vice-president of the Trump Organization to head of a fashion label to lifestyle entrepreneur had taken place before her father attained the presidency and seemed initially, to some, to bode well for her political (though unelected and nepotistic) role. More recently the curtailment of Trump's ability to perform family values on her terms suggests that when 'facts are semantically renegotiated to a greater extent than before' self-promotion activities can be exceedingly hazardous and subject to unwanted juxtapositions and interpretations.[43] I suggest that in the current plutonomy important fractures have emerged in Ivanka Trump's representability. The tension between Trump's self-representation and a caustic, critical social media ethos aptly illustrates 'the emergence of a digital culture that combines high levels of top-down algorithmic power concentrated in the hands of a few corporations with equally high levels of bottom-up insurgency capabilities distributed among a myriad of individual and collective actors'.[44] Finally the failure of *Women Who Work* as an effort to broadly speak on behalf of women and commercialise Ivanka Trump's authority in an even more multiplatformed way should give us hope that there are limits to public tolerance for the audacity of postfeminist branding. One of the things that makes Ivanka Trump a compelling figure for my purposes is the way she now seems to inspire the kind of schadenfreude we might expect to increasingly characterise celebrity relations in the era of deregulated plutocratic capitalism.

Notes

1. My focus here is on the US and UK, but it is worth noting that Trump is a figure of inspiration in China, where her associations with nepotism and corruption don't signify pejoratively: the former

is typically read as dynastic connection and the latter as common business practice. Javier Hernandez notes, 'Chinese companies have filed hundreds of trademark applications using her name.' Javier C. Hernandez, 'The "Goddess" Yi Wan Ka: Ivanka Trump Is a Hit in China', *New York Times*, 5 April 2017, <https://www.nytimes.com/2017/04/05/world/asia/ivanka-trump-china.html> (accessed 29 January 2020). In a more extended reflection on the significance of Trump's celebrity in China, Jiayang Fan writes, 'That such a vexed figure may serve as the role model for Chinese women who are just beginning to grapple with their identity in a society that has historically been hostile to their empowerment seems like a regression. Underneath the sexy sheen of commodified feminism is the notion that unless you are beautiful, privileged, and most important, part of an essentially (and, in Ivanka's case, literally) patriarchal setup, your success as a working woman is still very much probationary.' Jiayang Fan, 'China and the Legend of Ivanka', *New Yorker*, 11 April 2017, <http://www.newyorker.com/news/daily-comment/china-and-the-legend-of-ivanka> (accessed 29 January 2020).

2. Rosalind Gill, 'Post-Postfeminism?: New Feminist Visibilities in Postfeminist Times', *Feminist Media Studies* 16, no. 4 (2016), 614 (original emphasis).
3. Gary Gutting and Nancy Fraser, 'A Feminism Where "Lean In" Means Leaning on Others', *New York Times*, 15 October 2015, <https://opinionator.blogs.nytimes.com/2015/10/15/a-feminism-where-leaning-in-means-leaning-on-others> (accessed 29 January 2020).
4. Nathan Heller, 'The Multitasking Celebrity Takes Center Stage', *New Yorker*, 23 June 2016, <https://www.newyorker.com/culture/cultural-comment/the-organizational-celebrity> (accessed 29 January 2020).
5. Tanya Ann Kennedy, *Historicizing Post-Discourses: Postfeminism and Postracialism in United States Culture* (Albany: SUNY Press, 2017), 159.
6. Of course, that bond skews creepily as well, given Donald Trump's notorious comment that 'I've said that if Ivanka weren't my daughter perhaps I would be dating her'. This level of signification is well captured in comedian Bill Maher's repeated references to Ivanka as her father's 'daughter-wife'.
7. As Frank Bruni writes (in exasperation), 'In campaigning full-force for her father, she and her brothers seemed at once to be repaying a debt – they'd profited so enormously from the Trump name – and hopping aboard a ride to greater dividends still. But she stood out,

because she in particular insisted on a veneer of virtue. She alone marketed a persona of goodness.' Frank Bruni, 'Ivanka Trump's Bitter Scent', *New York Times*, 15 March 2017, <https://www.nytimes.com/2017/03/15/opinion/ivanka-trumps-bitter-scent.html> (accessed 29 January 2020).

8. Amy Davidson Sorkin, 'The Global Effort to Flatter Ivanka', *New Yorker*, 27 April 2017, <https://www.newyorker.com/news/amy-davidson/the-global-effort-to-flatter-ivanka> (accessed 29 January 2020).
9. For a fuller discussion of the popular culture of first daughterhood, see Jia Tolentino, 'Ivanka Trump and the Ways that We Imagine First Daughters', *New Yorker*, 14 January 2018, <https://www.newyorker.com/culture/cultural-comment/ivanka-trump-and-the-ways-that-we-imagine-first-daughters> (accessed 29 January 2020).
10. In late April 2017, in the wake of her appointment as special advisor to the president and her appearance at the W20 women's summit in Berlin, coverage of Trump seemed to change. Television comedian John Oliver produced a detailed piece examining Trump and Jared Kushner's wealth and power and Amy Davidson wrote an extensive piece in the *New Yorker*. In the UK press suspicion of Trump took an even more detailed form as in the case of Jess Cartner Morley's account of the significance of Trump's mismatched earrings at the W20. Calling her 'a virtuoso of visual messaging', Cartner-Morley observed that Trump's mimicking of a popular trend was a performance of the 'independent-minded, creative-thinking outlook, an identity Ivanka Trump deliberately flirts with. We should all be scared of Ivanka's earrings, because they represent what makes her the most terrifying of all the Trump circle, which is her Bladerunner-replicant-like ability to make you believe – just for a second – that she is a bit like us.' Jess Cartner Morley, 'Why We Should All Be Afraid of Ivanka Trump's Mismatched Earrings', *The Guardian*, 27 April 2017, <https://www.theguardian.com/fashion/2017/apr/27/why-we-should-all-be-afraid-of-ivanka-trumps-mismatched-earrings> (accessed 29 January 2020).
11. Robin Pogrebin, 'Might Ivanka Trump Speak Up If Her Father Guts the Arts?', *New York Times*, 19 February 2017, <https://www.nytimes.com/2017/02/19/arts/might-ivanka-trump-speak-up-if-her-father-guts-the-arts.html> (accessed 29 January 2020).
12. Susan Chira, '"You Focus on the Good": Women Who Voted for Trump, in Their Own Words', *New York Times*, 14 January 2017, <https://www.nytimes.com/2017/01/14/us/women-voters-trump.html> (accessed 29 January 2020).

13. Karin Wahl-Jorgensen, 'Public Displays of Disaffection: The Emotional Politics of Donald Trump', in Pablo J. Boczkowski and Zizi Papacharissi (eds), *Trump and the Media* (Cambridge, MA: MIT Press, 2018), 80.
14. Laura Favaro, '"Just Be Confident Girls!": Confidence Chic as Neoliberal Governmentality', in Ana Sofia Elias, Rosalind Gill and Christina Scharff (eds), *Aesthetic Labour: Rethinking Beauty Politics in Neoliberalism* (London: Palgrave Macmillan, 2017), 296.
15. Ibid., 283.
16. Catherine Rottenberg, 'Neoliberal Feminism and the Future of Human Capital', *Signs: Journal of Women in Culture and Society* 42, no. 2 (2017), 329–48.
17. Suzanne Leonard, *Wife, Inc.: The Business of Marriage in the Twenty-First Century* (New York: New York University Press, 2018), 12.
18. Eschewing the reality television forms (not to mention sex tapes) so critical to the celebrity of Hilton and Kim Kardashian, Trump has been keen to present herself as a business school graduate and entrepreneur with a rather chaste sexual identity.
19. Diane Negra, 'Celebrity Nepotism, Family Values and E! Television', *Flow* 3, no. 1 (2005), <https://www.flowjournal.org/2005/09/celebrity-nepotism-family-values-and-e-television> (accessed 29 January 2020).
20. Jon Kraszewski writes that 'the New York City accent in the Trump family has gone through three phases: Donald's father, who grew up working class and retained that speech pattern, even though he became wealthy; Donald, who still holds many speech patterns from this dialect; and Trump's children, who are a third-generation moneyed class who no longer have a New York City accent.' Jon Kraszewski, *Reality TV* (New York: Routledge, 2017), 65.
21. For another instance see Cathy Lew's mock interview with Trump, 'The Ivanka Trump Guide to Style', in which in response to the question 'How do you define style?' Trump is fictitiously quoted: 'It's a diamond-encrusted watch that doesn't lose its lustre when you're baking chocolate-chip cookies with your children. It's a fitted blazer that inspires confidence whether you're jetting to a playdate or jetting to a meeting you're not authorized to attend.' Cathy Lew, 'The Ivanka Trump Guide to Style', *New Yorker*, 11 March 2017, <https://www.newyorker.com/humor/daily-shouts/the-ivanka-trump-guide-to-style> (accessed 29 January 2020).
22. Jodi Kantor, Rachel Abrams and Maggie Haberman, 'Ivanka Trump Has the President's Ear. Here's Her Agenda', *New York Times*, 2 May 2017, <https://www.nytimes.com/2017/05/02/us/politics/ivanka-trump.html> (accessed 29 January 2020).

23. Meghan Keneally and John Santucci, 'Ivanka Trump Taking Formal Role in Administration amid Ethics Concerns', ABC News (United States), 29 March 2017, <https://abcnews.go.com/Politics/ivanka-trump-taking-formal-role-administration/story?id=46454858> (accessed 29 January 2020).
24. See Kate Aronoff, 'No, Ivanka Trump Will Not Moderate Her Father. She Will Just Strengthen Him', *The Guardian*, 5 April 2017, <https://www.theguardian.com/commentisfree/2017/apr/05/ivanka-trump-donald-trump-cbs-progressive-white-house> (accessed 29 January 2020).
25. Julie A. Wilson and Emily Chivers Yochim, *Mothering through Precarity: Women's Work and Digital Media* (Durham, NC: Duke University Press, 2017), 14.
26. Ibid., 22.
27. See Jill Filipovic, who reads such photos as a form of message delivery for Donald Trump, who 'ran a campaign of aggrieved masculinity, appealing to men who feel their rightful place in society has been taken from them.' Jill Filipovic, 'The All-Male Photo Op Isn't a Gaffe. It's a Strategy', *New York Times*, 27 March 2017, <https://www.nytimes.com/2017/03/27/opinion/the-all-male-photo-op-isnt-a-gaffe-its-a-strategy.html> (accessed 29 January 2020).
28. Joanna Pitman, *On Blondes* (London: Bloomsbury, 2003).
29. Sarah Banet-Weiser, *Authentic™: The Politics of Ambivalence in a Brand Culture* (New York: New York University Press, 2012), 56.
30. Rottenberg, 'Neoliberal Feminism and the Future of Human Capital', 340.
31. Ibid., 345.
32. 'Ivanka Trump's Brand Building at the White House', *New York Times*, 1 March 2018, <https://www.nytimes.com/2018/03/01/opinion/ivanka-trump-donald-nepotism.html> (accessed 29 January 2020).
33. Jessica Valenti, 'The Eternal Uselessness of Ivanka Trump', *Marie Claire* (United States), 16 September 2017, <https://www.marieclaire.com/politics/a29434/ivanka-influence-over-trump> (accessed 29 January 2020).
34. Lindy West, 'The Ivanka Trump Guarantee', *New York Times*, 6 September 2017, <https://www.nytimes.com/2017/09/06/opinion/the-ivanka-trump-labor-women.html> (accessed 29 January 2020).
35. Sarah Ellison, 'Bland Ambition', *Vanity Fair*, October 2017, 153.
36. 'Ivanka Trump's Brand Building at the White House'.
37. 'Parents Upset over Ivanka Trump's Surprise School Visit in Connecticut', WABC-TV News, 19 December 2017, <https://abc7ny.com/2800798> (accessed 29 January 2020).

38. 'In May of 2018 the conjunction of the Trump Administration's efforts to save Chinese telecommunications company ZTE and the awarding of seven Chinese trademarks to Ivanka Trump's firm was widely noted.' Javier C. Hernández, 'Ivanka Trump Cited a "Chinese Proverb". China is Confused', *New York Times*, 12 June 2018, <https://www.nytimes.com/2018/06/12/world/asia/ivanka-trump-china-summit-korea.html>.
39. Ed Mazza, 'Ivanka Trump Called Out for "Cosplaying" as a Scientist in Latest Weird Photo Op', *HuffPost* (United Kingdom), 20 March 2018, <https://www.huffingtonpost.co.uk/entry/ivanka-trump-scientist-meme_n_5ab09c3ce4b0e862383abad5?ri18n=true> (accessed 29 January 2020).
40. See, for instance, Jesse Drucker and Agustin Armendariz, 'Ivanka Trump and Jared Kushner Had a Busy Year in Investing, Filing Shows', *New York Times*, 11 June 2018, <https://www.nytimes.com/2018/06/11/business/ivanka-trump-jared-kushner-investing.html> (accessed 23 March 2020); Jill Abramson, 'Now We Know the Outrageous Scale of the Trumps' White House Dividend', *The Guardian*, 13 June 2018, < https://www.theguardian.com/commentisfree/2018/jun/13/trump-white-house-donald-ivanka-jared-clinton> (accessed 29 January 2020).
41. Arwa Mahdawi, 'Is Ivanka the Worst Trump? Her Tweeted Portrait of "Perfect Motherhood" Seals It for Me', *The Guardian*, 29 May 2018, <https://www.theguardian.com/commentisfree/2018/may/29/is-ivanka-trump-worst-tweeted-portrait-border-agents>.
42. In a searing account of the way elites fortify their power while associating themselves with the prospects of social development, Giridharadas writes, 'All around us, the winners in our highly inequitable status quo declare themselves partisans of change.' Anand Giridharadas, *Winners Take All: The Elite Charade of Changing the World* (New York: Alfred A. Knopf, 2018), 5.
43. Pablo J. Boczkowski and Zizi Papacharissi, 'Introduction', in Boczkowski and Papacharissi (eds), *Trump and the Media*, 5.
44. Ibid., 5.

12
Trump and the Age of Hybrid Media Communicators

Alireza Hajihosseini

The 2016 election of Donald Trump as the forty-fifth president of the United States shocked the American political establishment. Few had correctly predicted the electoral success of a truly unorthodox political outsider and many were left pondering one simple question: how? More precisely, how exactly could a candidate that upended all political norms, eschewed all traditional campaign strategies and openly embraced divisive messages convince enough Americans in key battleground states to send him to the White House? Many have tried to answer that question. Academics have launched many research projects while columnists have penned numerous polemics in search of a clue. News organisations have dispatched numerous fact-finding missions to main streets across the proverbial 'Trump country' to report on an America they had overlooked. For scholars of political communication, however, the answers lie much closer to home. Trump's success at the ballot box could be explained by a wide body of scholarship on the dynamics of today's media system and the political actions it rewards.

With the benefit of hindsight, and now the initial shock has worn off, one can clearly see that Trump's election was less the beginning of a new form of political communication and more a by-product of a hybrid media system in which the lines between new and old media logics are increasingly blurred. Barriers to content creation and consumption have diminished, and the fall of traditional gatekeepers has enabled both political actors and the electorate to intervene in the political narrative creation process when they want and how they want. Candidate Trump had a unique ability to spot these trends thanks to his unique background as a reality TV star. President Trump has continued to exploit these dynamics to shape the news agenda in ways that benefit him.

Examining the media undercurrents that contributed to Trump's rise will not only add a nuanced layer to our understanding of Trump's America, it will also help us identify the next crop of political actors who are succeeding Trump in leveraging media trends to their benefit. Ironically, the most visible of them hail from the progressive left of American politics, a group that has arguably benefited most from Trump's presidency while being vociferously against his policies. This chapter will argue that Donald Trump's political success was in many ways a result of his astute understanding of the prevailing media logics of his time. It will then examine the media strategies employed by some of the up-and-coming stars in the Democratic Party to argue that politicians who have most successfully created new powerful brands are following a path that has been blazed by the current American president.

Political communication and media logic

Understanding how the fundamental dynamics of today's media system impact political communication requires a clear breakdown of some key concepts. As Lisa Gitelman argues, 'the media' isn't a singular unified body but rather should be viewed as

> socially realized structures of communication, where structures include both technological forms and their associated protocols, and where communication is a cultural practice, a ritualized collocation of different people on the same mental map, sharing or engaged with popular ontologies of representation.[1]

A medium, as a singular, can be seen as a 'vast clutter of normative rules and default conditions, which gather and adhere like a nebulous array around a technological nucleus'.[2] A media system is, therefore, a collection of different mediums that are not only defined by their individual modus operandi but also by their relationship to one another.

The normative rules and practices that govern the relationship between the different entities within a media system and inform its interaction with the social and political fields can be best captured by the concept of 'media logic'.[3] In other words, media logic refers to the underlying technologies, norms, behaviours and organisational forms that shape the power relations between political actors, media and publics.[4] It also encapsulates the shared understanding among the different actors operating within a media system about what constitutes publicly valued information and how that information should be communicated. Effective political communication, therefore, is that which adheres to the embedded expectations laid out by the media logic of the time.

In their seminal 1999 article 'The Third Age of Political Communication', Jay Blumer and Dennis Kavanagh categorised political communication since the end of World War II into three phases.[5] In the decades immediately after the war, the primacy of political parties' 'group-based loyalties' meant politicians did not need to work too hard to convince the public to trust them. The second period was dominated by television news, which brought with it an enlarged audience, an emphasis on visual communication, and the rise of pre-tested messages that were known to resonate with the electorate. The third age of political communication was characterised by media abundance and coincided with the spread of multi-channel television, 24-hour news channels and the rise of digital media. Blumer and Kavanagh identified five main trends that shaped political communication in this period.

First, the spread of different platforms put pressure on politicians to rely on professionals to get their message across. They needed help to understand the unique demands of different mediums. Communication strategists and experts soon became the heart of a political operation. Second, in a media system filled with many different outlets, politicians not only have to compete with their rivals for airtime but also have to deal with entertainment, sport and other more appealing content. Thus political messaging adopted a more 'infotainment' approach. Third, and perhaps most prescient given the time the paper came out, was anti-elitist populism. Blumer and Kavanagh argued that as the media system moved away from a top-down model where the political and media elite dictated what information should be shared, the opportunity arose for the public to actively engage in the political communication process. People were given a voice, sometimes quite literally with the rise of talk shows and audience panels, and that voice mattered as much as that of the elite. This was exacerbated by centrifugal diversification of the media, which enabled 'previously excluded voices to express their views and perhaps even be noticed by mainstream outlets' and changed how people received political messaging.[6] More channels and more options meant a compartmentalisation of the wider society into smaller groups driven by their own values, providing incentives to 'tailor' communication to them. Finally, they observed that media abundance leads to a 'pick and choose' culture where people have the ability and the option to tune into outlets that best reflect their already-held beliefs.

Blumer and Kavanagh provide a useful foundation for understanding the media logic that is prevalent in today's media system. Media abundance has indeed led to a fragmentation of audiences and birthed competing domains of public discourse that at times seem to occupy different realms of reality. Political communication has had to adapt itself to the trends outlined. It has become more professional, readily available on more channels, and capable of reaching people with pre-existing values and norms. But even Blumer and Kavanagh would agree that what is transpiring in today's media system is different to the trends of the third age. We need to inject another concept into the discussion to capture the real essence of today's media logic: hybridity.

The age of hybrid political communication

Throughout history all media systems have been a hybrid amalgamation of new and older media. As Adam Chadwick states:

> All older media were once newer and all newer media eventually get older. But older media of any consequence are rarely entirely displaced by newer media ... As successful newer media start to age, its physical characteristics as well as social norms that surround it start to become less visible. What was once awkward and contested becomes habitual and settled.[7]

While Chadwick clearly outlines the hybridity of previous media systems, it can be argued that today's media system is more hybrid due to the rapid advances in digital communication technology. The media abundance that was a defining feature of Blumer and Kavanagh's third age of political communication pales in comparison to what we are witnessing today, when more people have greater access to a wider variety of content than any other time in history. Social media platforms like Facebook, Twitter and Instagram have an almost insatiable appetite for content and the barriers to creating and distributing that content have almost disappeared. Not only is there an abundance of media, there is also an abundance of ways that media can be consumed.

But, while these digital newcomers have had a profound impact on patterns of media consumption, they haven't pushed the old media out of the picture. Rather, old and new media practices are constantly interacting and co-evolving as they combine the 'logics' of one another to form a new hybrid media logic. That is why media outlets such as CNN or the *New York Times* are now learning how to create content that works best for the logics of new media platforms like Snapchat or Facebook, be it creating more interactive tools for smartphone users or putting text on videos. On the other hand, platforms like Twitter are under increasing pressure to adopt some of the logics of older media such as verifying the source of information especially during breaking news situations.

The hybrid media logic encapsulates a number of emerging trends that are shaping today's political communication. First, there is greater opportunity for non-elite actors, be they activists or fringe groups, to intervene in the news-making process alongside established players. The technological and financial barriers to content creation and distribution have decreased. A story can originate on a messaging board or fringe website but quickly travel from the digital realm to the front page of a newspaper and the top story of a news bulletin. Second, older media's traditional role as gatekeepers of information has diminished. This has allowed politicians to connect directly with the electorate without the filter of the media and on their own terms. The lack of a centralised gatekeeper allows politicians, journalists and regular citizens to exploit the hybrid media logic to 'exert their power' and to push their version of events.[8]

Third, the increased fragmentation of the media landscape has hastened the 'pick and choose' culture that was first identified by Blumer and Kavanagh. On the plus side, people can choose what content they want to consume at a time of their own choosing and on their preferred devices. Less positive is the diminished value of truth and facts as anyone can easily access and consume content that supports their pre-existing position on issues regardless of their veracity. There is an active process of political narrative formation driven by traditional and non-traditional actors that feeds entrenched views and enables the existence of alternative realities. Fourth, the hybrid media logic awards virality and narrative episodes. The abundance of content and the accompanying cacophony of 'noise' means that political communication has to compete with a lot of distractions to break through. That is why political messages, be they a tweet or meme that goes viral, need to stand out.

Therefore, political actors who wish to connect effectively to the public, and in turn motivate them to take action, need to understand the logic of the hybrid media system and must satisfy its constant need for virality, trending moments and narrative episodes. Arguably, the original 'hybrid media actor' is none other than Donald J. Trump, the forty-fifth president of the United States.

The rise of Trump: books, TV shows and social media

Regardless of what anyone thinks about Trump's skills and effectiveness as president of the United States, there's no denying that he has always had an uncanny understanding of how to be an effective media player. Long before he tweeted his way to the White House, he understood the prevailing media logic of his time and exploited it to promote an image of himself that best fitted his personal, business and eventually political objectives.

Trump's journey to the top of the political and media world began in the 1980s when the deregulation of Reaganomics unleased a decade of cowboy capitalism and the brash celebration of wealth. By 1987, when Trump published *The Art of the Deal*, he had been a visible feature of the New York tabloid scene for years. He appeared on the front page of tabloids eighty-seven times in the fifteen years leading up to the millennium.[9] *The Art of the Deal* effectively packaged up an easily consumable narrative of Donald Trump the successful capitalist titan. Part memoir, part business advice, the book was the perfect medium for setting a suitable narrative at the time. It follows Trump as he leaves the comforts of the family real estate business in Queens and Brooklyn to make big moves in the heart of the business world, Manhattan. Trump is presented as a shrewd calculator who deftly overcomes bureaucratic barriers and takes advantage of government aid to achieve his lofty goals. He was the successful businessman, symbolising the riches of America.

The book was a major success. It reached number one on the *New York Times* bestseller list and stayed there for thirteen consecutive weeks, and it remained on the list for nearly a year.[10] However, the image of Trump that was depicted in the pages of the book was based on fiction. In a 2016 profile piece in the *New Yorker*, Tony Schwartz, the journalist who actually wrote the book and shared a byline with Trump, talks about how he 'created a character far more winning than Trump' actually was and how he 'sidestepped unflattering incidents and details'.[11] The most important myth that the book helped establish was that Donald Trump was a self-made man. But as numerous books and investigations have shown, that is far from the truth. A 2018 investigation by the *New York Times* based on financial records and tax returns showed how Donald Trump received at least $143 million from his father, Fred Trump, throughout his life using dubious tax practices.[12] In fact, whenever Trump ran into financial problems he was bailed out by loans from his father. The second myth that the book helped create was the idea that Trump's impressive business acumen allowed him to weave his way through the New York real estate swamp to find deals that would bring with them riches. Another recent investigation by the *New York Times* has shown that from 1985 to 1994, the period directly before and after the publication of *The Art of the Deal*, Trump's business empire was in a bleak financial predicament, and it claims that he 'lost more money than nearly any other individual American taxpayer'.[13] The entire origin story regarding Donald Trump that emerged in the mid-1980s and went on to dominate the narrative about him all the way to the White House was based on a myth.

Despite its inaccuracies, *The Art of the Deal* propelled Trump from the tabloid papers of New York into the national conversation. It had provided a useful foundational framework through which Donald Trump could be understood. But the medium that had an even bigger role in shaping the American public's understanding of Donald Trump was television, and specifically the reality TV show *The Apprentice*. The show premiered in January 2004 with a simple and straightforward premise. Each episode, contestants took part in an activity inspired by the world of business, be it selling products on the streets or opening an art gallery, and by the end of the episode the losing team would join Trump in the boardroom where one person would get fired. The last man or woman standing would be the winner, getting the chance to work for the Trump Organization and become an apprentice to the business genius that was Donald Trump. The show opened with shots of symbols of wealth cut to the tune of the 1973 R&B song 'For the Love of Money' by the O'Jays. In the intro scene Donald Trump is seen riding in the back of a limousine where he talks about his success:

> My name's Donald Trump, and I'm the largest real estate developer in New York. I own buildings all over the place, model agencies, the Miss Universe pageant. And private resorts like Mar-a-Lago, one of the most spectacular estates anywhere in the world. But it wasn't always so easy. About thirteen years ago, I was seriously in trouble. I was billions of dollars in debt. But I fought back, and I won big league. And I worked it all out.[14]

The Apprentice was created by Mark Burnett, best known by that point as the creator of *Survivor*, a groundbreaking reality TV show that places contestants on a remote location where they have to fend for themselves as part of tribes and the last person remaining on the island wins the ultimate prize. Long before he trained his lens on Donald Trump, Burnett had perfected the art of the spectacle.[15] Reality TV, pioneered by *Survivor*, brought with it a new media logic in which media spectacles were given primacy. These spectacles can be understood as 'those phenomena of media culture that embody contemporary society's basic values, serve to initiate individuals into its way of life, and dramatize its controversies and struggles, as well as its modes of conflict resolution'. Shows like *The Apprentice* and *Survivor* helped create a celebrity culture where the public came to connect with and emulate on-screen characters. They mediated reality and blurred the lines separating fact and fiction.[16] They created fictional universes with idealised images of the leading proponents.

As Patrick Radden Keefe wrote in *The New Yorker*, *The Apprentice*

> portrayed Trump not as a sleazy hustler who huddles with local mobsters but as a plutocrat with impeccable business instincts and unparalleled wealth – a titan who always seemed to be climbing out of helicopters or into limousines. 'Most of us knew he was a fake,' [Jonathon] Braun told me. 'He had just gone through I don't know how many bankruptcies. But we made him out to be the most important person in the world. It was like making the court jester the king.' Bill Pruitt, another producer, recalled, 'We walked through the offices and saw chipped furniture. We saw a crumbling empire at every turn. Our job was to make it seem otherwise.'[17]

Just like *Survivor*, *The Apprentice* was a ratings hit when it first came out. The season one finale drew twenty-eight million viewers, making it one of the most successful show finales ever. Americans were hooked and the 'avatar of prosperity' that was presented as Trump became the way many came to view him.[18] In fact, the 'show's camera operators often shot Trump from low angles, as you would a basketball pro, or Mt Rushmore. Trump loomed over the viewer.'[19] Quickly after the premiere of the first season, Trump began to understand the value of ratings and how a successful media spectacle can dominate the discussion. In an interview with Larry King that year he admitted he 'didn't know what demographics was four weeks ago. All of a sudden, I heard we were number three in demographics. Last night, we were number one. And that's the important thing.'[20]

If *The Art of the Deal* laid the foundations of Trump's myth, *The Apprentice* built the entire tower complete with the gilded name plates. The seven seasons of the show helped create a powerful image of Trump as the true embodiment of the American Dream. A man who, in his own words, had parlayed a small one-million-dollar loan from his father into a global real estate empire. He was the decisive executive making important decisions who millions of Americans had come to know through their TV screens. It also gave Trump the opportunity to understand the media logic of the time. He saw how the television medium emphasises ratings and requires the creation of fictional universes where the audience can connect with characters. As a celebrity TV star, he perfectly understood the imperative of 'dominating the news agenda, entering the news cycle and repeatedly re-entering it, with stories and initiatives so that subsequent news coverage is set on your terms'. He understood the utility of social media, such as Twitter, which he joined in May 2009, in allowing him the opportunity to enter the news cycle on his own terms.[21]

Trump employed the lessons he learned from years of being a media actor during the manufactured media spectacle surrounding President Obama's birth certificate. He first raised questions about it on an episode of ABC's morning show *The View* on 23 March 2011.[22] 'There is something on that birth certificate that he doesn't like,' Trump said during the appearance, which also included him musing about running for president someday. Days later he phoned into *Fox and Friends* and said he was now wondering whether or not Obama 'was even born in this country'. On 7 April in an appearance on NBC's *Today* show he claimed that if Obama was not born in the United States then he had pulled 'one of the great cons in the history of politics'.[23] Even after Obama released his long-form birth certificate on 27 April 2011, Trump was not convinced. On 6 August 2012, more than a year after Obama released his birth certificate, he tweeted, 'An "extremely credible source" has called my office and told me that @BarackObama's birth certificate is a fraud.'[24] In May 2014, Trump again contested the legitimacy of Obama's birth certificate and even questioned whether or not it was actually released. In an interview with Ireland's TV3 he said: "Well, I don't know, did he do it? Well, a lot of people don't agree with you and a lot of people feel it wasn't a proper certificate."[25] Two years later, again speaking with CNN's Wolf Blitzer, he didn't back down from his claims and when asked about them simply replied, 'Who cares?' He only publicly accepted Barack Obama was born in America in September 2016, five years after he first brought the issue to the public's attention, and during the presidential campaign. But reporting from the *New York Times* afterwards suggest that he still harbours doubts about the birthplace of his predecessor.[26]

The birther conspiracy media spectacle was in many ways Trump's dry run for his presidential campaign. He saw how, by making outlandish claims never backed by evidence, he could garner media attention and consistently dominate the airwaves. For years, he was given a platform on reputable news outlets to discuss his claims. By the time he came down the escalators in the Trump Tower lobby to announce his intention to run for president, a mere six months after he hosted his final season of *The Apprentice*, Donald Trump had perfected his skills as a true hybrid media actor.

From the minute he entered the race, he showed his ability to create a media spectacle that inserted him right in the middle of the national conversation. His announcement speech generated days of coverage given his incendiary comments regarding illegal immigration and his claims that he would build a wall on the US–Mexico border.[27] Adhering to the logics of the hybrid media system, he initially inserted himself in the conversation using rallies, conventional press briefings, and TV and radio appearances, but then he extended his narrative reach by using his social media platforms. Throughout the campaign, Trump used Twitter for talking directly to his supporters, to ensure that topics of his choosing were constantly trending and also for signalling his support for, at times, politically incorrect stances. Thus, even though he got negative coverage at times for sharing tweets that were deemed racist or insensitive he stood by them. That helped burnish his image as an authentic politician that was breaking away from the yoke of the political elite.[28] He also understood that media abundance requires increased media presence and made himself available to the media more than any of his competitors.[29] The media lapped it up. Stories on Trump and his often outlandish claims were a boon for the industry online and on TV. Even though a lot of outlets scrutinised his statements and challenged his claims, he still managed to garner attention and spread his message. In the process, Trump racked up approximately $2 billion of 'earned' media, boosting his electoral chances.[30]

Trump highlighted a number of key requirements for success in the new hybrid media system. First, it is important to have a brand and a strong origin story that people can recognise and connect with. For him, that brand and the myth surrounding him were fashioned over decades of being in the public eye and through the pages of a bestselling book and a popular TV show. He presented himself as a successful businessman who made it all on his own and would bring a wealth of business acumen to the role. Second, in the age of media abundance, you too need to be abundantly present at all times in order to dominate the news agenda. He inserted himself into the conversation at any given opportunity and fed off the ensuing media attention. Third, embrace the language and norms that your supporters are using on newer mediums. Over and over again, Trump retweeted, or reused memes, gifs and imagery being produced by his army of supporters online. That created a strong connection between the two and also showed them that he 'gets' where they are coming from.[31]

Trump laid the groundwork for a new crop of political actors to emerge who are using the same communication playbook to generate media attention, build a political brand and in turn create a loyal base. Ironically, one of the most visible actors within this new generation hails from the progressive left camp of the American political system: Alexandria Ocasio-Cortez.

AOC: the rising star of the hybrid media system

In May 2019, Netflix released a documentary titled *Knock Down the House*. The film follows the campaigns of four progressive Democratic women as they run for Congress in the 2018 midterm elections. They all challenge male incumbents, but only one succeeds: Alexandria Ocasio-Cortez. In June 2018, AOC, as she's known, defeated ten-term incumbent congressman Joe Crowley in the Democratic primary race and went on to represent New York state's 14th district in the United States Congress. Her victory shocked the national Democratic political machine and transformed her from a young woman working at a taqueria in lower Manhattan to a national political star and the youngest woman ever to be elected to the US Congress. While the film tells the story of other leading women as well, it is mainly focused on Ocasio-Cortez and is in many ways her origin story. If Trump had *The Art of the Deal*, Ocasio-Cortez has *Knock Down the House*. The impact of the movie cannot be overestimated. Today, many consumers are flocking to streaming platforms to consume content and a Netflix documentary has the combined myth-making power of a bestselling book and a TV show. The platform has nearly 150 million subscribers around the world and has established new norms and practices regarding how the public consumes media. The movie effectively shaped the public perception of Ocasio-Cortez in depicting her fairy tale rise to the heart of power in Washington, DC.[32]

Ocasio-Cortez's electoral success was, in large part, due to her strong grassroots campaign. Her message resonated with voters in her district. She ran on issues that mattered to people and was successful in painting her opponent as belonging to an out-of-touch political elite that is more interested in maintaining the status quo. But she also had an astute understanding of how the changing media system requires new approaches to political communication. According to a recent report from the Pew Research Center, 85 per cent of Americans now get news on their mobile devices. That's the same percentage as get news on desktops and laptops.[33] 'But of the people who access news on both desktop and mobile, 65 percent prefer consuming it on their mobile devices. That's up from 56 percent in 2016.'[34] The Pew report also found that the increase in mobile news consumption was driven by Democrats. No surprise then that a young digital and mobile media-savvy Democrat would find success in New York, America's largest media market.

From the early phases of her campaign, Ocasio-Cortez adopted a media strategy that took into account the logics of the hybrid media system. As a non-elite actor in an age of media abundance, she understood that she can enter into the political information cycle by appearing on multiple platforms no matter what their size and audience reach. She appeared on numerous podcasts, local talk shows and radio shows to raise her profile and to set the narrative that defined her and her candidacy. She bypassed traditional gatekeepers and connected directly with the electorate through livestreams on Instagram and Facebook. About two-thirds of American adults get news on social media sites with Facebook being the biggest social platform for news consumption.[35] These platforms use algorithms to determine what viewers like and show them content that matches stories or issues that they have previously engaged with. In effect, the 'pick and choose' trend that is characteristic of any media-abundant system has been automated by algorithms that are determined by behemoths like Facebook and YouTube. While this trend has serious implications for the spread of false information and the creation of filter bubbles, it has also made it easier for like-minded people in a community to find each other, connect and mobilise. Ocasio-Cortez not only used social media platforms for communicating with her followers and to raise her profile, she also relied on them for organising campaign meetups and other actions that translated online passion into tangible political action on the ground. Above all else, she understood that political communication in today's hybrid media system requires authenticity, virality and the ability to create personal connections with the audience.[36] A recent linguistic analysis carried out by RAND found that broadcast TV news, cable TV news and online news have all become more personal, emotional and interactive in recent years.[37] Successful political communication in this context, therefore, requires presenting policy ideas and social issues through personal frames and experiences.

The first example of Ocasio-Cortez's media prowess was the video she used to introduce herself to voters. The video presented an emotional narrative of a working-class activist going up against the entrenched wealthy elite that are bent on protecting the status quo, and it talked about issues using the personal frame of Ocasio-Cortez's experiences. It was produced in a mobile-friendly fashion and released on YouTube and linked to on other social media platforms. It quickly went viral, racking up 300,000 views within a day of release.[38] The video cost less than $10,000 to produce, but it established Ocasio-Cortez as an authentic voice of change. Afterwards, she tweeted, 'One great thing about our campaign video: not a single consultant was involved. I wrote the script. My family is the closing shot. That's my actual bodega.'[39]

Ocasio-Cortez's social media presence exploded after her election to Congress. She saw a 600 per cent increase in Twitter followers between the time she won her primary in June and February 2019, after approximately two months on the job.[40] Recent data show a continued upward trajectory in the number of her Twitter followers, making her one of the most popular Democrats on the platform. More importantly, she has a higher rate of interaction per tweet than any other politician, which suggests that she's dominating the conversation on the platform. She has used her Twitter page to constantly push back against her critics and to challenge them using all the tools of the platform, such as memes and emojis, without looking out of place. She has also used the platform to support her fellow progressive Democrats and even held a Twitter tutorial for Democrats in Congress.

Ocasio-Cortez's social media strategy goes beyond Twitter and Facebook. She has burnished her brand on Instagram as well with her livestreams where she engages with her followers and answers their questions while doing mundane tasks like putting together flatpack furniture or cooking. With these livestreams she is allowing her supporters to live vicariously through her and her time in the nation's capital. While critics might downplay these actions as political infotainment, in reality Ocasio-Cortez is creating her own political space for expression. She is not bound by party hierarchy or the gatekeepers of older media. She is creating the same level of emotional connection that Trump created with *The Apprentice*. For millions of Americans who watched *The Apprentice*, especially in the earlier series of the show, Trump personified the American Dream that they could aspire to. Ocasio-Cortez is presenting a modern, digitally savvy version of the American Dream. She's giving her viewers and her political followers a seemingly unfiltered look into policy making and politics and in turn creating new meaning about what it means to be a young American working for change.

Ocasio-Cortez's large social media presence has enabled her to shine a brighter media light on the issues that she's most passionate about and her legislative campaigns. In May 2019, as a freshman congresswoman, she teamed up with Senator Bernie Sanders to release her first legislative initiative, targeting high credit card interest rates.[41] While the pair held a traditional presser to announce their plan and its merits, followers of Ocasio-Cortez on Instagram and Facebook were able to accompany her behind the scenes as she made her way through the tunnels of Congress on her way to the rollout. These steps allowed Ocasio-Cortez, supported by a darling of the progressive left in Senator Bernie Sanders, to court greater media attention to the cause that she's championing and to her personal brand. She also understands that today's hybrid media system feeds off viral moments. News producers and editors are very cognisant of what is trending online and what stories are gathering momentum. They will commission digital writes, explainer pieces and TV segments that in turn help feed the virality. Therefore, a clip might first appear on a social media platform but by the end of the news cycle it will be the subject of multiple writes and video segments. Ocasio-Cortez and her media team are very aware of this dynamic. They have used strategic viral moments, such as her grilling pharmaceutical executives about drug pricing in the US compared to Australia or her talking about the role of dark money in American politics from the floor of the house, to repeatedly insert Ocasio-Cortez into the news cycle and to maintain the media focus on her brand and the issues she is identified with.

Yet it hasn't all been glowing reviews for Ocasio-Cortez. From the minute she emerged on the national stage she has been attacked and vilified by conservatives and their media allies. A *Washington Post* analysis of Fox News segments between 1 January and 15 February 2019 showed that AOC got more coverage than all Democratic candidates running for president in 2020, bar Elizabeth Warren.[42] What is fascinating about that period of analysis is that it covers the first couple of weeks of the political career of a junior Democratic congresswoman, not some seasoned veteran. She has been ridiculed for everything ranging from her clothing choices to her policy inexperience to her dance moves as an undergraduate. While those negative attacks have dragged down her national polling numbers especially among Republican voters, she hasn't backed down from the fight and continues to clapback on social media using 'slaying lewks' that further enrage her detractors while appeasing her fans.[43]

It is too soon to tell whether or not Ocasio-Cortez can translate her social media stardom to long-term political gain, but the mere fact that she captured the public's attention so effectively within less than a year of entering the political scene is testament to her power within the hybrid media system. Just like Trump, she has a strong origin story that's been depicted in the popular medium of the time. She rose to power as a non-elite actor who effectively intervened in the political communication process using newer media. She is a digital native who understands the norms and logics of newer media and leverages that to own the narrative about her and to enter the news cycle at convenient times. Like Trump, Ocasio-Cortez has a unique grasp of the media logic of her time.

Conclusion

The future of American politics belongs to politicians who understand and adopt the norms, values and requirements of the hybrid media system. They will have to know how to bypass traditional gatekeepers and enter the news cycle on their own terms. They have to be digitally savvy with an acute understanding of newer media platforms and the content that works on them. Above all else they have to come across as unfiltered and authentic. As trust in old societal structures – be they news institutions, political parties or religious organisations – continues to decrease, the public will increasingly look for leadership to a new breed of politicians who combine celebrity and authenticity. These new celebrity politicians will have a strong origin story and will know how to frame issues through personal narrative that translates well on social media platforms. They are clued into the trending discussions online and know how to insert themselves into them without looking out of place. Their brand will be enhanced on social media through viral moments that showcase their 'realness' or their passion about certain issues, or their ability to 'slay and clapback' against critics. But their gravitational pull will be strong enough to motivate their band of followers to look up from their smartphones to take action in the real world. These new hybrid media players will not only change the way aspiring politicians attain and hold power, they will fundamentally transform the dynamics governing media and politics.

Notes

1. Lisa Gitelman, *Always Already New: Media, History and the Data of Culture* (Cambridge, MA: MIT Press, 2006), 7.
2. Ibid., 7.
3. D. L. Altheide and Robert P. Snow, *Media Logic* (London: Sage, 1979).
4. For an excellent summary of the scholarship on media logic see Andrew Chadwick, *The Hybrid Media System: Politics and Power* (New York: Oxford University Press, 2013).
5. Jay G. Blumler and Dennis Kavanagh. 'The Third Age of Political Communication: Influences and Features', *Political Communication* 16, no. 3 (1999): 209–30.
6. Ibid., 221.
7. Chadwick, *The Hybrid Media System*, 23.
8. Ibid., 157.
9. 'What Do Old Tabloid Covers Reveal about the Rise of Donald Trump?', *The Economist*, 11 January 2019, <https://www.economist.com/prospero/2019/01/11/what-do-old-tabloid-covers-reveal-about-the-rise-of-donald-trump> (accessed 29 January 2020).
10. Jane Mayer, 'Donald Trump's Ghostwriter Tells All', *New Yorker*, 18 July 2016, <https://www.newyorker.com/magazine/2016/07/25/donald-trumps-ghostwriter-tells-all> (accessed 29 January 2020).
11. Ibid.
12. David Barstow, Susanne Craig and Russ Buettner, 'Trump Engaged in Suspect Tax Schemes as He Reaped Riches from His Father', *New York Times*, 2 October 2018, <https://www.nytimes.com/interactive/2018/10/02/us/politics/donald-trump-tax-schemes-fred-trump.html> (accessed 29 January 2020).
13. Russ Buettner and Susanne Craig, 'Decade in the Red: Trump Tax Figures Show Over $1 Billion in Business Losses', *New York Times*, 8 May 2019, <https://www.nytimes.com/interactive/2019/05/07/us/politics/donald-trump-taxes.html> (accessed 29 January 2020).
14. Available at <https://www.youtube.com/watch?v=Ozb0WYpusxU> (accessed 29 January 2020).
15. Patrick Radden Keefe, 'How Mark Burnett Resurrected Donald Trump as an Icon of American Success', *New Yorker*, 27 December

2018, <https://www.newyorker.com/magazine/2019/01/07/how-mark-burnett-resurrected-donald-trump-as-an-icon-of-american-success> (accessed 29 January 2020).
16. Douglas Kellner, 'Donald Trump, Media Spectacle, and Authoritarian Populism', *Fast Capitalism* 14, no. 1 (2017), <http://www.uta.edu/huma/agger/fastcapitalism/14_1/Kellner-Donald-Trump-Media.htm> (accessed 29 January 2020).
17. Keefe, 'How Mark Burnett Resurrected Donald Trump as an Icon of American Success'.
18. 'Trump Stories: The Apprentice', NPR, 11 October 2017, <https://www.npr.org/templates/transcript/transcript.php?storyId=555768139> (accessed 29 January 2020).
19. Keefe, 'How Mark Burnett Resurrected Donald Trump as an Icon of American Success'.
20. Ibid.
21. 'Trump on Twitter: A History of the Man and His Medium', BBC News, 12 December 2016, <https://www.bbc.com/news/world-us-canada-38245530> (accessed 29 January 2020).
22. See Sophie Tatum and Jim Acosta, 'Report: Trump Continues to Question Obama's Birth Certificate', CNN Politics, 30 November 2017, <https://edition.cnn.com/2017/11/28/politics/donald-trump-barack-obama-birth-certificate-nyt/index.html> (accessed 29 January 2020).
23. See Nick Gass, 'Trump Concedes Obama Was Born in the US', *Politico*, 15 September 2016, https://www.politico.com/story/2016/09/donald-trump-birtherism-campaign-statement-228261.
24. Donald Trump (@realDonaldTrump), Twitter, 6 August 2012, <https://twitter.com/realdonaldtrump/status/232572505238433794?lang=en> (accessed 29 January 2020).
25. See Andrew Kaczynski, 'Trump Questioned Obama Birth Certificate in 2014, Despite Campaign Statement', *BuzzFeed*, 15 September 2016, <https://www.buzzfeednews.com/article/andrewkaczynski/trump-questioned-obama-birth-certificate-in-2014-despite-cam> (accessed 23 March 2020).
26. German Lopez, 'Trump Is Still Reportedly Pushing His Racist "Birther" Conspiracy Theory about Obama', *Vox*, 29 November 2017, <https://www.vox.com/policy-and-politics/2017/11/29/16713664/trump-obama-birth-certificate> (accessed 29 January 2020).
27. Kellner, 'Donald Trump, Media Spectacle, and Authoritarian Populism'.
28. Michael Gurevitch, Stephen Coleman and Jay G. Blumler, 'Political Communication: Old and New Media Relationships', *Annals*

of the American Academy of Political and Social Science 625, no. 1 (2009), 164–81.
29. Callum Borchers, 'The Clinton Campaign's Totally Bogus Claim about Its Press Availability', *Washington Post*, 6 June 2016, <https://www.washingtonpost.com/news/the-fix/wp/2016/06/06/the-clinton-campaigns-totally-bogus-claim-about-its-press-availability> (accessed 30 January 2020).
30. Nicholas Confessore and Karen Yourish, '$2 Billion Worth of Free Media for Donald Trump', *New York Times*, 15 March 2016, <https://www.nytimes.com/2016/03/16/upshot/measuring-donald-trumps-mammoth-advantage-in-free-media.html> (accessed 30 January 2020).
31. Stephanie Mencimer, '"The Left Can't Meme": How Right-Wing Groups Are Training the Next Generation of Social Media Warriors', *Mother Jones*, 2 April 2019, <https://www.motherjones.com/politics/2019/04/right-wing-groups-are-training-young-conservatives-to-win-the-next-meme-war> (accessed 30 January 2020).
32. On Netflix's earnings see Seth Fiegerman, 'Netflix Adds 9 Million Paying Subscribers, but Stock Falls', CNN Business, 18 January 2019, <https://edition.cnn.com/2019/01/17/media/netflix-earnings-q4/index.html> (accessed 30 January 2020). For a breakdown on the Ocasio-Cortez documentary see Lucy Diavolo, 'Netflix's AOC Documentary, "Knock Down the House", Might Make You Want to Riot', *TeenVogue*, 1 May 2019, <https://www.teenvogue.com/story/netflix-aoc-documentary-knock-down-the-house-make-you-want-to-riot> (accessed 30 January 2020).
33. Elisa Shearer and Katerina Eva Matsa, 'News Use across Social Media Platforms 2018', Pew Research Center, 10 September 2018, <https://www.journalism.org/2018/09/10/news-use-across-social-media-platforms-2018> (accessed 30 January 2020).
34. Christine Schmidt, 'Americans Expect to Get Their News from Social Media, but They Don't Expect It to Be Accurate', Nieman Labs, 10 September 2018, < https://www.niemanlab.org/2018/09/americans-expect-to-get-their-news-from-social-media-but-they-dont-expect-it-to-be-accurate> (accessed 30 January 2020).
35. Shearer and Matsa, 'News Use across Social Media Platforms 2018'.
36. Sean Wise, '5 Social Media Moves That Prove Alexandria Ocasio-Cortez Is the Queen of Digital Emotional Intelligence', *Inc.*, 20 February 2019, <https://www.inc.com/sean-wise/5-social-media-moves-that-prove-alexandria-ocasio-cortez-is-queen-of-digital-emotional-intelligence.html> (accessed 30 January 2020).

37. Jennifer Kavanagh, William Marcellino, Jonathan S. Blake, Shawn Smith, Steven Davenport and Mahlet G. Tebeka, *News in a Digital Age: Comparing the Presentation of News Information over Time and across Media Platforms* (Santa Monica, CA: RAND, 2019), available at <https://www.rand.org/pubs/research_reports/RR2960.html> (accessed 30 January 2020).
38. Zaid Jilani, 'How a Ragtag Group of Socialist Filmmakers Produced One of the Most Viral Campaign Ads of 2018', *The Intercept*, 5 June 2018, <https://theintercept.com/2018/06/05/ocasio-cortez-new-york-14th-district-democratic-primary-campaign-video> (accessed 30 January 2020).
39. Available at https://bit.ly/2M0iRvh (accessed 30 January 2020).
40. Max Benwell, 'How Alexandria Ocasio-Cortez Beat Everyone at Twitter in Nine Tweets', *The Guardian*, 12 February 2019, <https://www.theguardian.com/us-news/2019/feb/12/alexandria-ocasio-cortez-twitter-social-media> (accessed 30 January 2020).
41. Gregory Krieg, Katie Lobosco and Ryan Nobles, 'Bernie Sanders and Alexandria Ocasio-Cortez Team Up on Credit Card Interest Rates', CNN Politics, 9 May 2019, <https://edition.cnn.com/2019/05/09/politics/bernie-sanders-aoc-credit-card/index.html> (accessed 30 January 2020).
42. Philip Bump, 'The Democrats Attracting the Most Attention on Fox News? Warren, Harris – and Ocasio-Cortez', *Washington Post*, 20 February 2019, <https://wapo.st/2M1jZyJ> (accessed 30 January 2020).
43. Wise, '5 Social Media Moves'.

13

'Reality Has a Well-Known Liberal Bias':[1]
The End(s) of Satire in Trump's America

Liam Kennedy

Is this a golden age of satire in the US or is satire dead? Both opinions have been strongly expressed in recent years, often pinioned to the election of Donald Trump and the effects of his presidency on the public sphere. For some, there has been a radical 'democratisation of satire', facilitated and shaped by new platforms on the Internet and social media, enjoining new producers and consumers. For others, partly due to this putative democratisation, 'satire is dead', killed off by fake news and disinformation and fatally compromised by its limited appeals to like-minded audiences in their bubbles or echo chambers.[2]

With the radical intensification of political and cultural polarisation and partisanship in the US there has been a seismic, paradigm-shifting shock to the public sphere. It has become a funhouse of distortions and distractions, disruptions and disinformation, and its regression is evidenced in the surfacing of obscene ideas, discourses and images that were once confined to margins or underworlds. The derealisation of political culture and communications signals a radical decline in the symbolic efficiency of liberal democracy and satire registers this. Traditionally, satire has functioned as a form of political communication that attacks but also relies on the solid-seeming reality secured by existing institutions and relations of power. In the era of Trump, though, Americans seem to have lost belief in a shared referential world. Can satire be effective if there is no underlying belief system?

Satire is commonly viewed as the most politically motivated and directed form of humour, combining play with critique, often with a moralising or reformist intent. Its critical impulse defines and differentiates it from its comedic cousins irony and parody – in Northrop Frye's trenchant definition, satire is 'militant irony'.[3] Satire is of course historically and culturally contingent, always in flux, its premises and targets shifting; it is neither inherently liberal nor inherently conservative and its politics are dependent on the contexts of its production, style and dissemination. Why has satire become so popular and pervasive in the US in the twenty-first century? The answers lie in the co-evolution of new communications technologies and transformations in the public sphere, political culture and civil society. This is to say that political satire is contingent on the relations between institutions and processes of governance on the one hand and those of media production and representation on the other, and as that ecosystem evolves the relationship between satire and its imagined community shifts. Today, with the rise of a networked society and advent of unregulated social media, institutions of news and other forms of authoritative cultural production have been severely disrupted and challenged, while new actors have emerged taking on narrative and information power. In this contemporary context the meaning and value of satire has come under review, reflecting broader apprehensions about the advent of 'fake news' and a 'post-truth' society and how these are reshaping civic and social engagement.

Underlying the differing views on the currency of satire is a common perception that there is a surfeit of material with satirical resonance circulating in American culture but there is doubt and disagreement about the purpose or impact of such material. The Internet has become so saturated with ironic and humorous material that it is difficult to tell what is serious intent and what is spoofing, and so any reference to satire can seem an inadequate categorising. For liberals, in particular, this seems to be part of a broader epistemic panic about the dismantling of norms and standards of political and civic discourse and the collapse of the myth of social progress. For liberals, satire holds out a dream of attack and pushback against the disruptors and especially the disruptor-in-chief; they tend to invest in satire as a critical weapon and an affective balm, and they like to define satire in ways that imagine it as a liberal or progressive form of communication, off limits to humourless conservatives. For conservatives, many of whom are invested in Trump's attack on 'elites', satire promises to be a key resource in fighting the culture wars, following the example of the alt-right's weaponisation of irony and meme culture. For both liberals and conservatives, satire is as much a reflection of their anxieties and prejudices as it is a critical mirror held up to authority.

Renaissance

Political satire is long established in the US and it has taken various forms, ranging from pamphlets during the Revolutionary War period to user-generated memes today. For much of this history, it was the preserve and tool of elites, even when its producers created the illusion of being the voice of the average American. In its recent history, since the 1960s, it has shape-shifted in relation to dramatic realignments of politics, media and civil society, presaging the satirical forms and energies of today.

In 1960, the election campaign of John F. Kennedy signalled the profound effect television would have on political culture, blurring it with entertainment and accelerating its transformation into spectacle. Norman Mailer, writing about Kennedy's media image as he campaigned, observed that the 'President is the lead actor in the national soap opera of the US' and Kennedy appealed to 'the dream life of the nation'.[4] Philip Roth, reflecting on the 1960 televised debates between presidential candidates Kennedy and Richard Nixon, lamented: 'The American writer in the middle of the 20th century has his hands full in trying to understand, and then describe, and then make credible much of the American reality . . . The actuality is continually outdoing our talents.'[5] Kennedy's election prefaced a decade of civil unrest and protest that was awash with satirical energies that moved beyond the conventional confines of traditional forms and genres. The counterculture of the 1960s incorporated forms of satire into its carnivalesque challenges to social, cultural and political authorities, much of this transgressive material emerging from the subcultural 'underground' in alternative magazines, performances and music, but also now moving into the mainstream culture and media which had often been its target. Its more overtly politicised and challenging forms included the agitprop activities of Paul Krassner and Abbie Hoffman, the stand-up comedy of Lenny Bruce and Dick Gregory, and the literary satire of Don Novello. The mainstreaming of satire was evident in television by the mid-1960s, with *That Was the Week That Was* (NBC 1964–5), followed by *The Smothers Brothers Comedy Hour* (CBS 1967–70), *Rowan and Martin's Laugh-In* (NBC 1968–73) and *Saturday Night Live* (NBC since 1975). While these programmes were innovative and occasionally pushed political boundaries, they generally neutered the sharper edges of countercultural satire.

Satire become comfortable within mainstream media and culture but would once again emerge as a more unsettling force in the early years of the twenty-first century. Already, through the 1990s, there were signs of a widening and deepening of partisanship and polarisation in political culture, as the culture wars that have their roots in the 1960s were reignited around the presidency of Bill Clinton. This shift in political culture was enabled in significant part by major transformations in media including the erosion of networked television and emergence of cable, the rise of talk radio and beginnings of the Internet, all hastening the fragmenting of public attention. It was the Bush presidency, though, and especially the effects of 9/11 on political culture in the US that sparked a new wave of satirical cultural production, most notably in late-night comedy shows that took energy from the platform of cable television. *The Daily Show* (Comedy Central since 1996; with Jon Stewart as host from 1999 to 2015) became a very influential example as it developed an admixture of political and news satire that became a popular genre. These shows were credited with displacing certain functions of the news media and rendering satire an engaged form of political communication, and with creating a community of dissent at a time when dissenting voices where being marginalised or silenced in the wake of 9/11 and the US commitment to wars in Afghanistan and Iraq. The growth of political satire in US media at this time also reflected the growing distrust in institutions and the widespread perception of American decline.[6]

The upsurge in political satire was notably liberal in impetus and address. In this it also reflected something of a liberal anxiety about political reality and particularly about the hubris of the Bush presidency, which dismissively viewed news media as a part of the 'reality-based community', alienated from and secondary to the workings of power.[7] It further reflected apprehension about the growing power of a conservative media that claimed to speak for 'real Americans'.[8] The comedian Stephen Colbert created a popular satirical persona of a hyper-conservative pundit who personified these distortions of reality. It was a performance he first honed on *The Daily Show* and then on his own show, *The Colbert Report* (Comedy Central, 2005–14). Colbert's satirical approach focused on the distrust of facts and pointedly parodied the wilful ignorance of Americans and particularly conservatives; he presented absurdities and small-mindedness as commonsense facts, lampooning the ascent of emotion over fact in American media and political culture. While criticising the George W. Bush administration he popularised the word 'truthiness': 'We're not talking about the truth; we're talking about something that seems like truth – the truth we want to exist.'[9] At the 2006 White House Correspondents' Dinner, when Colbert, in character, mocked the president and his administration and celebrated the obtuseness of a hyper-conservative worldview, his performance was widely lauded as speaking truth to power.

With the popularity of *The Daily Show* and its emerging satellites commentators began to refer to a 'renaissance' in satire.[10] Increasingly this form of satire was becoming a source of information and news, not just a critic of these. By 2015, comedians were being described as 'the new public intellectuals', and granted degrees of credibility and trust that were increasingly withdrawn from traditional institutions including government and news media.[11] Satire was now vaulted to gatekeeper status in the public sphere, with satirists 'filling some of the watchdog functions that journalists used to carry out'.[12] This was satire with a message, blurring lines between comedy, commentary and cultural criticism, on topics such as racism, misogyny, terrorism and climate change, and posing questions about identity politics, privilege and cultural authority. Liberal scholars and media commentators saw in satire the values they prized and identified with as writers. In the view of scholars Sophia McClennen and Remy Maisel, writing in 2014, satire represented 'one of the strongest voices of critical thought and democratic deliberation' and they opined that 'satire may be the only way we can save our democracy and strengthen our nation'.[13]

During the Obama administration, the liberal satirists appeared to have the high ground, but as watchdogs they may be said to have failed, for few grasped how radically the ground was shifting. Around talk radio and Fox News a conservative media ecosystem was being built that fostered alternative, illiberal perspectives and touted conservative values; it spoke very directly to Americans who felt culturally disenfranchised and many gravitated to it. It is also the case that Fox News proved a significant foil to the emergence and styling of liberal satirical news shows – it was often the butt of liberal comedy but also used this as leverage with its audience, and so a feedback loop was being formed. Lines were being drawn around liberal and conservative media spheres and echo chambers were already formulating communities with different realities, believing in different Americas. At the same time, online media were growing in a mostly unregulated way and beginning to form nodes and incipient networks of communication that referenced political matters, often irreverently and sometimes in a satirical form. The imageboard website 4chan, launched in 2003, was mostly invisible to mainstream culture and media commentators but would prove influential. From its origins as a site for sharing images of manga and anime it rapidly grew, taking in diverse Internet subcultures, populated by gamers and trollers, and forming and popularising memes as a new form of communication. In the final years of the Obama presidency trolling culture entered into mainstream media and online communications, and mocking humour and irony became powerful accelerants and smokescreens for lies and propaganda. The 2016 election was thus primed to be disruptive of norms and civility, blowing open the Overton window of tolerable political discourse.[14]

Catharsis

In the wake of the 2016 election, as many Americans struggled to come to terms with the election of Trump as president, humour was quickly seen as both a balm and a weapon. The veteran TV host David Letterman claimed that 'comedy is one of the ways that we can protect ourselves from' Trump.[15] Others promoted a more militant and offensive use of humour, seeking to weaponise satire as part of the 'Resistance'. The film maker and provocateur Michael Moore called for 'an army of satire' to attack and undermine Trump; he tweeted, 'Satire is truth, but what is it when it becomes real? A more dangerous brand of satire is needed and an Army of Satirists Will Defeat Trump.'[16] The term 'renaissance' was widely used again as across media and genres there were claims that satirical energies had been invigorated by the election of Trump. Few would have disagreed with *Doonesbury* creator Garry Trudeau's observation that it would be 'comedy malpractice' not to cover Trump, observing that the new president '*is* satire, pure and uncut, free for all to use and enjoy'.[17]

Late-night comedy became the bellwether of this trend and the intensified focus on political satire proved a ratings hit for many of the hosts, with the shows also being well rewarded in the Emmys in 2017 and 2018. *The Daily Show*, now helmed by Trevor Noah, and its offshoots – *The Late Show with Stephen Colbert* (CBS since 2015), *Last Week Tonight with John Oliver* (HBO since 2014) and *Full Frontal with Samantha Bee* (TBS since 2016) – led the way, while *The Tonight Show Starring Jimmy Fallon* and *Late Night with Seth Myers* (both NBC since 2014) also pushed into more political material, with Trump usually the butt. *Saturday Night Live* spearheaded the satirical attacks on Trump and his administration, attracting interest in its cold openings that regularly focused on Trump, with Alec Baldwin's impersonation of the president receiving especial attention. Broader media began to produce regular coverage of the TV shows, furthering their cultural significance as a reference point for many. Trump's early presidency also gave rise to satirical coverage in other media, including a cartoon on Showtime, *Our Cartoon President*, Twitter accounts such as @TrumpDraws, and a growing number of books in various genres.

Underlying many of these satirical representations of Trump in late-night shows and other media was the promise of exposing hypocrisies and laying bare the real intent or machinations of the new president and his administration. In part, this was an extension of the acts of witnessing and speaking truth to power that had become a feature of satire's appeal during the Bush presidency. In the case of Trump, it involves not only imagining incompetence but also feeding conspiracy theories about the ulterior motives behind the president's constant disruptions, including the idea that these are designed to create an illusion of incompetence. In these ways satire fed into a desire for compensatory narratives that would explain Trump's election and continued authority, and also stoked fantasies about his inevitable fall. This was a remarkably sustained illusion given that there was no evidence that political satire had slowed Trump's race to the presidency. During the election liberal media celebrated satirical barbs directed at Trump in hyperbolic terms, as 'takedowns' that 'destroyed' or 'demolished' or 'eviscerated' the presumptive Republican forerunner, but still he galloped to victory.[18] That it was so sustained indicates that comedy and satire in particular took on key purposes for a traumatised citizenry, functioning as vectors for wish fulfilment and catharsis.

For all the satirical activity in the first year of Trump's presidency, or more likely because of it, questions about the quality and efficacy of these shows' promotion of political satire soon began to emerge and sections of liberal and progressive commentators called them out as 'lazy' and 'ineffective'.[19] For a growing number of commentators the satire felt strained or misjudged, too reliant on repeated tropes and motifs, such as the routines and memes that infantilised Trump, caricaturing him as a baby or toddler that is out of control or being mollified by handlers.[20] Others criticised the tendency to rely on reference humour that too often consists of pointing at Trump's actions or statements in an arch or ironic way, or quoting his own language and especially his tweets.[21]

More and more voices complained that Trump was 'resistant' to satire, arguing that he embodies irony and hyperbole, that he was a 'already a walking caricature of himself', and that it is impossible to 'shame the shameless'.[22] The writer and producer Armando Iannucci, who created the HBO satire *Veep*, called Trump 'a self-basting ironist' and while this echoed Trudeau's comment that Trump '*is* satire', Iannucci more pointedly sees this as a problem for satirists: 'Just read him and you have found the joke about him. It comes out in what he says, which leaves people like me slightly redundant other than just to point it out.'[23] In such complaints there is an inference that reality is outrunning the imagination of the satirists. Ben Greenman, reviewing a satirical literary take on Trump in the *New York Times*, observes that 'if reality consistently beats you to your punch you are not writing satire'.[24] The challenge was starkly acknowledged by the makers of the TV show *South Park* shortly after Trump's election. During the election they had run a season in which a central character mimicked Trump but found themselves confounded by the absurdity of the Trump-driven news cycle. Co-creator Trey Parker explained:

> In the last season, we were really trying to make fun of what was going on, but we couldn't keep up . . . What was actually happening was much funnier than anything we could come up with, so we decided to back off and let [politicians] do their comedy and we'll do ours.[25]

After a year of the Trump presidency, many commentators were arguing that it had not only warped reality but eroded the sense of a shared reality and that this neutered satirical comedy. Jo Miller, producer and writer of *Full Frontal with Samantha Bee*, makes a similar point: 'When it comes to jokes, they depend on a shared reality. A joke that is built on an untrue or only partially true premise isn't funny. Which is why partisan "comedy" isn't funny. It puts an agenda before truth and is merely tedious.'[26]

As humourists have become more conscious of these shortcomings and challenges, they have pushed back against expectations about the role of political comedy. Some recalled that in his penultimate *Daily Show* in August 2015 Jon Stewart lamented that 'my years of evisceration have embettered nothing'.[27] More recently, his replacement at the *Daily Show*, Trevor Noah, remarked, 'I was fascinated that people said, "Your job now is to stop Trump" . . . I don't know how Americans were tricked into believing that is possible.' He added that satire may give viewers of the show 'a false sense of activism, because people experience a catharsis and they go, "Yeah, we've done our job, we've retweeted that clip."'[28] Stephen Colbert reflects, 'I have never had any illusion that what I am doing is changing the world. We do it late at night, and maybe you sleep better because of it.'[29]

While quick to disown the idea that political satire will 'stop Trump', some of the comedians have defended the value of their work and sought to address the perceived limitations of the genre in their methods. Since giving up his persona as a facetious conservative pundit (on taking over as host of *The Late Show* in 2015) Colbert has retained his sharp focus on parodying wilful ignorance. He argues that it remains important to provide correctives to Trump's distortions of reality and has dubbed Trump a 'heretic against reality' who 'lives in this fantasy world where only his emotions count and therefore only his reality is real'.[30] In this, Colbert has maintained a strong investment in imaginatively addressing and validating his audience as part of a 'reality-based community'. John Oliver's *Last Week Tonight* has also developed its approach with some consciousness of the challenges of satirising Trump and his administration. Over time Oliver has tended to avoid many direct references to Trump and to move outside the news cycle of the moment, purporting to take a longer view with more investigative pieces on single issues and based on rigorous fact-checking. Tactically, he says, 'What you don't want to do is narrate things that [Trump] said and then just tell a joke off each thing. You want to try and show why that actually matters.'[31] Like *South Park*'s creators before them, these shows have recognised the dilemma of focusing too directly or exclusively on Trump's absurdities and angled their satirical commentary on more tangible features of Trump's America. Yet, both approaches announce limitations even as they seek to address them; both tend towards the moral high ground in prizing seriousness of purpose over gratuitousness but still have to overcome the in-built ephemerality of the late-night show genre, and they show little sign of effective political intervention or reach beyond partisan audiences.

The often hollow satirical performances and rhetoric of the late-night hosts reflect the strains of the transformed relationship between media and politics. The extent of that shift may be observed in the 2018 White House Correspondents' Association (WHCA) dinner, when Michelle Wolf played comic host twelve years after Colbert mocked President Bush and his administration.

The most notable difference in 2018 was the absence of the president, who was represented by his press secretary, Sarah Huckabee Sanders. The deeper change, though, was in the ways in which Wolf's performance and responses to it more transparently revealed the occasion as a pseudo-event of establishment authority and vanity. Wolf's twenty-minute monologue, filled with mockery and obscenities, excoriated Trump, his administration and the mainstream media. The media reaction was mostly predictably partisan but among liberal media it was curiously conflicted, with many criticising Wolf for a lack of decorum and praising Sanders for not walking out[32] A notable feature of these criticisms was their efforts to maintain a fiction of civility that had already been exposed and transgressed by Trump and his associates and to attempt to shore up distinctions between news and comedy that had already collapsed. Where Colbert's pitch-perfect ironic performance in 2006 could be celebrated as speaking truth to power, Wolf's made many liberals uncomfortable by seemingly stepping over bounds of irony and civility to enjoin the bad faith of the Trump presidency. In the furore that followed the WHCA refused to defend Wolf and issued a statement saying:

> Last night's program was meant to offer a unifying message about our common commitment to a free press while honoring civility, great reporting and scholarship winners, not to divide people. Unfortunately, the entertainer's monologue was not in the spirit of that mission.[33]

The statement underscores the fiction of civility in political discourse and echoes the disavowal by liberal commentators of the obscenities, which is to say their refusal to acknowledge or accept their complicity in this fiction.[34]

Conservative commentators were quick to express faux outrage at Wolf's speech even as they mocked the 'phony' civility of liberal political discourse, and Trump sought to turn the event to his advantage, telling a crowd in Michigan the following day it was evidence that 'they hate you' and describing Wolf as a 'filthy "comedian"'.[35] The ease with which Trump turned satire into propaganda and expressed casual obscenity and denigration spoke to the new landscape and rules of political communication.

Conservative satire and meme culture

It is often observed that American comedians are rarely politically conservative and that there is no tradition or culture of political satire on the American right, though reasons to support such observations rarely move beyond supposition. Some commentators have mused that political humour 'might have an inherently liberal bias' but this devolves into a vague notion that conservatives prefer to uphold rather than attack institutions.[36] To be sure, the landscapes of politicised stand-up comedy and of late-night chat shows are dominated by liberals or progressives, but this is not evidence of a conservative lack of humour. Rather, as we have seen, it speaks to the hegemonic forms mainstream liberal culture takes. We need to look to what platforms and locales and in what forms and styles conservative humour is produced and disseminated and consider the nature of satire within it.[37] Liberal dismissal of conservative comedy is myopic in refusing to acknowledge that there is an outpouring of satirical material from conservative, often alt-right, sources on the Internet and in social media, only fractions of which enter the mainstream liberal media sphere.

Most liberal commentators were blindsided by the growth and deployment of trolling and meme culture in support of Trump's election campaign and the indirect support it lent him by spreading distrust in media and government. While much of this developed as a chaotic, uncontrolled process, the alt-right was a significant agent in helping to animate and radicalise a toxic online counter-public, with attacks on the 'establishment' and 'political correctness' directing its transgressive energies against progressive ideas and representatives. Irony and satire are favoured devices of this alt-right discourse, which has increasingly infiltrated more mainstream media and political communications, thereby warping political discourse. Central to the advent and advance of this counter-public has been the deployment of meme culture. A meme, first defined by Richard Dawkins as a 'unit of cultural transmission', is now generally understood to be an image or text that spreads virally on the Internet and is often comic in content or form, referencing or riffing off available media content including political communications.[38] They often have markers, such as in-jokes, symbols, words or phrases, that first emerged in online subcultures and which have been widely mainstreamed. Pepe the Frog is a now infamous example, the cartoon frog having morphed from a figure in a little-known online comic to one of the most popular memes on the Internet.[39] Memes are participatory and intertextual forms of cultural production, picking up meaning as they spread virally, while also disseminating a semiotic repertoire and creating online communities of users. Due to their 'vernacular creativity' and immediacy, memes have become the dominant currency of comic and satirical online discourse, and due to their anonymity and potential for viral acceleration they have proved to be engines of racism, xenophobia and misogyny.[40] Key to this deployment is that memes blur the boundaries between declarative and satirical intent and so offer an ironic veil for abuse – 'lol', 'It's just a joke'. 4chan has a boilerplate that signifies this: 'The stories and information posted here are artistic works of fiction and falsehood. Only a fool would take anything written here as fact.'[41] This statement itself is laced with irony, an example of how bigotry masquerades as satire in alt-right communications.

Trump's polarising election campaign developed a symbiotic relationship with alt-right meme culture. While the originating desire to create chaos and mock marginalised groups that animated much of alt-right trolling became more focused on support for Trump as an agent of chaos and mockery, the Trump campaign began to leverage the power of memes as forms of political communication. In September 2016, following the publication of Hillary Clinton's description of Trump supporters as a 'basket of deplorables' and the ensuing outcry, many satirical memes circulated that referenced the phrase and the hashtag #basketofdeplorables trended on Twitter. A Reddit user published a meme of the faces of Trump's inner circle photoshopped onto actors in the poster image for the film *The Expendables*, with the title changed to *The Deplorables*. Front and centre is the face of Donald Trump while to his left the actor's face has been replaced with Pepe the Frog, now an alt-right icon, in a Trump wig. Donald Trump Jr posted the meme on Instagram and it was widely disseminated by alt-right communities whose leaders would later boast, 'We memed Trump into power.'[42]

'REALITY HAS A WELL-KNOWN LIBERAL BIAS'

Figure 13.1. 'The Deplorables' meme. (Source: Donald Trump Jr (@donaldjtrumpjr), Instagram, 11 September 2016, <https://www.instagram.com/p/BKMtdN5Bam5/?utm_source=ig_embed>, accessed 30 January 2020)

Trump's first public use of a meme was when in July 2017 he tweeted an image made by a Reddit user that depicts him body-slamming a wrestler whose head has been replaced by the CNN logo. Trump's endorsement of the meme was a significant moment in the short history of meme culture as it signalled support for online trolling and spurred meme producers to be creative in their attacks on mainstream media and politics. 'That's when the game changed,' notes a leading 'memesmith' called CarpeDonktum, 'and memes went from being crummy images to these high-fidelity ones.'[43] There are alt-right sites, such as Reddit's The Donald, which act as online laboratories for meme development and others, such as Infowars, that have meme contests and many users keen to create the next viral meme attack on progressive targets and receive Trump's endorsement. Trump has not only endorsed alt-right meme producers and trolls; he has actively courted them, inviting several to a White House 'Social Media Summit' in July 2019, and he sees them as important to his media strategy for the 2020 election.[44]

The growth and popularity of memes is indicative of how not only the political economy of media is shifting but the driving forces of political humour are no longer secured within establishment institutions. A concomitant indicator of these shifts is the demise of professional political cartoonists, in part displaced by amateur meme creators. There are some who lament this trend and they are often dismissive of memes as forms of satirical communication.[45] To be sure, memes exist in a more ephemeral environment and most have a very short life span but they should be understood as a fundamentally different form of cultural production to political cartoons. The latter are generally produced within conventionalised formats and styles and discursive boundaries shaped not only by the history of the genre but by the political economy of media and doxa of the public sphere. There are clear demarcations between author and audience and the cartoon is produced and understood as an individual expression often in signature style shared with a knowing audience. Precisely because they are so conventionalised and exist in a recognised niche of mainstream political culture, they have limited room for transgressive expression and are policed accordingly – the cartoonist Rob Rogers was fired from the *Pittsburgh Post-Gazette* for a critical illustration of Trump.[46]

Unlike cartoons, memes are 'multi-accentual' and participatory in their production; remixing is a core feature of meme culture, often requiring a degree of subcultural knowledge. In this they reflect the polyvalence and 'discursive integration' of the Internet content they remediate.[47] Meme producers can appropriate and repurpose images and text that denigrate or negatively represent their identity, and so irony is commonly used in meme production as it plays off very different meanings of the same content – an example is the alt-right's appropriation and reclaiming of the 'basket of deplorables' remark by Hillary Clinton. So, memes utilise satire in ways that can reflect political cartooning in style but are very different in impulse and impact.

There has been a tendency on the left to dismiss memes as a form of political communication while the right seem convinced they are a valuable form of information warfare and represent a new cultural battleground that progressives have struggled to fight on. As Stephanie Mencimer writes:

> Well-funded conservative groups are making a more organized push to train young internet-savvy right-wingers in the art of meme-making, enlisting a growing army in what they see as the coming meme war of 2020 . . . And it's clear that when it comes to political memes, the left – which has never taken them very seriously – is trailing the right badly, and falling even further behind.[48]

There is even a subgenre of memes titled 'the left can't meme' and little evidence that progressive activists have been as aggressive or organised as the right in incorporating memes into their training or getting to grips with the viral violence of alt-right trolling. There are a growing number of anxious observations by liberal and progressive commentators that the alt-right has targeted Generation Z as a pliable online public to indoctrinate via 'memetic warfare', using satire and irony as lures to activate and direct their perceived apolitical nihilism and encourage the identity play of conservative trolling.[49]

A key part of what perplexes liberals and leftists is the erasure of boundaries between satire and propaganda and the difficulties of deducing intent. That discomfort is evident in responses to a mocking video made by right-wing online comedian Allie Stuckey in July 2018. The video faked an interview with then congressional candidate Democrat Alexandria Ocasio-Cortez in which Ocasio-Cortez appeared not to know the answers to questions posed by Stuckey. It was produced by the digital CRTV network, which streams conservative content, and was widely disseminated on Facebook. It was simply and effectively produced by creating a split screen, with Stuckey on the left asking questions and Ocasio-Cortez on the right answering different questions spliced from a different interview. Liberal commentators took note when the video reached over one million views on Facebook, with some referring to it as a 'hoax' and complaining that it was not labelled satire. *Intercept* journalist Robert Mackey tweeted. 'Manipulated video to create entirely fake video presented as real,' to which Stuckey responded:

> Lol . . . It was never presented as real. The 'entire point' was for it to look edited. We don't have to say 'SATIRE' just so people who don't notice that we clearly spliced her PBS interview to make a comedic point can feel okay.[50]

Discussing the video on Fox's *Tucker Carlson Tonight*, Stuckey expanded this argument:

> Of course, it was intended to be seen as a joke. Satire has played a very important part in political dialogue for a long time, and I'm certainly not apologetic for playing a part in that. And this particular tactic that we use, we certainly didn't come up with it ourselves. We have seen comedians since the 1970s and 1980s doing similar things. It was never meant to actually be deceived [*sic*], but it was supposed to be very obvious that it was satire.[51]

The video and the responses it generated illuminate some of the ways in which the relationship between humour and politics has shifted with online cultural production. The video producer argues it is 'very obvious that it was satire', but this is not obvious in an environment where context trumps intent and the response to the video is indicative of the ambiguity that surrounds so much politicised humour on the Internet. The split screen symbolises the satirical bent of the video, the ironic point of tension between the said and unsaid – such discordance is the base of the humour of the piece, but it is also ambiguous and so the conversation is about intent. Liberals can claim it is fake and intended as a political smear and that conservatives are calling it a joke in order to hide behind humour, while conservatives can claim it was intended as satire and that liberals cannot take a joke. This deep ambiguity has become so common it has popularised the axiom of 'Poe's law', which states that without clear indication of intent it is impossible to distinguish between satire and extremism in online communications.[52]

Conclusion

Both the currency and the crisis of satire today reflect a significant disruption of norms of political communication in a chaotic media ecosystem where viral memes and tweets shape public opinion. Satire is not dead, rather it has evolved to take on new forms in this frenzied environment and in doing so it illuminates some of the bubbles and blind spots in a traumatised liberal hegemony. Satire in Trump's America is more politically and culturally distributed than at any time since the 1960s and its new licentiousness has revealed the persistence of uncivil discourses and opinions among the American public. It may be that the scale of this distribution portends a near future of 'a news–satire singularity', a world where 'satire is not so much dead as unidentifiable'.[53] Some commentators are now asking if it is necessary 'to regulate satire' and Facebook has taken to marking selected articles as satire, but these are belated and inadequate responses to the erosion of 'reality-based community' in the US.[54] As with so much else in Trump's America, reality is not what it used to be.

Notes

1. 'Stephen Colbert – White House Correspondents' Association Dinner' (2006), available at <https://www.c-span.org/video/?c4519958/stephen-colbert-white-house-correspondents-association-dinner> (accessed 30 January 2020).
2. See Eamonn Forde, 'In a World of Fake News What Happens to Satire?', *Big Issue*, 23 November 2018, <https://www.bigissue.com/latest/in-a-world-of-fake-news-what-happens-to-satire>; Adam J. Smith, 'Twitter Has Democratised Satire – but It Has Lost Its Potency in the Process', *Reaction*, 12 October 2018, <https://reaction.life/twitter-democratised-satire-lost-potency-process>; 'President Trump Is Making Satire Great Again', *The Economist*, 11 February 2017, <https://www.economist.com/united-states/2017/02/11/president-trump-is-making-satire-great-again>; Anne Quito, 'Satirical Art in the Trump Era: Why It's Important to "Shame the Shameless"', *Quartz*, 19 October 2018, <https://qz.com/1424380/art-as-witness-satirical-illustration-flourishes-in-the-trump-era>; David Zurawik, 'Maher, Baldwin, Oliver, Colbert: Political Satire Thrives in Trump Era', *Baltimore Sun*, 18 February 2019,

<https://webcache.googleusercontent.com/search?q=cache:ulf6Fc_sKzQJ:https://www.baltimoresun.com/opinion/columnists/zurawik/bs-fe-zontv-maher-oliver-political-satire-20190218-story.html+&cd=17&hl=en&ct=clnk&gl=ie>; David Macaray, 'The Death of Political Satire', *CounterPunch*, 16 August 2019, <https://www.counterpunch.org/2019/08/26/the-death-of-political-satire>; Justin E. H. Smith, 'The End of Satire', *New York Times*, 8 April 2019, <https://www.nytimes.com/2019/04/08/opinion/the-end-of-satire.html (all accessed 30 January 2020).

3. Northrop Frye, *Anatomy of Criticism* (Princeton: Princeton University Press, 1957), 223.
4. Norman Mailer, 'Superman Comes to the Supermarket', *Esquire*, November 1960, <http://www.esquire.com/news-politics/a3858/superman-supermarket> (accessed 30 January 2020).
5. Philip Roth, 'Writing American Fiction', *Commentary*, March 1961, <https://www.commentarymagazine.com/articles/writing-american-fiction> (accessed 30 January 2020).
6. Commentators in books and op-eds sent out dire warnings, from Robert Putnam's thesis in *Bowling Alone* (2000) that social intercourse and community in the US had collapsed to George Packer's argument in *The Unwinding* (2013) that the social contract had been shredded – the common theme was civic decline. 'In the space of a generation', Packer wrote, America 'has become more than ever a country of winners and losers, as industries have failed, institutions have disappeared and the country's focus has shifted to idolise celebrity and wealth.' Robert D. Putnam, *Bowling Alone: The Collapse and Revival of American Community* (New York: Simon & Schuster, 2000); George Packer, *The Unwinding: An Inner History of the New America* (New York: Farrar, Straus & Giroux, 2013), jacket statement.
7. In 2004 a top aide to President Bush (later identified as Karl Rove) told journalist Ron Suskind that journalists like him were in 'the reality-based community' and went on, 'We're an empire now, and when we act, we create our own reality. And while you're studying that reality – judiciously, as you will – we'll act again, creating other new realities, which you can study too, and that's how things will sort out. We're history's actors . . . and you, all of you, will be left to just study what we do.' Ron Suskind, 'Faith, Certainty and the Presidency of George W. Bush', *New York Times Magazine*, 17 October 2004, <https://www.nytimes.com/2004/10/17/magazine/faith-certainty-and-the-presidency-of-george-w-bush.html> (accessed 30 January 2020).

8. The discourse of 'real Americans' was famously promoted by Sarah Palin when she was running as the vice-presidential nominee in 2008. She said she and presidential nominee John McCain 'believe that the best of America is in these small towns that we get to visit, and in these wonderful little pockets of what I call the real America, being here with all of you hardworking, very patriotic . . . pro-America areas of this great nation.' Rosa Brooks, 'The "Real" America, Really', *Los Angeles Times*, 23 October 2008, <https://www.latimes.com/archives/la-xpm-2008-oct-23-oe-brooks23-story.html> (accessed 30 January 2020).
9. Quoted in Adam Sternbergh, 'Stephen Colbert Has Americans by the Ballots', *New York Magazine*, 16 October 2006, <http://nymag.com/news/politics/22322/index1.html> (accessed 30 January 2020).
10. Amber Day, writing in 2011, proclaimed there was 'a renaissance taking place in the realm of political satire'. Amber Day, 'Why More Americans Are Being Informed and Entertained by Satire than Ever Before', *Huffington Post*, 16 February 2011, <https://www.huffpost.com/entry/why-more-americans-are-be_b_824064> (accessed 30 January 2020).
11. Megan Garber, 'How Comedians Became Public Intellectuals', *The Atlantic*, 28 May 2015, <https://www.theatlantic.com/entertainment/archive/2015/05/how-comedians-became-public-intellectuals/394277> (accessed 30 January 2020).
12. Alison Dagnes, *A Conservative Walks Into a Bar: The Politics of Political Humor* (New York: Palgrave Macmillan, 2012), 11–12.
13. Sophia A. McClennen and Remy M. Maisel, *Is Satire Saving Our Nation? Mockery and American Politics* (New York: Palgrave Macmillan, 2014), 6.
14. The 'Overton window' refers to the range of ideas or policies the public will tolerate. See Maggie Astor, 'How the Politically Unthinkable Can Become Mainstream', *New York Times*, 26 February 2019, <https://www.nytimes.com/2019/02/26/us/politics/overton-window-democrats.html> (accessed 30 January 2020).
15. David Marchese, 'In Conversation: David Letterman', *Vulture*, 5 March 2017, <https://www.vulture.com/2017/03/david-letterman-in-conversation.html> (accessed 30 January 2020).
16. Michael Moore (@MMFlint), Twitter, 3 January 2017, <https://twitter.com/mmflint/status/816480558444412930> (accessed 30 January 2020).
17. 'Trudeau: Three Decades of Doonesbury and the Donald', *Newsday*, 3 November 2016 (original emphasis), <https://webcache.googleusercontent.com/search?q=cache:ChTB1k5CkBUJ:https://www.newsday

.com/opinion/garry-trudeau-three-decades-of-doonesbury-and-the-donald-1.12549247+&cd=1&hl=en&ct=clnk&gl=uk&lr=lang_en%7Clang_fr> (accessed 30 January 2020). Of course, Trump has long been a subject of satirical mockery: *Spy* magazine famously depicted him as a 'short-fingered vulgarian' and *Doonesbury* itself featured him as a character over thirty years.

18. See Adam Felder, 'The Limits of the Late-Night Comedy Takedown', *The Atlantic*, 17 April 2016, <https://www.theatlantic.com/entertainment/archive/2016/04/late-night-comedy/475485> (accessed 30 January 2020).

19. See Jesse David Fox, 'Trump Is One of the Worst Things Ever to Happen to Comedy', *Vulture*, 21 December 2017, <https://www.vulture.com/2017/12/donald-trump-jokes-bad-comedy.html>; Ron Charles, 'Liberal Satire Is Getting Dangerously Lazy in the Trump Era', *Washington Post*, 2 November 2018, <https://www.washingtonpost.com/entertainment/books/liberal-satire-is-getting-dangerously-lazy-in-the-trump-era/2018/11/01/fed766ee-ddd9-11e8-b3f0-62607289efee_story.html> (both accessed 30 January 2020).

20. On the Twitter feed @TrumpDraws, Trump spends his time in the White House doing childish drawings and scribbles. In *Trump's ABC*, the cartoonist Ann Telneas portrays Trump as a petulant red-faced toddler.

21. See Charles, 'Liberal Satire Is Getting Dangerously Lazy'. Several books have been published that are based on Trump's tweets, for example Rob Sears, *The Beautiful Poetry of Donald Trump* (Edinburgh: Canongate, 2017).

22. See Quito, 'Satirical Art in the Trump Era'; Jack Holmes, 'The Death of Shame, or the Rise of Shamelessness?', *Esquire*, 31 January 2018, <https://www.esquire.com/news-politics/a15940835/trump-shame-shamelessness> (accessed 30 January 2020); Max Boot, 'Trump's Superpower Is His Shamelessness', *Washington Post*, 12 February 2019, <https://www.washingtonpost.com/opinions/2019/02/12/trumps-superpower-is-his-shamelessness> (accessed 30 January 2020).

23. David Sanderson, 'Rise of Trump Makes Satire Unnecessary, Says Armando Iannucci', *The Times*, 1 October 2018, <https://www.thetimes.co.uk/article/rise-of-trump-makes-satire-unnecessary-says-armando-iannucci-vpdncxr9f> (accessed 30 January 2020).

24. Ben Greenman, 'Is Satire Possible in the Age of Trump?', *New York Times*, 8 March 2019, <https://www.nytimes.com/2019/03/08/books/review/mark-doten-trump-sky-alpha.html> (accessed 30 January 2020).

25. Monique Schafter, 'Donald Trump Too Hard to Satirise, Say South Park Creators Trey Parker and Matt Stone', ABC News (Australia), 2 February 2017, <https://www.abc.net.au/news/2017-02-02/donald-trump-too-hard-to-satirise-say-trey-parker-and-matt-stone/8236338> (accessed 30 January 2020).
26. Dahlia Lithwick, 'Constitutional Crisis of Comedy', *Slate*, 25 May 2017, <https://slate.com/news-and-politics/2017/05/mike-birbiglia-on-how-donald-trump-is-killing-comedy.html> (accessed 30 January 2020).
27. Felder, 'The Limits of the Late-Night Comedy Takedown'.
28. Richard Zoglin, 'The Late Night Comics Are Going after Trump', *Fortune*, 15 September 2016, <https://fortune.com/2016/09/15/donald-trump-late-night-samantha-bee> (accessed 30 January 2020).
29. David Marchese, 'Stephen Colbert on the Political Targets of Satire', *New York Times Magazine*, 31 May 2019, <https://www.nytimes.com/interactive/2019/06/03/magazine/stephen-colbert-politics-religion.html> (accessed 30 January 2020).
30. Brian Hiatt, 'The Triumph of Stephen Colbert', *Rolling Stone*, 29 August 2018, <https://www.rollingstone.com/tv/tv-features/stephen-colbert-late-show-rolling-stone-interview-716439> (accessed 30 January 2020). In his interview with David Marchese, Colbert observes: 'It's almost as if the president is trying to cast a spell to confuse people so they cannot know the true nature of reality, and what we do is pick apart the way in which the [expletive] was sold to you. I think that's why it's going well. Our job is to identify the [expletive], and there's never been more. It's a transformation of the poison into something entertaining.' Marchese, 'Stephen Colbert on the Political Targets of Satire'.
31. Adam Epstein, 'John Oliver Is Staying Sane by Turning Away from Trump's "Fire Hose of Bullshit"', *Quartz*, 13 February 2018, <https://qz.com/quartzy/1205974/last-week-tonight-host-john-oliver-is-staying-sane-by-turning-away-from-trumps-fire-hose-of-bullshit> (accessed 30 January 2020).
32. See tweets from Peter Baker, 'Unfortunately, I don't think we advanced the cause of journalism tonight' (@peterbakernyt, Twitter, 29 April 2018, <https://twitter.com/peterbakernyt/status/990437494440321024>) and Maggie Haberman, 'That @PressSec sat and absorbed intense criticism of her physical appearance, her job performance, and so forth, instead of walking out, on national television, was impressive' (@maggieNYT, Twitter, 29 April 2018, <https://twitter.com/maggieNYT/status/990428993542414336>) (both accessed 30 January 2020). Many criticised Wolf's remarks

on Sanders's appearance while not mentioning her comments on the press secretary's propensity to tell lies nor her charge that female members of the Trump administration have been covering for the president's sexism. See Hadley Freeman, 'How Sarah Sanders Became Trump's Liar-in-Chief', *The Guardian*, 13 November 2018, <https://www.theguardian.com/us-news/2018/nov/13/sarah-sanders-lies-white-house-female-face> (accessed 30 January 2020).

33. 'Trump Blasts Michelle Wolf's Correspondent's Dinner Remarks about Sarah Huckabee Sanders', CBS News, 30 April 2018, <https://www.cbsnews.com/news/trump-blasts-michelle-wolfs-correspondents-dinner-remarks-about-sarah-huckabee-sanders> (accessed 30 January 2020).

34. Which may be why Wolf said of the media's relationship with the president: 'You pretend like you hate him, but I think you love him. I think what no one in this room wants to admit is that Trump has helped all of you. He couldn't sell steaks or vodka or water or college or ties or Eric, but he has helped you. He's helped you sell your papers and your books and your TV. You helped create this monster, and now you're profiting off of him.' Aaron Blake, 'The Most Provocative Thing Michelle Wolf Said', *Washington Post*, 30 April 2018, <https://www.washingtonpost.com/news/the-fix/wp/2018/04/30/the-most-provocative-thing-michelle-wolf-said> (accessed 30 January 2020).

35. David Smith, 'White House Correspondents' Dinner: Michelle Wolf Shocks Media with Sarah Sanders Attack', *The Guardian*, 29 April 2018, <https://www.theguardian.com/us-news/2018/apr/29/white-house-correspondents-dinner-michelle-wolf-stuns-media-with-sarah-sanders-attack> (accessed 30 January 2020).

36. Oliver Morrison, 'Waiting for the Conservative Jon Stewart', *The Atlantic*, 14 February 2015, <https://www.theatlantic.com/entertainment/archive/2015/02/why-theres-no-conservative-jon-stewart/385480> (accessed 30 January 2020).

37. Talk radio, for instance, has much humour that plays an important part in bonding listening communities, but the humour is not that of liberal stand-ups and late-night hosts; it is relatively lacking in irony while fulsome in hyperbole and mockery. See Morrison, 'Waiting for the Conservative Jon Stewart'.

38. Richard Dawkins, *The Selfish Gene* (Oxford: Oxford University Press, 1976).

39. Priscilla Frank, 'The Strange Internet Journey of Pepe the "Chilled-Out Stoner Frog"', *HuffPost*, 30 September 2016, <https://www.

huffpost.com/entry/matt-furie-pepe-frog-meme_n_57ed3a6fe4b0c2407cdc4298> (accessed 30 January 2020).
40. Ryan M. Milner, 'Media Lingua Franca: Fixity, Novelty, and Vernacular Creativity in Internet Memes', *Selected Papers of Internet Research* 14 (2013), <https://journals.uic.edu/ojs/index.php/spir/article/view/8725/6943> (accessed 30 January 2020).
41. Emma Grey Ellis, 'Can't Take a Joke? That's Just Poe's Law, 2017's Most Important Internet Phenomenon', *Wired*, 6 May 2017, <https://www.wired.com/2017/06/poes-law-troll-cultures-central-rule> (accessed 30 January 2020). For the alt-right, as Alice Marwick observes, 'irony has a strategic function. It allows people to disclaim a real commitment to far-right ideas while still espousing them.' Jason Wilson, 'Hiding in Plain Sight: How the "Alt-Right" Is Weaponizing Irony to Spread Fascism', *The Guardian*, 23 May 2017, <https://www.theguardian.com/technology/2017/may/23/alt-right-online-humor-as-a-weapon-facism> (accessed 30 January 2020).
42. Orie Givens, 'Trump, Clinton, and the Deplorable Picture', *Advocate*, 14 September 2016, <https://www.advocate.com/election/2016/9/14/trump-clinton-and-deplorable-picture> (accessed 30 January 2020).
43. Charlie Warzel, 'Meet the Man behind Trump's Biden Tweet', *New York Times*, 6 April 2019, <https://www.nytimes.com/2019/04/06/opinion/internet-meme-joe-biden-trump.html> (accessed 30 January 2020).
44. Katie Rogers, 'White House Hosts Conservative Internet Activists at a "Social Media Summit"', *New York Times*, 11 July 2019, <https://www.nytimes.com/2019/07/11/us/politics/white-house-social-media-summit.html> (accessed 30 January 2020).
45. Sergio López argues that in the 'fast-paced environment of the internet, memes emerged as a one-dimensional illustration; they don't engage with the issue ... Print political cartoons, on the other hand, tend to engage with the socio-political context, participating more substantially to the debate' and instigating 'internal reflection among the audience'. Sergio López, 'Revival of Satire: Our Life in Memes', *PETRIe* (no date), <http://www.petrieinventory.com/revival-of-satire-our-life-in-memes> (accessed 30 January 2020).
46. Michael Cavna, 'Pittsburgh Post-Gazette Fires Anti-Trump Cartoonist, Mayor Says It Sends "Wrong Message about Press Freedoms"', *Washington Post*, 14 June 2018, <https://www.washingtonpost.com/news/comic-riffs/wp/2018/06/14/pittsburgh-post-gazette-fires-anti-trump-cartoonist-and-mayor-says-it-sends-wrong-message-about-press-freedoms> (accessed 30 January 2020).

47. Viveca S. Greene, '"Deplorable" Satire: Alt-Right Memes, White Genocide Tweets, and Redpilling Normies', *Studies in American Humor 5*, no. 1 (2019), 31–69.
48. Stephanie Mencimer, 'The Left Can't Meme: How Right-Wing Groups Are Training the Next Generation of Social Media Warriors', *Mother Jones*, 2 April 2019, <https://www.motherjones.com/politics/2019/04/right-wing-groups-are-training-young-conservatives-to-win-the-next-meme-war> (accessed 30 January 2020).
49. Ibid.
50. Robert Mackey, 'Fake Interview with Alexandria Ocasio-Cortez was Satire, Not Hoax, Conservative Pundit Says', *The Intercept*, 24 July 2018, <https://theintercept.com/2018/07/24/conservative-network-says-fake-interview-alexandria-ocasio-cortez-satire> (accessed 31 January 2020).
51. 'Can't Take a Joke', *Tucker Carlson Tonight*, Fox News, 25 July 2018, <https://archive.org/details/FOXNEWSW_20180726_040000_Tucker_Carlson_Tonight/start/540/end/600> (accessed 31 January 2020).
52. Poe's law 'postulates that sincere extremism online (manifesting as bigotry, conspiracy theorizing or simply being wrong about something) is often indistinguishable from satirical extremism'. Whitney Phillips and Ryan M. Milner, *The Ambivalent Internet: Mischief, Oddity and Antagonism Online* (Cambridge: Polity, 2017), 78–9.
53. Gavin Haynes, '"An Absolutely Disgusting Article": Is Satire Funnier When the Targets Don't Get the Joke?', *The Guardian*, 24 May 2018, <https://www.theguardian.com/us-news/2018/may/24/michael-cohen-the-onion-satire-news-mistake-reality> (accessed 31 January 2020).
54. Smith, 'The End of Satire'. On Facebook's struggles to classify satirical news, see Erik Wemple, 'Facebook Working on Approach to Classify Satirical News Pieces', *Washington Post*, 5 March 2018, <https://www.washingtonpost.com/blogs/erik-wemple/wp/2018/03/05/facebook-working-on-approach-to-classifying-satirical-news-pieces> (accessed 31 January 2020).

14
Spectacle of Decency: Repairing America after Trump

Scott Lucas

> As democracy is perfected, the office of the President represents, more and more closely, the inner soul of the people . . . On some great and glorious day, the plain folks of the land will reach their heart's desire at last, and the White House will be occupied by a downright moron. (H. L. Mencken, 1920)[1]

To simply apply Mencken to Donald Trump, forty-fifth president of the United States, is misguided. The Sage of Baltimore, evaluating the 1920 presidential campaign between Warren Harding and James Cox, assessed, 'Of the two, that one wins who least arouses the suspicions and distrusts of the great masses of simple men'[2] – not exactly a trait that fits Trump's self-promotion. Yes, significant questions may be asked about Trump's intelligence. But as many revelled and continue to revel in the distrust of his controversial persona, it is the manner of his achievements – or those of his advisors, fronted by Trump – that is more pertinent.

At the least, Trump's campaign knew of Russian efforts to intervene in the 2016 presidential election. It may have colluded with Moscow's officials in that intervention. Trump may have obstructed justice to try and bury investigation of that intervention.[3] Yet to date, Trump has paid no political price for any benefit from this unprecedented attempt by a foreign power to affect a US vote.[4] He has refused to provide tax returns and financial information that could bear on conflicts of interests between his businesses and his political office.[5] His officials, notably his daughter Ivanka and his son-in-law Jared Kushner, have been denied security clearances because of their financial affairs – but continue to carry out sensitive duties and receive classified information.[6]

Trump's policies have included 'zero tolerance' of immigration, with separation of children from parents to be detained hundreds and even thousands of miles away,[7] and pursuit of the vanity project of a 30-foot-tall wall entailing a 'national emergency' and a record-setting shutdown of the federal government.[8] His denial of climate change has been accompanied by not only withdrawal from international environmental accords but also the shredding of regulations and end to scientific research.[9] He has tried to dismantle America's healthcare system and to restrict services from public assistance to student loans.[10] To implement these policies, and/or out of personal belief, Trump has stigmatised migrants as 'animals'.[11] He has effectively endorsed white supremacists,[12] and encouraged Islamophobia, from his retweets of faked videos to his linking of America's first Muslim legislators to the 9/11 attacks.[13] He has bragged about sexually accosting women,[14] and he has insulted those who say they have suffered sexual abuse.[15] He has mocked Caribbean and African countries as 'shitholes', as his administration denies temporary residence to people from those areas.[16]

Then there is the assault on the American system. Even while trying to fill the Supreme Court with staunch conservatives, Trump has assailed judges – both those trying cases related to his businesses and those ruling on administration policies – as corrupt, uninformed, incompetent or 'Mexican'.[17] Trying to neuter congressional opposition, he has claimed that Democratic legislators are subversives and extremists.[18] He has sought to pack the independent Federal Reserve with his political appointees, and blasted the body over interest rate decisions.[19] To undermine the Russia investigation, Trump has compared US intelligence services to Nazis.[20] He has repeatedly derided and lied about the FBI, insulting and forcing out its top officials including director James Comey.[21] He has continued the assault on the independent team of special counsel Robert Mueller. These agencies, Trump asserts, are all part of a 'deep state coup' against him.[22]

Yet not only is Trump likely to complete his term in office, but he is already running for re-election in 2020. His average approval rating has remained between 39 and 43 per cent since January 2018 – still among historical lows for presidents, but not sinking to a critical level and still close to the minority 46 per cent that put him in the White House.[23] How do Trump and his team get away with it? The answer lies in spectacle.

Trump the showman

Mencken had more than a few words about spectacle to accompany his pessimism: 'The whole aim of practical politics is to keep the populace alarmed (and hence clamorous to be led to safety) by menacing it with an endless series of hobgoblins, all of them imaginary.'[24] More than forty years later, in a quicker world of media, Daniel Boorstin updated the spectacular of everyday politics: 'Demanding more than the world can give us, we require that something be fabricated to make up for the world's deficiency.' This was, Boorstin asserted, 'our demand for illusions'.[25] He labelled this not-so-new world one of the 'pseudo-event', a 'happening' staged to be reported. But here Boorstin was off the mark. There was nothing 'pseudo' about the event, which in its staging was definitely 'real'. What was significant – as, in the subsequent media generation, Jean Baudrillard assessed[26] – was that the 'reality' of the staged event could overtake and empty meaning from the political issue with which it was supposedly concerned.

It is unlikely that Donald Trump has ever read Mencken, Boorstin or Baudrillard, but he has an innate sense of the 'event'. Trying to establish himself as the brilliant real estate developer remaking a battered New York City in the 1970s, he invited reporters to his apartment of opulence. They responded with celebrity portraits:

> He is tall, lean and blond, with dazzling white teeth, and he looks ever so much like Robert Redford. He rides around town in a chauffeured silver Cadillac with his initials, DJT, on the plates. He dates slinky fashion models, belongs to the most elegant clubs and, at only 30 years of age, estimates that he is worth 'more than $200 million'.[27]

This opulence was not given to him. Trump benefited from today's equivalent of $413 million in trusts set up by his father Fred and from tax manipulation, possibly to the extent of fraud. However, in Trump's narrative, he spun his wealth from a loan of 'only' $1 million from Dad.[28] (Nor did Trump mention the cases of racial discrimination, settled out of court, against both him and Fred.[29])

Trump's adventure with casinos in Atlantic City was another 'event'. More importantly, when that led to a series of six bankruptcies, he was saved by an even more important image: that of the super-boss on the reality TV show *The Apprentice*. The failed businessman was replaced by the aggressive Donald of the ghost-written *The Art of the Deal* in the 1980s.[30] The persona was complemented by perhaps the consummate combination of business and 'sport', masculinity and arrogance. In 2007, Trump was a recurring guest star on the World Wrestling Experience (WWE), the mega-million-dollar spectacle, cast as the mogul trying to take the WWE from long-time owner Vince McMahon. In the climactic episode, a battle for control of the enterprise through their proxy wrestlers, Trump body-slammed McMahon and then stripped him of his masculine authority by shaving his head in the ring. An estimated 1.2 million people bought pay-per-view to watch 'this spectacle of excess'.[31]

Trump, whose franchises now ran beyond hotels from a 'university' to steaks, was everywhere. He would pose as his own supposed spokesman to give statements to reporters.[32] He crashed the stage at charity events, even though he had not made a donation, and used Trump Foundation money to buy items.[33] He was a regular guest on shock jock Howard Stern's radio programme, more often reviewing his sexual exploits, wives and ex-wives than discussing politics.[34] He took to Twitter to spread outrageous but effective lies, from climate change as a Chinese hoax to Barack Obama being born outside the US.[35] Years later, running for president, Trump displayed a moment of honesty, or rather brash confidence, as he recognised his ability to use and manipulate spectacle: 'I have the most loyal people. I could stand in the middle of 5th Avenue and shoot somebody and I wouldn't lose voters.'[36]

Spectacle and media before Trump

Of course, spectacle long predates Donald Trump in American politics. Mencken had a thought or two about this, such as 'a national political campaign is better than the best circus ever heard of, with a mass baptism and couple of hangings thrown in'.[37] From the Lincoln–Douglas encounters of the 1850s to the glad-handing at rallies, from the combined celebration-negotiation of party conventions to the centrepiece of the presidential debates – launched by Kennedy and Nixon and established by 1976 – the myth and reality of the US politics is built on the manufactured event.

But the sweep of the spectacle was widened by the changes in media technology and media culture from the 1980s. The advent of 24/7 news coverage was accompanied by the Reagan administration's abolition of the 'fairness doctrine' – the Federal Communications Commission's requirement that holders of broadcast licences presented public issues in an honest, equitable and balanced manner.[38] Cable and then satellite networks across the political spectrum, but particularly on the conservative side, were unleashed to push opinion and to promote candidates in the guise of 'fair and balanced' reporting and analysis. In 1988, the Republican campaign of George H. W. Bush used giant posters and video of Willie Horton, who absconded while on weekend release from prison in Massachusetts and committed a series of crimes, to tie Democratic opponent Michael Dukakis to menacing African-American rapists and murderers.[39] More than a decade later, supporters of George W. Bush spread the rumour that Bush's primary rival John McCain was the father of an illegitimate half-black child, turning the South Carolina contest – and thus the Republican nomination – in their favour.[40] Barack Obama, whose campaign benefited from innovation with platforms such as YouTube, was not immune from 21st-century social media conspiracies alleging he was a foreign-born Muslim communist.[41]

Trump and his advisors did not create the social media spectacle but they found new territory for exploitation. The candidate and the campaign placed Twitter rumours which were immediately amplified by supporters unconcerned with veracity.[42] They employed Cambridge Analytica for unprecedented data mining that supported Facebook ad campaigns seeking maximum effect.[43] They liaised with WikiLeaks – and possibly Russian military intelligence – over the dissemination of material, including hacked emails and documents, which could damage Democratic opponent Hillary Clinton.[44]

Trump had prepared for years with his Twitter persona, which began in 2009 to advertise a book in his name but soon rested upon his provocative and often inflammatory commentary. In 2015, he matched this with the PR launch of his campaign. With paid onlookers watching, Trump descended on the Grand Escalator of New York's Trump Tower to Neil Young's 'Rockin' in the Free World' (a song-grab that later brought a 'Fuck You, Mr Trump' from the Canadian artist). He began with one of his grandiose claims, saying of the unseen audience 'There's never been a crowd like this', and immediately rambled with a combination of jeremiad and aggressive posturing that he – and only he – could save the US from treacherous foreigners with their thieves, drug dealers and rapists:

> Our country is in serious trouble. We don't have victories anymore. We used to have victories, but we don't have them. When was the last time anybody saw us beating, let's say, China in a trade deal? They kill us. I beat China all the time. All the time.
>
> When did we beat Japan at anything? They send their cars over by the millions, and what do we do? When was the last time you saw a Chevrolet in Tokyo? It doesn't exist, folks. They beat us all the time.
>
> When do we beat Mexico at the border? They're laughing at us, at our stupidity. And now they are beating us economically. They are not our friend, believe me. But they're killing us economically.[45]

The press grabbed the campaign's exceptionalist 'Make America Great Again' but the spectacle was never about America as much as it was about Trump. With almost no attention to issues – and little capability on Trump's part to address them – the campaign was built on and sharpened a persona developed during forty years of New York City celebrity, *The Apprentice* and the WWE. The man who boasted on 11 September 2011 that his building was 'now the tallest' in New York City became the candidate, declaring, 'I think

I could have stopped [9/11] because I have very tough illegal immigration policies.'[46]

With these tactics, part bullying and part self-promoting narcissism, Trump – effectively a third-party candidate within the Republican primaries – garnered free airtime across all channels, a vital asset given his funding-strapped campaign. Equally important, it permitted him to pull off political sleights of hand as he built his voting. The entrenched member of a New York and national elite, propelled by his father's money, portrayed himself – and was often portrayed by the media – as the leader of a populist movement of the excluded.[47] The man who had gone through six bankruptcies, including over his failed casino ventures, represented himself as the multi-billionaire whose acumen would be transferred to the US government. And, cutting against the notion of consensus in American politics, Trump was a divider, aligning 'his people' against all the other Republican hopefuls – Low Energy Jeb, Little Marco, Lyin' Ted – as well as the supposed enemies inside and outside the US. He insulted characters, body parts and families, to the point of saying that Senator Ted Cruz's father was involved in the assassination of John F. Kennedy.[48]

Playing the heel

The spectacle of professional wrestling turns upon the 'babyface' and the 'heel'. The babyface – good and upstanding – ostensibly represents the good and upstanding us against the villainous heel, who resorts to insult, derogation and dirty tricks to win at all costs. But in the course of the play, many in the crowd may become more enamoured of the heel than of the clean-cut, clean-speaking babyface. Or, as with the Trump–McMahon drama in 2007, there may be no babyface, only two heels each trying to be more deviously effective than the other.

So, Trump's political spectacle galvanised a significant minority in 2016. He boasted that he manipulated the tax system, but justified it as winning over an illegitimate government.[49] He stepped up his insults of opponents, ending up with a boast in the Republican debates about the size of his penis.[50] He asked Russian officials, who already were interfering in the election, to hack Hillary Clinton's emails.⁵¹ Trump was loud, coarse and amoral if not immoral. But rather than repelling potential supporters, his show won over many of them as 'their' guy.

During the general election against Clinton, there were moments when the heel's act almost fell apart. Belatedly, some media outlets began to question a potential free pass for Trump with the unchallenged airtime for his displays.⁵² He drew criticism when he moved from rivals to 'everyday' Americans as targets, notably when he derided the parents of a Muslim marine who died in service in Iraq.⁵³ His finances drew more scrutiny, notably in David Fahrenthold's exposés of Trump's misuse of Trump Foundation funds – using it to buy expensive portraits of himself and National Football League memorabilia and then taking money from it for his campaign.⁵⁴

In October, Trump faced a critical point with the resurrection of a 2005 *Access Hollywood* segment in which, joined by celebrity reporter Billy Bush, he bragged about sexually accosting women: 'I just start kissing them. It's like a magnet. Just kiss. I don't even wait. And when you're a star, they let you do it. You can do anything. Grab 'em by the pussy. You can do anything.'⁵⁵ Trump's poll numbers dipped, and leading Republicans, including members of Congress, stayed away. But even the emergence of fifteen women alleging sexual misconduct could not silence, let alone defeat, him. He doubled down on the aggressive rhetoric:

> The establishment and their media enablers wield control over this nation through means that are very well known. Anyone who challenges their control is deemed a sexist, a racist, a xenophobe and morally deformed.
>
> They will attack you, they will slander you, they will seek to destroy your career and your family, they will seek to destroy everything about you, including your reputation. They will lie, lie, lie, and then again they will do worse than that, they will do whatever is necessary. The Clintons are criminals, remember that. They're criminals.⁵⁶

For Trump was not necessarily seen as a bully of babyfaces, at least for those persuaded by his heel's act. Captain Humayun Khan might have given his life in Iraq, but his parents were suspect because they were Muslim. Gonzalo Curiel, the judge in the case against Trump University – ultimately settled by the Trump Organization for $25 million – was guilty of being 'Mexican', even though he was born in Indiana. And Hillary Clinton was guilty of being Hillary – be it a conviction of cold and insensitive behaviour; of the 33,000 deleted emails; of supposed complicity in an attack on the US consulate in Benghazi, Libya, in October 2012; of the activities of the Clinton Foundation; or of covering for the infidelities of husband Bill. So, the heel could stalk his opponent across the platform as she tried to speak in the second presidential debate. He could claim that it was her case of pneumonia, rather than his sexual behaviour, that was disqualifying for the White House. And, even as he faced legal questions about his taxes and his business interests, he could lead his rallies in shouts of 'Lock Her Up!'

On 13 October 2016, less than four weeks before the vote, First Lady Michelle Obama delivered a powerful speech in New Hampshire. Responding to Trump's defence of his sexual behaviour, albeit without using his name, she said: 'This is not normal. This is not politics as usual. This is disgraceful. It is intolerable. And it doesn't matter what party you belong to – Democrat, Republican, independent – no woman deserves to be treated this way.'[57] But whatever the merits of Obama's 'They go low, we go high', on 8 November the heel won. The spectacle of going low may not have brought Donald Trump the most votes, but through the mechanics of the Electoral College, it brought him the White House.

Spectacle of chaos

Donald Trump's presidential term started with a failure of spectacle. The crowd for his inauguration was estimated at less than a third of the 1.5 million on the Washington Mall for Barack Obama's first ceremony eight years earlier.[58] Trump responded in Trumpian fashion, trying to portray the gathering as the largest in inaugural history, despite videos, photographs and National Park Service data confirming the relatively sparse audience. He ordered White House press secretary Sean Spicer to lie – later defended by White House counsel Kellyanne Conway as 'alternative facts' – in a briefing of the media. He demanded the editing of official inaugural photos 'to depict more spectators in the crowd'.[59] The episode fused spectacle and ego in a challenge to the American system. Whenever Trump met reporters, he foisted upon them copies of the Electoral College map from 9 November, falsely declaring that his was the largest victory margin in presidential history. (It is forty-sixth out of fifty-eight presidential elections.)[60] Trying to cover his loss in the popular vote, he made unfounded accusations that up to five million fraudulent votes were cast for Hillary Clinton.[61] And, worried that stories of Russian interference in the election would mar his win, he began a series of interventions that would amount to an obstruction of justice.[62]

Governance devolved into a round-the-clock cycle of manufacturing Trump's preferred 'reality'. He woke about 6 a.m. to watch his favourite morning spectacle, the puff opinions of *Fox and Friends*, sometimes calling the show – and, on one occasion, paying a surprise visit – to whip up a narrative. Led by the programme's daily agenda, he then posted his first tweets of the day, praising himself and railing against supposed enemies from Democrats to immigrants to national healthcare.[63]

In its first week in office, the administration tried to roll out its first spectacular policy initiative. Almost overnight it announced an executive order to ban entry into the US by citizens of seven mainly Muslim countries. Trump staged an elaborate ceremony of signing his name on the executive order, telling the press, 'Protection of the nation from foreign terrorists' entry into the United States. Big stuff.'[64] Looking on were chief strategist Steve Bannon and his assistant Stephen Miller, who saw the Muslim ban as the first step in policing and regulating those living in America or those hoping to come on a permanent or even a temporary basis.

But here spectacle met its possible limits. Legally the step was challenged in the courts, who blocked the order within a week. Judge Ann Donnelly ruled that the ban 'violates . . . rights to due process and equal protection guaranteed by the United States constitution'.[65] Judge James Robart, issuing a national restraining order, concluded that there was no support for the administration's argument that 'we have to protect the US from individuals from the seven countries'.[66] Even before this, activists countered with their humanitarian spectacle. They mobilised at US airports from New York to San Francisco. Demonstrators held 'NO MUSLIM BAN' placards and lawyers worked pro bono to advise those who might be turned back or detained by the authorities. The effort worked, at least in the short term: as the ban was stayed by the 9th Circuit Court, enthusiastic welcomes were given to Muslim visitors.[67]

However, if the administration had been checked in its display, it could try to seize advantage while planning others. Trump used Twitter to deride the courts: 'The opinion of this so-called judge, which essentially takes law-enforcement away from our country, is ridiculous and will be overturned!'[68] Executive orders were scheduled in the following weeks to cut back environmental, health and safety regulations; to declare 'free speech and religious liberty'; to undermine Obamacare; and to command 'Buy American and Hire American'.[69] The administration so favoured this fusion of spectacle and presidential fiat that, combined with repeated setbacks in its attempts to scrap Obamacare completely, its first major legislative victory would not come until December with a $1.5 trillion tax cut. The outcome was a policy of whim rather than consideration, seeking to grab the daily news cycle and obscure stories of the chaos. Trump was so enamoured of a Twitter presidency that he used the platform to order a halt to transgender personnel in the US military, to challenge North Korea with 'fire and fury', and to threaten an end to the North American Free Trade Agreement and the NATO alliance.[70]

Staff and agencies tried to pull Trump back. Chiefs of staff Reince Priebus and John Kelly tried to organise access to the president and to keep his announcements in line with the US government's positions. A trio of generals – Kelly, defence secretary James Mattis and H. R. McMaster – sought order from the chaos, agreeing to arrange their official travel and vacations so at least one was in Washington at any time.[71] But the effort was doomed by Trump's self-confidence in his impulses, coupled with an abject lack of knowledge. Six months into the administration, his national security chiefs organised a detailed briefing on topics from NATO to Afghanistan to America's nuclear posture. Trump set aside their presentations to demand a ten-fold increase in the US nuclear arsenal and to order the firing of the commander of forces in Afghanistan. Frustrated secretary of state Rex Tillerson told staff that Trump was a 'fucking moron'; McMaster thought Trump was an 'idiot with the brain of a kindergartner'.[72]

Trump and his advisors almost welcomed the chaos rather than dealing with it. Press Secretary Spicer finally gave up covering for Trump's controversies and was replaced as communications director by Anthony Scaramucci, best known for organising New York events for hedge fund managers. Scaramucci's tenure lasted ten days, distinguished by his battles within the White House and profanity-laced description to a reporter with the promise, 'They'll all be fired by me. I fired one guy the other day. I have three to four people I'll fire tomorrow.'[73] Scaramucci did not survive to dismiss anyone, but his rival, Reince Priebus, was toppled in the summer. Even Steve Bannon was not safe: he was pushed out in August.

Far from seeing this as a setback, Trump appeared to revel in the assurance of his primacy in the news cycle. 'A great day in the White House!' he tweeted after Scaramucci's dismissal.[74] He stepped up his confrontations with the media – now labelled as the 'enemy of the people'[75] – with the courts and with his own agencies: 'It's a shame what's happened with the FBI. It's a very sad thing to watch.'[76] His comfort zone was his Mar-a-Lago resort in Florida, where he spent much of his time and hosted leaders such as China's Xi Jinping and Japan's Shinzo Abe. Even more importantly, there were the spectacles of rallies across the country. Wilfully exaggerating the sizes of the audiences, Trump would whip them into joy, anger or fury as he repeated his vilification of Hillary Clinton – bringing the renewed cry of 'Lock Her Up!' – and introduced new adversaries: 'truly dishonest people in the media'; dissenting protesters ('thugs', in contrast with the white supremacist marchers at Charlottesville whom he absolved); and NFL players who raised social issues by taking a knee during the National Anthem before games – 'Get that son of a bitch off the field.'[77]

The limits of spectacle

But spectacle had its limits, namely the challenges of institutions in the US system. Despite a GOP majority in both houses of Congress, the administration still could not scrap Obamacare;

roll back the rights of non-citizens such as the 'Dreamers', about 800,000 residents who came to the US as children with undocumented immigrant parents; or even pass a budget. The $1.5 trillion tax cut bill was pushed through in December, but only at risk to the US economy from the burden of a spiralling federal government debt. Then there was Trump–Russia. Trump failed to quash the investigation of his 2016 campaign and transition's links with Russian officials and their intermediaries such as WikiLeaks. He tried to halt the inquiry into Michael Flynn, the campaign staffer and then national security advisor forced to resign because of phone calls with Russian ambassador Sergei Kislyak in December 2016; fired FBI director James Comey; and harassed attorney general Jeff Sessions to take control of the investigation. But each step only increased scrutiny of Trump and added obstruction of justice to the list of possible offences. Just before he took office, Trump had compared the US intelligence services to Nazis. Now he and his allies claimed the agencies were conspiring with Democrats and the 'fake news media' in a 'deep-state coup' attempt. No lie on social media was too big about special counsel Robert Mueller and his team of '18 Democrats', current or former FBI and CIA officials, and Hillary Clinton. No irony was out of bounds. Trump, who had long relied on the legal counsel of Joseph McCarthy's right-hand man Roy Cohn, portrayed himself as the victim of a McCarthyite 'witch hunt'.[78]

Trump survived, under pressure but always attacking. Senior FBI officials such as deputy director Andrew McCabe were dismissed. The trio of generals trying to contain Trump fell: National security advisor H. R. McMaster in March 2018, White House chief of staff John Kelly in December, and defence secretary Jim Mattis in the same month after Trump impulsively ordered the withdrawal of all US troops from Syria.[79] The hardline advisors and Trump's insatiable desire for the grand gesture combined with their tactics for the 2020 re-election campaign. In the shelter of his rallies, Trump demanded The Wall, the 30-foot-tall concrete or steel barrier along much of the US–Mexico border. His 'zero tolerance' policy separated almost 3,000 children from migrant parents, sending them hundreds or thousands of miles away.[80] When the institutional barrier of Congress refused to allocate funds for The Wall, he called a 'national emergency' so he could take money from the military, covering the declaration with a series of lies.[81] The right to claim asylum was curbed for victims of gang violence and domestic abuse and withdrawn from thousands of other migrants.[82] More discreetly, plans were drawn up by advisor Stephen Miller to force about 25 per cent of legal immigrants out of the US.[83]

In March 2019, Trump faced perhaps his greatest challenge to date. After twenty-two months of investigation, Special Counsel Mueller – although denied a face-to-face interview with Trump and restricted in his inquiry into key Trump aides – issued a 448-page report on the Trump–Russia links and Trump's obstruction of justice. The administration tried to get out in front with a pre-emptive display. Attorney general William Barr, appointed in February, first put out a four-page memorandum and then held a press conference to spin – and arguably distort to the point of deceit – the findings in favour of Trump.[84] Without apparently reading the report, Trump declared, 'No Collusion, No Obstruction, Complete and Total EXONERATION.'[85] Once more, institutions and spectacles collided. Despite Barr's dedicated efforts, Trump could not bury the report. Because Democrats controlled the House of Representatives after the 2018 midterm congressional elections, they could pursue 'major hearings'. The White House and attorney general countered by blocking subpoenas, taking the contest into the courts and counting on Republican legislators to assist, to the point of declaring that it was the Democrats who had colluded with the Russians in 2016 and the FBI who had enabled them.[86]

And Trump and his inner circle counted on Twitter and the rallies. The invective escalated against the supposed 'enemies', declaring an attempted 'coup' by current and former officials. Order after order on immigration and asylum was issued, as Trump boasted about his 'sick idea' to flood Democratic-led sanctuary cities with immigrants.[87] If courts blocked his efforts, they were derided as 'stupid', 'horrible', 'ridiculous', 'incompetent', 'a laughing stock' and a 'complete and total disgrace'.[88] Democrats and other political opponents were labelled as 'extremists'. Trump said four Democratic congresswomen of colour – three of whom were born in the US, two of whom were the first Muslim congresswomen in American history – should 'go back' to their countries.[89] Republican leaders, worried that Trump's racism had crossed the line into causing electoral damage, advised him, 'Argue that the four congresswomen hated America and were welcome to leave for that reason.'[90]

In 2019, Mencken's forecast of a century ago is part fulfilled. Trump may be limited intellectually. He may have uttered more than 10,000 lies since taking office. Yet it is not the moron who is in the White House. It is the showman. Moreover, even the cynic's darkest words do not capture the threat beyond the circus. If this was spectacle alone, the show would be over by January 2025 at the latest, with Trump departing at the end of a second term. But the showman's patter, and the policies that it seeks to enable, are now a fundamental challenge both to institutions and to the ideals that supposedly animate them. A successor could try to emulate and even enhance the show and all its consequences.

What is to be done?

On 21 January 2017, the day after the failure of Trump's inaugural, there was a far different spectacle in Washington, in US cities and towns, and around the world. Millions of people rallied in the Women's March. This was a combination of protest, joy and playfulness with issues. From pink 'pussy hats' to placards such as 'We Are Stronger than Fear', the marchers turned Trump's rhetoric and actions against him. They enshrined reminders of his misogyny and his sexual aggression. They held to the light his declarations of climate change as hoax and his description of Hillary Clinton as 'nasty woman'. They did so not in anger, but in a satire that never detached itself from hope. They did so with a respect and uplift not of the slogans of division, but of the necessity of issues. The demonstrations were not just about women's rights but also about the environment, the preservation and pursuit of accessible healthcare, recognition and respect of LGBT and minority rights, and a quest for economic policies benefiting all rather than a Trumpian few.[91] Six months after Michelle Obama said 'When they go low, we go high', this was a spectacle of decency.[92] Of course, this type of spectacle could not be reproduced daily like a Trump tweet, soundbite or rally. The showman still held that advantage. However, it held out the prospect of the alternative: an appeal to the mass did not have to exalt the divisive, the insulting and the petty. And it did not have to tear at the American system but could uphold it as, while flawed, valuable and capable of reform.

Just over two years later, Donald Trump gave a delayed State of the Union address to both houses of Congress. His spectacle had been foiled initially by an institutional battle over his theatrics: House speaker Nancy Pelosi withheld the invitation because of Trump's record-setting shutdown of the federal government to get his Wall with Mexico. Having relented to end the shutdown, without a penny for The Wall, Trump tried to regain the showman's supremacy. He sheltered in the safety of the introductions of World War II veterans and Apollo 11 astronaut Buzz Aldrin. He claimed credit for everything from the American economy to the release of inmates. He railed against the 'partisan investigation' over Trump–Russia. But then he was confounded by an unexpected turn in the spectacle. With his chequered personal and political record over women's rights, he reached for self-congratulation: 'No one has benefited more from our thriving economy than women, who have filled 58 per cent of the new jobs created in the last year.' One hundred and thirty-one female Democratic legislators leapt to their feet. They whooped, danced and high-fived each other. They celebrated. Appearing surprised and unsettled, Trump exclaimed, 'You were not supposed to do that.' He tried to regain attention to himself: 'All Americans can be proud that we have more women in the workforce than ever before.' The dancing surged. Alexandria Ocasio-Cortez of New York gave a hip shake. Trump tried one more time: 'We also have more women serving in Congress than ever before.' Every eye on them rather than the president, the women hugged each other, waved and danced some more.[93] This too was the spectacle of decency.

Conclusion

In 1968, amid protests and social unrest in France, Guy Debord published *The Society of the Spectacle*. He portrayed 'spectacularisation', in which the production and circulation of images inverts social realities and transforms citizens into spectators, as the economy dominates the ethos and purpose of the state. These images not only divert us from reality, they overtake 'reality' by detaching the spectator from any hold on what is definitely true. 'Disinformation' becomes more than a deliberate process of deception by state authorities or other groups trying to wield or seize power; it is the construction of 'unanswerable lies'.[94]

As Donald Trump's rise from *The Apprentice* to the WWE to the 2016 campaign embodied and extended spectacle, some scholars and commentators looked to Debord. Thomas Lynch summarised, 'In spectacular society, truth becomes elusive.'[95] But the analysis appeared to end in a cul-de-sac. Robert Zaretsky wrote:

> The spectacle swallows us all . . . Whether we love Trump or hate him, is it possible we are all equally addicted consumers of spectacular images he continues to generate? Have we been complicit in the rise of Trump, if only by consuming the images generated by his person and politics?[96]

Lynch invokes Slavoj Žižek to worry that responses to Trump are only part of a spectacle which reinforces rather than challenges his exercise of power: 'Satirisation of the new president risks making the task of analysing the Trump presidency into just another television spectator sport, with the unanticipated consequence of further normalising the practices and processes contributing to his victory.'[97]

The problem lies in Debord's binary: 'The spectacle in its generality is a concrete inversion of life and, as such, the autonomous movement of non-life.'[98] The assumption is that spectacle is empty of a meaning or value other than that which is constructed and conferred by those holding power. In the US since the late twentieth century, society has pivoted around the spectacular figure, from Ronald Reagan to Barack Obama, the event, from the O. J. Simpson trial to Hurricane Katrina, and the shock and awe of a war such as the 2003 invasion of Iraq. In the Trumpian era, all stems from the perpetual watching of Donald Trump and of the disinformation which he puts forth each day. We are the passive consumers of spectacle's complete colonisation of 'politics, culture, and everyday life'.⁹⁹ Searching for a way out, both Lynch and Zaretsky posit their own binary. Lynch calls for an 'alternative vision to the spectacular politics at work today, one in which civility and generosity figure large'.¹⁰⁰ Zaretsky writes, 'The unfolding of national protests and marches, and more important the return to local politics and community organizing, may well . . . shatter the spell of the spectacle.'¹⁰¹

But why must protests, marches and our networks which put forth issues be devoid of spectacle? The message in pink of the Women's March was that celebration and humour go hand in hand with activism. As one woman summarised on a poster, 'Bitches Get Shit Done.' Her partner's adjacent sign affirmed, 'I Also Feel Strongly About This.'¹⁰² Rather than submitting to a supposed colonisation by spectacle, the challenge is to acknowledge and then take control of the political, bound up with the expression and interaction of the social, cultural and artistic. Laura Conway of T\lt West, a Denver artistic community, started a discussion in January 2018, by converting spectacle as phenomenon to an instrument of empowerment:

> When is the use of spectacle a democratizing force and when is it not? . . . If spectacle can be a dangerous weapon when put in the wrong hands, how can we rethink its hold on our society and move forward as media consumers, as artists, and – perhaps most importantly – as citizens?¹⁰³

Soon before Mencken suffered a stroke in 1948, unable to write again, he famously quipped, 'Democracy is the art and science of running the circus from the monkey cage.'¹⁰⁴ Debord committed suicide in 1994. One was cynical to the end about the spectacle; the other was defeated by it.

Donald Trump, in his manipulation of the spectacular, and social media have magnified the threat. But spectacle does not mean sinking into the position of spectator. To the contrary, it can be part of empowerment. In the mass movement that followed the Parkland shootings of February 2018, survivor Emma Gonzalez, speaking for the hundreds of thousands who rallied, spoke powerfully in response:

The people in the government who were voted into power are lying to us. And us kids seem to be the only ones who notice . . . to call BS.

Companies trying to make caricatures of the teenagers these days, saying that we are all self-involved and trend-obsessed and they hush us into submission when our message doesn't reach the ears of the nation – we are prepared to call BS.

Politicians who sit in their gilded House and Senate seats funded by the NRA telling us nothing could have been done to prevent this — we call BS.

They say tougher gun laws do not decrease gun violence. We call BS. They say a good guy with a gun stops a bad guy with a gun. We call BS.

They say guns are just tools like knives and are as dangerous as cars. We call BS.

They say no laws could have prevented the hundreds of senseless tragedies that have occurred. We call BS.

That us kids don't know what we're talking about, that we're too young to understand how the government works. We call BS.[105]

Notes

1. H. L. Mencken, 'Bayard vs. Lionheart', *Baltimore Evening Sun*, 26 July 1920, reprinted at <https://www.newspapers.com/clip/21831908/hl_mencken_article_26_jul_1920_the> (accessed 31 January 2020).
2. Ibid.
3. Robert S. Mueller III, 'Report on the Investigation into Russian Interference in the 2016 Presidential Election' (Mueller report), March 2019, available at <https://www.documentcloud.org/documents/5955118-The-Mueller-Report.html> (accessed 31 January 2020).
4. Scott Lucas, 'TrumpWatch Video Special: This Ain't Columbo – Mueller's Suspect Likely to Get Away with The Crime', *EA WorldView*, 25 July 2019, <https://eaworldview.com/2019/07/trumpwatch-video-special-this-aint-columbo-mueller-suspect-likely-to-get-away-with-the-crime> (accessed 31 January 2020).
5. Stephen Dinan, 'Steven Mnuchin, Treasury Secretary, Rejects Democrats' Demand for Donald Trump Tax Returns', Associated Press, 7 May 2019, <https://www.apnews.com/ea346c47374d-162d5e37626408ac61bb>.

6. Maggie Haberman, Michael S. Schmidt, Adam Goldman and Annie Karni, 'Trump Ordered Officials to Give Jared Kushner a Security Clearance', *New York Times*, 28 February 2019, <https://www.nytimes.com/2019/02/28/us/politics/jared-kushner-security-clearance.html> (accessed 31 January 2020).
7. Caitlin Dickerson, '"There Is a Stench": Soiled Clothes and No Baths for Migrant Children at a Texas Center', *New York Times*, 21 June 2019, <https://www.nytimes.com/2019/06/21/us/migrant-children-border-soap.html> (accessed 31 January 2020).
8. Scott Lucas, 'TrumpWatch, Day 785: Trump Issues Veto for His "National Emergency" and the Wall', *EA WorldView*, 16 March 2019, <https://eaworldview.com/2019/03/trumpwatch-day-785-trump-issues-veto-national-emergency-the-wall> (accessed 31 January 2020).
9. Helena Bottemiller Evich, 'Agriculture Department Buries Studies Showing Dangers of Climate Change', *Politico*, 23 June 2019, <https://www.politico.com/story/2019/06/23/agriculture-department-climate-change-1376413>; Lisa Friedman, 'New EPA Plan Could Free Coal Plants to Release More Mercury into the Air', *New York Times*, 28 December 2018, <https://www.nytimes.com/2018/12/28/climate/mercury-coal-pollution-regulations.html> (both accessed 31 January 2020).
10. Scott Lucas, 'TrumpWatch, Day 796: Trump Administration Tries to End Obama Care through Courts', *EA WorldView*, 27 March 2019, <https://eaworldview.com/2019/03/trumpwatch-day-796-trump-administration-tries-to-end-obamacare-through-courts>; Katie Lobosco, 'Betsy DeVos Faces New Lawsuit over Student Debt Forgiveness', CNN, 25 June 2019, <https://edition.cnn.com/2019/06/25/politics/betsy-devos-borrower-defense-lawsuit/index.html> (both accessed 31 January 2020).
11. 'Trump Calls Some Illegal Immigrants "Animals" in Meeting with Sheriffs', CBS News/YouTube, 16 May 2018, <https://youtu.be/3tmT7-dhOWs> (accessed 31 January 2020).
12. Andy Campbell, 'Trump Defends "Both Sides" Charlottesville Comments with a New Falsehood', *HuffPost* (UK), 26 April 2019, <https://www.huffingtonpost.co.uk/entry/trump-defends-both-sides-charlottesville-comments-with-a-new-falsehood_n_5cc30c9de4b08846403d585d> (accessed 31 January 2020).
13. Hasan Patel, 'Katie Hopkins and Donald Trump Whip Up Muslim-Phobia – and They May Have Pulse of UK's Tory Leaders', *EA WorldView*, 18 June 2019, <https://eaworldview.com/2019/06/katie-hopkins-and-donald-trump-whip-up-muslim-phobia-and-they-may-have-pulse-of-uks-tory-leaders> (accessed 31 January 2020).

14. 'Trump's Uncensored Lewd Comments about Women from 2005', CNN/YouTube, 8 October 2016, <https://youtu.be/FSC8Q-kR44o> (accessed 31 January 2020).
15. 'Trump Mocks Dr Christine Blasey Ford's Senate Testimony', CBS News/YouTube, 3 October 2018, <https://youtu.be/AWv1ipoi-c8> (accessed 31 January 2020).
16. Josh Dawsey, 'Trump Derides Protections for Immigrants from "Shithole" Countries', *Washington Post*, 12 January 2018, https://www.washingtonpost.com/politics/trump-attacks-protections-for-immigrants-from-shithole-countries-in-oval-office-meeting/2018/01/11/bfc0725c-f711-11e7-91af-31ac729add94_story.html> (accessed 24 January 2020).
17. Trump tweeted, 'The opinion of this so-called judge. . .' (Donald J. Trump (@realDonaldTrump), Twitter, 4 February 2017, <https://twitter.com/realdonaldtrump/status/827867311054974976> (accessed 31 January 2020)) and 'A very sad time for America' (Donald J. Trump (@realDonaldTrump), Twitter, 3 July 2019, <https://twitter.com/realdonaldtrump/status/1146245459268263938> (accessed 31 January 2020)). See also Sean Sullivan and Jenna Johnson, 'Trump Calls American-Born Judge "a Mexican", Points Out "My African American" at a Rally', *Washington Post*, 3 June 2016, <https://www.washingtonpost.com/news/post-politics/wp/2016/06/03/trump-calls-american-born-judge-a-mexican-points-out-my-african-american-at-a-rally> (accessed 31 January 2020).
18. Scott Lucas, 'TrumpWatch, Day 906: Trump's Twitter Racism v. Democratic Congresswomen', *EA WorldView*, 15 July 2019, <https://eaworldview.com/2019/07/trumpwatch-day-906-trumps-twitter-racism-v-democratic-congresswomen> (accessed 31 January 2020).
19. Trump tweeted, 'The Fed "raised" way too early and way too much.' Donald J. Trump (@realDonaldTrump), Twitter, 29 July 2019, <https://twitter.com/realDonaldTrump/status/1155829888701673472> (accessed 31 January 2020). See also Frida Ghitis, 'Trump's Attacks on the Fed Are About to Get Worse', CNN Business, 29 July 2019, <https://edition.cnn.com/2019/07/29/perspectives/fed-independence-powell-trump-authoritarian-populists/index.html> (accessed 31 January 2020).
20. 'Trump Compares Intel Leaks to Nazi Germany', CBS News/YouTube, 11 January 2017, <https://youtu.be/ZsZG-u2BzOU> (accessed 31 January 2020).
21. Eric Tucker, 'The Comey Firing, as Retold by the Mueller Report', Associated Press, 24 April 2019, <https://www.apnews.com/4ff1ecb621884a728b25e62661257ef0> (accessed 31 January 2020).

22. Trump tweeted, 'Why didn't Robert Mueller & his Band of 18 Angry Democrats spend any time investigating Crooked Hillary Clinton, Lyin' & Leakin' James Comey, Lisa Page and her Psycho lover, Peter S, Andy McCabe, the beautiful Ohr family, Fusion GPS, and many more, including HIMSELF & Andrew W?' Donald J. Trump (@realDonaldTrump), Twitter, 24 July 2019, <https://twitter.com/realdonaldtrump/status/1153992334054440960> (accessed 31 January 2020). See also 'Trump Claims Attempted Coup, Says It Started Long before Robert Mueller', Global News/YouTube, 26 April 2019, <https://youtu.be/zUGBp99mobc> (accessed 31 January 2020).
23. 'How Unpopular/Popular is Donald Trump?', *FiveThirtyEight*, January 2017–July 2019, https://projects.fivethirtyeight.com/trump-approval-ratings (accessed 31 January 2020).
24. H. L. Mencken, *In Defense of Women* (Mineola, NY: Dover, [1918] 2003), 29.
25. Daniel Boorstin, *The Image: A Guide to Pseudo-Events in America* (New York: Atheneum, [1961] 1978), 9.
26. Jean Baudrillard, *The Gulf War Did Not Take Place* (Bloomington: Indiana University Press, 1995).
27. Judy Klemesrud, 'Donald Trump, Real Estate Promoter, Builds Image as He Buys Buildings', *New York Times*, 1 November 1976, 41, <https://www.nytimes.com/1976/11/01/archives/donald-trump-real-estate-promoter-builds-image-as-he-buys-buildings.html> (accessed 31 January 2020).
28. David Barstow, Suzanne Craig and Russ Buettner, 'Trump Engaged in Suspect Tax Schemes as He Reaped Riches from His Father', *New York Times*, 2 October 2018, <https://www.nytimes.com/interactive/2018/10/02/us/politics/donald-trump-tax-schemes-fred-trump.html> (accessed 29 January 2020).
29. Morris Kaplan, 'Major Landlord Accused of Antiblack Bias in City', *New York Times*, 16 October 1973, 1.
30. Michelle Lee, 'Fact Check: Has Trump Declared Bankruptcy Four or Six Times?', *Washington Post*, 27 September 2016, <https://www.washingtonpost.com/politics/2016/live-updates/general-election/real-time-fact-checking-and-analysis-of-the-first-presidential-debate/fact-check-has-trump-declared-bankruptcy-four-or-six-times>; Philip Bump, 'Trump's Money Problems Were Well Known in the 1990s. Then Came *The Apprentice*', *Washington Post*, 8 May 2019, <https://www.washingtonpost.com/politics/2019/05/08/trumps-money-problems-were-well-known-s-then-came-apprentice> (both accessed 31 January 2020).

31. 'The Battle of the Billionaires Takes Place at WrestleMania 23', WWE/YouTube, 19 July 2011, <https://youtu.be/5NsrwH9I9vE> (accessed 31 January 2020). The term 'spectacle of excess' is from Roland Barthes's seminal essay on wrestling, 'The World of Wrestling', in *Mythologies* (New York: Hill & Wang, [1957] 1972). See also Christina M. Blankenship, 'President, Wrestler, Spectacle: An Examination of Donald Trump's Firing Tweets and *The Celebrity Appresident* as Response to Trump's Media Landscape', *Journal of Communication Inquiry*, 19 March 2019, <https://doi.org/10.1177/0196859919833785> (accessed 31 January 2020).
32. Callum Borchers, 'The Amazing Story of Donald Trump's Old Spokesman, John Barron – Who Was Actually Donald Trump Himself', *Washington Post*, 13 May 2016, <https://www.washingtonpost.com/news/the-fix/wp/2016/03/21/the-amazing-story-of-donald-trumps-old-spokesman-john-barron-who-was-actually-donald-trump-himself> (accessed 31 January 2020).
33. David A. Fahrenthold, 'Trump Boasts about His Philanthropy. But His Giving Falls Short of His Words', *Washington Post*, 29 October 2016, <https://www.washingtonpost.com/politics/trump-boasts-of-his-philanthropy-but-his-giving-falls-short-of-his-words/2016/10/29/b3c03106-9ac7-11e6-a0ed-ab0774c1eaa5_story.html> (accessed 31 January 2020).
34. 'Donald Trump: The Howard Stern Interviews 1993–2015', Factbase, <https://factba.se/topic/howard-stern-interviews> (accessed 31 January 2020).
35. Trump tweeted, 'The concept of global warming was created by and for the Chinese' (Donald J. Trump (@realDonaldTrump), Twitter, 6 November 2012, <https://twitter.com/realdonaldtrump/status/265895292191248385> (accessed 31 January 2020)) and, 'Let's take a closer look at that birth certificate. @BarackObama was described in 2003 as being "born in Kenya"' (Donald J. Trump (@realDonaldTrump), Twitter, 18 May 2012, <https://twitter.com/realDonaldTrump/status/203568571148800001> (accessed 31 January 2020)).
36. ABC News, 'Donald Trump Says He Could "Shoot Somebody" without Losing Votes', ABC News/YouTube, 23 January 2016, <https://youtu.be/rMmiLWDpCno> (accessed 31 January 2020).
37. Quoted in 'Script: Mencken – October 3 2015', *A Prairie Home Companion with Garrison Keillor*, <https://www.prairiehome.org/story/2015/10/03/script-mencken-october-3-2015.html> (accessed 31 January 2020).

38. Victor Pickard, 'The Strange Life and Death of the Fairness Doctrine: Tracing the Decline of Positive Freedoms in American Policy Discourse', *International Journal of Communication* 12 (2018), 3434–53.
39. Video available at 'Willie Horton 1988 Attack Ad', <https://youtu.be/Io9KMSSEZ0Y> (accessed 31 January 2020).
40. Jennifer Steinhauer, 'Confronting Ghosts of 2000 in South Carolina', *New York Times*, 19 October 2007, <https://www.nytimes.com/2007/10/19/us/politics/19mccain.html> (accessed 31 January 2020).
41. Josh Rogin, 'In Facebook Postings, OPSEC Spokesman Rips "Communist-in-Chief Hussein Mao-bama"', *Foreign Policy*, 21 August 2012, <https://foreignpolicy.com/2012/08/21/in-facebook-postings-opsec-spokesman-rips-communist-in-chief-hussein-mao-bama> (accessed 31 January 2020).
42. Zhiwei Jin, Juan Cao, Han Guo, Yongdong Zhang, Yu Wang, and Jiebo Luo, 'Detection and Analysis of 2016 US Presidential Election Related Rumours on Twitter', in Dongwon Lee, Yu-Ru Lin, Nathaniel Osgood and Robert Thomson (eds), *Social, Cultural, and Behavioral Modeling: 10th International Conference, SBP-BRiMS 2017, Washington, DC, USA, July 5–8, 2017, Proceedings* (Cham, Switzerland: Springer, 2017), 14–24.
43. Matthew Rosenberg, Nicholas Confessore and Carole Cadwalladr, 'How Trump Consultants Exploited the Facebook Data of Millions', *New York Times*, 17 March 2018, <https://www.nytimes.com/2018/03/17/us/politics/cambridge-analytica-trump-campaign.html> (accessed 31 January 2020).
44. Mueller report, Vol. I, 44–60.
45. 'Donald Trump Presidential Campaign Announcement Full Speech (C-SPAN)', C-SPAN/YouTube, 16 June 2015, <https://youtu.be/apjNfkysjbM>; Sarah Grant, 'Neil Young Onstage: "F—k You, Donald Trump"', *Rolling Stone*, 11 June 2016, <https://www.rollingstone.com/politics/politics-news/neil-young-onstage-f-k-you-donald-trump-106918> (both accessed 31 January 2020).
46. 'Donald Trump Calls Into WWOR/UPN 9 News on 9/11', Fox5NY/YouTube, 12 September 2016, <https://youtu.be/PcKlPhFIE7w>; 'Donald Trump Says He Will "Unify" the Republican Party', Fox News/YouTube, 20 October 2015, <https://youtu.be/cCFvVbU3ULA> (both accessed 31 January 2020).
47. Michael Lind, 'Donald Trump, the Perfect Populist', *Politico*, 9 March 2016, <https://www.politico.com/magazine/story/2016/03/donald-trump-the-perfect-populist-213697> (accessed 31 January 2020).

48. Nolan D. McCaskill, 'Trump Accuses Cruz's Father of Helping JFK's Assassin', *Politico*, 3 May 2016, <https://www.politico.com/blogs/2016-gop-primary-live-updates-and-results/2016/05/trump-ted-cruz-father-222730> (accessed 31 January 2020).
49. 'Trump Brags about Not Paying Taxes: "That Makes Me Smart"', GOOD Magazine/YouTube, 26 September 2016, <https://youtu.be/uBZR1-onmAo> (accessed 31 January 2020).
50. 'Donald Trump: Look at Those Hands . . . There's No Problem', Fox News/YouTube, 4 March 2016, <https://youtu.be/N9QYZ6qha1s> (accessed 31 January 2020).
51. 'US Election: Trump Encourages Russia to Find Clinton Emails', BBC News, 27 July 2016, <https://www.bbc.co.uk/news/election-us-2016-36907541> (accessed 31 January 2020).
52. Nicholas Confessore and Karen Yourish, '$2 Billion Worth of Free Media for Donald Trump', *New York Times*, 15 March 2016, <https://www.nytimes.com/2016/03/16/upshot/measuring-donald-trumps-mammoth-advantage-in-free-media.html> (accessed 31 January 2020).
53. Maggie Haberman and Richard A. Oppel Jr, 'Donald Trump Criticizes Muslim Family of Slain US Soldier, Drawing Ire', *New York Times*, 30 July 2016, <https://www.nytimes.com/2016/07/31/us/politics/donald-trump-khizr-khan-wife-ghazala.html> (accessed 31 January 2020).
54. David A. Fahrenthold and Danielle Rindler, 'Searching for Evidence of Trump's Personal Giving', *Washington Post*, 7 November 2016, <https://www.washingtonpost.com/graphics/politics/2016-election/trump-charity-donations>; David A. Fahrenthold, 'How Donald Trump Retooled his Charity to Spend Other People's Money', *Washington Post*, 10 September, 2016, <https://www.washingtonpost.com/politics/how-donald-trump-retooled-his-charity-to-spend-other-peoples-money/2016/09/10/da8cce64-75df-11e6-8149-b8d05321db62_story.html> (both accessed 31 January 2020).
55. 'Trump's Uncensored Lewd Comments about Women from 2005', CNN/YouTube, 7 October 2016, <https://youtu.be/FSC8Q-kR44o> (accessed 31 January 2020).
56. 'FNN: Donald Trump Delivers "Major Speech" – DENIES Groping Allegations – in West Palm Beach', Fox 10 Phoenix/YouTube, 13 October 2016, <https://youtu.be/TZ_eV2TRlOg> (accessed 31 January 2020).
57. 'First Lady Michelle Obama Live in Manchester, New Hampshire', Hillary Clinton/YouTube, 13 October 2016, <https://youtu.be/SJ45VLgbe_E> (accessed 31 January 2020).

58. Tim Wallace, Karen Yourish and Troy Griggs, 'Trump's Inauguration vs. Obama's: Comparing the Crowds', *New York Times*, 20 January 2017, <https://www.nytimes.com/interactive/2017/01/20/us/politics/trump-inauguration-crowd.html> (accessed 31 January 2020).
59. 'Jimmy Kimmel's FULL INTERVIEW with Sean Spicer', *Jimmy Kimmel Live*/YouTube, 13 September 2017, <https://youtu.be/bZJpwidiMco>; 'Kellyanne Conway: Press Secretary Sean Spicer Gave "Alternative Facts"', NBC News/YouTube, 22 January 2017, <https://youtu.be/VSrEEDQgFc8>; Gregory Wallace, 'National Park Service Edited Inauguration Photos after Trump, Spicer Calls', CNN Politics, 9September 2018, <https://edition.cnn.com/2018/09/07/politics/trump-inauguration-photos/index.html> (all accessed 31 January 2020).
60. Harrison Jacobs, 'Trump Paused a Discussion about China's President to Hand Out Copies of the 2016 Electoral Map', *Business Insider*, 28 April 2017, <https://www.businessinsider.com/trump-2016-electoral-map-reuters-interview-xi-jinping-china-2017-4?r=US&IR=T>; Jugal K. Patel and Wilson Andrews, 'Trump's Electoral College Victory Ranks 46th in 58 Elections', *New York Times*, 18 December 2016, <https://www.nytimes.com/interactive/2016/12/18/us/elections/donald-trump-electoral-college-popular-vote.html> (both accessed 31 January 2020).
61. Eli Rosenberg, '"The Most Bizarre Thing I've Ever Been a Part Of": Trump Panel Found No Widespread Voter Fraud, Ex-Member Says', *Washington Post*, 3 August 2018, <https://www.washingtonpost.com/news/politics/wp/2018/08/03/the-most-bizarre-thing-ive-ever-been-a-part-of-trump-panel-found-no-voter-fraud-ex-member-says> (accessed 31 January 2020).
62. Mueller report, Volume II.
63. David Choi, 'Trump Schedules His Meetings around "Fox and Friends" Segments, According to Former White House Official', *Business Insider*, 31 July 2018, <https://www.businessinsider.com/trump-fox-new-and-friends-schedules-meetings-2018-7?r=US&IR=T> (accessed 31 January 2020).
64. Rachael Revesz, 'Donald Trump Signs Executive Order to Ban Refugees and All Visitors from Muslim-Majority Countries', *The Independent*, 27 January 2017, <https://www.independent.co.uk/news/world/americas/donald-trump-executive-order-muslims-immigrants-ban-refugees-rebuild-military-a7550516.html> (accessed 31 January 2020).

65. Adam Liptak, 'Long Legal Fight Looms over Limits of Presidential Power', *Seattle Times*, 29 January 2017, <https://www.seattletimes.com/nation-world/long-legal-fight-looms-over-limits-of-presidential-power> (accessed 31 January 2020).
66. Mark Landler, 'Appeals Court Rejects Request to Immediately Restore Travel Ban', *New York Times*, 4 February 2017, <https://www.nytimes.com/2017/02/04/us/politics/visa-ban-trump-judge-james-robart.html> (accessed 31 January 2020).
67. Lauren Gambino, Sabrina Siddiqui, Paul Owen and Edward Helmore, 'Thousands Protest against Trump Travel Ban in Cities and Airports Nationwide', *The Guardian*, 30 January 2017, <https://www.theguardian.com/us-news/2017/jan/29/protest-trump-travel-ban-muslims-airports> (accessed 31 January 2020).
68. Donald J. Trump (@realDonaldTrump), Twitter, 4 February 2017, <https://twitter.com/realdonaldtrump/status/827867311054974976?lang=en> (accessed 31 January 2020).
69. '2017 Donald Trump Executive Orders', Federal Register, <https://www.federalregister.gov/presidential-documents/executive-orders/donald-trump/2017> (accessed 31 January 2020).
70. Trump tweets, 'After consultation with my Generals and military experts, please be advised that the United States Government will not accept or allow...' (Donald J. Trump (@realDonaldTrump), Twitter, 26 July 2017, <https://twitter.com/realDonaldTrump/status/890193981585444864> (accessed 31 January 2020)); 'What good is NATO...' (Donald J. Trump (@realDonaldTrump), Twitter, 11 July 2018, <https://twitter.com/realdonaldtrump/status/1017093020783710209> (accessed 27 February 2020). See also 'Donald Trump: North Korea "Will Be Met with Fire and Fury"', NBC News/YouTube, 8 August 2017, <https://youtu.be/1bt4t05m_j0>; Martin Pengelly, 'Trump Threatens to Terminate Nafta, Renews Calls for Mexico to Pay for Wall', *The Guardian*, 27 August 2017, <https://www.theguardian.com/us-news/2017/aug/27/donald-trump-camp-david-nafta-mexico-wall-canada> (both accessed 31 January 2020).
71. Kim Sengupta, 'Trump Has Fallen Out with His Military Chiefs – and This Is What It Means for American Security', *The Independent*, 5 September 2018, <https://www.independent.co.uk/voices/donald-trump-fallen-out-us-military-chiefs-mattis-kelly-mcmaster-a8524056.html> (accessed 31 January 2020).
72. Courtney Kube, Kristen Welker, Carol E. Lee and Savannah Guthrie, 'Trump Wanted Tenfold Increase in Nuclear Arsenal, Surprising

Military', NBC News, 11 October 2017, <https://www.nbcnews.com/politics/donald-trump/trump-wanted-dramatic-increase-nuclear-arsenal-meeting-military-leaders-n809701>; Zack Beauchamp, 'H. R. McMaster Reportedly Thinks Trump Is an "Idiot" with the Brain of a "Kindergartner"', *Vox*, 20 November 2017, <https://www.vox.com/world/2017/11/20/16680190/hr-mcmaster-trump-idiot-kindergartner> (both accessed 31 January 2020).

73. Ryan Lizza, 'Anthony Scaramucci Called Me to Unload about White House Leakers, Reince Priebus, and Steve Bannon', *New Yorker*, 27 July 2017, <https://www.newyorker.com/news/ryan-lizza/anthony-scaramucci-called-me-to-unload-about-white-house-leakers-reince-priebus-and-steve-bannon> (accessed 31 January 2020).

74. Donald J. Trump (@realDonaldTrump), Twitter, 31 July 2017, <https://twitter.com/realdonaldtrump/status/892147656319004672> (accessed 31 January 2020).

75. Michael M. Grynbaum, 'Trump Calls the News Media the "Enemy of the American People"', *New York Times*, 17 February 2017, <https://www.nytimes.com/2017/02/17/business/trump-calls-the-news-media-the-enemy-of-the-people.html> (accessed 31 January 2020).

76. 'Trump: "It's a Shame What's Happened with the FBI"', ABC News, 15 December 2017, <https://abcnews.go.com/Politics/video/trump-shame-happened-fbi-51813146> (accessed 31 January 2020).

77. 'President Trump's Full Rally in Phoenix', CNN/YouTube, 23 August 2017, <https://youtu.be/pfTvvLObtSc>; 'Trump's Huntsville Speech in 3 Minutes', *Washington Post*/YouTube, 25 September 2017, <https://youtu.be/mWyXyqxxAM4> (both accessed 31 January 2020).

78. Marie Brenner, 'How Donald Trump and Roy Cohn's Ruthless Symbiosis Changed America', *Vanity Fair*, August 2017, <https://www.vanityfair.com/news/2017/06/donald-trump-roy-cohn-relationship> (accessed 31 January 2020). On 18 May 2017 Trump tweeted, 'This is the single greatest witch hunt of a politician in American history!' Donald J. Trump (@realDonaldTrump), Twitter, https://twitter.com/realdonaldtrump/status/865173176854204416 (accessed 31 January 2020).

79. Paul Sonne, Josh Dawsey and Missy Ryan, 'Mattis Resigns after Clash with Trump over Troop Withdrawal from Syria and Afghanistan', *Washington Post*, 20 December 2018, <https://www.washingtonpost.com/world/national-security/trump-announces-mattis-will-leave-as-defense-secretary-at-the-end-of-february/2018/12/20/e1a846ee-e147-11e8-ab2c-b31dcd53ca6b_story.html> (accessed 31 January 2020).

80. Dara Lind, 'The Trump Administration Just Admitted It Doesn't Know How Many Kids Are Still Separated from Their Parents', *Vox*, 5 July 2018, <https://www.vox.com/2018/7/5/17536984/children-separated-parents-border-how-many> (accessed 31 January 2020).
81. Scott Lucas, 'TrumpWatch, Day 759: Facing Tough Fight, White House Lies over Trump "National Emergency"', *EA WorldView*, 18 February 2019, <https://eaworldview.com/2019/02/trumpwatch-day-759-facing-tough-fight-white-house-lies-trump-national-emergency> (accessed 31 January 2020).
82. Katie Benner and Caitlin Dickerson, 'Sessions Says Domestic and Gang Violence Are Not Grounds for Asylum', *New York Times*, 11 June 2018, <https://www.nytimes.com/2018/06/11/us/politics/sessions-domestic-violence-asylum.html> (accessed 31 January 2020).
83. Tal Kopan, 'Sources: Stephen Miller Pushing Policy to Make It Harder for Immigrants Who Received Benefits to Earn Citizenship', CNN, 7 August 2018, <https://edition.cnn.com/2018/08/07/politics/stephen-miller-immigrants-penalize-benefits/index.html> (accessed 31 January 2020).
84. Elaina Plott, 'Bill Barr Already Won', *The Atlantic*, 23 July 2019, <https://www.theatlantic.com/politics/archive/2019/07/mueller-testimony-barr-narrative/594547> (accessed 31 January 2020).
85. Donald J. Trump (@realDonaldTrump), Twitter, 24 March 2019, <https://twitter.com/realdonaldtrump/status/1109918388133023744> (accessed 31 January 2020).
86. Glenn Kessler, 'Did Hillary Clinton Collude with the Russians to Get "Dirt" on Trump to Feed It to the FBI?', *Washington Post*, 9 February 2018, <https://www.washingtonpost.com/news/fact-checker/wp/2018/02/09/did-hillary-clinton-collude-with-the-russians-to-get-dirt-on-trump-to-feed-it-to-the-fbi> (accessed 31 January 2020).
87. 'Trump: "My Sick Idea" to Send Migrants to Sanctuary Cities', NBC News/YouTube, 28 April 2019, <https://youtu.be/ZGaO4TZoiPA> (accessed 31 January 2020).
88. 'In His Own Words: The President's Attack on the Courts', Brennan Center for Justice, 5 June 2017, <https://www.brennancenter.org/analysis/his-own-words-presidents-attacks-courts> (accessed 31 January 2020).
89. Donald J. Trump (@realDonaldTrump), Twitter, <https://twitter.com/realdonaldtrump/status/1150381394234941448> (accessed 31 January 2020).

90. Michael Scherer, Josh Dawsey, Ashley Parker and Seung Min Kim, '"He Always Doubles Down": Inside the Political Crisis Caused by Trump's Racist Tweets', *Washington Post*, 21 July 2019, <https://www.washingtonpost.com/politics/he-always-doubles-down-inside-the-political-crisis-caused-by-trumps-racist-tweets/2019/07/20/b342184c-aa2e-11e9-86dd-d7f0e60391e9_story.html> (accessed 31 January 2020).
91. Scott Lucas, 'US & Beyond Pictures: The Women's Marches', *EA WorldView*, 22 January 2017, <https://eaworldview.com/2017/01/us-beyond-pictures-the-womens-marches> (accessed 31 January 2020).
92. 'Michelle Obama: "When They Go Low, We Go High"', CNN/YouTube, 25 July 2016, <https://youtu.be/mu_hCThhzWU> (accessed 31 January 2020).
93. Scott Lucas, 'State of the Union: The Women in White Stole Trump's Night – And Will Haunt Him for the Rest of the Year', *The Conversation*, 6 February 2019, <https://theconversation.com/state-of-the-union-the-women-in-white-stole-trumps-night-and-will-haunt-him-for-the-rest-of-the-year-111276> (accessed 31 January 2020).
94. Guy Debord, *The Society of the Spectacle*, 2nd ed. (Detroit: Black & Red, 1984).
95. Thomas Lynch, 'President Donald Trump: A Case Study of Spectacular Power', *Political Quarterly* 88, no. 4 (2017), 612–21.
96. Robert Zaretsky, 'Trump and the "Society of the Spectacle"', *New York Times*, 20 February 2017, <https://www.nytimes.com/2017/02/20/opinion/trump-and-the-society-of-the-spectacle.html> (accessed 31 January 2020).
97. Lynch, 'President Donald Trump'.
98. Debord, *The Society of the Spectacle*, 12.
99. Douglas Kellner, 'Guy Debord, Donald Trump, and the Politics of the Spectacle', in Marco Briziarelli and Emiliana Armano (eds), *The Spectacle 2.0: Reading Debord in the Context of Digital Capitalism* (London: University of Westminster Press, 2017), 1–14.
100. Lynch, 'President Donald Trump'.
101. Zaretsky, 'Trump and the "Society of the Spectacle"'.
102. Sage Lazzaro, 'The 35 Absolute Best Signs from the Women's March', *Observer*, 23 January 2017, <https://observer.com/2017/01/best-signs-from-the-womens-march> (accessed 31 January 2020).
103. Laura Conway, 'The Lure of Spectacle in Politics & Art', T\lt West, January 2018, <https://www.tiltwest.org/item/the-lure-of-spectacle-in-politics-art> (accessed 31 January 2020).

104. H. L. Mencken, *A Mencken Chrestomathy* (New York: Knopf Doubleday, [1949] 1982), 622.
105. 'Emma Gonzalez's Powerful March for Our Lives Speech in Full', Guardian News/YouTube, 24 March 2018, <https://youtu.be/u46HzTGVQhg> (accessed 31 January 2020).

Index

Access Hollywood, 342
alt-right, 102–3, 321–5, 322n
alternative reality, 8, 18–19
America First, 5, 29–30, 100
American expansionism, 155–6, 168
American leadership, 31–2
Anton, M., 37, 89–90, 97, 98
Appadiurai, A., 141, 142

Badiou, A., 8
Baker, P., 9
Bakhtin, M., 136–7
Bannon, S., 98–9
Baudrillard, J., 337
birther conspiracy, 298–9
Bishop, B., 9
Boorstin, D., 337
Brands, H. W., 162
Brexit, 97
Bush, G. H. W., 178
Bush, G. W., 139–40, 189, 225–6, 228–90

Caesarism, 60–1, 64, 66
celebrity politicians, 305
Chadwick, A., 292–3
China, 27–8, 31, 207–8

Clancy, T., 188
clash of civilisations, 179, 184–6
climate change denial, 182–3
Clinton, B., 27, 28, 162
Clinton, H., 96, 112, 270–1
Colbert, S., 314, 318, 319
conjunctural analysis, 3, 55–6
cruel optimism, 277
Cuba, 231
Cultural Front, 67–9
cultural Marxism, 91–2
culture wars, 313

Danner, M., 2
Debord, G., 350
decline (of US), 5–6, 39, 160, 209, 236, 313n
democracy promotion, 211, 224–38
Denning, M., 67–8
Dred Scott decision, 42

economic equality, 165–7
ethnic nationalism, 177–9
Evangelical voters, 117–18
exceptionalism (American), 155, 233

INDEX

Fallows, J., 152
fantasy, 7, 35–6, 38–9, 137–8, 270
4chan, 315, 322
Fox News, 315
Fukuyama, F., 28

Georgian crisis, 194–5
Gessen, M., 2, 10, 10n
Gest, J., 255, 259, 263
globalisation, 138, 140
globalism, 25–9
Gonzalez, E., 352
Gossip Girl, 272–3
Gramsci, A., 3, 55–64, 70, 87
grand strategy (of the US), 25, 29, 33–5, 40, 41, 159, 205, 210, 215–17

Habermas, J., 97
Hall, S., 54–70
Havel, V., 177
Hemon, A., 10, 10n
Higgins, R., 90–3
hillbilly, 254
Hillbilly Elegy, 247–63
Hochschild, A. R., 39, 251, 255, 262
hybrid media system, 289, 292–4, 300, 301, 304, 305

Iannucci, A., 317
illiberal democracy, 23
illiberal hegemony, 25, 32–4, 40, 41
immigrant (figure of), 39–41, 44
Infowars, 323
Isenberg, N., 259, 261, 262

Jackson, A., 42–4
Judis, J. B., 23n

Kaplan, R., 186–8
Kavanaugh, B., 120
Kennan, J., 161
Kennedy, J. F., 4, 312
Knock Down the House, 300–1

Labour Party, 57–9, 61, 63
Lepore, J., 157, 168
Letterman, D., 273–4, 316
Lewis, B., 184–5
liberal democracy, 3, 5, 23–4, 232–3, 235–6, 310
liberal hegemony, 25–9, 32, 74, 165, 327
liberal world order, 26, 206, 216

McCain, J., 190–1, 194–6
McCain, M., 282
Madison, J., 158
Mailer, N., 4
Make America Great Again, 100, 204
Manafort, P., 196–7
Mead, W. R., 29, 42
Mearsheimer, J. J., 26, 165
media logic, 291–3
memes, 321–5, 327
Mencken, H. L., 335, 337, 339, 352
#MeToo movement, 120
middle class, 64, 94
Mills, C. W., 36n
Moore, M., 316

natal alienation, 42
nation of immigrants, 4–5, 41
National Endowment for Democracy (NED), 234
neoliberalism, 86, 93–5, 262
New Right, 81, 85

INDEX

Niebuhr, R., 152
Noah, T., 318
North Atlantic Treaty Organisation (NATO), 192, 214

Obama, B., 5, 7, 35, 36–9, 45, 146, 153n, 226–30
Obama, M., 343
Obamacare, 37
Ocasio-Cortez, A., 300, 303–5, 325
Oliver, J., 319
O'Toole, F., 7–8
Overton window, 315

Packer, G., 6, 313n
Palin, S., 191–2
partisan politics, 117, 310
Patriot Act, 189–90
Pepe the Frog, 322
Poe's law, 326
political communication, 289–94, 301–2, 305, 310, 313, 320, 321, 322, 325, 327
populism, 7, 23
Posen, B., 25, 28–9, 34–5
post-truth, 2, 8
postfeminism, 268–9, 272, 277
Powell, L. F., 84
Powell Memorandum, 84–6
public sphere, 310
Putnam, R., 6, 313n

Rabelais, F. 135
racial contract, 36–7
Reagan, R., 84, 157–8, 167
Reddit, 323
Rice, S., 31n

Rondon, A. M., 7
Russian intervention in 2016 election, 197, 335

satire, 310–27, 351
Saturday Night Live, 316
South Park, 318
spectacle, 296–9, 337–52
Stuckey, A., 325

Tea Party, 123, 251, 252
Thatcherism, 54–64, 70
The Apprentice, 296–7, 338
The Art of the Deal, 295–6, 338
The Colbert Report, 314
The Daily Show, 313, 314, 316, 318
Trump, D.,
  and illiberalism, 5, 24, 27, 34, 35, 39, 40, 41, 42
  anti-immigration stance, 39–41, 44
  leadership style of, 31
  as media actor, 294
  political appeal of, 83
  rallies, 39
  sexism of, 113
Trump, I., 268–83, 336
Trumpism, 55, 64, 79, 83, 92, 93, 97, 98, 100, 205

Ukranian crisis, 195–7

Vance, J. D., 247–63
Venezuela, 229–30, 231, 234

Wallace, G., 84
Warren, E., 166
White House Correspondents Association dinner, 314, 319–20

white males, 249, 255–7
white nationalism, 6–7
white settler colonialism, 32, 43–5
white women voters, 110–12
white working class, 247–63
Williams, W. A., 156
Wilson, W., 32
Wilsonianism, 222–5, 228, 230, 231, 233, 237
Wolf, Michelle, 319–20

women, political activism of, 118–24
Women Who Work, 277–8, 283
Women's March, 118–19, 349, 352
World Wrestling Experience, 338

Younge, G., 141

Zakaria, F., 23

EU representative:
Easy Access System Europe
Mustamäe tee 50, 10621 Tallinn, Estonia
Gpsr.requests@easproject.com